An Introduction to Sustainable Transportation

An Introduction to Sustainable Transportation

Policy, Planning and Implementation

Preston L. Schiller, Eric C. Bruun
and Jeffrey R. Kenworthy

First edition published in 2010
by Earthscan
2 Park Square, Milton Park, Abingdon, Oxon OX14 4RN

Simultaneously published in the USA and Canada
by Earthscan
711 Third Avenue, New York, NY, 10017, USA

Earthscan is an imprint of the Taylor & Francis Group, an informa business

ISBN-13: 978-1-844-07664-2 (hbk)

Typeset by Domex e-Data, India
Cover design by Susanne Harris

A catalogue record for this book is available from the British Library

Library of Congress Cataloging-in-Publication Data

Schiller, Preston L.
  An introduction to sustainable transportation : policy, planning and implementation /
Preston L. Schiller, Eric C. Bruun, and Jeffrey R. Kenworthy.
      p. cm.
  Includes bibliographical references and index.
  ISBN 978-1-84407-664-2 (hardback) – ISBN 978-1-84407-665-9 (pbk.)
1. Transportation–Environmental aspects. 2. Sustainable development.
I. Bruun, Eric Christian II. Kenworthy, Jeffrey R., 1955- III. Title.
  HE147.65.S35 2010
  388'.049–dc22
                              2009052802

Printed and bound in the United States of America by
Edwards Brothers Malloy

Contents

List of Figures, Tables and Boxes

Figures

Tables

Boxes

Acknowledgements

The authors are deeply indebted to Susanne Lynette Seales for her dedicated assistance with editing, formatting, graphics preparations and all her other work that helped to bring this project to conclusion. The authors also thank the editorial staff of Earthscan Publishing for all their dedicated help. We are especially indebted to Jonathan Sinclair Wilson and Rob West for their early interest and encouragement of this project. We thank Todd Litman for his comments on some of the early chapter drafts. We also thank Mike Ferro, James Hillegas, Eric Manners and Susanne Lynette Seales for their original contributions of material for several boxed items in the text. Thanks to John Whitelegg and John Maryon for permission to republish sections of articles published in journals under their editorship. A special thanks to Andy Singer for the use of his fabulous car-toons.

Eric C. Bruun would like to thank the many people who helped and inspired him, including those who furnished photos or diagrams for this work.

Jeffrey R. Kenworthy would like to sincerely thank his research assistant, Ms Monika Brunetti, for her indispensible part in compiling the updated cities data that appear in this book. He would also like to thank innumerable people around the world who continue to contribute to his ongoing data collection on cities and without whose help it would not be possible to create the comparative data on cities to be found in various parts of this book. These people are far too many for any to be named; but each and every one of them is owed a debt of gratitude for taking the time out of their busy days to answer emails for data. They know only too well who they are! Hopefully, in books like this and other publications that bring together some of these data, there is some value added for them by being able to see their own city in comparison to others.

Preston L. Schiller would like to thank the co-authors and the many encouraging individuals and supportive institutions and organizations whom he met trekking and bicycling along the path of sustainable transportation. These include, but are not limited to, John Adams; Bruce Agnew; Don Alper; Mayor Dan Pike and City Council members Barbara Ryan and Jack Weiss of Bellingham; Meeky Blizzard; Peter Boothroyd; Hal B. H. Cooper, Jr.; Leroy Demery; Hank Dittmar; Mike Ferro; Wes Frysztacki; Richard Gilbert; David L. A. Gordon; Spense Havlick; John Holtzclaw and many Sierra Club transportation activists; Jane Jacobs; Jane Holtz Kay; several individuals inside the city halls and within the communities of Kingston, Ontario, and Kirkland, Washington; Charles Komanoff; James Howard Kunstler; Chris Leman; the Library of Congress and the libraries of the US Department of Transportation (USDOT), Queen's University, Kingston, Ontario, and Western Washington University; Tom Matoff; Anne Vernez Moudon; Peter Newman; Michael Replogle; Anne Roberts; numerous students at Huxley College of the Environment at Western Washington University and the School of Urban and Regional Planning at Queen's University, Kingston, Ontario; Will Toor; Tony Turrittin; Richard Untermann; Ellen Vanderslice; and Bob Whitson and others at GO Boulder.

Preston dedicates his portion of this book's effort to his children, Jacques-Philippe Colgrove Schiller and Lena Catherine Schiller Hanson, their spouses and their children, and to his beloved *principessa*, who warms him after cold bicycle rides and inspires him to continue working for sustainable transportation – Nancy Elena van Deusen.

Foreword

Hank Dittmar

It is a privilege to be asked to introduce this important book concerned with the vital and often overlooked question of the relationship between how we get around and the sustainability of our cities, towns and our planet. Along with the authors, I have laboured for many years to try to get the message across that our environment is shaped just as much by our transportation and land use patterns as by our energy sector or by industries like agriculture, mining or fishing.

This has been a difficult message to get across, and Preston Schiller, Eric Bruun and Jeff Kenworthy have all combined careful research with principled advocacy in service of the planet. I hope that this book receives the attention it deserves despite the fact that sustainable transportation is often viewed unsympathetically by many in the environmental community, who view the answer either through the lens of regulating the automobile or as a question of getting the prices right.

The past two or three years have seen a breakthrough in understanding about transport and urban issues, with high-speed rail under serious discussion in the United States, England and Canada, and increased public interest in public transport and cycling, especially in difficult economic times.

An Introduction to Sustainable Transportation is thus an especially timely work, and it deserves to reach a wide audience. Preston Schiller, Eric Bruun and Jeff Kenworthy have assembled an encyclopaedic and useable catalogue of the theory, technique and practice needed for recovery from the twentieth century's long delusion about hypermobility, and it comes not a moment too soon!

2008 was the first year in which more than half the people on the planet lived in urbanized areas, and according to the United Nations Environment Programme the flood of people from rural areas in the Global South to the exploding megacities and regional capitals of Africa, South America, and South and East Asia is expected to continue and accelerate over the next decade. In fact, of the 2.2 billion people to be added to the world's population by 2030, 2.1 billion of them are expected to be living in cities, driven there by the promise of an increased standard of living. To many this will mean joining the middle class, and this will mean sprawl and automobility.

An alternate version of improved quality of life for the Global South is desperately needed, and as this book demonstrates, that vision can increasingly be found not only in Portland, Freiburg, and Vancouver, but also in Surubaya, Bogota and Seoul. This is a world where accessibility is favoured over mobility, where amenities, services and neighbourhoods are advantaged over highways and bypasses, and where green modes are designed to be convenient, reliable and ubiquitous. Above all, it is a vision of a world where mobility is seen as a means to an end, not an end in itself.

At the same time, this book will give hope to local leaders and planners in North America, Europe, Australia, New Zealand and the Middle East, where the go-go economy of the last decade has hit the skids and with it the endless drive for sprawl, fuelled by the illusion of an endless need for suburban housing and the possibility of an endless supply of motorways. The Dubai debt crisis followed hard on the heels of the bursting of the housing bubble, and it is telling that Dubai went from a town to automotive gridlock in less than

20 years, much accelerating the rate at which it happened in cities like Los Angeles or Atlanta. One hopes that planners the world over will take this lesson and adopt different patterns of growth.

Indeed, another way forward towards a greener economy is emerging, and investment in sustainable transportation is increasingly recognized as one of the most effective ways not only to stimulate the economy but also reinforce the benefits of metropolitan agglomeration. Driven by the global climate crisis, the coming investment in high-speed rail, commuter railways, trams, streetcars and busways, alongside the reconfiguration of urban street networks for all users will help to create a new skeletal framework for more sustainable cities.

The prescription offered in this book is a positive one. All too often solutions to our environmental problems seem to require donning a hair shirt and promising abstinence. The exemplars cited by Schiller, Bruun and Kenworthy to the contrary point to a future where there are more and better choices available, and where rather than transport being a burden and a problem, access becomes a pleasure, and improved quality of life the outcome.

Hank Dittmar *is the Chief Executive of the Prince's Foundation for the Built Environment, and is a Senior Research Associate at Oxford University. He was formerly Chairman of the Congress for the New Urbanism and President of Reconnecting America, and served as Executive Director of the Surface Transportation Policy Project. He is the co-author of the 2004 book* New Transit Town *and author of the 2008 book* Transport and Neighbourhoods.

Introduction and Overview

This book is an effort to illuminate how to move towards sustainability in transportation. It addresses the question of how to shape transportation planning, policy-making and citizen activities in a direction of greater social and environmental benefit to society and Planet Earth. The general discussion of sustainable transportation to be found in current literature is much less developed than the general discussion of sustainability. Transportation is one of the most basic of human activities linked to almost all daily routines, from employment and obtaining essential services to shopping and recreation. It is intimately linked to land-use planning and urban design. It provides many benefits to individuals, but aspects of it pose serious problems for the environment and society. Almost all of the motorized ways or modes in which individuals, goods or materials move around our cities and Planet Earth consume considerable amounts of energy and resources, most of which are not renewable. Most of these modes are highly dependent on fossil fuels and are deeply implicated in the processes of greenhouse gas emissions and their atmospheric accumulation. This book explores the ways in which many transportation benefits can be retained, while its social and environmental burdens are reduced.

Goals of sustainable transportation

Sustainable transportation aims at promoting better and healthier ways of meeting individual and community needs while reducing the social and environmental impacts of current mobility practices. It attempts to achieve these through reducing resource inputs, waste outputs and minimizing transportation's often deleterious effects on the public realm. It is about adapting the techniques and technologies most appropriate to the type of service needed. It is about making important everyday destinations, such as shopping, employment, basic services and recreation, closer and more accessible, rather than increasing mobility in order to overcome inaccessibility. It is about healthier ways of getting around communities – ways that improve the individual's health through more activity: the few minutes' walk to the transit stop or station or the pleasant bicycle trip to the store. It attempts to find ways of improving the health of communities through lowering traffic and its accompanying pollution and safety hazards.

Technical and technological factors, such as improved fuel efficiency, reduced motor emissions or systems that control traffic flow on major highways, are important; but they are not the essence of sustainable transportation. Sustainable transportation involves taking many dimensions of transportation and land-use planning into account simultaneously, as well as public visioning processes aimed at describing the future we desire, and then taking the steps necessary to attain that vision. Sustainable transportation is essentially a societal, rather than strictly technical, process that depends upon planning, policy, economics and citizen involvement.

Sustainable transportation aims at lowering financial costs to society and to the individual through lessening dependence upon automobiles as the main mode of individual mobility. At present, it appears that we are at the early stages of a significant change, or 'paradigm shift', in the ways in which transportation is conceived, planned, financed and implemented. The shift is away from automobile-oriented planning that emphasizes system growth – or 'bigger is better' – towards emphasizing appropriate modes, infrastructure and technologies that may tend towards 'smaller is beautiful' or 'closer is beautiful', and slowing our increasingly hyper-mobile societies.

Why this book?

In preparation for the writing of this book the authors reviewed numerous transportation texts. It was perceived that there was a great need for a relatively succinct and basic work that addressed the wide range of issues involved in making transportation more sustainable. The shortcomings of conventional transportation planning, policy-making and public participation needed to be subject to critique in the context of a wider view of how transportation could become more sustainable.

While there are many excellent works summarizing transportation planning, both conventional and sustainable, none available presented an accessible treatment of each by individuals without advanced education in maths, engineering or the physical sciences. Nor do these books provide a comparison of their significant differences, less yet an indication of how to effectively mobilize planning, policy-making and citizen participation in the arduous but rewarding task of moving from business as usual (BAU) to sustainable transportation (ST) – hence the need for this text and its effort to create a work intended to be of use to more than one type of reader.

Students

It is hoped that students of transportation, policy and environmental issues will benefit from this book. Students are often already aware of many of the issues, but may need more background and depth material in their efforts to master the subject matter and apply it to their broader areas of study. Students have unique opportunities to apply their learning to practice in everyday community living, as well as bringing their life experiences and practices to bear on their studies. By walking, bicycling or taking transit to their classes, students can model sustainable transportation. By working to attain university-wide transit pass programmes or a walking- and bicycling-friendly campus community, students can change community and institutional practices and planning in the direction of sustainability. One of the exemplary cities chosen for analysis in Chapter 9 is Boulder, Colorado, in the US, a university and research centre that has chosen to move in the direction of sustainable transportation.

Planners

Public- or private-sector planners and planning consultants are very well situated to help move transportation towards greater sustainability. People working in the transportation field, whether their background is in planning, engineering, policy or another discipline, often have a deep understanding of the ways in which planning and transportation programmes work. They are well situated to inform and educate the public and policy-makers about the range of available options and planning modalities, as well as their consequences. Many planners are already uncomfortable with BAU, but need more resources to make the transition to sustainable transportation; it is hoped that this work will be a resource for them in that effort.

Policy-makers and decision-makers

People who are in a position to influence public policy – how resources are invested, programmes developed, laws and regulations formulated and how planning receives guidance – are well situated to help direct transportation in the direction of sustainability. In the private sector, management can influence decisions about whether facilities are located in car-dependent or transit-friendly sites, and union leadership can influence decisions about whether employees insist on free parking or accept a range of transportation benefits, including transit passes or in-lieu-of-parking rewards. Visionary and brave leaders have played a central role in the stories of several of the cities presented as exemplars of sustainable transportation. The authors have been inspired by their interactions with some of these bold elected officials who have taken seriously the concepts of leadership and 'politics as a vocation' in the original sense of that word: a calling, not just a job.

Engaged citizens

Possibly the most important, and most neglected, resource for sustainable transportation is the citizenry. Whether as a neighbourhood resident with transportation concerns or as a user of transit, streets or paths, the citizen's point of view is often taken for granted in planning and policy processes. Often the ways in which governmental entities undertake public outreach or consultation leave much to be desired with regard to creating effective partnerships with the citizens who are the subjects of projects. Sometimes concerned citizens throw up their hands and simply reject any and all change, fearing that it will only worsen their neighbourhood or their commute. But citizen input, involvement and energy is crucial to successful planning and project realization. Several of the exemplary communities and projects presented in this book have succeeded, in the main, because visionary citizens helped government to focus on problems, as well as to develop sustainable solutions.

It is hoped that interested, engaged and involved citizens, who often form the 'cement' of sustainability planning, will find this book useful in their efforts. The accessibility of this book should broaden the number of concerned citizens who can absorb the material and issues without the barriers of specialized jargon and advanced engineering mathematics.

Point of view: Values, commitments, 'objectivity' and documentation

This work does not shy away from presenting its material from the point of view of individuals committed to the values of environmental and social sustainability. The light of that commitment, which motivates the authors' research, teaching and civic engagement, will not be hidden under an epistemologically questionable bushel of 'objectivity'. That commitment does not excuse the authors from carefully analysing issues and documenting their assertions while presenting a broad array of references. Where making points about situations where there is demonstrated excess or disingenuousness, the text pulls no punches in its tone and outlook. This is especially the case in the 'car culture' discussion, where it is easier to demonstrate some of these excesses in a more colourful way. While there is much to criticize in current conventional planning and policy-making, examples of efforts that are moving some cities towards sustainable transportation are presented. Not all the news is bad and there is room for hope.

Much of the material presented in this book involves the integration of research results of the authors and the inclusion of some of their ongoing research, not previously published. In addition, one of the major research problems in sustainable transportation is the lack of synthesis of a very diverse and rapidly expanding information base. This book, therefore, is also a serious research enterprise in drawing together a huge amount of technical, social, economic, environmental and cultural material into a policy-relevant synthesis, of use to all of the aforementioned potential readers.

Overview of the book

Chapter 1 opens with a discussion of definitions of sustainable transportation, as well as the problems of defining such a phenomenon. It then turns to the planet's high level of mobility, persons and freight, which is encouraged by an overemphasis and overdependence on 'automobility' in many, but not all, parts of the world. This phenomenon has been termed 'hypermobility'. Automobile dependence is seen to have led to serious inequities between and within societies. A minority of the planet's populace drive and create disproportionate pollution and energy consumption, while a majority are greatly disadvantaged in their efforts to gain access to basic needs. Such inequities also affect wealthy societies.

Chapter 2 builds upon the first chapter and presents an analysis of the evolution of communities from walking cities to transit cities and then, for many, to automobile cities, with the concomitant development of a 'car culture' that has come to dominate and guide a large portion of transportation consciousness and unconsciousness. The creation of the car culture and its bolstering in everyday popular media, such as movies, music and music videos, radio, television, literature and advertising, is explored, including examples of campaigns to get young girls to become 'Mustang Sally' or have guys feel good about getting their oil changed. The value and meaning of the frequent traffic reports that permeate daily radio are questioned, and tourism, the fly-drive and recreational vehicle (RV) phenomena are scrutinized. A former advertising agency executive presents a critique of the ways in which 'cars are us'. Portraits of car-stuck and car-free families are drawn, indicating that in some communities the two may coexist in the same neighbourhood with very differing consequences for their daily lives and their communities.

Chapter 3 explores the rich area of transportation history. Its purview includes land modes, water travel and aviation, telecommunications, and aspects of infrastructure development, especially roads. It demonstrates the centrality of walking to human evolution and existence and how, for thousands of years, human communities were designed to maximize access to important resources and minimize travel. It includes several boxed items presenting perspectives on topics ranging from Inca roads to Sherlock Holmes assisting a young woman bicyclist in distress, and how the experience of a small city with the development of the US interstate highway system embodies many of the contradictory notions of what the new highways would bring. The interesting history of bicycling, and its role in 'paving the way' for the automobile, is explored. A table of selected historic timelines for several modes and transportation innovations (see Table 3.1) helps the reader to grasp the vast time period over which these developed, as well as the rapidity of the pace of change during the 19th and 20th centuries.

Chapter 4 brings to the present, analyses and compares the various modes by which people move around within their communities and across longer distances. These include walking, bicycling, motorized two- and three-wheelers, personal motor vehicles (PMVs), buses, urban rail transit, intercity rail, airplanes and ships. It examines modes in the context of their interaction with infrastructure needed or available, as well as trip purposes. It defines and describes modes beyond the physical characteristics of specific vehicles, drawing attention to how vehicles are deployed and viewed by users. It begins a discussion, continued in Chapter 6, of the effects of different modes on the consumption of urban space and the limits to the numbers of automobiles that a city can support. It examines the various factors which are assessed by travellers, including out-of-pocket costs and the characteristics of modes chosen or preferred. It analyses the energy efficiency of numerous modes and vehicles within modal categories and compares the discussion of vehicular energy efficiency with the discussion of the energy efficiency of cities, which is seen to vary with urban form. It also points to the huge modal 'overkill' for many transportation chores in wealthy countries, while many in poor countries still carry backbreaking loads and use pack animals.

Chapter 5 presents key aspects of freight movement, its supply chains and logistical systems. It highlights the variety of freight transport modes and necessary infrastructure, including trains, trucks, airplanes and ships. It explores issues such as moving more freight from trucks to trains, why it is so cheap for producers to globalize many aspects of their production chains, and why companies are willing to pay very high rates sometimes just to save one or two days of shipping time. Volumes and distance trends for freight flows are analysed. Globalization of trade is shown to push freight transport in the opposite direction of sustainable development. Possible reforms that could be taken to move freight transport towards greater energy efficiency, balance, localization and sustainability are explored.

Chapter 6 explores aspects of economics and investment strategies that could help in efforts to move transportation towards a more sustainable direction. Among the topics surveyed and analysed are the serious shortcomings of BAU transportation economics, particularly the neglect of positive and negative impacts that are not monetary; the need to reduce motor vehicle pollution and other harmful impacts through 'getting the prices right' and de-subsidization; why it is necessary to subsidize some modes that are serving important environmental and social purposes; the questionable practices of investing public funds in parking and highway expansions, including high-occupancy vehicle (HOV) lanes; why private commercial and residential parking, in general, but especially 'free parking', should be reduced and managed and priced differently than it conventionally is; the ways in which BAU investment analyses and strategies work against sustainable transportation and some of the corrective measures than can be taken; and the need to weigh economic considerations carefully with regard to environmental and social considerations to keep the 'bottom line' from dominating all decision-making.

Chapter 7 addresses how policy-making and public participation can be moved away from their conventional status quo in maintaining forms to more rewarding change-oriented forms, where public policy truly precedes and shapes planning, takes the lead in setting a sustainability agenda, and where citizens are involved in shaping policy and planning in creative and effective ways. Examples of the key roles that political leadership and energized and well-prepared citizens have played in several locales are described. The systematic differences between conventional versus sustainable approaches to policy and participation are analysed, and several examples of cities, large and small, moving in the direction of sustainable transportation are tabulated. Various formats and strategies, including deliberative democracy, for effective public participation are described, along with several case examples of successful efforts, as well as a description of a citizen effort that headed transportation away from a more sustainable strategy.

Chapter 8 presents a critique of conventional 'predict and provide' planning and builds upon the necessity of moving towards 'deliberate and decide' planning. The chapter opens with a 'lessons learned' from previous chapters. It then proposes a new paradigm for integrating the many factors that comprise planning, and discusses how the types of policy-making and participation reforms presented in the previous chapter can be incorporated within it. There is discussion of the crucial role of 'mobility management': the managing of existing resources and services. The notion of 'going beyond' sustainable transportation planning to the repair, regeneration and renewal of major transportation institutions, including public transportation providers and society itself, is presented along with a possible agenda for sustainable transportation.

Chapter 9 reviews the efforts towards sustainable transportation in six cities of very different sizes and with very different socio-economic and cultural frameworks. It looks at the key pillars of their achievements, what sets the cities apart from other cities in special ways, and how the cities have achieved their successes. It also provides some quantitative snapshots of each city, incorporating some new research results, so that readers have a basic picture of the current state of the land-use transportation system in each place. Collectively these exemplars cover many of the issues and approaches addressed in Chapter 8, including the development of superior transit systems, the integration of land uses with those systems, the provision of excellent conditions for walking and cycling, reductions in road capacity, the greening of the urban environment and the role of leadership and civil society in forging such changes in transportation and urban planning.

The book concludes with a discussion of the most vital actions, preparations and measures that need to be taken at several levels to move from conventional business as usual transportation to sustainability. Chapter 10 attempts to draw out some common threads and themes, which can be found in many of the successful examples of sustainable transportation in this book – for example, the need for leaders who lead, citizens who participate in effective and well-informed ways, and institutions that are transformed is presented.

At the end of the book, Appendix 1 provides a transit primer, with information about some of the more recent developments in transit technologies and planning, while Appendix 2 outlines a resources toolbox, listing web addresses for numerous sources of information about data sources and organizations involved in sustainable transportation. An index also assists readers in locating specific topics in the text.

1

A Highly Mobile Planet and Its Challenges: Automobile Dependence, Equity and Inequity

Sustainable transportation

This chapter presents an approach to characterizing, defining and exploring a few of the major issues associated with transportation and efforts to move it towards greater sustainability. Several differences between conventional approaches to transportation, business as usual (BAU) and sustainable transportation (ST) are delineated. A brief treatment of the expansiveness and extensiveness of freight and passenger mobility and some aspects of transportation infrastructure are presented in order to put some of the issues surrounding these into a broad, even global, perspective. Two major issues confronting ST, automobile dependence and (in)equity, are discussed in depth.

What is sustainable transportation about?

ST emerged from three main sources:

1   Concerns about transportation's burdens and the counterproductivity of much conventional highway-oriented planning began to emerge around the planet from the 1970s onward as pollution increased and the often destructive effects of highway expansion upon cities attracted more attention (Stringer and Wenzel, 1976; Gakenheimer, 1978; Newman and Kenworthy, 1989).
2   The recognition in some places that reducing traffic in cities through traffic calming (deliberately slowing personal motor vehicles, or PMVs) and pedestrianization (excluding PMVs from certain streets) had many benefits for mobility and the environment, including reductions in vehicular traffic ('traffic evaporation') and traffic-related injuries, especially those of pedestrians and bicyclists, and increases in the numbers of people walking, bicycling and using public transportation. These will be discussed further in other parts of the book, especially in Chapters 8 to 10.

3   The growth of sustainability awareness, especially following the Brundtland Commission's report (WCED, 1987) on sustainable development as 'development which meets the needs of current generations without compromising the ability of future generations to meet their own needs'.

These three strands led to a lively discussion about ST and many excellent efforts to describe, characterize or define it since the 1990s.[1] While all efforts to define a field as complex as ST are fraught with difficulty, one of the more useful definitions is that of the University of Winnipeg's Centre for Sustainable Transportation. An ST system is one that:

- allows the basic access needs of individuals and societies to be met safely and in a manner consistent with human and ecosystem health, and with equity within and between generations;
- is affordable, operates efficiently, offers choice of transport mode and supports a vibrant economy;
- limits emissions and waste within the planet's ability to absorb them, minimizes consumption of non-renewable resources, limits consumption of renewable resources to the sustainable yield level, reuses and recycles its components, and minimizes the use of land and the production of noise.[2]

Common threads in various efforts examining ST emphasize that sustainability with regard to passenger transportation (freight is discussed in Chapter 5) should:

- meet basic access and mobility needs in ways that do not degrade the environment;
- not deplete the resource base upon which it is dependent;
- serve multiple economic and environmental goals;
- maximize efficiency in overall resource utilization;
- improve or maintain access to employment, goods and services while shortening trip lengths and/or reducing the need to travel; and
- enhance the liveability and human qualities of urban regions (Schiller and Kenworthy, 1999, 2003).

Differences between sustainable transportation and business as usual

The dominant transportation paradigm until now has emphasized single-mode mobility – whether automobiles, planes or huge cargo ships; 'hard path' approaches relying upon facility expansion – whether roads, parking, ports or runways; and financing that often masks the full costs and environmental consequences of its arrangements. The paradigm of conventional transportation planning and policy may be termed BAU. The differences between BAU and ST will be visited many times throughout this book. Some of the major points of comparison are presented in Table 1.1.

Table 1.1 Comparison of business as usual and sustainable transportation

Business as usual (BAU)	Sustainable transportation (ST)
Emphasizes mobility and quantity (more, faster)	Emphasizes accessibility and quality (closer, better)
Emphasizes one mode (uni-modality, automobility)	Emphasizes plurality (multi-modality)
Often lacks good connections between modes	Emphasizes interconnections (inter-modality)
Accommodates and accepts trends	Seeks to interrupt and reverse harmful trends
Plans and builds based on forecasts of likely demand (predict and provide)	Works backwards from a preferred vision to planning and provision (deliberate and decide)
Expands roads to respond to travel demand	Manages transportation or mobility demand
Ignores many social and environmental costs	Incorporates full costs within planning and provision
Transportation planning often in 'silos' disconnected from environmental, social and other planning areas	Emphasizes integrated planning combining transportation with other relevant areas

Source: Preston L. Schiller

Unsustainable transportation: The magnitude of the problem

The challenge facing the shift from BAU to ST is great. It touches upon almost every aspect of life: ecosystem health, liveability of communities, access to jobs and services, and the costs of basic goods, including foodstuffs, to identify a few. One way of understanding the world that BAU in transportation has led to is to consider the magnitude of personal and freight mobility and the increasing length and dispersion of trips. The concept of 'hypermobility' is very useful in this regard.

Hypermobility

The magnitude of the mobility of persons and freight and the vast trip distances generated by such mobility are presented in Box 1.1 and Table 1.2. BAU in transportation has meant that more roads have been built and expanded, which has not led to less traffic congestion. It has led to more driving, longer trips for people and freight, more sprawl, and more land and energy consumption (Newman and Kenworthy, 1989, pp94–110; Whitelegg, 1997). The magnitude of personal and freight movement has been characterized by John Adams as 'hypermobility'. Building upon the work of Ivan Illich (1973, 1976), Wolfgang Sachs (1992) and others, he has described the serious environmental and social consequences of allowing this phenomenon to continue unchallenged:

- more dispersion of society; more sprawl and destruction of natural areas; longer distances to destinations;
- more societal polarization and inequity between the highly mobile and those denied the benefits of mobility and accessibility; more crime;
- more danger for those not in cars, especially children and other vulnerable persons; more fat, less fitness;
- less social and cultural diversity and variety; less democratic politically; less participation (Adams, 1999, 2000).

An attempt to capture a snapshot of the magnitude of this issue is presented in Box 1.1 and Table 1.2.

Box 1.1 Passenger motorization: A very mobile planet with plenty of roads

Each day Planet Earth's motorists drive their 737 million personal motor vehicles (PMVs) a total of 30 billion kilometres (18 billion miles), creating 60 billion passenger kilometres (pkm) travelled, and by the year's end a total of 10 trillion kilometres (6 trillion miles) and 20 trillion pkm of travel have been recorded on their odometers. In the US, which leads the world in personal motorized mobility, motorists daily record 13 billion vehicle kilometres travelled (vkt), or 8.2 billion vehicle miles travelled (vmt), adding 20.5 billion pkm, or 13 billion passenger miles (pmi), of travel so that by the year's end they have added 5.5 trillion vehicle kilometres (vkm), or 3.5 trillion vehicle miles (vmi), and 7.2 trillion pkm (4.5 trillion pmi) to the odometers of their fleet of 230 million PMVs. While the US constitutes only 4 per cent of the world's population, American motorists own one third of the planet's automobiles, about seven to eight times the rate of vehicle ownership for most of the rest of the world, and account for over half the planet's driving.

Interspersed among the hundreds of millions of personal vehicles clogging the millions of miles/kilometres of the planet's streets and roads, some 100 million trucks and lorries, ranging from small to medium to very large 18-wheelers and double and triple rigs, are busily hauling their loads, accounting for some 8 trillion tonne kilometres (tkm) per year. Churning across the oceans, a fleet of tens of thousands of cargo ships (mostly containerized) and tankers are hauling freight and fuel for a total of 45 trillion tonne kilometres annually. A larger fleet of tugs and merchant vessels transports a somewhat lesser amount of cargo along the inland waterways of the major continents.

In the skies above the roads and waterways, thousands of commercial airplanes account for 24 million flights each year, logging 6 billion pkm (3.3 billion passenger miles travelled, or pmt) travelled each day, accumulating to over 2 trillion pkm annually. The US accounts for 10 million annual flights, almost half the global commercial aviation fleet and half of the world's pkm flown, when its domestic and international flights are combined. A rapidly growing amount of freight, accounting for 200 billion tkm annually, is being carried in the holds of the commercial aviation fleet as well as by fleets of specialized air freight carriers.

Bon voyage! Bonne route!

Figure 1.1 Huge highways and their interchanges devour and divide the landscape

Source: Preston L. Schiller

Ironically, much more is known about motorized movements of persons and goods across the planet than is known about non-motorized movement: people walking or bicycling – although these are the dominant trip modes on Planet Earth. Table 1.2 presents pertinent statistics about the magnitude of personal and freight mobility around our very busy planet. Wherever possible the most recent data and data from the same year were used; but that was not always possible as data for a particular year may not be available until a few years later. Since there is no precise accounting of the total mileages and of world roads and pavements, expert estimates were used.

Complexity of the issue

Transportation has many impacts; environmental, social equity, economic, cultural, land use and urban form are but a few important ones. Currently, some of these impacts are beneficial, as when people find it easier to get to medical help in an emergency; but many are not beneficial or are even extremely harmful, as when transportation-generated pollution threatens human health and even the survival of life on Planet Earth. Many of transportation's deleterious impacts stem from the lack of integrated planning, flawed policy-making and not including effective public participation. Transportation's impacts and what can be done about them will be examined in greater depth in subsequent chapters. For now we will touch on some of the most common issues and dimensions in preparation for the following discussions.

The variety of issues, the many dimensions of society that are affected, the diversity of actors and interests – all of these make ST an extremely interesting area of endeavour and action. Among the many important factors and dimensions that shape ST, and which vary from one society to another, are:

- culture and social organization;
- economics;

- political and social equity issues;
- environmental concerns;
- policy and planning;
- interest groups.

Table 1.2 The hypermobility index (with apologies to *Harper's Magazine* and John Adams)

World roads, paved–unpaved, of kilometres/miles paved–unpaved (millions)	15/9; 25/15
US roads, paved–unpaved, linear kilometres/miles paved–unpaved (millions)	4.2/2.6; 2.2/1.4
US lane kilometres/miles (includes width of multilane roads) (millions)	13.4/8.4
World automobile (PMV) population (millions)	737
US automobile (PMV) population (millions)	230
World human population (millions)	6784
US human population (millions)	307
Automobiles (PMVs) per 1000 persons (world)	100
Automobiles (PMVs) per 1000 persons (US)	750
World passenger kilometres/miles by PMV daily (billions)	60/36
US passenger kilometres/miles by PMV daily (billions)	20.5/12.3
World vehicle kilometres/miles by PMV annually (trillions)	10/6
US vehicle kilometres/miles by PMV annually (trillions)	5.5/3.5
World passenger kilometres/miles by PMV annually (trillions)	23/12
US passenger kilometres/miles by PMV annually (trillions)	7.2/4.5
World truck (lorry, large and medium sized) population (millions)	100
US truck (lorry) population, large tractor–trailer/medium–large (millions)	2/6.2
World freight movement by truck (lorry) tonne kilometres (tkm)/tonne miles (tmi) (trillions)	8/5.3
US freight movement by truck (lorry) tkm/tmi (trillions)	1.9/1.3
World freight total (water, road, rail, air) tkm/tmi (trillions)	58/38
World freight by water, mostly oceanic, tkm/tmi (trillions)	43/28
World freight movement per person tkm/tmi (thousands)	8700/5750
US freight movement per person, tkm/tmi (thousands)	17,520/12,000
Canada freight movement per person, tkm/tmi (thousands)	25,810/17,000
EU25 freight movement per person, tkm/tmi (thousands)	8160/5400
China freight movement per person, tkm/tmi (thousands)	5300/3500
Japan freight movement per person, tkm/tmi (thousands)	4500/3000
World commercial aviation flights annually (millions)	24
US commercial aviation flights annually (millions)	10
World commercial aviation passenger kilometres/miles, 2005 (trillions)	3.7/2.2
US domestic commercial aviation passenger kilometres/miles 2004 (billions)	891/557
World commercial aviation passenger kilometres/miles daily (billions)	10/6
US commercial aviation passenger kilometres/miles daily (billions)	2.4/1.5

Source: BTS (2006); US Bureau of Transportation Statistics (2006); World Bank (2006); Chafe (2007); Gilbert and Perl (2008); US Census Bureau (2008); *Automotive Digest* (2009); Richard Gilbert (pers comm, 2009)

These and related factors will be addressed in several places in this book. Several of these factors come together in two major challenges confronting ST: the overdependence on automobility in daily life and the inequities created and maintained by BAU.

The problems of automobile dependence

The patterns of transportation and urban land use associated with high levels of automobile dependence present an array of environmental, economic and social problems for the sustainability of cities, as summarized in Table 1.3 (Newman and Kenworthy, 1999). Some problems are relevant to multiple categories, but for convenience are placed in only one category. For example, the problem that auto dependence has gradually reduced many transit systems to mere shadows in the overall transportation system (e.g. in many US cities, especially those in the south such as New Orleans) clearly has severe environmental, economic and social outcomes, but appears here under environmental problems. Similar comments can be made about urban sprawl and many of the other dilemmas. This section provides a brief overview of this array of problems with some selected quantification where appropriate.

HIGHWAYS DIVIDE HABITATS

Source: Andy Singer (www.andysinger.com)

Figure 1.2 'Highways divide habitats'

Table 1.3 Problems associated with automobile dependence

Environmental problems	Economic problems	Social problems
Oil vulnerability	Congestion costs	Loss of street life
Urban sprawl	High urban infrastructure costs for sewers, water mains, roads, etc.	Loss of community in neighbourhoods
Photochemical smog	Loss of productive rural land	Loss of public safety
Acid rain	Loss of urban land to pavement	Isolation in remote suburbs with few amenities
High greenhouse gases – global warming	Poor transit cost recovery	Access problems for those without cars or access to cars and those with disabilities
Greater storm water runoff problems	Economic and human costs of transportation accident trauma and death	Road rage
Traffic problems: noise, neighbourhood severance, visual intrusion, physical danger	High proportion of city wealth spent on passenger transportation	Anti-social behaviour due to boredom in car-dependent suburbs
Decimated transit systems	Public health costs from air and other pollution	Enforced car ownership for lower-income households
	Health costs from growing obesity due to sedentary auto lifestyles	Physical and mental health problems related to lack of physical activity in isolated suburbs

Source: Jeffrey R. Kenworthy

Environmental problems

Automobile-dependent cities have high levels of private transportation energy use, as shown in Figure 1.3, which compares per capita consumption of energy for private transportation in cities in the US, Canada, Australia and New Zealand, high-income Asia, Eastern Europe, the Middle East, Africa, low-income Asia, Latin America and China.[3]

An average American city of 400,000 inhabitants uses as much energy for private passenger transportation as an average Chinese city of 10 million people. Cities in the US, Canada and Australia are therefore highly vulnerable to events in the Middle East associated with oil, as the overthrow of Iraq demonstrates. As a consequence of high energy use, 'automobile cities' also produce large quantities of greenhouse gases and emissions such as carbon monoxide, volatile hydrocarbons and nitrogen oxides, which contribute to the formation of photochemical smog. Figure 1.5 shows automotive smog emissions for the same groups of cities outlined above.

Sulphur dioxide (from transportation and industry), when mixed with precipitation causes acid rain, which results in the acidification of inland waters and kills native forests (e.g. the Black Forest in Germany and Switzerland). Like all air pollution and other pollution, such emissions do not respect national boundaries and therefore strengthen the need for regional and transnational agreements about abatement strategies.

Automobile-dependent cities also lose large quantities of productive land or natural areas to suburban sprawl every year. With the peaking of world oil production, cities increasingly need to retain as much near-city agricultural production as possible to minimize the energy content of food. The recent phenomenon of the '100 mile restaurant' in the US and the '100 kilometre restaurant' in Canada is partly a response to this issue.

The covering of vast areas of urban land with pavement for roads and parking and the construction of extensive low-density housing areas creates huge amounts of water runoff, which can cause flooding as well as polluted water from the oil and brake residues that build up on the pavement. Los Angeles is a prime example of this, where in some areas up to 70 per cent of the land area is covered with roads and parking; the remainder comprises

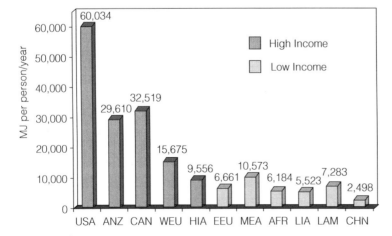

Figure 1.3 Private passenger transport energy use per capita in world cities, 1995

Note: CAN = Canada; ANZ = Australia and New Zealand; WEU = Western Europe; HIA = high-income Asia; EEU = Eastern Europe; MEA = Middle East; AFR = Africa; LIA = low-income Asia; LAM = Latin America; CHN = China.

Source: based on Kenworthy and Laube (2001)

buildings, and its expansive aqueduct system is sealed in concrete to separate it from ground contamination, but is nevertheless badly polluted from pavement runoff.

Traffic noise, neighbourhood severance and deterioration of the public realm are a major feature of auto-dependent environments. Traffic noise pervades every aspect of life from intrusion into dwellings and workplaces to the inability, in some cases, to converse in public. Since the automobile began to dominate urban transport systems, neighbourhoods have been carved into two by large freeways and roads have been widened, making it impossible for neighbours to maintain contact across their own streets. The US Federal Highway Program, which saw thousands of miles of freeways carved into the urban fabric, destroyed hundreds of thousands of homes across the country and resulted in the fragmentation of intact well-functioning urban neighbourhoods, especially working-class ones, built on easy contact among neighbours. The public realm has suffered immeasurably as streetscapes have become dominated by parking, roads and the other paraphernalia of auto dependence, including high levels of visual intrusion from auto-scale advertising signs, or '100 km/hr architecture' as Jan Gehl, the famous urban designer, calls it (Whitelegg, 1993; Newman and Kenworthy, 1999).

Finally, one of the most insidious problems created by auto dependence and its attendant land uses is the spiralling decline of transit systems. Figure 1.7

Figure 1.4 A California service station proudly proclaims its mission as the 'Smog Shop'

Source: Preston L. Schiller

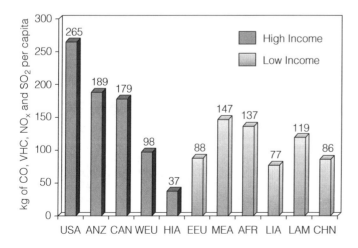

Figure 1.5 Transportation emissions per capita in world cities, 1995

Note: CAN = Canada; ANZ = Australia and New Zealand; WEU = Western Europe; HIA = high-income Asia; EEU = Eastern Europe; MEA = Middle East; AFR = Africa; LIA = low-income Asia; LAM = Latin America; CHN = China.

Source: based on Kenworthy and Laube (2001)

Figure 1.6 Aerial view of older neighbourhood with wide streets and large parking lots, Seattle, Washington

Note: Seattle grew as a transit city with a well-articulated street grid and streetcar system, and then began to destroy its streetcar lines, widen streets for more traffic lanes and clear areas for large parking lots, as shown in this view of an older north Seattle neighbourhood; most automobile cities have allowed parking lots to be their major form of 'open space', their suburbs even more so.

Source: Preston L. Schiller

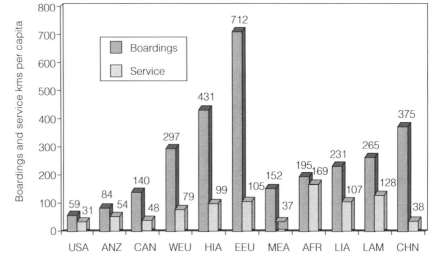

Figure 1.7 Transit system service provision and use per capita in world cities, 1995

Note: Vertical scale is annual boardings and vehicle kilometres per capita. Abbreviations as in Figure 1.9, opposite.

Source: based on Kenworthy and Laube (2001)

shows the annual transit service provision in vehicle kilometres provided per capita and the annual boardings per capita in groups of cities around the world. As can be seen, the US and Australian cities, and, a little less so, the Canadian cities, have low levels of transit use and service. This is not because people in these cities are necessarily less willing to use transit if excellent services are provided, but rather because entire urban systems have been built around the car, resulting in the progressive marginalizing of transit systems that have become less and less able to compete in speed terms with cars, or, indeed, in most of the other factors that influence people's mode of choice, such as level of service and frequency.

Economic problems

Automobile cities suffer a number of economic impacts, such as congestion costs in terms of lost time and the high costs of urban infrastructure for the extra distances that must be traversed for water, sewage and drainage systems, roads, and a variety of social infrastructure such as schools, medical centres and community halls that must be duplicated as the city spreads. In the meantime, vast areas of existing urban infrastructure remain underutilized due to demographic changes and are begging for revitalization through better transit and higher densities (Newman and Kenworthy, 1999).

Figure 1.8 'Waiting for the Interurban'

Note: These folks have been waiting so long for the Interurban train to return to their Fremont, Seattle (Washington), neighbourhood that they have all turned into clay.

Source: Preston L. Schiller

There are also issues such as the loss of productive rural land and urban land to sprawl and pavement. The excessive use of land in cities for the movement of cars to cater for upwards of 80 per cent of daily trips, when other less resource-consuming options are available, has a significant opportunity cost.

Transit systems in auto-dependent cities also tend to have lower operating cost-recovery ratios – that is, the percentage of operating costs that are recovered from fare box revenues (see Figure 1.9). In 1995, US transit systems had the lowest recovery of all cities, at 36 per cent.

There are large economic costs associated with road accidents and deaths in cities. About 45,000 people die on US roads per year, equivalent to a full-scale war. Road accidents cost developing countries US$100 billion per annum,

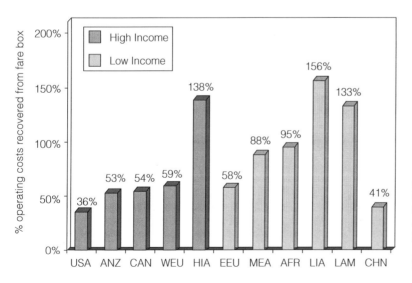

Figure 1.9 Transit operating cost recovery in world cities, 1995

Note: CAN = Canada; ANZ = Australia and New Zealand; WEU = Western Europe; HIA = high-income Asia; EEU = Eastern Europe; MEA = Middle East; AFR = Africa; LIA = low-income Asia; LAM = Latin America; CHN = China.

Source: based on Kenworthy and Laube (2001)

compared to all incoming aid to developing countries of US$50 billion.[4] Road accident costs worldwide are conservatively estimated to be US$518 billion.[5]

But the biggest cost to cities of dependence on cars comes when one adds up all the operating and infrastructure investment costs for both private and public transportation and normalizes it according to wealth (i.e. as a percentage of gross domestic product – GDP). These data consider all operating costs of both private passenger transport and transit, as well as a five-year average investment cost for roads and transit all added together. The results are shown in Figure 1.10 and they clearly demonstrate that in the developed or wealthy countries with comparable wealth, it is the auto cities that are paying the biggest price tag to maintain daily access to the needs of everyday life, while the transit-, walking- and bicycling-oriented European and wealthy Asian cities spend a lot less. Since transportation is a cost that should be minimized, this lower expenditure gives these cities a competitive advantage. And the data show the relatively small proportion of city wealth that is expended on transit, irrespective of its significance.

Other, perhaps less obvious, economic impacts of automobile dependence include the effects of obesity on the health system from lack of physical activity, including walking. A Rutgers University study by Reid Ewing entitled *Does Sprawl Make You Fat?* pursued this question. The US, the world's most auto-dependent society, has over 30 per cent of its population officially obese, the highest in the world (Frank et al, 2003). In 2008 it was announced in the UK that there was to be a pilot programme in Manchester to pay people to exercise. This was being considered on the grounds that the costs to the health system for treating obesity / physical inactivity-induced health problems are so great that it would be cheaper to simply pay people to exercise to avoid such medical conditions.[6]

Of course, air pollution from transportation also causes many health-related problems and even death in extreme cases, which carry an economic impact. The most obvious examples of this are the well-known 'smog events'

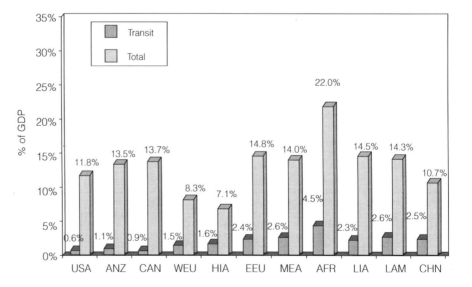

Figure 1.10 Proportion of city wealth spent on passenger transportation and the transit component in world cities, 1995

Note: CAN = Canada; ANZ = Australia and New Zealand; WEU = Western Europe; HIA = high-income Asia; EEU = Eastern Europe; MEA = Middle East; AFR = Africa; LIA = low-income Asia; LAM = Latin America; CHN = China.

Source: based on Kenworthy and Laube (2001)

in Los Angeles when surface ozone levels or photochemical smog reach dangerous levels and people are warned to stay indoors and not to exercise heavily. Photochemical smog also has other well-documented economic impacts, such as deterioration of paint on buildings, negative impacts upon car tyres and the killing of leafy row vegetables and citrus crops.

Social problems

Perhaps less obvious than the environmental and economic issues are a host of social issues for cities linked to excessive dependence upon automobiles. Table 1.3 lists these problems, a majority of which can be traced back to the automobile's deleterious effect on the public realm and the nature of human interactions in auto-based societies. This is an important dimension, not only for the direct effects which these social problems incur, but also because they relate to human capacity to respond to the demands of ST. If, as is argued below, people lose the capacity to function in a participatory society, lose their sense of being 'citizens', then it is more difficult to enact the kind of policies and programmes needed to address these problems. Therefore a more detailed discussion of these social dimensions of auto dependence is provided here.

Low-density auto-dependent suburbs where there are few, if any, small local shops and where little walking occurs can suffer from a lack of community feeling and a loss of street life that was common in North American and Australian suburbs only some 40 to 50 years ago. Numerous authors over many years have pointed to many problems associated with creating urban environments with a poor sense of belonging and a lack of natural surveillance. Jane Jacobs was most articulate in her defence of lively and active city streets, especially in their capacity to help form a community and enhance public safety (Jacobs, 1961).

Other literature points strongly to the influence that attractive, safe and walkable environments have on the development of children, especially their capacity for independence and unassisted travel.[7] Defensive urban environments such as in gated communities and many low-density suburbs are designed for cars not children, nor do they assist in the formation of friendly, interactive neighbourhoods. Lasch (1991), referring to Jane Jacobs, reminds us of the important role played by the public realm in cities. He describes it thus:

> The myth that playgrounds and grass and hired guards or supervisors are innately wholesome for children and that city streets, filled with ordinary people, are innately evil for children boils down to a deep contempt for ordinary people ... people must take a modicum of public responsibility for each other even if they have no ties to each other. (Lasch, 1991, p64)

He continues further, raising the idea of Los Angeles as the archetypal 'privatized' city, lacking in the normal sustaining and civilizing influence of a decent urban environment:

> City streets, as Jacobs reminds us, keep the peace and instruct the young in the principles of civic life. Neighborhoods recreate many features of village life

celebrated in American folklore ... Neighborhoods provide the informal substructure of social order, in the absence of which everyday maintenance of life has to be turned over to professional bureaucrats. In Los Angeles, a city deliberately designed to maximize privacy, we see how this hyperextension of the organizational sector is the necessary consequence of the retreat from the neighborhood. (Lasch, 1991, p65)

We can find endless examples in cities of gated, unfriendly human environments that are the logical extension or expression of a declining public realm in cities. On the other hand, cities can give expression to cultural values associated with social interaction and shared space which result in entirely different patterns of urban community and means of transport. For example, in central cities such as Stockholm (Sweden), Freiburg (Germany) and San Jose (US), urban spaces present the kind of real public environments that encourage independence in children and convey the sense that a city is a safe and interesting place. In many Swedish urban and suburban environments, other values of community, interaction and safe streets are expressed, such as in the Skärpnack development in Stockholm and in Angered Centrum in Gothenburg. Such environments encourage children's independence and development. The role of an attractive public realm that functions from a human perspective is paramount in delivering such urban qualities (Kenworthy, 2000).

The decline of the public realm in cities is well depicted in Mike Davis's (1990) book *City of Quartz*, a detailed portrayal of the decline of Los Angeles (and a metaphor for urban America, more generally), which turns primarily on the destruction of the public realm and the descent into what he calls 'Fortress LA' and the 'ecology of fear'.

In an interview about his work, Davis describes Los Angeles as:

... a megalopolitan sprawl ... economically and ecologically moribund, ravaged by social polarization and racial tensions that have provided fertile ground for the criminalizing of non-whites, urban youth and the homeless; militarizing of a notoriously brutal police force; the privatizing of public space; and the proliferation of fortified suburban enclaves whose lawns bristle with warnings of 'armed response'. (cited in Dery, 1995, p43)

Davis also provides a disturbing picture of the logical consequences of ignoring the public realm in cities through automobile-based planning:

A future urban America in which the government and private sectors have abdicated any vestige of responsibility to the dispossessed; where public space and civil rights have been willingly relinquished by homeowners fearful of racial unrest and gang violence; and where upper- and middle-class citizenry has incarcerated itself in gated communities, or on family outings in surveilled, privately patrolled malls, 'historic districts' or theme parks ... Universal Studios has constructed a 'parallel urban reality' called City Walk, repackaging 'the best features of Olvera Street, Hollywood and the West Side' in what its designer calls 'easy, bite-sized pieces' for consumption by tourists and residents who don't need the excitement of dodging bullets ... in the third world country that Los Angeles has become. (cited in Dery, 1995, pp43–44)

He goes on to speak further about the problems in Los Angeles related to a neglected public realm:

> ... the malling of public space [generates] the definition of new forms of criminality, to the extent that the social spaces that people – particularly kids – use are now these pseudo-public spaces, malls and their equivalents. Increasingly, the only legal youthful activities involve consumption, which just forces whole areas of normal teenage behaviour off into the margins ... Irvine, which is the last generation's absolute model utopia of a master-planned community, is producing youth pathologies equivalent to those in the ghettos simply because in the planning of Irvine there was no allotted space for the social relationships of teenagers, nowhere for them lawfully to be ... So you get these seemingly random irrational acts of violence.[8] (cited in Dery, 1995, pp45–46)

Other critics of American suburbs have focused on the problems of creating urban environments that are, in their view, 'unreal', false and illusory places (Kunstler, 1996), which deny the very nature of what it means to live in a city with all the attendant responsibilities of being a citizen and not just an individual maximizing his or her private benefits. Kunstler (1996, p32) states:

> From its inception the chief characteristic of the American suburb was not of an organically real town, nor a civic place, but a place of fantasy and escape ... those who lived in such suburbs [believed] that they could conduct their industrial activities without suffering any of the unpleasant consequences these activities typically entailed. Along with the suburb itself as a physical artifact, this notion of freedom from the consequences of one's social behavior has also persisted in the mental life of Americans.

The public realm under the above philosophies or outlooks has become a place that is often very hostile. The private automobile and its requirements for roads and parking structures has been instrumental in this transformation of the public environments of cities into places unsuitable for human beings, where up to two thirds of the land is under pavement. In Los Angeles, planning for the automobile has created bypassed neighbourhoods that are breeding grounds of discontent, which have sometimes bubbled over into riots, such as those in 1967 centred on Watts. Such neighbourhoods today present a challenging picture with their dilapidated, hostile streets and threatening public transport stations, such as along the Los Angeles Blue Light Rail Transit (LRT) line.

The downtown area of Los Angeles is also a place designed to allow cars free passage and presents an unpleasant, if not hostile, face to pedestrians. Fearing further riots, streets in the Los Angeles central business district (CBD) are under constant video surveillance and many buildings can be secured at the touch of a button, including steel plates to protect vulnerable plate glass windows near ground level. This is further evidence to support Davis's view of the city as a fortress and fear-driven environment.

Such problems are not peculiar to American cities, but are apparent in Australian cities, perhaps in a more subtle way. For example, social commentator Hugh Mackay (1994) states that:

If you've decided to be a two- or three-car household, you've already established some fundamental patterns for your own life in the 21st century. For a start, you've increased the probability that you will continue to be a stranger to neighbours you never meet on the footpath. We may complain about the loss of a sense of belonging to a local community; but, by our perfectly understandable enthusiasm for the car, we've taken such giant strides away from a communal life that we can hardly expect the community to re-emerge all by itself ... The fear of urban violence ... has already gripped many older people and many parents of young children ... But many of us have already decided to create a climate of fear, which is conducive to violence, by teaching our children to avoid eye contact with strangers and by staying away from public spaces, such as streets and parks, which if only we thronged them would remain safe.

Rather derogatively, Mackay (1993) also refers to suburban life in Australia today as 'caving' in the following way:

> ... an ultimately defensive form of escapism: a retreat to the comfort, privacy and, above all, security of home base ... There is a growing emphasis on entertainment and recreation equipment being installed in the home to minimize the need to go out ... as the sense of neighbourhood community gradually broke down in the 1970s and 1980s, we developed a compensatory obsession with the notion of privacy, which, in turn, further fuelled the fortress mentality.

Beyond the social, economic and environmental problems associated with automobile dependence there are serious problems of social injustice and inequity. In the following section, unequal access to transportation or urban amenities and necessities fostered or maintained by current BAU arrangements is explored.

Equity and auto dependence

Effective access to amenities and services in cities is a key measure of the performance of the urban transportation system. A fundamental principle, then, of sound urban and transportation planning is the delivery of effective 'access for all' without discrimination as to income, physical ability, housing location, mode of travel or any other factor (Schaeffer and Sclar, 1975). Effective and equitable access means many different things – for example, the difference between an easy and difficult commute. It may even, under certain circumstances, mean the difference between getting a job or not. It can make the difference between easy travel to schools, shops, medical services, recreational facilities and entertainment or a cumulative deprivation leading to real social problems. Access, in other words, profoundly affects the quality of urban life. It is an essential good, which depends on the effectiveness of transportation systems and, as transportation and urban theorists increasingly stress, on better urban spatial organization, which reduces the need for expensive private motorized movement.[9]

The transportation systems that help to supply access can be expensive in terms of public, environmental and other external costs. The question, then, of how transportation costs are distributed between individuals and households is very important because this distribution of costs, along with the distribution of access-related goods and services themselves, determines the equity of access which urban systems deliver (Rawls, 1971). In the absence of commonly accepted standards relating to minimum household or individual entitlements – or acceptable levels of inequality – no firm judgement about equity or justice is possible (Newman et al, 1992).

Transportation and locational disadvantage

Reduced capacities to use or afford automobiles are clearly a key factor in determining what can be termed transportation disadvantage. Land-use planning and investment in urban infrastructure can minimize or exacerbate both the extent and the intensity of transportation disadvantage. For example, where those unable to use or afford automobiles live closer to employment and other essential services, or where there is access to regular and reliable transit, these vulnerabilities may not lead to serious access problems. On the other hand, if people find themselves in more remote fringe locations where travel distances are typically longer and transit systems are often reduced to poor demand-responsive bus systems, access problems can be great. The twin sceptre of transportation and locational disadvantage comes into play.

Economic forces over many years in many auto-oriented societies (and others, including many developing cities) have caused increasing numbers of aspiring homeowners to settle in the less well-serviced urban fringe where land is cheap. In wealthy auto-based societies, this is manifested in endless tracts of poor-quality, low-density suburban housing with few transportation options other than the automobile and few amenities (Newman et al, 1992). In developing cities such as those in Latin America, millions of people seeking a better life in giant cities, such as Rio de Janeiro or São Paulo, simply inhabit slums or *favela*, or, at best, very poor makeshift housing areas, where they then flood into the employment-rich areas on informal or very low-grade formal bus systems, sometimes transferring onto metro or commuter rail systems, where those exist, and where they can afford to pay the fares (Vasconcellos, 2001).

In Australian cities, where inner areas were traditionally the address for poorer working-class populations, they have now mostly become the province of the rich. There is a mixed picture in the US where both poorer and wealthier households can be seen inhabiting fringe regions of metropolitan areas and still the inner cities have many low-income neighbourhoods (but this is changing with the gentrification of many older areas in US cities across the country in recent years).

Many households of low to middle income in outer areas face the choice of using poor transit or of devoting an increasing proportion of limited household income to the high costs of auto-ownership and use. Where low-density peripheral expansion or BAU continues, auto dependence becomes increasingly built into the form and fabric of the city. In essence, the capacity to afford and use automobiles becomes the key to the enjoyment of adequate and equitable access in the modern automobile-dependent city (Newman et al, 1992). Schaeffer and Sclar (1975, p6) analysed this interplay of urban form and transportation in their famous study *Access for All* and drew attention to its ethical implications:

The automobile has given improved mobility to the middle class, middle aged. But these owner drivers have not merely gained new mobility through the car; they have also rearranged the physical location patterns of society to suit their own private needs, and unwittingly in the process destroyed and limited the mobility and access of all others.

In cities in the US, these issues also have a racial dimension. Very often transportation disadvantage and inequity are centred in communities with African-American and Hispanic populations. In the early era of freeway expansion, many of the expansive roads were built in ways that concentrated minority populations within the 'walls' of surrounding expressways with most of the old connecting streets severed by the new limited-access roads. There are problems of insufficient access to transit and poor transit services, as was seen, in particular, in New Orleans, where so many low-income people were unable to escape the devastation of Hurricane Katrina because there was simply no transportation to allow them to do so. Unemployment in such communities can be high, while the lower paid and unskilled jobs (which are often part time) are frequently located in areas that demand long commutes. Automobile commuting is not economically rational relative to the amount of money being earned; where commuting on transit is not feasible, people are essentially excluded from the job markets. Thus, transportation assumes the complicating dimension of racial inequality in such situations and is an urgent issue to address.[10]

The sub-prime mortgage meltdown in the US, with its toxic loans, was concentrated in amenity-poor auto-based suburbs where people were already stretching budgets to make mortgage payments. The record oil prices of 2008 pushed these areas over the edge economically, with disastrous effects both for families and, indeed, the global economy.

The equity implications in an automobile-dependent city are that those who must manage without automobiles suffer not just from a lack of mobility, but also accessibility because they must travel in an urban environment that is hostile to alternative modes. Dispersed and low-density urban forms have placed important journeys beyond safe and easy walking and bicycling distance, and beyond the time reach of transit (Schaeffer and Sclar, 1975). Illich (1973) was one of the first to recognize technologically driven exclusion of alternatives to the automobile as a 'radical monopoly' (Newman et al, 1992).

Location and equity of access

Although a substantial portion of auto-ownership costs are fixed, most transportation costs vary with distance travelled. Notwithstanding differences across income groups, all will contain some households who must travel longer distances than others. Location is critical in determining this and, generally speaking, those living in outer and fringe urban zones will be spending more on transportation than those living closer to urban centres. For wealthier households, who choose more remote locations for the sake of environmental amenity, this may not be a problem. But for poorer households, who may be going into debt to make ends meet, it can seriously exacerbate the difficulties and stresses of more generalized financial hardship and the relative deprivations described above (Newman et al, 1992).

Speaking from an Australian point of view in the 1980s, to emphasize the longstanding nature of the whole equity problem of automobile dependence, Morris (1981, p39) states:

> Transport assumes a larger share of total household spending in non-metropolitan centres and especially in the outer suburbs of large cities ... increased transport spending has significant effect on household finances, particularly in outer suburban areas where families tend to be on low to middle incomes and are already faced with heavy cumulative commitments, such as housing and hire purchase payments.

Analysis of fuel consumption patterns in Sydney, Melbourne and Perth strongly confirms these observations (Newman et al, 1990). Per capita fuel use is significantly different between individual suburbs.[11] One recent study that tends to bring all this together and highlights the problems is that from Dodson and Sipe (2006), in which they produced a new index called VAMPIRE: Vulnerability Assessment for Mortgage, Petrol and Inflation Risks and Expenses. The VAMPIRE index is constructed from four indicator variables obtained from the 2001 Australian Bureau of Statistics Census, combined to provide a composite mortgage and oil vulnerability index for Australian cities. The variables are:

1 *Auto dependence*: proportion of those working who undertook a journey to work by car (driver or passenger);
2 *Proportion of households with two or more cars*;
3 *Income level*: median weekly household income;
4 *Mortgages*: proportion of dwelling units that are being purchased (either through a mortgage or a rent/buy scheme).

The VAMPIRE map for Melbourne is available on the web.[12] It clearly shows the equity problem in modern cities. The amenity- and transit-rich, high-value, culturally attractive and now high-income inner areas of Australian cities have a very low vulnerability to mortgage costs, fuel prices and inflation risks. Wealthy people who have the greatest capacity to pay for accessibility and mobility now live in areas where transportation needs are at a minimum and are thus highly privileged. Lower-income households live in amenity- and transit-poor areas farthest from the core city and

Figure 1.11 Transit, pedestrians and bicyclists all share Amsterdam's car-free centre

Source: Preston L. Schiller

significant centres, where transportation needs and costs are highest, but they have the least capacity to pay. The only variant to this pattern is along the suburban rail lines, which have fingers into the far outer suburbs. Location near these lines lessens one's vulnerability.

Summary

This discussion of equity in relation to auto dependence has highlighted three dimensions of transportation disadvantage and inequitable access in cities:

1   The transportation disadvantage associated with incapacities to afford or use automobiles: in an urban environment in which alternative transportation modes have been effectively eliminated in many areas or are declining, this is perhaps the most crucial inequality.
2   The question of transportation costs borne by households and individuals: transportation, and private automobiles, in particular, are expensive. Lower-income households able to reach across the threshold of auto-ownership may experience greater strain and be forced to make greater sacrifices than those enjoying higher incomes.
3   The added burdens imposed by distance and poor location: notwithstanding the high fixed cost of auto-ownership, the costs of transportation vary with distances travelled. Those living closer to city centres and significant sub-centres around cities, especially those built around rail stations where access to a rich array of services is highest, are significantly better off in all income groups, whether they depend on automobiles or on centralized transit systems. Such issues in the US often have an added racial dimension that urgently needs to be addressed.

Some key questions arise from all this. How close to universal auto-ownership can we realistically go, given the more or less intractable individual human limitations of income, age, physical and mental ability and so on? Conversely, how large is the population of those unable to use automobiles likely to be in the future? In the US and Australia during the early 1990s, around half the population did not have motor vehicle licences (Zuckerman, 1991), so the idea of a unitary common good, often cited in the 1950s and 1960s about the benefits of new roads and more automobiles, hardly can be justified now or, indeed, then.

It is perhaps finally worth drawing attention to the fact that many households do not have access to two or more automobiles. In urban Australia, for example, less than about half of the households enjoy the luxury of two or more autos. When one adds vulnerable individuals in one-auto households to the half million or so households who have no automobile, the problems of equitable access loom much larger. Certainly, significant vulnerable populations – the young, the old and disabled and, in some cases, significant proportions of the female population – are often very disadvantaged in automobile-dependent cities. These groups are frequently also poor and are likely to be permanently excluded from ready access to important activities or locations (Newman et al, 1992).

Figure 1.12 Sprawl development invades the beautiful mountains of the San Francisco Bay area (California)

Source: Preston L. Schiller

Importantly and, finally, even if it were possible to achieve universal auto-ownership, the other environmental, social and economic costs of auto dependence are so great that urban systems cannot sustain endlessly expanding private mobility. Everything then points to the fundamental need for a radical rethink of the urban transportation issue and its basic tenets – a sustainability-driven approach.[13]

Conclusions

This chapter has analysed several of the key issues and challenges for ST. The sheer magnitude of travel and freight movement in everyday life, its impacts and benefits and the consequences of overdependence on automobility, with its accompanying inequities experienced under BAU transportation, mean that sustainable transportation has its work cut out for itself. The next chapter is an exploration of the 'car culture', the system of beliefs and values that maintain hypermobility, automobile dependence and inequity.

Questions for discussion

- Discuss the strengths and limitations of the definition of sustainable transportation. How might you change it?
- Is transportation planning and provision (infrastructure, transit, etc.) in your community oriented towards business as usual (BAU) or sustainable transportation (ST)? Cite examples.
- Identify and discuss some examples of automobile dependence and hypermobility in your community and daily life.

Notes

1   These include Tolley (1990), Whitelegg (1993, 1997), CST (1998), Bannister (2000) and Benfield and Replogle (2002).
2   See http://cst.uwinnipeg.ca/.
3   All graphs in this section based on these cities are drawn from Kenworthy and Laube (2001).
4   For more, see www.fiafoundation.com/policy/road_safety/news/g8_poverty_gains_ threatened_by_road_crash_costs.html.
5   For more, see www.factbook.net/EGRF_Economic_costs.htm.
6   For more, see www.telegraph.co.uk/news/uknews/1576430/Obesity-crisis-get-paid-to-lose-weight.html.
7   See Lynch (1977), van Vliet (1983), Wohlwill (1985) and Kenworthy (2000).
8   Davis interviewed in Dery (1995).
9   See Goodwin et al (1991), Mohr (1991), Newman et al (1992), Calthorpe (1993) and Katz (1994).
10 See Rothschild (2009). Also, Morgan Spurlock's television series *30 Days* dealt with this issue in the first episode of the first season, where he attempted to live on minimum wage for 30 days, using mass transit to get to several jobs from his out of the way apartment.
11 For example, Fremantle and Padbury are extremes in Perth and indicate that average households spent three times as much on fuel in the low-density outer suburbs as in the compact mixed land-use area of Fremantle.
12 See www.98.griffith.edu.au/.../Dodson2006ShockingTheSuburbs_ATRF.pdf, Figure 7.
13 See Whitelegg and Haq (2003), especially Chapters 1 and 25.

References and further reading

Adams, J. (1999) 'The social implications of hypermobility', in *OECD, Project on Sustainable Transportation (EST): The Economic and Social Implications of Sustainable Transportation*, Proceedings of the Ottawa workshop, 20–21 October 1998, OECD Publications, Paris, pp95–134

Adams, J. (2000) 'Hypermobility', *Prospect*, March, pp27–31

Automotive Digest (2009) 'World automobile population 2005–2020', *Automotive Digest*, www.automotivedigest.com/content/displayArticle.aspx?a=55782, accessed 14 September 2009

Bannister, D. (2000) 'Sustainable urban development and transport: A Eurovision for 2020', *Transport Reviews*, vol 20, no 1, pp113–130, http://dx.doi.org/10.1080/014416400295365, accessed 15 September 2009

Benfield, F. K. and Replogle, M. (2002) 'The roads more traveled: Sustainable transportation in America', *Environmental Law Review*, vol 32, p10633, www.eli.org

BTS (Bureau of Transportation Statistics) (2006) *National Transportation Statistics 2006*, US Department of Transportation, Research and Innovative Technology Administration, Washington, DC, www.bts.gov/.../national_transportation_statistics/2006/pdf/entire.pdf, accessed 14 September 2009

Calthorpe, P. (1993) *The Next American Metropolis: Ecology and Urban Form*, Princeton Architectural Press, Princeton, NJ

Chafe, Z. (2007) 'Transportation and communication', *Worldwatch Institute*, November, www.worldwatch.org/taxonomy/term/517, accessed 14 September 2009

CST (Centre for Sustainable Transportation) (1998) *Sustainable Transportation Monitor*, no 1, Toronto, Ontario

Davis, M. (1990) *City of Quartz: Excavating the Future in Los Angeles*, Vintage, London

Dery, M. (1995) 'Downsizing the future: Beyond blade runner, an interview with Mike Davis', *Future Noir 21-C*, no 3, pp43–47, www.otthollo.de/JONA/.../Davis%20Downsizing%20 the%20Future.pdf, accessed 15 September 2009

Dodson, J. and Sipe, N. (2006) 'Shocking the suburbs: Urban location, housing and oil vulnerability in the Australian city', Griffith University, Urban Research Program, Research

Paper 8, www.98.griffith.edu.au/.../Dodson2006ShockingTheSuburbs_ATRF.pdf, accessed 14 September 2009

Frank L., Engelke P. and Schmid T. (2003) *Health and Community Design: The Impact of the Built Environment on Physical Activity*, Island Press, Washington, DC

Gakenheimer, R. (ed) (1978) *The Automobile and the Environment: An International Perspective*, MIT Press, Cambridge, MA

Gilbert, R. and Perl, A. (2008) *Transport Revolutions: Moving People and Freight without Oil*, Earthscan, London

Goodwin, P. E., Hallett, S., Kenny, F. and Stokes, G. (1991) *Transport: The New Realism*, Transport Studies Unit, Oxford University Press, Oxford, UK

Illich, I. (1973) *Tools for Conviviality*, Calder and Boyars, London

Illich, I. (1976) *Energy and Equity*, Marion Boyars, London

Jacobs, J. (1961) *The Death and Life of Great American Cities*, Random House, New York, NY

Katz, P. (1994) *The New Urbanism: Toward an Architecture of Community*, McGraw Hill, New York, NY

Kenworthy, J. R. (2000) 'Building more livable cities by overcoming automobile dependence: An international comparative reviews', in R. Lawrence (ed) *Sustaining Human Settlement: A Challenge for the New Millennium*, Urban International Press, Newcastle-upon-Tyne, pp271–314

Kenworthy, J. R. and Laube, F. (2001) *The Millennium Cities Database for Sustainable Transport*, UITP, Brussels, and ISTP, Murdoch University, Perth

Kunstler, J. H. (1996) *Home from Nowhere: Remaking Our Everyday World for the 21st Century*, Simon & Schuster, New York, NY

Lasch, C. (1991) 'Liberalism and civic virtue', *Telos*, vol 88, pp57–68

Lynch, K. (ed) (1977) *Growing Up in Cities: Studies of the Spatial Environment of Adolescence in Cracow, Melbourne, Mexico City, Salta, Toluca and Warszawa*, MIT Press, Cambridge, MA, and UNESCO, Paris

Mackay, H. (1993) *Reinventing Australia: The Mind and Mood of Australia in the '90s*, Angus and Robertson, Sydney

Mackay, H. (1994) 'The future stops here', *The Weekend Australian: The Weekend Review*, 3–4 September, p16

Mohr, R. (1991) 'Time, space and equity', Discussion paper prepared for the Australian Council of Social Service (ACOSS), Sydney

Morris, J. (1981) 'Urban public transport', in P. N. Troy (ed) *Equity in the City*, George Allen and Unwin, Sydney

Newman, P. W. G. and Kenworthy, J. R. (1989) *Cities and Automobile Dependence: A Sourcebook*, Gower Technical, Aldershot, UK, and Brookfield, VT

Newman, P. W. G. and Kenworthy, J. R. (1999) *Sustainability and Cities: Overcoming Automobile Dependence*, Island Press, Washington, DC

Newman, P. W. G., Kenworthy, J. R. and Lyons, T. J. (1990) *Transport Energy Conservation Policies for Australian Cities: Strategies for Reducing Automobile Dependence*, Institute for Science and Technology Policy, Murdoch University, Perth, Western Australia

Newman, P., Kenworthy, J. and Vintila, P. (1992) 'Housing, transport and urban form', Background Paper 15 + Appendices for the National Housing Strategy, Commonwealth of Australia, Canberra

Rawls, J. (1971) *A Theory of Justice*, The President and Fellows of Harvard College, Cambridge, MA

Rothschild, E. (2009) 'Can we transform the auto-industrial society?', *The New York Review of Books*, vol 56, no 3, www.nybooks.com/articles/22333, accessed 3 July 2009

Sachs, W. (1992) *For Love of the Automobile: Looking Back into the History of Our Desires*, University of California Press, Berkeley, CA

Schaeffer, K. and Sclar, E. (1975) *Access for All: Transportation and Urban Growth*, Penguin, Baltimore, MD

Schiller, P. and Kenworthy, J. R. (1999) 'Prospects for sustainable transportation in the Pacific Northwest: A comparison of Vancouver, Seattle and Portland', *World Transport Policy and Practice*, vol 5, no 1, pp30–38

Schiller, P. and Kenworthy, J. R. (2003) 'Prospects for sustainable transportation in the Pacific Northwest', in J. Whitelegg and G. Haq (eds) *The Earthscan Reader on World Transport Policy & Practice*, Earthscan, London

Stringer, P. and Wenzel, H. (1976) *Transportation Planning for a Better Environment*, Plenum Press, New York, NY

Tolley, R. (ed) (1990) *The Greening of Urban Transport: Planning for Walking and Cycling in Western Cities*, Belhaven Press, London

US Bureau of Transportation Statistics (2006) *National Transportation Statistics 2006*, US Department of Transportation, Research and Innovative Technology Administration, Washington, DC, www.bts.gov/.../national_transportation_statistics/2006/pdf/entire.pdf, accessed 14 September 2009

US Census Bureau (2008) *FT 920 US Merchandise Trade Selected Highlights*, www.census.gov/foreign-trade/balance/c5700.html#2009, accessed 5 August 2009

Vasconcellos, E. (2001) *Urban Transport, Environment and Equity: The Case for Developing Countries*, Earthscan Publications, London

Vliet, W. van (1983) 'Children's travel behaviour', *Ekistics*, vol 298, pp61–65

WCED (World Commission on Environment and Development) (1987) *Our Common Future*, Brundtland Commission, www.unece.org/oes/nutshell/2004-2005/focus_sustainable_development.htm, accessed 22 February 2008

Whitelegg, J. (1993) *Transport for a Sustainable Future: The Case for Europe*, Belhaven Press, London

Whitelegg, J. (1997) *Critical Mass: Transport Environment and Society in the Twenty-First Century*, Pluto Press, London

Whitelegg, J. and Haq, G. (eds) (2003) *The Earthscan Reader on World Transport Policy and Practice*, Earthscan, London

Wohlwill, J. F. (1985) 'Residential density as a variable in child development research', in J. F. Wohlwill and W. van Vliet (eds) *Habitats for Children: The Impacts of Density*, Lawrence Erlbaum Associates, Publishers, Hillsdale, NJ

World Bank (2006) *World Development Indicators*, World Bank, Washington, DC, http://devdata.worldbank.org/wdi2006/contents/cover.htm, accessed 13 September 2009

Zuckermann, W. (1991) *End of the Road: The World Car Crisis and How We Can Solve It*, Lutterworth Press, Cambridge, and Chelsea Green Publishing Company, Post Mills, VT

2

Automobile Cities, the Car Culture and Alternative Possibilities

Introduction

The previous chapter provided definitions of sustainable transportation (ST) and explored two of its major challenges: automobile dependence and equity, and inequity in transportation. This chapter explores how cities evolved from walking cities to automobile cities and how a car culture developed, along with greater dependence on automobiles. The chapter investigates several facets of the car culture and contrasts two versions of everyday life: an automobile-dependent family and neighbourhood is compared with the life of a car-free family in a traffic-calmed neighbourhood.

Walking cities, transit cities and automobile cities[1]

Walking cities

Urban life extends back thousands of years and over this long period of time all cities were basically dependent upon walking for their circulation needs (Kostof, 1991). Many walking cities were also walled cities and all growth had to be accommodated by increasing densities and intensifying the mixture of land uses. In Europe, the walking city was dominant up until around 1850, when walking or, at best, horse-drawn transport was the chief means of movement. These were slow forms of transport and in order for the city to remain accessible, all destinations had to be available within about half an hour, travelling at about 5km/hr. The cities therefore remained small and dense, with highly mixed land uses. The surrounding countryside was preserved for farming or natural open spaces such as wood lots and forests (Newman and Kenworthy, 1999). Walking cities are conceptualized in Figure 2.1.

The walking city was characterized by narrow, often winding streets and provided for an inherently egalitarian transport system. Some people had horses and carriages; but the advantages afforded by this were more related to comfort than any major accessibility benefit. No one in a walking city was locationally disadvantaged in a transport sense, which cannot be said for cities today, designed around the automobile. As described in Chapter 1, in automobile cities, many people who live in the outer suburbs and urban fringe in order to find cheap land discover that their access needs are difficult to meet by any mode apart from the car. Such people live with enforced car ownership due to their location within the city and are especially disadvantaged with respect to walking (Newman et al, 1992). The Chinese city is still today largely a walking and cycling environment; but this is changing very dramatically as millions of people avail themselves of cars, and the environment for pedestrians and cyclists is severely disrupted (Kenworthy and Hu, 2002; Kenworthy and Townsend, 2002).

Today there are many examples from around the world of walking cities that became overrun with cars during the 1950s and 1960s, but which, over a period of time, have gradually reclaimed their walking qualities (e.g. Freiburg and Munich in Germany and Copenhagen in Denmark). In 1967, Copenhagen began to gradually remove a few per cent of central city parking spaces every year until they had transformed their city centre back into its traditional walking city form (Gehl and Gemzøe, 1996).

Transit cities

The transit or public transport city emerged in the industrial world around 1850 with the advent of new transport technologies – namely, the revolutionary steam train and electric tram. Preceding these modes were the horse-drawn tram operating on wooden tracks and the steam tram, pulled by chains, which were powered from a stationary steam engine. These modes facilitated faster travel (on average, a jump from about 5km/hr to 15km/hr) and, hence, bigger cities, although all urban development had to remain within an easy walk or bicycle trip of the tram stops or rail stations. These cities, therefore, still had quite high densities of land use and there was a well-defined 'edge' to urban settlements (nodes around rail stations and tight corridors around tramlines). A high-density, mixed-use urban form also meant that there were still a very large number of trips that could be conveniently accomplished on foot or bicycle, and the public environments of cities (their streets, squares and other places) were still very people oriented (Newman and Kenworthy, 1999). Figure 2.2 conceptualizes the urban form of the typical transit city, showing the two clear types of urban form of tram-based inner suburbs and distinct nodes or urban villages around railway stations on the steam train and later electric rail lines.

This type of city gained ascendancy in the industrial world, and during the period from about 1850 to 1940 it tended to be the dominant type of city form in industrialized countries. In other less developed parts of the world where new technologies did not take off in the way in which they did in the Western world, the walking city remained dominant. These cities have had a less well-defined period of public transport development, if any. Certainly, most of them have not been shaped significantly by a period of extensive and enduring urban rail development (trains or trams), although some, such as Bangkok, did have these modes (Poboon, 1997; Barter, 1999). Rather, in recent years (from about the 1970s onwards) they have tended to develop directly from pedestrian-oriented cities with some bus-based public transport systems into cities where motorcycles and cars have begun to take the upper hand. In the process, the rights of pedestrians and cyclists have been trampled on through the removal of footpaths for widened roads, the severance of neighbourhoods by freeway and toll road infrastructure, and the creation of a hostile, highly dangerous public realm dominated by traffic (Kenworthy, 1997).

The influence of transport technologies on the quality of public spaces in cities and the nature of social relations is clearly seen in the kinds of attractive and interactive public realms that have been created in many cities where transit systems have been given priority in city development. For example, in Zurich's Bahnhofstrasse, and in many other cities, urban space is shared between trams and pedestrians and private space spills out into the public realm. Transit, by its nature, involves people mixing together in shared space and is an important factor in helping to shape social relations.

Automobile cities

Whatever one's particular outlook is on what the automobile has done for urban societies, it is universally agreed that it has brought enormous change. Figure 2.3 provides a conceptual diagram of the archetypal automobile city, showing the enormous expansion of developed area relative to the walking and transit cities, which its use has facilitated.

The automobile facilitated the uninhibited outward expansion of the city because people and businesses were no longer constrained to the fixed-track public transport systems or walking-scale environments of earlier times. Development became footloose and could occur anywhere that a section of black top could be laid down. The automobile's much greater speed allowed the city to get much bigger again, and densities of development dropped dramatically. Through the exercise of modern town planning principles, land uses became segregated into zones, and travel distances for all trip purposes increased dramatically. The car began to displace public transport and non-motorized modes and today achieves modal shares for all daily trips in the range of 80 to 95 per cent in automobile cities in North America and Australia. This type of city became the dominant form in the US and Australia and, to a slightly lesser extent, in Canada from the mid 1940s onward (Kenworthy and Laube, 1999; Newman and Kenworthy, 1999).

Many countries in other parts of the world such as Asia, whose cities have traditionally had high-density walking-oriented urban forms, are developing their own characteristic style of automobile city forms, particularly in outer regions. This is especially true where there is little planning to control the use of cars and, indeed, little effective public planning control over urban land uses (e.g. in Bangkok and Kuala Lumpur). In the high-density mixed-use parts of the city, where land uses would normally facilitate high levels of walking and non-motorized transport, these modes are so unattractive due to lack of facilities, noise, fumes and danger that they have been, or are being, decimated. Such cities suffer particularly high levels of transport deaths, many of them of non-motorized mode users (and also motorcyclists) (Barter, 2000).

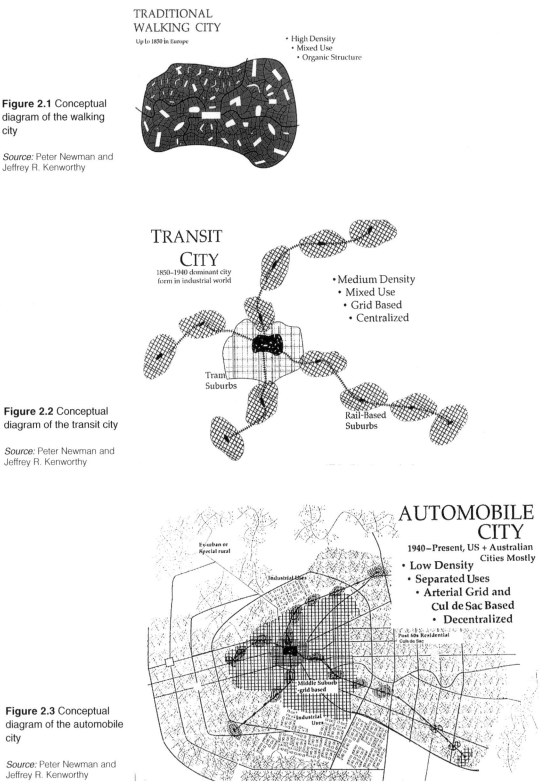

Figure 2.1 Conceptual diagram of the walking city

Source: Peter Newman and Jeffrey R. Kenworthy

Figure 2.2 Conceptual diagram of the transit city

Source: Peter Newman and Jeffrey R. Kenworthy

Figure 2.3 Conceptual diagram of the automobile city

Source: Peter Newman and Jeffrey R. Kenworthy

Additional lessons from city types

Kenworthy's depictions of automobile dependence, equity and inequity issues in Chapter 1, and the transportation evolution of cities from walking to transit and automobile above, provide a very helpful backdrop for a discussion of the relationship of 'car culture', to be discussed immediately below, and how urban life is organized. A few additional points may be added to his analysis:

- The walking city respected topography, and it tended to create communities within which walking was relatively easy. Fine grid street patterns were also common (e.g. Greece, Japan and China).
- Accessibility and proximity were the organizing principles of life in the walking city.
- Transit provided solutions to population growth and the need to separate residences from unhealthy industrial pollution. This separation, understandable in the context of the 19th and 20th centuries, led to building codes and zoning enforcing segregated land uses long after it was necessary – as in recent decades when re-urbanization and infill are so greatly hampered by this 'weight of the past'. While transportation equity was not as great as in the walking city, most sectors of the population maintained reasonably good access to jobs and other necessities.
- Transit cities were able to expand or extend themselves along transit routes while still generally respecting their topography and the need for strong centres. This also allowed some relief from the overcrowding of pre-transit industrial cities. While transit cities generally maintained a strong urban centre, they allowed for the development of sub-centres around transit nodes, also easily accessible by foot or bicycle modes. Not all trips for services and shopping needed to have the central business district (CBD) as a destination, nor did they just rely on one mode.
- The automobile allowed cities to expand without limits and without respect to topography. The automobile climbed hills that streetcars had shunned. The grid of arterial streets and expressways, rather than the lines of rail transit routes, became the defining and organizing features of mobility. The automobile city has created great mobility opportunities for some segments of the population while generating or maintaining serious inequities in mobility and accessibility for the rest of the population.

Figure 2.4 A conclave of pink Cadillacs: Rewards for very productive cosmetics salespersons

Source: Preston L. Schiller

The following vignette, in Box 2.1, illustrates the extreme dependence that can shape life in automobile cities.

Box 2.1 Automobile dependence in the neighbourhood

It is a typical weekday morning and Phil Erup and Minnie Vann march out their door into his-and-her sports utility vehicles (SUVs), en route to their respective worksites about 3 miles (5km) distant from their house. First they drop off Carla, their robust teenager, at her school a few short blocks away because they think that walking, even in a quiet residential neighbourhood, is inherently dangerous. En route they pass the nearly empty school bus weaving through the dozens of parents' cars jamming the street at the school. Next they drop off their four-year-old, Tim, at a daycare centre 1 mile (1.6km) away from their neighbourhood because the city's zoning code does not allow for daycare facilities in their immediate neighbourhood. Phil and Minnie work only a few blocks apart in the centre of town, and there is bus service every 15 minutes connecting their neighbourhood to the town centre; but each feels compelled to drive and to have a vehicle at work. Often the family drives to and through a fast food outlet, eating in the car while on their way elsewhere. They have installed a rear-seat DVD monitor to occupy the children while they are chauffeured. Saving time for family activities is the reason that Phil and Minnie drive everywhere; but they never seem to have much time outside of the car or the TV room.

One street over, bored retiree Ernie Edsel wonders what's new in the neighbourhood this morning and fires up his large sedan for his daily exploration. It has been two years since he became widowed and his life is rather lonely. If he had chosen to walk he might have had a little human contact, perhaps even met a potential companion, but he's gotten out of the walking habit.

Up the hill at the university Jack and Jill dutifully take notes in a lecture on climate change and then drive down the hill to the health club. The fuel that their car consumes for its short workout will greatly exceed the number of calories they shed in their own workouts. All over town teenagers are driving about, one hand on the wheel, the other clutching a mobile phone. Occasionally they drive through the fast food purveyors to visit their friends who work there to support their cars so that they can drive to school, drive to work after school, and support their cars, so they can drive to school, drive to work after school ...

Source: Schiller (2002)

The vignette in Box 2.1 illustrates the way in which many people are organizing their daily lives and communities around the automobile. The phenomenon of drive-to/drive-through/drive-for-all is turning almost everywhere in the US and parts of Canada into a nowhere of ugly strips and malls, vast parking lots and barren roadways (Kunstler, 1993). About half of the priority recommendations made by the US Public Health Service's Centers for Disease Control for combating the current epidemic of obesity and inactivity address increasing physical activity, walking, bicycling, transit use and community design; another way of stating their recommendations is to urge citizens to drive less and for communities to accommodate less driving and automobile-oriented design

(CDC, 2009). And Health Canada (Starky, 2005; Health Canada, 2006) warns that Canadians are following close behind.

While the vignette's examples may seem far fetched and possible only in the extreme example of the automobile-dependent US, statistics indicate that in many metropolitan areas of Canada, Europe and even Asia, driving for all sorts of trips is on the increase. There are notable exceptions: several cities and urban areas where automobile dependence is being challenged with varying degrees of success, and these are discussed in several places in this text, especially in Chapter 9. A heavy degree of automobile dependence is not inevitable. Even in automobile-dependent communities, it is possible for a combination of factors, including policy changes, to encourage the lessening of this dependence in neighbourhoods, workplaces and the wider community. Chapter 9 presents several exemplary efforts to move to transportation sustainability and Chapter 8 contains examples of how a more desirable future could be attained.

Car culture

The complex of social factors that buttress and maintain automobile dependence may be termed the 'car culture'. This term is used in the tradition of scholars of automobility, such as James Flink (1975, 1988). Car culture includes such factors as:

- cultural, philosophical and institutional underpinnings – critique and criticism of the automobile's symbolism, belief systems, mediating factors and roles of institutions such as education, industry and government;
- role of the mainstream media – broadcast (radio, television), print, cinema and web-based in shaping perceptions and values surrounding the automobile;

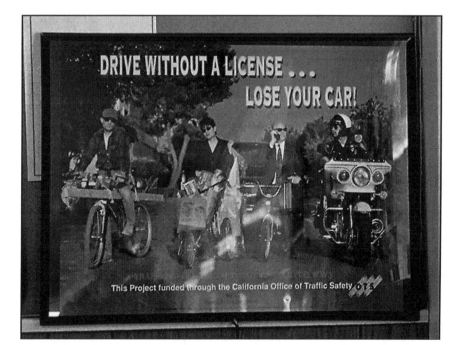

Figure 2.5 'Lose your license, become a bicyclist', warns the California Office of Traffic Safety

Source: Preston L. Schiller

- advertising – the packaging, selling and promotion of the automobile;
- music, music videos and popular entertainment;
- literature (automobile travel as a theme);
- carchitecture – the ways in which buildings are designed to accommodate automobiles and show their most important features to passing motorists, as well as the enshrining of automobile aesthetics;
- tourism – much of which is dependent upon motoring, especially in the wealthier countries.

Critique and criticism of the car culture

While a fair degree of philosophical, political and cultural criticism accompanied the rise of automobility in the late 19th and early 20th centuries, its pace and depth grew in the decades immediately following World War II. Early criticism tended to focus on the elitist aspects of automobility, especially before Fordism made the automobile an item of mass consumption in industrially advanced nations, and then moved to criticism of its effects on urban life, especially its reckless takeover of streets and the killing and harming of pedestrians. This aspect of criticism became somewhat blunted as the walking and bicycling public gradually submitted itself to traffic regulation – the early ideological cloak of automobile hegemony (Norton, 2007, 2008).

The reach of automobility, in terms of ownership, driving and highway construction, expanded greatly in the late 1940s and 1950s. While welcomed at first by cities large and small, the large new expressways dumping more and more traffic into cities were experienced as destroyers of urban life. Reactions to the lack of fit between standards designed for intercity highways and city needs set in earlier in Europe than in the US. The Marshall Plan guiding US post-World War II assistance in Europe had encouraged the construction of large expressways into and through many of the war-damaged cities that it aimed to rebuild. Its housing counterpart, the building of large Le Corbusier-style residential towers, triggered strong reactions among many advocates of a more traditional approach to transportation and land-use planning.

The 1960s were a time of massive road expansion and major protest and reaction against their destruction of the urban fabric, especially in the US. Jane Jacobs's *The Death and Life of Great American Cities* (1961) provided an incisive critique of the destructiveness of 1950s and 1960s business as usual (BAU) transportation, especially in its destructive impacts upon cities. Her masterful work, as influential for popular thinking about pedestrians, street life, neighbourhoods, cities and transportation as was Rachel Carson's (in her seminal 1962 work *Silent Spring*) for the early environmental movement, inspired civic activists and urban researchers across the US and Canada as well as many other countries.

The 1970s witnessed a full flowering of critique and criticism of automobility and the car culture. Prominent among these were the critiques of Ivan Illich, whose seminal thinking on these matters was published in the incisive and pithy *Energy and Equity* (Illich, 1976). Illich's thinking on this topic had already been circulating, stimulating widespread discussion and influencing parallel critiques, such as that of the French social and political philosopher André Gorz (1973). Their overlapping critiques, with Illich's much more highly developed, should be consulted in full while a few key points are included here:

- The perceived gains derived by higher-speed, higher energy-consuming modes are illusory because the financial and time commitments demanded to support them, especially at the level of the traveller, create dependence and consume more time than lower-speed, lower-energy modes. The perceived benefits of higher speeds are actually offset by the amount of time people must labour to afford them, as well as the greater time commitment to travel created by greater trip distances.
- While automobility may be perceived as a mass and, therefore, 'democratic' phenomenon in industrial countries, it actually expands social and economic inequity.
- In industrially less developed countries the greater speed of travel achieved by elites comes at the expense of the walking and bicycling masses.

The work of Illich and Gorz attracted the attention of automobility and car culture critics and advocates for alternatives to these throughout the 1970s and subsequent decades. Among those who expanded upon their central themes were John Adams, who developed the very important notion of 'hypermobility', the excessive amount of travel fostered by destinations made more distant by urban sprawl combined with the 'mobility culture' (Adams, 1999, 2000); and John Whitelegg's systematic development of the notion of 'time pollution': the ways in which excessive mobility robs people of valuable time in a variety of insidious ways (Whitelegg, 1993, 1997).

The reactions against automobility and highway expansion that created numerous critiques in the 1970s (see Chapter 7) were followed by several important works, some academic and some for a general audience, during the 1980s and 1990s. These were often built upon notions introduced by Illich and Gorz. Academic critique of automobility and highway expansion was aided by increasingly sophisticated analysis of traffic data that led to conclusions indicating that road expansion, often justified by traffic engineers and highway interests as the 'cure' for congestion, actually created more congestion than might have otherwise occurred. This well-documented phenomenon has come to be known as generated, or induced traffic, sometimes popularly referred to as the 'field of dreams' effect after the cryptic saying from the film of that title – 'if you build it, they will come'.

The opposite effect, if you un-build it (or reduce road capacity), the result is that traffic diminishes. This has been documented and is known as 'traffic degeneration', 'trip degeneration' or 'traffic evaporation' (Roberts, 1992). Other voices added the dimension of sensitivity to urban design and urban form to the mix. Researchers Peter Newman and Jeffrey Kenworthy analysed the relationship between urban form, infrastructure and automobility (Newman and Kenworthy, 1989, 1999), and found that the more that cities attempted to accommodate automobility through road expansion and a variety of traffic engineering gimmicks oriented to keeping traffic flowing freely, the more congestion, sprawl and pollution they created. For wider audiences, architecture and planning critic Jane Holtz Kay (1997) and New Urbanism advocate James Howard Kunstler (1993, 1996) wrote passionately and perceptively about urban sprawl, automobile-oriented design and the culture of car-centred convenience.

Box 2.2 Cars are us

Michael Ferro[2]

For most of us denizens of the industrial West, the car fills our lives completely, inside and out. The car pervades our thinking as much as it encloses our bodies and organizes the cities and towns in which most of us live.

The psychologist Lev Vygotsky was one of the first to note that the mind is culturally determined. Vygotsky observed that our practical day-to-day activities require particular mental processes. Cars, because we drive them, ride in them, have to dodge them and cannot avoid seeing them or hearing about them, are fundamental units of our mental life. We may, for example, refer to the 'Cadillac' or the 'Mercedes Benz' of any number of completely unrelated things.

Driving a car or riding in one produces a particular consciousness in which other drivers and riders, as well as pedestrians and bicyclists, are transformed into exotic creatures different from us, with incomprehensible needs, rights and ways of being. Car consciousness pervades our lives because driving is not a luxury or an occasional or exceptional activity, but an essential tool for existing in the US and many places in the world.

In the US, the car has come to embody a conception of individualism whose roots might be traced to the talks and writings of Ralph Waldo Emerson, in which he focused on the virtue of following one's own thoughts and intuitions and the avoidance of a superficial conformity. The isolation of the car driver allows a person to see himself as empowered and in control. This has long been a theme in popular culture, in literature and films as well as advertising. Our pervasive mythology of the 'road trip' means that we view the act of driving as an adventure of self-discovery and personal character development. The great size of the US, its abundance of open space and relative under-population, has given personal mobility a special sort of meaning and emphasizes our exceptionalist character.

During the early 20th century in the US, the consumption of consumer goods made by corporations became a new basis for defining the individual. The new art and science of advertising were chief ingredients of this development. With regard to the car, corporate consumerism reached a new level of cultural dominance with Sloanism in the 1930s. Henry Ford previously had made automotive-industrial production very efficient. Alfred Sloan of General Motors (GM) came up with the idea of creating new car models each year focused on functionally trivial styling and comfort features. Various car models were advertised to specific groups of buyers to maintain and increase consumption. Sloanism encouraged economic waste by defining cars as disposable objects of fashion.

Sloanism continues today in full force in the car industry as in other businesses which encourage consumption and waste. In 2006, US car companies, including dealers, spent over US$18 billion in advertising, down a few per cent from the previous year. To put this in perspective, this is twice the amount of federal public transit funding for that year (FHWA, 2006). Today's Sloanist car-marketing techniques include cars, such as 'hybrids', designed to be sold to those drivers who enjoy thinking of themselves as environmentally conscious and responsible.

We can only be astounded when looking at just how dominant a role the car plays in the US economy. It is the industry with the highest economic output. In the 25 years from 1978 to 2002, which includes some recession years, the car industry has typically constituted about 3.5 per cent of our gross domestic product (GDP). Direct employment attributable to the car industry was 3.5 million in 1998 and was 6.6 million including all indirect economic activities. The value-added productivity for the average job in the US in 2000 was US$73,000. In car manufacturing, value-added productivity during that year was US$292,000. In 2000, remuneration per employee for domestic industry as a whole was US$43,500. For the car industry, remuneration per employee was US$69,500.

Contradictions abound in our car-embodied selves. Love and death coexist uncomfortably. The freedom of the road inevitably implies the entrapment of traffic and the official commands of traffic signs and signals and painted lines. We have learned to feel safe from the world as it actually is in these devices, which hardcore motorcyclists wittily refer to as 'cages'. Cars are made ever more comfortable and quiet, their air-conditioning units filtering what we breathe as their audio systems numb us to the realities of mechanical noise. Because we must drive, and we cannot easily think of how not to do so, we are also numb to the realities of cars as agents of death from crashes and other 'accidents', the waging of wars for oil, the poisoning of the environment, the epidemic of disease due to lack of exercise and the potential calamity of climate change.[3]

The mainstream media and the car culture

The media, print and broadcast are extremely dependent upon the automobile industry and related industries and services for advertising revenues and generally do not engage in criticism directed at any aspects of 'automobiledom'. Most critique of automobility and the car culture is communicated through print, books and periodical articles and print-related media such as websites and publications that are often associated with political and environmental organizations (see Appendix 2). Critique sometimes emerges in the mainstream broadcast media in special programmes and documentaries. Some 'alternative newspapers' will publish criticism of the car culture and a few mainstream newspapers and magazines offer token critique space in their opinion sections and a rare special feature. Often these emerge in response to an article or editorial extolling the wonders of automobility or criticizing

Figure 2.6 'Automobiles: The myth, the reality'

Source: Andy Singer (www.andysinger.com)

some aspect of advocacy for improved walking, bicycling or public transportation (Engler, 2009). Some radio stations or networks offer occasional opportunities for voices that differ from BAU. Only rarely does a critique surface in cinema, commercial radio or television. An exception was the documenting of the destruction of most US streetcar systems and the struggle against urban freeways in *Taken for a Ride* by Jim Klein and Martha Olson (1996). When criticism does emerge in the mainstream broadcast media, it is often in the form of comedy or satire, such as Steve Martin's *L.A. Story* (1991) that includes scenes spoofing how Angelenos drive 100 feet (30m) to visit neighbours, receive guidance in life and love from traffic billboards, and engage in the sport of freeway shootouts.

Movies and TV: The automobile as star and sponsor

Cinema has had a long love affair with the automobile, and television has enjoyed multiple serial relationships with cars. From the earliest days of silent cinema to the era of James Dean and *Rebel Without a Cause*, the automobile was associated with numerous themes, from emotional to utilitarian, appealing to a mass audience: pursuit; escape; rescue; endangerment; travel and leisure; power; social class distinction and competition; reward for work ethic adherence; power; domination; self-destruction; gender; sexuality; romance; and eroticism. Automobile racing has been an important aspect of the car culture and cinema since the earliest days of automobility and film. The chaos of urban traffic has been mirrored in fantasy mayhems created by gangsters, motorized heists, motorcycle gangs and road warriors. For those inured to vehicular violence and for people who appreciate the dark side of the car culture there are films such as *Death Race 2000* and *Crash* – and, lest we forget, the intergalactic hot-rodding of *Star Wars* and George Lucas's earlier paean to hot-rodding, *American Graffiti* (Hey, 1983; Smith, 1983).

The love affair has turned into one of Hollywood's longest lasting marriages in a city and industry infamous for romantic turnovers and frequent divorce. With or without formal encouragement from the auto industry, Hollywood, on film and in its lifestyle, glamorized and romanticized the automobile. The automobile industry, especially in the US, quickly picked up on the power of the images projected on the silver screen and began to sponsor films advertising its wares and shaping its customer market. Present and future motorists and buyers were reached by short industry-produced films often shown as part of the screenings of feature films. Children learned about the wonderful machines and how to be good pedestrians by getting out of the way of automobiles through educational films produced and distributed by the auto industry and its allies, such as automobile clubs and self-proclaimed safety agencies.

The love affair carried over into television, Hollywood's sibling – although they have become more like twins joined at the hip than the rival siblings they once were. Many of the early TV programmes in the US were sponsored by automobile manufacturers or allied industries such as petroleum companies, tyre manufacturers and automobile servicing chains. Not only did cinema and, later, television, help to popularize the automobile, the automobile and all the related industries trailing in its comet tail have, in turn, helped to sustain the film and TV industry through various forms of sponsorship. The huge audiences

---

Box 2.3 We just want to change your oil

Personality interacts with the brand to influence how the customer feels about a company. The personality also determines whether a brand furthers the customer's emotional understanding of a company. For example, if the brand personality is open and friendly, it can make customers feel secure and comfortable. A good example of this is Saturn Corporation's Welcome Center in Spring Hill, Tennessee, US, where Saturn car owners can go to get to know Saturn or its national network of car clubs, which are communities of Saturn owners …

Can your customers identify with the personality?

Just like in person-to-person interactions, customers will respond to a brand personality that they can relate to. A brand that has a 'playful' personality attribute may appeal to customers who want to be perceived as not taking their lives too seriously. For example, a recent commercial for Jiffy Lube featured the slogan 'We don't want to change the world; we just want to change your oil'.

Source: LePla (2002)

---

at cinemas and in front of televisions provide great opportunities for automobile advertising – overt and covert.

Most advertising aims at the creation or exploitation of a relationship: an identification, an association between product and consumer. Some advertising aims to create a feeling of satisfaction among consumers that they have been smart in their choices – even after learning that they have purchased a product that is defective, dangerous or environmentally harmful.[4]

The same company that doesn't want to change the world does not seem to want to change thinking about automobile dependence either. A flyer mailed by Jiffy Lube asks: 'Think traffic is bad? Try walking.' Evidently the acceptance of traffic at the expense of walking is aimed to make potential customers feel better about driving, especially if it is to get their oil changed.

The many themes associated with the automobile enumerated at the beginning of this section afford advertising a rich opportunity to turn fantasy and emotional valence into product sales. This has led to the phenomena of automobiles placed at the centre of much covert or embedded advertising, product placement and branded entertainment. These phenomena, often aimed at children and teenagers, despite scathing critiques by Naomi Klein (2002) and Susan Linn (2004), continue unabated as the current campaign by Ford to target young women with the Mustang branding iron (see Box 2.4) demonstrates. And it appears that Bollywood is hurriedly following Hollywood down the asphalt wedding aisle of embedding automobile advertising clandestinely in films (Thanawala, 2007; Indiantelevision.com, 2008).

If the Ford campaign succeeds, young women might soon be racing their new Mustangs against Bill Clinton's 1967 vintage model and Barbie's Corvette. And young Dick and Jane of the reading primers of an earlier era will need to update their cheering for playmate Sally from 'Run, Sally, run!' to 'Ride, Sally, ride!'[5]

Box 2.4 'Ride, Sally, ride' replaces 'Run, Sally, run'

In an effort to target the young girls' market, Ford has launched the Pony Girl for Mustang – an auto-inspired lifestyle aimed at teenage girls.

According to Zandl Group, the Mustang is the most desired auto for the female demographic at the age [of] 8 [to] 16. The program will introduce branded products for two groups: one aimed at tweens (8 [to] 12) and the other [aimed] at older girls (13 [to] 16).

The main categories being explored are apparel, accessories, home decor, stationery, jewelry, cosmetics and back-to-school partners.

Brandweek's Becky Ebenkamp describes the program: 'A colorful style guide pairs Mustang's iconic galloping pony silhouette with other girly icons, such as butterflies, flowers and stars.'

Aspirational taglines including 'Untamed Heart', 'Run Free', 'A Pony Is Forever' and 'Let Loose' are offered for declarations on T-shirts in playful vintage-inspired fonts. Depending on the category, products will hit the market in either late 2009 or early 2010.

Ford and Beanstalk, the auto-makers' licensing agency, will meet with retailers and chain specialty stores to discuss distribution about the licensing show. 'Mustang is a mass market brand – it's sort of the affordable muscle car,' said John Nens, director of global brand licensing for Ford Motor Co. 'Licensing is all about reflecting the brand, and this one is about value.'

'[Licensing is] a way for young girls to get a piece of a Mustang before they're old enough to obtain a driver's license', said Rachel Terrace, director [of] brand management at Beanstalk.

Ford has more than 350 licensees and an automotive program that generates more than US$1 billion worth of retail sales annually.

Source: PPN (2009)

Radio and cars

The relation between automobiles, radio and car culture is somewhat different than that between automobiles and the visual broadcast media. As yet, most countries that license motorists do not allow them to watch TV while driving – although screens are available for some models allowing backseat passengers to watch videos. Computer-controlled automobiles that would free motorists from paying attention to traffic have been proposed but have not yet been developed. Radio was introduced into automobiles fairly early in their history (see Chapter 3), first for emergency and police purposes and then shortly afterwards for mass consumption and entertainment while motoring. Radio requires forms of attentiveness and imagination somewhat different from the visual broadcast media. Nevertheless, radio represents a significant opportunity for automobile advertising, especially in automobile-dependent societies where most commute or spend their leisure in cars.

The automobile figures prominently in US and Canadian radio, even in US public radio programming as the popularity of National Public Radio's (NPR's) Car Talk programme demonstrates. Many radio programmes target specific

Box 2.5 Turn off the traffic rap

Many, perhaps most, Americans and quite a few Canadians wake to traffic reports every morning. Eggs are poached, granola munched and pre-commute nausea developed as multi-vehicle pileups, overturned trucks and stalled cars blocking freeways are reported.

Overhead in noisy helicopters or in front of traffic monitoring screens, traffic jockeys, whose main credentials derive from voice training courses, are shaping perceptions of the 'best' way to get to work. Some of the commercial traffic reporting services have names that might mislead listeners into assuming a link with a government agency. The fact that their sympathetic and concerned voices are brought to us courtesy of automobile advertising may explain why their reports centre on car traffic with only an occasional transit tidbit. Generally ignored are all the options that should be emphasized singularly or in combination in an urban area: mass transit, bicycling, carpooling and walking.

Radio traffic rappers may be encouraging or 'inducing' unnecessary driving when they pronounce a freeway to be 'wide open' or promote a 'good time to drive'. While promising motorists to help to keep them rolling, they maintain the myth that a solution is just around the next curve and not to worry: continue to commute in your nearly empty cars.

Traffic spinning is intruding into daily life in insidious ways. Each morning and afternoon some public radio stations devote up to 40 per cent of local news minutes to traffic. Many commercial radio stations devote even more time to traffic. TV news provides graphic traffic reports with live coverage from hovering helicopters of police pursuing errant motorists.

Perhaps it is time to face the fact that there are no technological fixes for the automobile which will ease congestion and allow motorists to break their destructive driving patterns. Perhaps it is time to shape a viable and balanced urban system. Perhaps it is time to switch stations and turn off the traffic rap.

Source: adapted from Schiller (1992)

Figure 2.7 *'The traffic report'*

Source: Andy Singer (www.andysinger.com)

mobile audiences, from all-night truck drivers to rush hour commuters. Traffic reports are a prominent feature on the airwaves in many North American cities during daytime hours and every few minutes during rush hours. While the efficacy of these reports is open to question, they continue to be a popular item on many commercial and even public funded stations.

Music and the car culture

Popular music has a strong affinity for automobile themes and imagery. The relation has been fortified through powerful car radios and CD players whose audio systems seem to be designed for destroying neighbourhood tranquility or, at least, the hearing of listeners. Many television and radio programmes devoted to popular music ranging from the *Grand Ole Opry* to MTV have been associated with automobility. Radio and televised opera was associated with automobility from the 1920s to early 1960s *Voice of Firestone* to Texaco's (later Chevron Texaco) sponsorship of radio broadcasts of the New York Metropolitan Opera from 1940 to 2004. The relationship between motoring and music has been exceptionally close in the US where motorists in 1905 could sing 'In my merry Oldsmobile', 'Get your kicks on Route 66' in the 1940s, 'See the USA in your Chevrolet' with Dinah Shore in 1952, drive your Oldsmobile 442 to the beach to surf with the Beach Boys or chase Maybellene and her pink Cadillac with Chuck Berry in the 1960s. More socially conscious souls could join Joni Mitchell in her 'Big yellow taxi: They paved paradise and put up a parking lot' lament. The relationship between the car and rock-and-roll has been extremely close and intense with the automobile industry recognizing this in many ways, including the Ford Motor Company's major donation to help create the Rock-and-Roll Hall of Fame Museum in Cleveland, Ohio (Belasco, 1983; Berger, 2001, p220). The relationship between the automobile and car culture only strengthened through the decades that have led to the rise of hip hop, often strongly associated with automobile and limousine imagery.

Car culture in literature

The automobile and car culture have captured the attention of cultural critics, fiction writers and poets ranging from Booth Tarkington, F. Scott Fitzgerald and Carl Sandburg to Jack Kerouac, Tom Wolfe, Karl Shapiro and Allen Ginsburg (Goldstein 1998). It has been the focus of many artists' work, as well as an important symbol and metaphor for the work of many others. The road trip provides the structure for many novels and poems preceding the automobile, and it has been an especially fertile literary vehicle since 1900. John Steinbeck developed several automobile motifs in *The Grapes of Wrath*, some focused on the Joad family's dependence on their ancient vehicle to deliver them from the destruction of the Dust Bowl to the promised land of California, while others focused on the automobile as symbolizing class differences, as in the contrast between the wealthy landowners' fancy convertibles and the broken-down jalopies of the migrants. Late in his career Steinbeck set off with his dog in a pick-up truck and camper on a long exploration recounted in *Travels with Charley: In Search of America* (Berger, 2001, pp221–226; Smoak, 2007). While erotic adventure is often part of road trip literature, some authors such as J. G. Ballard, whose work *Crash* was also made into a deeply disturbing film, have used automobility as the vehicle for exploring the horrific and perverse side of the relation between automobility and sexuality (Lewis, 1983, pp233–234; Parchesky, 2006).

The oddity of being a pedestrian in an automobile and TV world was a theme in many of the writings of Ray Bradbury, including *Fahrenheit 451*. The story and (later) short play *The Pedestrian* was inspired by his experience of police harassment for the 'crime' of walking around Los Angeles one evening. The story's central character, Leonard Mead, is arrested for being a pedestrian and resisting mandatory enslavement to TV by robotic police, and committed to the 'Psychiatric Center for Research on Regressive Tendencies' for rehabilitation back to TV addiction (Bradbury, 1966, 2001).

'Carchitecture': Reshaping architecture and urban design for automobile cities

The term 'carchitecture' is often used, sometimes derisively, to denote the ways in which the built environment has been reshaped to accommodate automobiles. It is sometimes employed to denote the ways in which automobiles are designed, although that usage will not be addressed here. Accommodating automobility and designing buildings and residences to display their most important features to passing motorists have been master trends in architecture and urban design throughout the 20th and into the 21st century. The ways in which projects as different as Le Corbusier's 'Radiant City' and Frank Lloyd Wright's 'Usonian' vision for 'Broadacre City' profoundly shaped the design and redesign of cities and suburbs to accommodate or even promote automobility have been masterfully examined in Peter Hall's *Cities of Tomorrow* (1988, especially Chapters 7 and 9). At the level of residential design, modernist architects over many decades blurred the distinction between living space and automobile space as garages and carports moved onto and into houses and replaced porches and formal entranceways (Kihlstedt, 1983).

Figure 2.8 Hotel garage entries across the sidewalk are typical of 'carchitecture', San Francisco central business district

Source: Preston L. Schiller

'Futurama': We have seen the future and it drives![6]

Over many decades General Motors (GM) developed a vision of an automobile-centred world that went far beyond the reach of its factories and dealerships. GM's landscape, urban and rural, was to be dominated by superhighways that were, of course, never congested. In city centres, superhighways directly entered high-rise buildings. This expression reached its fullest form in the Futurama exhibit designed by Norman Bel Geddes for GM's pavilion at the New York World's Fair of 1939. In 1964 GM returned to its vision for the future of mobility that went beyond superhighways to the conquest of rainforests and outer space.[7]

Counterpoised to the vision of a superhighway future was the critique and vision of urbanologist and regional planning advocate Lewis Mumford, whose life and works parallel the Bel Geddes and GM elaborations (Ellis, 2005). Today, the ruins of automobile industry cities such as Detroit and Flint, Michigan, provide a sobering reminder of the dark and perhaps inevitable side of Futurama (see discussion of Flint in Chapter 8). Mumford's influence can be sensed, along with that of Jane Jacobs, in the current interest in renewing and revitalizing cities and de-emphasizing automobility.

Tourism: The car culture evolves into the fly-drive and recreational vehicle cultures

Tourism presents special problems and questions for sustainability and ST. There are numerous issues involving the extent to which tourism is harmful to the environment and socially harmful to many of its destinations in less wealthy nations (Whitelegg, 1997, especially Chapter 6). Tourism transportation may have several components and there are a number of complex issues around how tourism is defined and measured. Better data seems to exist for tourism that crosses national borders and for travel by airlines than for domestic tourism – especially that done by private motor vehicles (Page, 1998; Hall, 2008). Tourism is rapidly growing, and travel by the most harmful modes (aviation and personal motor vehicles, or PMVs) is similarly increasing, fuelled to a certain extent by the large subsidies given to

Figure 2.9 Recreational vehicles (RVs) and sports utility vehicles (SUVs) gather to spawn along the California–Oregon coast

Source: Preston L. Schiller

automobiles and commercial aviation, which can lead to the phenomenon of low-cost airfares with large environmental price tags. The largest component of international tourism is air travel between North America and Europe, although Latin American, Caribbean and Asian destinations are rapidly increasing their shares. For some long-distance tourist travel, over 90 per cent of a vacationer's energy footprint was the air travel component (Hall, 2008, pp204–205). The fact that US residents drive much more than residents of other countries, including motoring for leisure and tourism, has led some researchers to conclude that 'most of the world's tourism takes place within the US' (Gilbert and Perl, 2008, pp90–91).

Racing is another interesting aspect of the car culture that has been discussed above in the context of the automobile and broadcast media. The relation between the early motorist associations, in the US and Europe, is discussed in Chapter 3. In the US, millions of people drive substantial distances annually to watch hundreds of others race cars and, occasionally, motorcycles around and around a track. Many millions more watch the cars zoom and crash on TV, interrupted by frequent automobile and fast food advertising. National Association for Stock Car Auto Racing (NASCAR) tracks are highly profitable ventures and they have been strategically located to draw visitors from large regional catchment areas (Mooradian, 2000; ISC, 2009). Racing tracks often attract fans who arrive and stay in their recreational vehicles (RVs).

Sales of RVs and RV travel have been growing in the US and Europe. A small but growing number of US residents have taken to living year round in RVs and are accommodated by an increasing number of special facilities termed 'RV parks', as well as in public campgrounds, some in wilderness areas. RVs often bring along off-road vehicles (ORVs) such as small motorcycles or snow machines, in order to explore and further pollute natural areas. The rapid increase of ORVs (especially in North America), whose emissions are generally less controlled than those of on-road vehicles, is a growing concern of environmental agencies.

Not everyone is attracted to weekend jet-setting, excessive driving in or out of town, or motorsports and RV travel. Some are trying to fashion a different existence emphasizing more sustainable forms of travel, as the vignette in Box 2.6 demonstrates.

Box 2.6 A car-free family, a quieter neighbourhood

On a typical weekday morning Bill Buspass strolls with his eight-year-old son, Walker, a couple of other parents and several other neighbourhood youngsters to a primary school a few blocks away in an effort called the 'walking school bus'. Bill then catches his bus to work at the far end of town. His partner, Cindy Cycler, and their daughter, Vela, mount their bicycles and ride together for a few blocks until Vela turns off to ride the last few blocks to her middle school. Cindy then turns onto the bicycle and pedestrian trail that leads from their neighbourhood to her employment destination 2 miles (3km) away. At Vela's school the parents' association has also been actively encouraging parents to have their children walk or cycle to school. Parents who drive students to and from school are consigned to an area a half-block from the school entrance in order to keep the area near the school entrance safe for cyclists and pedestrians.

Bill's employer offers him a transit pass in lieu of free parking at the worksite. Cindy's employer offers employees a small monthly stipend for not driving to work, as well as a changing room with a shower at the office. The stipend is paid out of a fund established by charging parking fees to employees who drive to work. This has reduced the amount of parking at the office and the employer has been able to expand office space and staff without adding more. In conjunction with the local transit agency, a 'guaranteed ride home' is offered to any employee who commutes by foot or bike or bus who needs to attend to an urgent family situation during the workday.

Because Bill and Cindy no longer own an automobile, they converted their garage into an apartment, which they have rented to a senior citizen. In exchange for a partial reduction in the monthly rent, the surrogate grandparent keeps an eye on Walker and Vela after school until Bill or Cindy arrive home from work. Their renter, too, is car free and finds it convenient to walk to some of the nearby shops and services in the nearby small commercial district or take the frequent bus downtown for other needs. Cindy and Bill de-paved their no longer needed driveway and transformed it into a garden. All along their street trees have been planted as part of an 'urban forest' city initiative in the 'planter strip' between the sidewalk and street. When mature, the trees help to shade the street pavement and the house in the summer.

It has been a few years since the city and the local university began a concerted effort to reduce driving and parking and improve walking, bicycling and transit. The city changed its housing regulations to encourage slightly more density close to the university as long as it did not result in extra cars at a residence. A universal bus pass and greatly improved transit connections to the university followed. Transit ridership grew dramatically. The city accelerated its programme of sidewalks and bicycle lanes and separated paths for pedestrians and bicyclists. Within a few years it became possible to safely and comfortably reach almost any destination in town by walking or bicycling, or on the improved bus system. The transit system began co-operating with neighbouring transit agencies so that express services were created linking the major towns of the region, and the region began improving its regional bus and rail services so that one could use public transportation between larger and smaller cities. Many of the students began selling their automobiles and buying the bargain bus and rail passes for weekend and holiday travel.

Cindy and Bill have noticed less traffic on their streets, which are now available for a variety of uses. Many of the teenagers who used to whiz around the neighbourhood in automobiles received as gifts for their 16th birthdays have taken advantage of the available asphalt to establish basketball street courts. A few parents have set up somewhat shorter basketball hoops for the smaller children. And the city now encourages neighbours to organize summer block parties and close off a street to motor vehicles completely for a day. Downtown merchants, impressed by the new level of pedestrian and bicyclist activity on their streets, are discussing creating pedestrian zones.

On the way home from work Cindy stops at the community food co-operative to fill her bicycle panniers with needed groceries. Once a month, Bill and Cindy use a vehicle from the car-share co-operative to do a major shopping trip. By purchasing many of their staples in bulk quantity they also reduce the transportation and packaging components of their shopping basket. Because the food co-op offers a special discount for people who walk or cycle to the store, and a delivery service, as well as charging a fee for parking in its lot, it was able to expand its site into its parking lot.

The car-share vehicle comes in handy for the occasional out-of-town trip to visit relatives when the train or intercity bus is not a viable option. The car-share co-op owns several different types of vehicles, from very small, very fuel-efficient town cars to station wagons and small vans for special needs such as moving, hauling large items or camping. Bill and Cindy's monthly membership fee plus the rates they pay for short-term or even weekend rental still come to considerably less than the many thousands of dollars they used to spend on insurance, licence fees, payments and fuel for their car – which they were using less and less over time. The money they save from living 'car free' and the income they derive from the conversion of their garage to a rental allow them to create college savings funds for their children.

The vignette in Box 2.6 demonstrates that the automobile dependence depicted in Box 2.1 is not inevitable. Communities, families and individuals can organize their lives to lessen their dependence upon driving. With supportive government programmes aimed at improving local transit, walking and bicycling infrastructure, and improved intercity public transportation, many trips can be conveniently and enjoyably made without a personal motor vehicle.

Another curious area of the car culture is 'drive-to transit'. In recent decades, transit agencies have been attempting to lure riders, usually in suburbs, but sometimes in cities themselves, with free or cheap parking at a parking lot or structure serviced by one or more transit routes. Park & Ride probably grew out of the parking provided at outlying suburban and small town regional (or commuter) rail stations. Box 2.7 explores this matter.

Box 2.7 Drive-to transit: Park & Ride, Kiss & Ride and the tiring of the transit planning mind

There are several issues surrounding Park & Rides (P&Rs) and other forms of drive-to transit:

- Drive-to transit access adds to emissions: it adds two more polluting cold-starts per day and in some areas the drive to the P&R is as long as or longer than the transit trip.
- Parking lots, whether for transit or other less noble uses, have many undesirable effects associated with all forms of pavement: heat entrapment, polluted runoff, ground water recharge interference, etc.
- A critique of Seattle-area Park & Ride investment estimated that the average P&R stall has an opportunity cost of 'in the range of US$5 to $15 per day depending on site-specific costs' (Schiller, 1997, pp16–17).
- When multiplied by the thousands of P&R stalls that might exist in an urban area, the costs and opportunity costs involved, including maintenance, operation and security, could be better applied to improving local bus services and transit centres, and providing more passenger shelters and bicycle facilities along routes (Strathman and Dueker, 1996).
- Even its drive-through 'cousin', the Kiss & Ride area at P&Rs or transit centres, where chauffeured riders are deposited (and perhaps kissed by the automobile driver as a reward for taking transit), entails traffic and emissions impacts.
- There is a social equity issue: these expensive investments reward those who can afford to drive at the expense of improving walking-and-waiting (bus stops) facilities for those who do not.

The P&R might be a useful facility in remote corners of a region where improving local transit and bicycling access to a major route may not be feasible. When done in well-developed areas or within city limits, in lieu of improved local feeder services, it can only be taken as an indication of the transit planning mind grown tired – very tired.

Figure 2.10 Transit facility dwarfed by parking, South Kirkland Park & Ride lot

Note: Drive-to transit involves costly Park & Ride lots generating traffic and pollution; often the traffic of the P&R interferes with bus access and egress. See if you can locate the transit facility dwarfed by the parking lot.

Source: Eric C. Bruun

Conclusions

This chapter has presented a present-day perspective on how most cities evolved through different transportation stages, from walking cities to transit cities and on to automobile cities. Many are attempting to move away from automobile domination and are trying to recapture favourable aspects of walking and transit cities. Some, many in developing countries, have made a leap from walking cities to automobile and motorcycle cities without ever having developed significant transit systems. Automobile cities nurture the car culture, which can pervade almost all aspects of daily life. The next chapter explores the history of sustainable and unsustainable transportation, how diverse modes and transportation patterns developed, and why some of its lessons need to be learned again.

Questions for discussion

- Discuss the transportation situation of your community in light of the discussion of walking cities, transit cities and automobile cities.
- Discuss whether and to what extent you or individuals close to you are experiencing 'time pollution'.
- Identify and discuss some aspects of the 'car culture' that you encounter in your community.

Notes

1   The section 'Walking cities, transit cities and automobile cities' and its accompanying figures have been the effort of Jeffrey R. Kenworthy, with some material (e.g. Figures 2.1–2.3) drawn from previous joint work, such as in Newman and Kenworthy (1999).

2   Michael Ferro recovered from his years in advertising in Michigan by becoming a Sierra Club and bicycling activist in Seattle. He has since returned to his origins in the San Francisco Bay area.

3   For more, see Rothschild (1973), Newman and Holzman (1993), McAlinder et al (2003), FHWA (2006), Nielsen Media Research (2007), Ladd (2008), O'Hagan (2009) and Seiler (2009).

4   This aspect of advertising is akin to Irving Goffman's sociological concept of 'cooling the mark out' after a 'sting' – in this case the consumer is conned through an act of questionable consumption and then 'cooled out' by feel-good advertising. See www.tau.ac.il/~algazi/mat/Goffman--Cooling.htm and the film *The Sting*.

5   The 1991 film *The Commitments* featured the song 'Mustang Sally', whose refrain was 'Ride, Sally, ride'.

6   This, of course, is a play upon the famous quote attributed to Beatrice and Sidney Webb upon returning from a visit to 1930s Stalinist Russia: 'I have seen the future and it works!'

7   GMC (1940): for Part 1, see www.youtube.com/watch?v=74cO9X4NMb4; for Part 2, see www.youtube.com/watch?v=WU7dT2HId-c&feature=related; for 1964–1965, see www.youtube.com/watch?v=2-5aK0H05jk&feature=related.

References and further reading

Adams, J. (1999) 'The social implications of hypermobility', in *OECD, Project on Sustainable Transportation (EST): The Economic and Social Implications of Sustainable Transportation*, Proceedings of the Ottawa Workshop, 20–21 October 1998, OECD Publications, Paris, pp95–134

Adams, J. (2000) 'Hypermobility', *Prospect*, www.prospectmagazine.co.uk/2000/03/hypermobility/, accessed 1 September 2009

Barter, P. A. (1999) *An International Comparative Perspective on Urban Transport and Urban Form in Pacific Asia: Responses to the Challenge of Motorisation in Dense Cities*, PhD thesis, Murdoch University at Perth, Australia

Barter, P. A. (2000) 'Urban transport in Asia: Problems and prospects for high-density cities', *Asia–Pacific Development Monitor*, vol 2, no 1, pp33–66

Belasco, W. (1983) 'Motivatin' with Chuck Berry and Frederick Jackson Turner', in D. L. Lewis and L. Goldstein (eds) *The Automobile and American Culture*, University of Michigan Press, Ann Arbor, MI

Berger, M. L. (2001) *The Automobile in American History and Culture: A Reference Guide*, Greenwood Press, Westport, CN

Bradbury, R. (1966) *The Pedestrian: A Fantasy in One Act*, Samuel French, New York, NY

Bradbury, R. (2001) 'The pedestrian', in R. Bradbury (ed) *A Medicine for Melancholy*, Perennial–HarperCollins, New York, NY (originally published elsewhere in 1951)

CDC (Centers for Disease Control) (2009) 'Recommended community strategies and measurements to prevent obesity in the United States', in *MMWR Recommendations and Reports*, 24 July, 58(RR07), www.cdc.gov/mmwr/preview/mmwrhtml/rr5807a1.htm, accessed 1 September 2009

Ellis, C. (2005) 'Lewis Mumford and Norman Bel Geddes: The highway, the city and the future', *Planning Perspectives*, vol 20, no1, pp51–68

Engler, G. (2009) 'A critical mess? Yes it is. If we lock up all those responsible for current traffic problems, the traffic jams would be gone', *Vancouver Sun*, 15 August

FHWA (Federal Highway Administration) (2006) *Revised Apportionment of Fiscal Year (FY) 2006 Surface Transportation Program Funds*, US Department of Transportation, www.fhwa.dot.gov/, accessed 1 September 2009

Flink, J. J. (1975) *The Car Culture*, MIT Press, Cambridge, MA

Flink, J. J. (1988) *The Automobile Age*, MIT Press, Cambridge, MA

Gehl, J. and Gemzøe, L. (1996) *Public Spaces, Public Life*, City of Copenhagen, Copenhagen

Gilbert, R. and Perl, A. (2008) *Transport Revolutions: Moving People and Freight without Oil*, Earthscan, London

GMC (1940) *Futurama*, GM Corporation, US, acquired through InterLibrary Loan: OCLC Number 4920548, Wesleyan University, lender, catalogue number 607.34 G286f

Goldstein, L. (1998) 'The automobile and American poetry', in D. L. Lewis and L. Goldstein (eds) *The Automobile and American Culture*, University of Michigan Press, Ann Arbor, MI

Gorz, A. (1973) 'The social ideology of the motorcar', *Le Sauvage*, September–October, http://rts.gn.apc.org/socid.htm, accessed 1 September 2009

Hall, D. (2008) 'Transport, tourism and leisure', in R. Knowles, J. Shaw and I. Docherty (eds) *Transport Geographies: Mobilities, Flows and Spaces*, Blackwell Publishing, Oxford, UK

Hall, P. (1988) *Cities of Tomorrow: An Intellectual History of Urban Planning and Design in the Twentieth Century*, Basil Blackwell, Oxford, UK

Health Canada (2006) *It's Your Health – Obesity*, www.hc-sc.gc.ca/hl-vs/iyh-vsv/life-vie/obes-eng.php, accessed 1 September 2009

Hey, K. (1983) 'Cars and films in American culture, 1929–1959', in D. L. Lewis and L. Goldstein (eds) *The Automobile and American Culture*, University of Michigan Press, Ann Arbor, MI

Hoyle, B. and Knowles, R. (eds) (1998) *Modern Transport Geography*, second revised edition, John Wiley and Sons, Chichester, UK

Illich, I. (1976) *Energy and Equity*, Marion Boyars, London

Indiantelevision.com (2008) 'GM to launch new TVC for Chevy: Announces "cashless ownership"', www.indiantelevision.com/mam/headlines/y2k8/mar/marmam52.php, accessed 15 August 2009

ISC (International Speedway Corporation) (2009) *Industry Overview*, http://ir.iscmotorsports.com/phoenix.zhtml?c=113983&p=irol-industryoverview, accessed 15 September 2009

Jacobs, J. (1961) *The Death and Life of Great American Cities*, Penguin Books, Harmondsworth, UK

Kay, J. H. (1997) *Asphalt Nation: How the Automobile Took Over America, and How We Can Take It Back*, Crown Publishers, New York, NY

Kenworthy, J. R. (1997) 'Automobile dependence in Bangkok: An international comparison with implications for planning policies and air pollution', in T. Fletcher and A. J. Michael (eds) *Health at the Crossroads: Transport Policy and Urban Health*, John Wiley and Sons, Chichester, UK

Kenworthy, J. R. and Hu, G. (2002) 'Transport and urban form in Chinese cities: An international and comparative policy perspective with implications for sustainable urban transport in China', *DISP*, vol 151, pp4–14

Kenworthy, J. R and Laube, F. B. (1999) *An International Sourcebook of Automobile Dependence in Cities, 1960 to 1990*, University Press of Colorado, Niwot, CO

Kenworthy, J. R. and Townsend, C. (2002) 'An international comparative perspective on motorisation in urban China: Problems and prospects', *IATSS Research*, vol 26, no 2, pp99–109

Kihlstedt, F. (1983) 'The automobile and the transformation of the American house, 1910–35', in D. L. Lewis and L. Goldstein (eds) *The Automobile and American Culture*, University of Michigan Press, Ann Arbor, MI

Klein, J. and Olson, M. (1996) *Taken for a Ride*, New Day Films, http://www.newday.com/films/Taken_for_a_Ride.html, accessed 15 September 2009

Klein, N. (2002) *No Logo*, Picador, New York, NY

Knowles, R., Shaw, J. and Docherty, I. (eds) (2008) *Transport Geographies: Mobilities, Flows and Spaces*, Blackwell Publishing, Oxford, UK

Kostof, S. (1991) *The City Shaped: Urban Patterns and Meaning Through History*, Bulfinch Press, Little, Brown and Company, New York, NY

Kunstler, J. H. (1993) *The Geography of Nowhere*, Simon & Schuster, New York, NY

Kunstler, J. H. (1996) *Home from Nowhere: Remaking Our Everyday World for the 21st Century*, Simon & Schuster, New York, NY

Ladd, B. (2008) *Autophobia: Love and Hate in the Automotive Age*, University of Chicago Press, Chicago, IL

LePla, J. (2002) 'Give your company a personality test', www.workz.com/content/view_content.html?section_id=469&content_id=5212), accessed 16 August 2009

Lewis, D. L. (1983) 'Sex and the automobile: From rumble seats to rockin' vans', in D. L. Lewis and L. Goldstein (eds) *The Automobile and American Culture*, University of Michigan Press, Ann Arbor, MI, pp123–133

Lewis, D. and Goldstein, L. (eds) (1983) *The Automobile and American Culture*, University of Michigan Press, Ann Arbor, MI

Linn, S. (2004) *Consuming Kids: The Hostile Takeover of Childhood*, New Press, New York, NY

McAlinder, S. P., Hill, K. and Swiedic, B. (2003) *Economic Contribution of the Automotive Industry to the US Economy – An Update*, Center for Automotive Research, Ann Arbor, MI

Mooradian, D. (2000) 'NASCAR attendance doubles during past decade', www.allbusiness.com/services/amusement-recreation-services/4557259-1.html, accessed 15 September 2009

Newman, F. and Holzman, L. (1993) *Lev Vygotsky: Revolutionary Scientist*, Routledge, London

Newman, P. W. G. and Kenworthy, J. R. (1989) *Cities and Automobile Dependence: A Sourcebook*, Gower Technical, Aldershot, UK, and Brookfield, VT

Newman, P. W. G. and Kenworthy, J. R. (1999) *Sustainability and Cities: Overcoming Automobile Dependence*, Island Press, Washington, DC

Newman, P. W. G., Kenworthy, J. and Vintila, P. (1992) 'Housing, transport and urban form', Background Paper 15 + Appendices for the National Housing Strategy, Commonwealth of Australia, Canberra

Nielsen Media Research (2007) *Nielsen Monitor-Plus Report: US Advertising Spending Rose 4.6 Per Cent in 2006*, www.nielsenmedia.com, accessed 1 September 2009

Norton, P. D. (2007) 'Street rivals: Jaywalking and the invention of the motor age street', *Technology and Culture*, vol 48, pp331–359

Norton, P. D. (2008) *Fighting Traffic: The Dawn of the Motor Age in the American City*, MIT Press, Cambridge, MA

O'Hagan, A. (2009) 'A car of one's own', *London Review of Books*, vol 31, no 11, www.lrb.co.uk/v31/n11/ohag01_.html, accessed 1 September 2009

Page, S. (1998) 'Transport for recreation and tourism', in B. Hoyle and R. Knowles (eds) *Modern Transport Geography*, second revised edition, John Wiley and Sons, Chichester, UK

Parchesky, J. (2006) 'Women in the driver's seat: The auto-erotics of early women's films', *Film History: An International Journal*, vol 18, no 2, pp174–184

Poboon, C. (1997) *Anatomy of a Traffic Disaster: Towards a Sustainable Solution to Bangkok's Traffic Problems*, PhD thesis, Murdoch University at Perth, Australia

PPN (Product Placement News) (2009) 'Ford branded products for teenage girls', www.productplacement.biz/200904173051/News/Branded-Entertainment/ford-branded-products-for-teenage-girls.html, accessed 16 August 2009

Roberts, J. (1992) *Trip Degeneration*, TEST, London

Rothschild, E. (1973) *Paradise Lost: The Decline of the Auto-Industrial Age*, Random House, New York, NY

Schiller, P. L. (1992) 'Turn off the traffic rap', *Eastside Week*, Seattle, WA, 13 May, p2

Schiller, P. (1997) *Parking – A Primer: How to Improve Communities while Promoting Alternatives to Driving*, ALT-TRANS, Washington Coalition for Transportation Alternatives, Seattle, WA

Schiller, P. L. (2002) 'Lift your right foot, now!' *The Every Other Weekly*, Bellingham, WA, 7–20 March, p8

Seiler, C. (2009) *Republic of Driver: A Cultural History of Automobility in America*, University of Chicago Press, Chicago, IL

Smith, J. (1983) 'Runaway match: The automobile in the American film, 1900–1920', in D. L. Lewis and L. Goldstein (eds) *The Automobile and American Culture*, University of Michigan Press, Ann Arbor, MI

Smoak, S. (2007) *Framing the Automobile in Twentieth Century American Literature: A Spatial Approach*, PhD thesis, University of North Carolina at Greensboro, NC

Starky, S. (2005) *The Obesity Epidemic in Canada (PRB 05–11E)*, Economics Division, Parliamentary Information and Research Service (PIRS), Library of Parliament – Bibliotheque du Parlement, Ottawa, ON, www.parl.gc.ca/information/library/prbpubs/prb0511-e.htm, accessed 1 September 2009

Strathman, J. G. and Dueker, K. J. (1996) 'Transit service, parking charges, and mode choice for the journey to work: An analysis of the 1990 NPTS', *Journal of Public Transportation*, fall, pp13–38

Thanawala, S. (2007) *Embedded Advertising: A New Revenue Model for Cinema*, FICCI (Federation of Indian Chambers of Commerce) Frames 2007, www.exchange4media.com/FICCI/2007/ficci_fullstory07.asp?news_id=25457, accessed 15 August 2009

Vanderbilt. T. (2008) *Traffic: Why We Drive the Way We Do (And What It Says About Us)*, Alfred A. Knopf, New York, NY

Whitelegg, J. (1993) *Transport for a Sustainable Future: The Case for Europe*, Belhaven Press, London

Whitelegg, J. (1997) *Critical Mass: Transport, Environment and Society in the Twenty-First Century*, Pluto Press, London

3

History of Sustainable and Unsustainable Transportation: From Walking to Wheels and Back to Walking

Transportation history: The intersection of modes, infrastructure and society

The history of transportation is a fascinating and vast field spanning millennia from early human evolution to the exploration of space. Its purview includes walking and human evolution, early experience with marine and river travel, the use of animals for transport, the impact of the wheel and early mechanization, roads, the motor age, telecommunications, popular culture and space travel. It sheds light on issues such as the relation of mobility to community, economic development and daily activity. Sustainable transportation has emerged as an important issue in recent decades, although aspects of sustainability are as ancient as mobility itself. This chapter will sketch the outlines of some of the important themes and issues relevant to sustainable transportation (ST) and suggest ways in which planning and policy-making should be informed by them. It will focus principally on land transport and major forms of transportation and infrastructure, but it will also review aspects of the history of maritime–water travel, telecommunications and aviation necessary for an understanding of subsequent chapters.

Among the major themes and issues explored are:

- Modal development, competition, succession: how modes developed and competed with each other; how some modes, or varieties of the same general mode, prevailed and others did not; how several modes reflected a desire for easier, speedier, more reliable and affordable travel but were not necessarily concerned about sustainability – as has been the case with those most dependent upon fossil fuels and land consumption.
- Relations between modes, infrastructure, community form and travel: in order for certain modes to succeed, changes in infrastructure were needed. Modes, infrastructure, community design and social and cultural factors interacted in complex and sometimes unpredictable ways.

Table 3.1 Transportation timeline

Dates	Walking	Water	Mechanical, roads, infrastructure	Aviation	Telecom
3–7 million years ago	Bipedalism begins				
8000–15,000 years ago	Early permanent settlements				Fires, smoke signals, drums, horns, flags
8000–5000 BCE	Animal transport; cities and walking	Dugouts, rafts	Sled, sleigh; wheel emerges		
4000 BCE–400 CE		Boats, sails, canals	Wheel spreads; Diolkos wagonway; Roman, Silk roads	Icarus-Daedalus Myth	
400–1400	Pilgrimages, tours, crusades	Vikings; crusades; sea trade routes expand	Caravan routes expand; Inca roads (1200–1500)		
1400–1700		Oceanic exploration	Intercity coaches and mail; Pascal's Paris bus (1662); Short rail-wagonways at mines/ports	da Vinci drawings (1487)	
1700–1800		Canals–locks; motorization (1783)	Watt's steam engine (1765-1769), Roads–Bridges Engineering School – France (1747)	Balloons (1783)	(Early) semaphores
1800–1860		More canals–locks; Erie–US (1825), early Welland–Canada (1829–1848)	Draisine-velo (1817); transit in UK, FR and US (1820s); railways; UK, US (1830s); Stephenson's locomotive (1829) French improve roads, Parisian Boulevards	First glider flight (1853)	Telegraphs; early wireless and fax experiments (1830–40s) English Channel Cable (1851)
1860–1870	Millions of marching soldiers (US)	Suez Canal (1869)	Railways major factor in US Civil War; pedal velo 'boneshaker'		Caselli's telefax (1861); telegraph cable, US–UK (1866)
1870s	Foot soldiers (EU)		Railways expand; high wheeler cycle; early 'Good Roads'		Bell's telephone (1876)
1880s			Safety bicycle; auto production begins; more 'Good Roads'		Hollerith's punch cards
1890–1910			Street railways; automobile mass production (Fordism)	Manned flight	Tesla, Marconi wireless; early fax
1910–1920 (and WWI)	Millions of foot soldiers	Submarines, Panama Canal (1914)	Auto production–ownership increase, trucks and tanks (WWI)	Military aviation	

Table 3.1 Transportation timeline *(Cont'd)*

Dates	Walking	Water	Mechanical, roads, infrastructure	Aviation	Telecom
1920s		Early aircraft carriers	'Car culture' spreads; tractor-trailer trucks; highway/auto interests dominate Good Roads movement	Air freight; dirigibles; rocketry	Analog computers; 2-way mobile radio (AU); wireless transoceanic fax; newspaper fax; TV (UK)
1930s	Poor and unemployed march		Great Depression; auto-migrants (US); Superhighways (Germany, Italy, US)	Airlines expand; DC-3 developed	Desktop calculators
1940s (and WWII)	Millions of soldiers and refugees on foot	Naval warfare; shipping and troop transport	Transit at capacity; commuters, war efforts	Aviation expands; civilians bombed	Large mainframe digital computers; commercial TV (US)
1950s	European cities embrace, then reject US urban design	First container ships; freight intermodalism	Suburbanization; transit services decline; auto-ownership and driving expand, cheap fuel; expansion of highway building, especially in US and Europe	Airports, airlines expand; jets; Sputnik (1957)	Digitization, fibre optics, microwaves, integ. circuitry; small mainframes, mag. disk, transistor–satellite era begins; Atlantic cable
1960s	Peace and civil rights marches	Cargo containerizing, intermodalism expand	Major increase in driving, roads, automobile ownership, suburbanization; anti-highway movements	Space and moon explored–militarized	Telstar (1962); first email (1965); early internet (1969)
1970s	Walking to school declines		Oil embargo; renewal of interest in energy efficiency and transit; Amtrak (US 1971), ViaRail (CA1978) founded; driving and roads increase; traffic restraint grows in Europe	Expansion of air cargo–express services	Mobile phones; first Apple I computer (1976)
1980s	Euro cities begin pedestrianization		Rail double-stack containers; TGV-HSR France (1981); EU improves bicycle planning and facilities		Al Gore 'invents' internet; digital network; PCs (1983), Macs (1984
1990s	Pedestrian interest grows in US		ISTEA; more funding for transit, walking, cycling (US)	Stealth bombers attack Iraq (1991)	Digitality, mobility, connectivity, videoconferencing
2000–present	Lack of walking and obesity become health concerns	Shippers explore sail assistance	Transit ridership-investment grows globally; Europe and Asia expand passenger rail; Amtrak funds cut, restored; road pricing interest (US); congestion pricing in Europe grows	Energy costs, security issues; Concorde ends; jumbo jets developed	Text messaging, videophones, Obama's Blackberry

- How modes interact with land use, infrastructure, environment and societal and cultural factors are important considerations for planning and policy-making especially as rapid changes occur – or need to occur. Some modal, infrastructure and urban forms are more compatible with sustainability goals than are others, and some modes work together in a sustainable manner to achieve energy efficiency, less fossil-fuel dependence and more compact communities than do others.

In order for transportation to play a significant role in achieving sustainability it is necessary to understand more of its history in order not to repeat mistakes of the past. The main transportation modalities whose history will be explored in this chapter are those related to:

- walking;
- water and maritime travel;
- sleds and related mobility devices;
- animal-assisted transport;
- wheeled apparatus;
- mechanization and motorization;
- air travel;
- communications and telecommunications.

Walking: The original affordable, healthful and sustainable mode

While much of pre-history and paleo-history is subject to debate and speculation, it appears that the transformation of mobility from the prone positioning of tetrapedalism, using feet and arms together, to erect feet-only bipedalism began millions of years ago. Bipedalism has been credited for evolutionary advances in physical and cognitive development and human tool-making. Walking was mostly a slow-paced group activity. It was another long slow walk until about 500,000 years ago when *Homo sapiens* became distinguished from *Homo erectus* and began to gather in very early seasonal communities. Human development then took another long slow walk until some 20,000 years ago when our predecessors began to gather in permanent settlements. A somewhat quicker walk led to the development of early civilizations some 10,000 years ago.[1] Walking remained the primary mode even as humans developed rudimentary ways of travelling across water, used animals to lighten their loads, or developed types of sleds and sleighs (Lay, 1992, p25, *passim*).

Early water and marine

Travel between coastal communities, along river systems and across large bodies of water resulted in increased trade, population exchanges and early forms of warfare. These developments, in turn, spurred improvements in the technology of water travel, which expanded its range, efficiency and hauling capacities. Aquatic and shoreline food sources, along with the new opportunities for trade, played a role in the development of settlements and cities. By about

5000 years ago several civilizations were building oar-powered complicated boats, some with sails and oars. Such ships could carry sizeable crews and cargoes and played an important role in the transport of food and the military, and the political and administrative development of early states. Even as navigational skills and ship technologies improved, the uncertain conditions of weather, as well as the health difficulties of long voyages, made such forms of travel risky. Transatlantic crossings in the centuries of conquest and colonization of the Americas claimed a fair percentage of lives, and those transported as slaves had especially high rates of mortality.[2]

Animals, sleds and sleighs lighten the load

The domestication of animals and their subsequent use for carrying materials began between 5000 and 15,000 years ago. Among the animals domesticated by humans and then used for work, mobility and war were dogs, donkeys, horses, camels, yaks, goats, llamas, alpacas and elephants. Sleds, useful for dragging loads, could be made more efficient by placing them on rollers or logs and using animals as their domestication developed (Lay, 1992, pp19–26; Derry and Williams, 1993, pp191–192).

Wheels, early vehicles and travel – mostly local and for necessity

The wheel developed in Mesopotamia about 7000 years ago and spread across many civilizations and cultures over the next few millennia, from Europe to India and China. Civilization was not dependent upon the wheel: several societies with complex systems of mobility developed without the wheel, as in the pre-Columbian Americas. Nor was the wheel suited for all cultures and terrains. The wheel opened numerous possibilities in the movement of persons and larger loads for those cultures that adopted it. As the wheel improved, the devices it supported became more differentiated: hand carts, animal-drawn wagons and chariots.[3]

Travel remained difficult even after the domestication of animals, wheeled transportation and boats and navigation improved. Most land travel was still on foot as animals were used more for packing loads and pulling wagons than for riding. Travel beyond the horizon was rare and reserved for special occasions and necessities. Avocational travellers were especially rare and often attached themselves to organized expeditions and caravans rather than risking solo travel. Some early explorers and geographers collected their travel observations in written or oral records that became renowned in the ancient world, shaping mythology and literature.

Figure 3.1 Modernity meets tradition: Hauling rocks in a carreta in today's Costa Rica

Source: John Redmond Stevens

Voluntary travel included the pilgrimage, which interpreted the vicissitudes of travel in religious metaphor. Shrines at Jerusalem, Bethlehem, Mecca, Spain's Santiago de Compostela and sacred sites in India and China have endured for centuries. Gruelling pilgrimages, some involving forms of self-punishment, exist to this day in Latin America, the Middle East and elsewhere. Chaucer's *Canterbury Tales: The Tale of a Merry Pilgrimage to the Site of the 12th-Century Martyrdom of St. Thomas Becket* became a pillar of English literature. More recently, between 1953, when she became alarmed by the nuclear menace of the Cold War, and 1981, when she was killed in a car crash, 'Peace Pilgrim' walked 50,000 miles (80,000km) or more across the US, Canada and Mexico distributing her pacifist literature and messages.[4]

Box 3.1 Walking: The pilgrims' preferred mode

Susanne L. Seales[5]

Most religious pilgrimages are undertaken on foot. The medieval church instructed pilgrims to shed worldly goods, wear humble garments, take up wooden staffs and walk hundreds to thousands of miles between starting points in France and the major shrines of Santiago de Compostela (a popular tourist pilgrimage in today's world) and Rome. Some travel by boat was allowed if necessary. Pious men and women, rich and poor, pursued the miraculous benefits of direct contact with relics along the routes and at their final destinations. Intended as a religious act, pilgrimages also became a conduit through which secular ideas were shared across Europe. Spreading along the routes' shrines, monasteries and cathedral schools, ideas disseminated and contributed to increased intellectual activity of the so-called 12th-century Renaissance. Without the yearly flow of penitent walkers the Middle Ages would truly have been dark.

Obtaining the permission of their liege lord, and presenting themselves to the local clergy as penitential sinners, poor and rich alike undertook a journey that was viewed as a metaphorical process of rebirth into a realm blessed by God and the saints. Dependent upon the charity of individuals and monastic lodges along the way, it took several months to travel the routes from France to the great shrines in Spain and Italy, and, if the sea routes were not an option, potentially years to reach the Holy Land. Wealthy pilgrims often found a way around the strict rules and rode horses. The poor walked and the disabled were given dispensation to ride donkeys.

In addition to church information, educated pilgrims consulted guidebooks, such as the 12th-century *Codex Calixtinus*, which gave advice and detailed information about difficult terrain, dangers and the shrines en route and at their destination. Upon arriving at the main shrines in Santiago de Compostela, Rome, Canterbury or Jerusalem, pilgrims were said to have felt great joy at the culmination of their efforts. Hymn-singing monks attended the weary and aching pilgrims at their destinations as they presented themselves for much sought-after saintly blessings, often receiving a handful of cockle shells as a memento. Then, on weary feet, they returned home across the hundreds to thousands of miles they had just crossed, most walking, a few riding, and all believing that they had for a brief instant touched the power of God.[6]

Eternal congestion: Vehicles and pedestrians don't mix well

Transportation innovations did not always fit well with settlement patterns. Early traffic jams and conflict between pedestrians and noisy wheeled conveyances on the streets of ancient Rome are a frequently used anecdote in transportation circles, reminding us that traffic congestion and noise are as enduring as the 'Eternal City'

(Mumford, 1961, pp218–219). Animals used for transport competed for space and resources with animals quartered in cities for food. The manure from urban animals became a public health problem. Raised sidewalks were constructed for walking above the muck and manure. Most older streets were too narrow for both vehicles and pedestrians. Over time, the design of expanding cities and new settlements changed to better accommodate horse-drawn vehicles.

Mechanization and motorization transform travel and society

The history of transportation during the Early Modern and Modern eras[7] illuminates the interplay and quickened pace of technical, political and economic factors, including the Western ambition to travel further and faster. Over many centuries, wheels, wagons and carriages improved and were better able to withstand the vicissitudes of travel along the primitive roads of the Middle Ages and Early Modern Era. Travel by water followed a similar trajectory, with improvements in design, navigation and sailing techniques, which improved speed and manoeuvrability. The modal developments that occurred during this time, many of which continued into the Modern Era, transformed transportation and notions of travel. These included:

- increased speed of vehicles;
- increased load carrying capacity;
- travel became relatively easier, more comfortable and less uncertain compared to earlier eras.

These developments transformed the societies experiencing them in several ways:

- Perceptions of distance and travel hardship changed, and travel became less discouraging. By the end of the 19th century, the mentality of travel motorization beginning with the phenomenon of railway travel and then the somewhat later experience of automobile travel led to the perception of the 'annihilation of space and time' (Schivelbusch, 1986, pp33–44; Sachs, 1992, pp6–12).
- Demographics changed as populations grew, dispersed more and entered into more exchange.
- Both colonial expansion and internal migration from rural areas to growing cities became easier.
- Access to goods and services generally increased.
- Perceptions of the environment and landscape changed: geography became less of a constraint, the consumption of energy resources, from wood, peat and whale oil to fossil fuels, greatly increased. Land previously in a more natural state was increasingly converted to crops and other uses to feed growing urban populations.

From hot air to steam: Balloons, rails and early steamships

During the 18th century the technology of several modes began to change. The first human-carrying hot air balloon was launched in Paris in 1783 and instigated a series of efforts aimed at air travel, which culminated in the beginnings of aviation during the early 20th century. Wheeled coaches were pulled by horses along tracks in the earliest form of rail transit: the 'omnibus'.[8] Primitive steam engines were developed for mining and transportation in the late 17th and early 18th centuries and improved towards the end of the 18th and early 19th centuries. Steam-driven boats slowly developed during the late 18th century and by the beginning of the 19th century were successfully used, albeit in a small way, for ships carrying passengers and freight. Steamships were used more for river and coastal routes where they could frequently stop for fuel: wood in the early days, coal later in the 19th century. Transoceanic steamships were slower in development due to their inefficient engines and the bulkiness of the wood or coal needed; they were not a major factor in ocean shipping until the latter part of the 19th century.

At the beginning of the 19th century, steam engines were developed to power both road and rail vehicles, with the success and refinement of rail applications spreading much faster than road applications. The success of steam rail locomotion was due in great measure to the improvements made by engineering genius George Stephenson, whose 'Rocket' locomotive won the competition for the first modern railway line that linked Liverpool and Manchester in 1829.[9] Railroads, too, made the transition from wood to coal, but not before decimating many of the forests of England, New England and wherever else early railroading spread.

Nineteenth-century motorization, along with engineering improvements to waterways[10] and roads, bridges and tunnels, made possible a major expansion of transportation's capabilities. Modern imperialism was fuelled by fossils, and the global logistics of military and cargo transportation were shaped by the strategic location of coal and (later) oil depots. In many ways transportation became less sustainable as it became more dependent upon non-renewable resources and an ever expanding reach.

One interesting 19th-century invention and its infrastructure needs is instructive about the complex relation between modal innovation, competition and succession, infrastructure, transportation politics and how the culture of mobility can divert progress away from the path of sustainability.

Bicycling: The sustainable path almost taken

While the rush to motorization and fuel consumption was occurring, a highly promising mechanized – but not motorized – mode was being developed: bicycle development began early in the 19th century and reached most of its modern form within one hundred years. Its timeline is summarized in Table 3.1.

Contrary to the popular myth of its invention by Leonardo da Vinci, the bicycle began as a wheel-assisted walking or running machine, the 'velocipede' (Latin for 'fast foot') or 'Draisine' after its German founder, Karl (von) Drais. It was simply an inlined two-wheeled device with a crossbar for sitting and a steering bar. A forester with an inventor's streak, Drais developed this horseless conveyance after witnessing several seasons of agricultural failures, beginning in 1812, and the climate effects of the volcanic eruption of Mount Tambora, Indonesia, in 1815. Horses could not be maintained during these failures and a substitute was needed for making the rounds of fields and forests (Economy-point.org, 2006; Huttman, 2009).

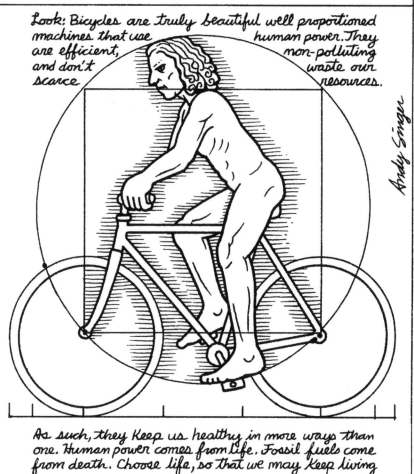

Figure 3.2 'da Vinci revisited'

Source: Andy Singer (www.andysinger.com)

The primitive wooden wheels and frame of the Draisine allowed the interaction of striding and wheels to create faster and easier mobility than walking alone did. It was less expensive than travel by horse, but it depended upon a reliable road surface to a far greater degree than did either walking or horse travel. The 'mechanical horse' stimulated a great deal of interest in its early years, but it did not lead to widespread use.

Beginning a practice that survives today, albeit sometimes in different form, the bicycle challenged its competitors: the horse and rider or the horse-drawn carriage. Along good surfaces the Draisine acquitted itself well, occasionally surpassing or enduring better than its competition. But the Draisine did not perform well on the poor roads and streets of its day; it was an encumbrance going uphill and difficult to control downhill. Some media portrayals flattered the Draisine; but many more pilloried or satirized it. The popular term that stuck to it was 'hobbyhorse' or 'dandy-horse'. Generally seen as the domain of dandies and privileged university students, when early velocipedes took to sidewalks in search of smooth surfaces they drew the ire of the walking public and were banned. Many jurisdictions banned them from roadways because they were thought to frighten horses and interfere with traffic.

Between the 1820s and the 1850s, several mechanics (a catchall term of the period) and inventors turned their attention to improving the Draisine. Several of their three- and four-wheelers were more stable and better performing on the rutted roads and streets of the day; a few substituted a treadle-drive mechanism for striding, but all still shared with the two-wheeler the problems of having to be lugged up hills and poor downhill control. In 1821 Lewis Gompertz of Surrey, England, proposed a hand crank powering the front wheel, which would have significantly increased its speed, but was ignored. An early animal rights activist as well, he went on to invent several other transportation improvements oriented towards relieving the burdens of work animals. Drais and Gompertz illustrate that transportation was not always viewed by inventors as a 'thing in itself', and how inventions can spring from the desire to ameliorate a condition of human or animal difficulty or suffering. Still, the growth of bicycling was impeded in this era by a combination of poor roads and a technology that did not yet ensure easy use, safety and reliability.[11]

Cranking up the velocipede: Bicycling grows and crosses social and cultural boundaries

During the 1860s the addition of pedals and cranks to the velocipede's front wheel increased its speed, although its hard wheels and lack of suspension caused it to earn the nickname of 'boneshaker'. It attracted much interest, especially in the growing urban areas of England, North America and France, where it had first been widely introduced. The familiar competitions between human-powered cycles and horses and horse-drawn carriages ensued, as did contests among cyclists.

Other 'velorutions' were associated with the new velocipede. Cycling was the first popular athletic activity open to women on a large scale, which had implications for their participation in a range of athletic activities, clothing and the feminist movement. Occasionally, women were portrayed as getting the better of male cyclist or equine competitors. Advertisements for velocipedes often featured robust athletically attired women, symbolizing freedom or progress.[12]

During the 1860s and 1870s velocipedes seemed to be everywhere: city streets, country roads, indoor rinks, outdoor race-tracks, regular circuses,

Figure 3.3 A 19th-century wooden-wheeled velocipede attracts people to an antique store in Bruges, Belgium

Source: Preston L. Schiller

Box 3.2 Miss Smith's cycling adventure and Mrs Bloomer's sensible fashion trends

Susanne L. Seales[13]

Sir Arthur Conan Doyle's 'The adventure of the solitary cyclist'[14] is the story of an independent young woman who presents Sherlock Holmes with a very interesting case. According to Dr John Watson, Miss Violet Smith arrived at 221B Baker Street on 23 April 1895, and after a brief introduction, Holmes asked what was troubling her. '"At least it cannot be your health", said he, as his keen eyes darted over her, "so ardent a bicyclist must be full of energy"'(p527). He had deduced from one quick glance at her shoes 'the slight roughening of the side of the sole caused by the friction of the edge of the pedal' (p527). It is also possible that Holmes noticed Miss Smith's cycling skirt, with bloomers hidden underneath, sensible and popular fashions introduced by the American Mrs Amelia Bloomer around 1851. Victorian crinolines made cycling cumbersome and dangerous, whereas Mrs B's innovative designs presented women with garments that were liberating and safe as they peddled about town or country.

Having just arrived in London with her bicycle in tow, it is probable that Miss Smith was dressed in the late Victorian version of these garments, as were the growing number of independent young female cyclists of the time.[15] In addition to using her bicycle to get about town, Miss Smith used it twice a week to travel between the train station and her place of employment on a rural estate. She made these trips without an escort, and would have continued without hesitation but for the recent appearance of a sinister male cyclist along a deserted stretch of the route, which caused her to seek Holmes's assistance in identifying the man. Her employer, Mr Carruthers, had suggested switching to a horse and trap as a solution to her problem, and Holmes also hinted at safer modes when he asserted: 'It is part of the settled order of Nature that such a girl should have followers ... but for choice not on bicycles in lonely country roads' (p530). However, although the plot takes an ominous turn for the cycling protagonist, in the end one is left with the impression that Conan Doyle was not criticizing Miss Smith's choice of the bicycle as her mode of transportation. He left no doubts about the risks that a young female cyclist might face in certain settings; but he also left the reader with a strong sense of the physical and mental benefits in store for a lady who chose a bicycle over a horse-driven cart.

This stance is in stark contrast to other views about female cyclists in Victorian Europe and America. 'Against bloomers and bicycles', an 1897 article in the *New York Times*, discusses a bill introduced in the Kansas Legislature by Representative Lambert, which would 'prohibit women from wearing bloomers' or from appearing 'on a public thoroughfare riding astride a bicycle'. Citing 'eminent physicians', Lambert asserted 'that the bicycle habit destroys the health of women and unfits them for the important and sacred duties of motherhood'. Others criticized the popular cycling garments, such as in an 1895 article for *The Christian Commonwealth*, which stated that 'The "Coming Woman" is already here, and we are bound to say that we do not like her appearance. In fact, she looks more like a man than a woman.' However, many people of the late Victorian era accepted this new activity for women, including doctors who, contrary to Lambert's physicians, asserted the healthy benefits of cycling. There were also a number of articles published by feminists, such as Marguerite Merington, who in 1895 discussed a more liberated view of bloomer-clad women in *Scribner's Magazine*, stating that an 'absence of self-consciousness has characterized the woman cyclist from the outset'. Sir Arthur Conan Doyle clearly shared these views, and in the character of Miss Violet Smith he created the vision of an independent Victorian woman in sensible clothes and well-travelled shoes, taking to the city and country roads on her bicycle.[16]

bicycle circuses on high wires and tested in distance competitions. Inventors and promoters sought wide-ranging applications for this popular invention, from the whimsical balloon-assisted mountain velocipede (Herlihy, 2004, p145) to police patrols. Cycling clubs formed in many cities and towns and developed political agendas aimed at better treatment of cyclists and, most importantly, improved streets and roads.

A tilt towards the high wheeler: The bicycle 'improves' at the expense of widespread use

Into this milieu rode the high-wheeled bicycle.[17] The innovation of a high wheel was made possible by advances in metal wheel and frame manufacture and solid rubber tyres. One crank of the pedals achieved a greater distance and velocity than the smaller-wheeled velocipede. The rubber tyre afforded better traction and less bone-shaking than previous wheels, and the pedalist perched directly above the front wheel used leg power more effectively. The high wheeler's simpler and lighter frame was produced at a much lower cost. Most importantly, it was faster and allowed a greater range than its competitors. Perching upon such a contraption, navigating the still largely unimproved streets and roads, required skill, learning time and courage impractical for average riders. An epidemic of broken bones and head injuries trailed close behind the high wheelers. In a theme common to much of transportation's modern history, speed and distance trumped utility, accessibility, moderation and safety. Still, an expansion of high-wheeler manufacture ensued and eclipsed the velocipede.[18]

Increased head injuries were not the only social cost of the high wheeler. The skill and time needed to master riding the high wheeler effectively limited its ridership to younger men of means and leisure sufficient to master it. The age band of riders narrowed, with few parents willing to allow youngsters to mount it and even fewer older adults willing to chance an injury. And, most tellingly, far fewer women seemed interested or willing to ride such a difficult machine. Despite these drawbacks, the high wheeler flourished for a decade or more among those inclined to master it and accept its risks (Herlihy, 2004, pp182–221). High-wheeler groups on both sides of the Atlantic staged parades and processions to impress the public. Today a number of groups on both sides of the Atlantic as well as in Australia and New Zealand keep high-wheeler, velocipede and even Draisine riding alive – albeit many of the riders now wear helmets (IVCA, 2009).

Safety to the rescue

The poor condition of streets and roads, as well as the difficulties of mastering the high wheeler, limited its utility and adoption by a mass of the population during the 1870s. But the appetite for cycling was aroused, and by 1885 a vastly improved velocipede was introduced. It had smaller in-line wheels, took advantage of the technical improvements of the high wheeler, but added a chain-and-sprocket drive that allowed a significant mechanical advantage without a large drive wheel. The new bicycle became known as the 'safety' or 'diamond' frame because of its shape, lower height and greater ease in balance and manoeuvre. Many improvements followed and prices eventually stabilized between US$80 and $100 in the patent-disadvantaged US and between US$35 and $50 in England – a significant sum for the time, but far below the cost of a horse or carriage.

Women again took to the streets on two wheels, parents felt more comfortable encouraging their children to mount the safety, and several people of colour became famous bicycle racers in the US and Europe. Bicycle police patrols heroically chased criminals and reigned in runaway horse carriages; city bicycle courier services expanded; and safety cycling youths delivered a range of goods from telegrams to groceries. Bicycle manufacturers attempted to convince the military, with little success, of the many applications of their versatile product – although a short-lived company of African-American bicyclists was formed in the American West (Herlihy, 2004, pp259, 292–293). Romance was made mobile side by side or in tandem – as expressed in the 1892 American popular song 'Daisy Bell':

> Daisy, Daisy,
> Give me your answer do!
> I'm half crazy,
> All for the love of you!
> It won't be a stylish marriage,
> I can't afford a carriage
> But you'll look sweet upon the seat
> Of a bicycle made for two.

The bicycle found a sizeable niche in Western society and soon spread to popular use in Africa and Asia. In Europe it became well institutionalized and accepted as 'normal' for use by both sexes and all ages, in town and country. Bicycling was seen as part of the hygienic movement's healthy lifestyle, and at age 67 Leo Tolstoy took up cycling at the behest of his friends: it was believed to have eased his depression following the death of a young son.[19] Not all bicycling was seen as 'healthy'. Many poorer city dwellers resented the more well-to-do cyclists who earned the derogatory term 'scorchers' for zooming through neighbourhoods, sometimes injuring pedestrians and disrupting children at play in the street (McShane, 1994, pp118–119).

While the safety bicycle resolved the problem of ease and access for most, the poor conditions of streets and roads limited the use of the bicycle. In several countries, especially Britain, France and the US, cyclists led political movements that aimed to improve streets and roads. While the heyday of the bicycle preceded the mass introduction of the motor car, it was part of the dynamic of conquering distance by speed that launched the era of the automobile and airplane. The street and road improvement movements begun by bicyclists, especially the Good Roads movement in the US and the Road Improvements Association in England, became the spearheads of efforts that paved the way for the rise of automobility.[20] Before exploring the rise of the automobile it is necessary to examine the development of roads and streets – the infrastructural basis for walking, animal-assisted transport (wagons and carriages), bicycling and motor vehicles.[21]

Transportation infrastructure: From animal paths to 'Good Roads'

The earliest routes that bipeds trod as they stopped swinging from tree to tree and walked upright across savannas made use of animal tracks. Improving paths and trails probably began after humans formed permanent settlements and needed better connections with other settlements. Road improvements in cities and extending outwards began as early as 3000 to 4000 BCE in India and parts of

Mesopotamia. Improving roads was more common within settlements than between settlements. Road-building between settlements increased as commerce and the use of wheeled and animal-assisted vehicles developed. Road-building begins as a large-scale endeavour with the peak of the Roman Empire, roughly between 400 BCE and 400 AD. Built primarily to move large numbers of foot legions around the empire, the roads were also used for the transport of goods. Roman roads and bridges, many of which survive today, were extremely well built and stretched for 53,000 miles (85,000km). In comparison, today's vast US Interstate Highway System totals less than 50,000 linear miles (80,000km).[22]

For 1000 years after the end of the Roman Empire, road-building in Europe stagnated. Land transportation moved in the direction of connecting nearby towns and cities by the easiest routes and much of the Roman road system was abandoned. The movement of persons and goods by inland waterways, as well as by sea, continued to progress. Extensive road projects in other parts of the world included the Great Wall of China – actually a 5500 mile (8800km) network of elevated roadways for military movement to prevent invasions and protect the Silk Road running alongside part of it – and the vast Inca road network.

Box 3.3 Silk Road to the West, Horse Road to the East

Susanne L. Seales[23]

Since the earliest settlements, travel has been linked to trade, the exchange of ideas and warfare. A dialectic between city walls, symbols of isolation and defence, and caravan routes, symbols of expansion and exchange, shaped the ancient landscape and slowly improved long-distance travel between city states and regions. Recent aerial photos of the Middle East show a vast network of caravan routes scarring the desert landscape and connecting it to regions bordering the Mediterranean and Central Asia. Some of these routes date from circa 3000 BCE, and many were frequented by merchants and armies throughout the ancient past. Caravans were at times comprised of hundreds of individuals and pack animals, including camels, donkeys and horses that could withstand extreme desert and mountain conditions.

The Chinese also established land and sea routes for trade and warfare, and small amounts of their silk and pottery, and philosophical ideas, appeared in the West prior to the second century BCE. Around 125 BCE, however, Zhang Qian, a Han Dynasty envoy, led an expedition directly west into Central Asia in search of the fabled 'heavenly horses'. After his return, the Han emperor opened up the route that Qian had taken, enabling Chinese merchants to trade their goods more frequently for horses and other Western products, including Persian metalwork, cucumbers and grapes. This route connected with others in Central Asia and became known as the Silk Road in the West, where Chinese silk was highly prized, along with pottery, jade ornaments, cinnamon and camphor. From the Chinese perspective, though, it could have been called the Horse Road for the highly prized military animals they brought back.

Over the next few centuries, these routes would link up with those connecting Central Asia to the West, eventually extending the Silk Road across the approximately 4500 miles (7200km) from China to the Levant. Passing through often dangerous and difficult conditions, merchants travelled from both directions to trade in 'exotic' goods. During the 14th century, Marco Polo[24] accompanied a number of caravans going east and kept an extensive diary of his travels, which covered large sections of the Silk Road. The Muslim scholar, Ibn Battuta,[25] also travelled these routes during his 24-year trek from Tangier to China and back. Crossing deserts and mountains, and passing through numerous lands, the Silk Road was a major conduit for the exchange of goods and ideas between the East and West from ancient times through to the 19th century.[26]

Box 3.4 Inca roads

While most of the Roman roads deteriorated or were abandoned, civilizations in the Americas were busily building extensive and complicated road systems even though they did not use the wheel and used animals mostly for carrying loads rather than humans. The Aztec and Inca (sometimes spelled Inka) built extensive well-engineered road systems between 500 and 800 years ago. The Spanish conquerors and explorers of the 16th century marvelled at their accomplishments as they surpassed anything they had known in Europe. The Inca road network consisted of 23,000km (14,000 miles) extending from north-central Ecuador to central Chile through Peru and parts of Bolivia and Argentina. Its tolls and tributes were important sources of revenue for the Inca Empire and the roads were maintained by a complex system of work obligations. The older Olmec, Maya and Toltec civilizations also developed complicated communications and transportation systems; but much less is known of them than of the Incas.[27]

Roads outside cities in Europe and North America from colonial days until the 20th century were a hodgepodge of private and tolled routes, with some government-controlled routes maintained by a much resented and often ineffective system of mandatory fees and labour known as the 'corvee'. Overall, there was generally a lack of government interest in centrally directed systems of roads.[28] Some cities even had toll gates at their entries (Toronto, 2009). Napoleon Bonaparte's extensive road-building programme was exceptional, planned and designed for troop movements; following a French tradition, most roads were lined by trees to shade marching soldiers and horses. The early enhancement of trees had the interesting consequence of aestheticizing road travel for later users. The chaos of uneven road conditions, forced labour for maintenance and tolls over centuries made travel difficult and expensive and left travellers with an aversion to tolls and road privatization that has survived to modern times.

During the 19th century, with Paris leading, many European cities began beautifying their streets: creating boulevards, widening sidewalks, adding gutters, trees, public parks and promenades – for strollers and carriages. These amenities encouraged bicycling as it emerged. Street improvement became part of a more general urban and public health reform movement. Early forms of streetcars made their appearance: the horse-drawn omnibus at first, the cable car and electrified trams and trolleys later. The rise of urban transit played a significant role in allowing cities to expand and residents to travel without the restrictions of poor walking conditions in those parts where streets were unimproved – as was the situation in most North American cities. They also allowed all urban classes better access to parks and the natural areas at the edges of cities. In some cities special Sunday and holiday excursion streetcars and interurban trains took riders to parks and picnics.[29] These examples demonstrate the interconnectedness of transportation, urban design and social factors.

Bicycle boom and the Good Roads movement pave the way for early automobility

Bicycling became popular in 19th-century France due, in part, to its good roads. The popularity of cycling, bicycle tourism and racing in France brought attention to the need to improve roads further. France improved the status of road-building and civil engineering with the establishment of the École des Ponts et Chaussées (School of Bridges and Roads) in 1747. Most transportation attention and investment in England went into developing an extensive railroad system; yet roads were good enough to allow some bicycle travel and competitions between cities, thanks, in part, to the work of the British pavement innovator John McAdam after whom the type of pavement known as macadam was named (Hindley, 1971). While support for road improvements grew among bicycle advocates in France and Britain during the 1880s and 1890s, the strongest pro-roads movement developed in the rapidly growing cities of the US, whose streets were generally in poor condition.[30]

The 1890s Good Roads movement in the US began in the 1880s as an outgrowth of the League of American Wheelmen (LAW), aided by bicycle manufacturer Alfred A. Pope. During the 1890s, its advocacy joined together urban bicyclists with the growing largely rural and small town populist movement. Farmers exploited by monopolistic railways, while generally hostile to the 'city-slicker cyclists', were willing to join them because good roads were needed to move goods from farm to market. The movement was further complicated with railways lending support, including railcars used to 'spread the gospel of good roads', in the expectation that better roads would extend the reach of railroads into rural areas still dependent upon rail shipment.[31]

The launching of the Good Roads movement preceded the introduction of the automobile into the US; but by the time the movement became influential in the early 20th century, the automobile was fast becoming a major force in American life. The bicycle interests were weak relative to the more powerful coalition members: farmers, urban motorists and the rapidly growing automobile and road construction industries. By the end of World War I, most industrial nations, either at federal or state–provincial levels, had resolved to establish government funding streams to improve and expand roads. The bicyclists' efforts for good roads led to their being driven off the road by the more powerful motor vehicle interests.

The rise of automobility

Contrary to President Obama's claim to its US origins, the first successful automobile was patented in 1885 by Karl Benz in Germany. A three-wheeler, it incorporated a two-cycle motor and other mechanical features already patented by Benz (Healey, 2009). After successive refinements and limited production runs of several models, the ironically named 'Velo'[32] emerged in 1894 and became the largest produced automobile of its decade. Numerous competitors to Benz's 1885 model quickly emerged on both sides of the Atlantic. Among them were Daimler and Maybach's 1886 four-wheeler; France's Emile Levassor and Armand Peugeot 1890 model derived from Daimler; the Duryea brothers'

US model of 1893; and Henry Ford's 1899 effort, which led to the Model T of 1908 and a mode of mass assembly line production known as 'Fordism'. Former farm boy Ford had a special interest in freeing 'stuck in the mud' rural folk, and the reliable and relatively inexpensive Model T did just that. Many, perhaps most, of the automobile's early inventors and producers had roots in the bicycle industry, again illustrating an ironical connection between the bicycle and subsequent developments, like good roads, that challenged its viability.[33]

Box 3.5 Electric vehicles

The earliest electric motor vehicles were developed during the 1840s. Better storage batteries emerged between the 1860s and 1880s, as did an early electric bicycle. Electric automobiles were introduced in France and Great Britain in the 1880s, and in the 1890s in the US by former bicycle manufacturer Albert Pope in a poorly managed unsuccessful effort to create fleets of battery-powered taxicabs in several cities. The battery-powered vehicle had some utility and promise as an in-town vehicle. Many townswomen and a not few townsmen were attracted to it since a crank was not needed to start the motor, nor did one need to be a mechanic to keep it running. With the exception of the failed effort of the Pope Motor Company to develop a national market for mostly male-driven electric taxis, many of the electric car's earliest adapters were women – although some feminist scholars have criticized its gender-oriented marketing. It could travel 50 to 80 miles (84–134km) on a charge. The scarcity of charging facilities between towns, the time needed to recharge and the high purchase price limited its application as a touring vehicle. The emerging automobile culture valued speed and distance over less noise and pollution. In 1912 the electronic starter was introduced and the internal combustion vehicle began to outdistance its electric and steam rivals. Interest in electric vehicles dampened but never disappeared in the 20th century – an example of the survival of a modal theme. As will be discussed further in later chapters, the early years of the 21st century have seen a revival of interest in both electric automobiles and bicycles.[34]

From World War I to World War II:
Automobile and highway culture

As the automobile's popularity grew during the late 19th and early 20th centuries, an international 'car culture' enveloped it. Automobile clubs, the precursors of present-day automobile associations found around the globe, emerged on both sides of the Atlantic and, eventually, across the Pacific. Their original focus was organizing automobile racing and touring. Eventually the clubs merged their efforts with those of the manufacturing and road construction interests into 'highway lobbies' that campaigned successfully for road funding, standards and regulations. Some automobile clubs developed into insurance companies offering various services to motorists. Movies that once displayed heroines rescued on horseback and trains in motion now featured limousine luxury and car chases and stunts.[35]

Figure 3.4 Historic cable car at the Smithsonian National Museum of American History: The front metalwork protruding at an angle was lowered in operation in order to act as a 'pedestrian catcher'

Source: Preston L. Schiller

By the eve of World War I the development of mechanized and motorized transportation modes was well under way, with the automobile in the lead and the truck, small by today's standards, close behind.[36] This led to increased demands for improved and expanded roads. Fordism led to the availability of relatively affordable and useful automobiles for rural folks, family physicians and city dwellers. The bicycle and the automobile had emerged as modes for elites but soon became available to a wide range of social classes in many countries. Transit improvements, especially the streetcar, improved urban liveability as well as making suburbanization possible. Then came World War I (Jackson, 1985).

World War I demonstrated the importance of the automobile and truck for military uses and the versatility of the automobile industry to produce machines for war. Many ambulances were automobiles modified to serve a light-truck purpose and quickly proved their value. Trucks moved troops, armaments and materiel in ways that supplemented or supplanted rail transport. After World War I the domain of the motor vehicle and the highway spread rapidly. Consolidation and merger in the automobile sector occurred as it expanded and became a major employer in many industrial nations. The Fordist mode of production became pre-eminent and Sloanism influenced the design and marketing of automobiles. Political leadership on both sides of the Atlantic used expanding roads and increasing motorization as ways of appealing to the citizenry. The creation and standardization of road, street and traffic standards began.[37]

Motoring for the masses: Depression parkways, superhighways and Hoovervilles

By 1928 the automobile was so firmly a fixture in American life that Herbert Hoover's presidential campaign was popularly depicted as promising 'A chicken in every pot. And a car in every backyard, to boot.' Just a few years later the battered lived-in car of the *Grapes of Wrath* Joad family, driven out of Oklahoma by dust storms and overloaded with people and furniture, struggled to reach California's 'pastures of plenty'. At night, and while waiting for work, the Joads and many families in the same circumstance gathered in impromptu campgrounds called 'Hoovervilles' after the president who had promised them much but led them into the Great Depression.[38]

During the same period several European nations undertook large highway and motoring projects. In 1930s Germany, Hitler accelerated the expansion of the ambitious Autobahn network, begun more democratically in the 1920s. While the Nazi regime had the military value of the Autobahn network foremost in its thinking, it simultaneously developed the 'people's car', or Volkswagen, as a way of helping the masses experience the value of the superhighways. The Italian Autostrada network of high-speed roads, begun in the more democratic time of 1921, was expanded upon by the Fascist regime in 1930s but never achieved the scale of the Autobahn.[39]

In the US, motor parkways became important expressions of the new highway culture. The early 1900s Long Island Motor Parkway, originally known as the Vanderbilt Parkway, a 45 mile (75km) private toll road connecting Queens with wealthy Long Island suburbs, was intended to give its sponsor William K. Vanderbilt Jr. and his plutocratic neighbours a quick ride to New York City as well as a venue for their spectator-killing car-racing hobby. Later parkways, such as the 1930s federal Blue Ridge Parkway[40] or the many of Robert Moses's crafting, were designed for somewhat nobler purposes: scenic recreation, helping families get to the seashore, parks and mountains and – not to be ignored – providing commuters with the opportunity to drive to city jobs from their newly developed suburbs (Caro, 1975; Schivelbusch, 2007)

Meanwhile, public transportation systems were under siege by automobility and automobile interests. In the US many, if not most, streetcar systems had been built by developers or utilities in order to promote their realty or energy source. They had promised a perpetual five cent ride and regulatory agencies held them to it long after it was feasible to operate a quality service at such a low fare. Quality suffered greatly as services became more crowded and less well maintained, becoming easy targets for closure or replacement by buses regardless of the General Motors-led conspiracy or *Who Framed Roger Rabbit?*[41]

During World War II the industrial power of automobile manufacturing in several nations was retooled to produce trucks, troop carriers, tanks, cannons and even aircraft. Transit services achieved record ridership as automobile manufacture was suspended, fuel was rationed and large numbers of newly recruited women commuted by public transportation to defence production jobs.

1945 to 2000: Complication, confusion, new directions

The period from the end of World War II to the year 2000 presents a complex, somewhat contradictory and often confusing, array of transportation and land-use trends and counter-trends, movements and counter-movements. Only a few can be touched on here. Similarities and differences between Europe, Asia and the US are evident. As Table 3.1 indicates, the pace of transportation events was rapid during this period. In order to best understand these issues it is helpful to try to divide this period into three approximate phases that vary somewhat from country to country and continent to continent:

1   The first is post-war expansion of cities, rebuilding of bombed European and Asian cities, restoration and expansion of transportation infrastructure, and a rush to create more housing: 1945 to 1960.

2   The second is that of large-scale transportation infrastructure expansion: a heavy emphasis on highways in some nations, and a mixture of highways and public transportation emphases in others. Some abandonment or neglect of transportation infrastructure occurred under decolonization: 1960 to 1980.

3   The third is one of growing recognition of problems associated with motor vehicle dependencies and road expansion emphases with widely divergent reactions between urban and rural areas and within nations. Conflicts between developing in the public or private sector and local control versus globalization are in full play: 1980 to 2000.

Phase one: Rebuilding, 1945–1960

After World War II the automobile industry quickly resumed mass production. There was extensive government subsidization of housing, both public and private, in Europe, the US and many parts of Asia. It took many years for the cities hardest hit by the war to effectively rebuild and furnish adequate housing and infrastructure.

In Europe many cities were influenced by the US Marshall Plan to rebuild along the American model of urban freeways pushing into their centres, often consuming large swathes of land. After a few years of this experience many began to reconsider the wisdom of that strategy. Even as automobile ownership and affluence grew, many rebuilding and expanding cities returned to transportation and land-use patterns less dependent upon driving. Much suburbanization in Europe proceeded with more compact urban design and basic public transportation in place.

In the US much of the government loan-supported private housing was built in low-density mono-function suburban tracts. A long wedding of federally supported highway expansion with suburbanization began that led to the condition commonly termed 'sprawl'. Federal engineering standards for street widths, capacities, turning radii and service levels were extended beyond the interstate highways to cities and suburbs regardless of their local applicability or wisdom. Localities needed to adopt them as their street standards or face losing federal funding. The standards favoured motor vehicles at the expense of walking and bicycling and had little concern for promoting transit. During the 1950s the massive federal interstate highway system was begun.[42]

Phase two: Expansion, 1960–1980

In Europe many highway systems were expanded and suburbanization grew. While some far-sighted rail improvement efforts were begun in Japan, France and a few other countries, most of the expansion of transportation infrastructure occurred in the highway sector. The amount of freight transported by trucks grew significantly. Interest in pedestrianization and traffic calming began in several cities. Automobile ownership and use increased although some cities were beginning efforts to slow the growth of driving and increase the proportion of trips taken by transit, walking or bicycling. Public transportation was generally improved.

Box 3.6 How Interstate 5 came to Bellingham: You can't always get what you want – luckily!

James V. Hillegas[43]

Located 60 miles (100km) south of Vancouver, British Columbia, and 100 miles north of Seattle, Washington, Bellingham's setting reflects its region's beauty: it gazes at the San Juans and Vancouver Island to the west; to the east the sun rises over Mount Baker, the region's volcanic icon. Its history since World War II reflects several important North American themes: de-industrialization and the shift from a resource-based economy to a service economy; the decline of central business districts (CBDs) and the dispersion of commercial enterprise to the urban fringe; and confusion about traffic and highway planning.

The state's main north–south pre-1950s highway, Route 99, snaked through Bellingham and its CBD along a series of streets, its traffic flow broken by numerous signals, pedestrian crossings and intersections. Increasing congestion caused residents to begin to seek a solution in the 1940s. Echoing national sentiment, Bellingham planners, civic leaders and most residents saw road expansion as a way of increasing downtown property values and relieving traffic congestion while rejuvenating the central business district and industries along the city's waterfront. Perceiving this project in terms of competition with other West Coast states, in 1950 the *Bellingham Herald* asserted that the state that could build freeways more quickly and efficiently would win the race to become 'the New York of the West'.

Public sentiment welcomed state highway officials' early 1950s plan to build a limited-access highway through Bellingham. The city's civic and business leaders lobbied strenuously for a waterfront route to serve various industries, shipping terminals and the CBD. An interchange would serve the large cannery in the Fairhaven neighbourhood at the waterfront's south end and another would serve the large pulp mill at the water's edge of downtown. Residents and civic leaders did not express concerns about preserving the many historic buildings in Fairhaven and the CBD. State highway officials proposed a much less expensive route circumventing the waterfront and downtown core by about 1 mile. After much debate the state prevailed.

While the state legislature had already purchased some rights of way, the project was greatly accelerated when President Eisenhower signed the Federal Aid Highway Act of 1956 (PL84–627). Eisenhower claimed that the interstates would be an important benefit of American citizenship while improving safety, increasing efficiency and delivering wide-ranging economic benefits. He also appealed to Cold War fears by asserting the importance of this highway system to evacuate cities during an atomic attack by the Soviet Union – although some quick calculations might have challenged this possibility. The opening of the final section of Interstate 5 through Bellingham in 1966 brought shopping and residential centres to freeway interchanges; during the 1980s a mall just outside the (then) northern city limits drew shoppers from Canada and Bellingham's CBD. By the mid 1990s, Bellingham's downtown, waterfront and Fairhaven areas were mere ghosts of what they had been through the 1950s.

Ironically, the large Fairhaven cannery closed the same year as the opening of Interstate 5, a victim of industry changes and dwindling salmon harvests. The massive downtown pulp mill decreased its production and workforce steadily over the decades and closed its final operations in December 2007; the City and Port of Bellingham and Western Washington University plan to redevelop its 137 waterfront brownfield acres. Since 2000 there has been a veritable renaissance of interest and activity in both Fairhaven and the CBD: moderate density infill development; bicycle lanes; improved sidewalks; abandoned historic buildings renovated; new multi-storey mixed-use buildings in a style consistent with historic buildings; a boardwalk and trails connect Fairhaven with the CBD; and an attractive village green hosts outdoor cinema and a farmers' market where the Fairhaven interchange had been proposed in the 1950s. All along the route proposed by well-intended but short-sighted civic and business leaders for a 1950s freeway, residents are reconnecting to their waterfront and its parks, often on foot or bicycle. Lucky them.[44]

Figure 3.5 Once targeted for a freeway interchange in the 1960s, the commercial district of Fairhaven now features a village green ringed by a bookstore, café, restaurants and stores: Today's event features a multigenerational Chinese–American cultural celebration of the harvest moon

Source: Preston L. Schiller

The US experienced the consequences of highway and suburban expansion that had made it easier for people to flee rather than resolve the problems of cities. Increasingly severe air pollution and the 1973 energy crisis prompted government regulatory responses, mostly aimed at reducing certain 'criteria pollutants' from emissions, increasing fuel efficiency and some renewed interest in public transportation. Private railroads withdrew from intercity passenger services and Amtrak was created as a federal entity. The pace of abandonment of small freight rail lines increased. In Canada and the US there were several successful campaigns to stop or limit urban highway expansion; but efforts to substitute transit for highway expansions were successful in only a few cities. In most North American cities transit came to be viewed as a service provided to those without automobiles and ridership declined. This era saw many urban reactions and books critical of the highway expansion trajectory, especially in North America, as well as many publications with fresh ideas and approaches to balanced transportation.[45]

Phase three: Different approaches, 1980–2000

Awareness of the unsustainability of a highway and streets expansion approach to transportation grew between 1980 and 2000 throughout the planet. This period illustrates many conflicting trends and counter-trends, such as re-urbanization versus suburbanization, and globalization versus community sustainability strategies. Both suburbanization and globalization generally increase transportation by unsustainable modes.[46]

In Europe there was further refinement and expansion of passenger rail and urban transit systems. Resistance to traffic expansion in cities grew, as did concern over pollution and growth in truck traffic. Several countries and many cities increased their investment in bicycle facilities, with The Netherlands, Scandinavia and Germany in the lead. Different styles of privatization and deregulation emerged; some countries engaged in increased partnerships between public and private transportation entities and refocused regulatory efforts, while others, such as the UK, engaged in sweeping deregulation and transfer of public transportation assets to private interests. Pedestrianization and traffic calming were undertaken on a broad scale in many parts of Europe and Asia and attracted interest in North America.[47]

In Latin America the city of Curitiba began its sustainable transportation and development reforms that have led it to become a world model (Vasconcellos, 2001). Concern about the social and environmental impacts of transportation grew in North America. The governments of Canada and the US stepped up efforts to curtail transportation-related pollution; but both countries allowed their intercity passenger rail services to diminish. During the early 1990s a short-lived effort to reform US federal policy was initiated with the passage of the Intermodal Surface Transportation Efficiency Act (ISTEA).[48]

Recent history: 2000 to the present

Aspects of recent transportation trends and efforts will be addressed in several of the subsequent chapters, but it is necessary to note a few highlights here.

Around the planet there is growing awareness of transportation's implication in atmospheric pollution and greenhouse gas (GHG) accumulation, as well as growing concern about the various social and environmental problems associated with the globalization of commerce; but efforts to address these matters have yielded mixed results. Efforts persist and, as the exemplars of Chapter 9 indicate, there are many cities on several continents where efforts to achieve a greater degree of sustainability are succeeding. Some of the major contemporary issues fuelling sustainable transportation discussions are:

- how best to contain or interrupt traffic growth, and promote improvement and use of transit, walking, bicycling and railways;
- how best to curtail transportation emissions – there is growing awareness that 'tailpipe' solutions such as emissions controls and fuel-efficiency standards are insufficient and that reducing travel by automobiles and trucks will be necessary to meet climate change goals;
- how to break out of conventional approaches to transportation planning in order to attain sustainability.

Before proceeding to a detailed discussion of contemporary transportation modes, a brief history of three more important modes will be presented: railways, aviation or air travel and maritime.

Rail and railways

Chapter 4 will provide details on how rail transport is one of the most sustainable, energy-efficient and least polluting of modes for moving people and goods – especially when electrified. Expanding rail capacity, for passengers or freight, is an effective alternative to highway expansion. Its history sheds some light on why its use for this purpose is unevenly applied.

The earliest efforts to harness the mechanical advantages of a fixed guideway to move heavy loads by wheeled conveyance without lateral slippage in trackways date back to Greek and Roman antiquity (Diolkos wagon way about 2500 years ago) and can be found in European mining operations in the 16th and 17th centuries. Early trackways were generally fairly short in distance, often connecting a mining site with a nearby waterway. Rails were constructed of wood, later reinforced with cast-iron plates, and steel has been used since the latter half of the 19th century. By the early 1830s a number of short railways were in operation and improvements in trackage and locomotion railways grew exponentially for the next several decades in England, Europe and the US.[49]

Figure 3.6 Nineteenth-century rail bicycle and early form of railed mine ore hauler at the Museum of Transport and Technology, Berlin

Source: Preston L. Schiller

Most of the early American and British railways were privately developed in the spirit of *laissez-faire* capitalism; there was little in the way of government interference with its social and environmental consequences. If government was involved at all it was to clear obstacles from the paths of entrepreneurs, and rails were often lubricated with bribery and other quaint practices of the time. People adversely affected by the railways developed deep resentments that sometimes lasted for generations.

The 'growth spurt' of the railways in the mid to late 19th century in most industrially developed countries followed a variety of trajectories. Some closely resembled the trajectory of the UK and US, some were the products of colonialism and a few were shaped by public policy to serve a wider public interest. Canadian railway development was fragmented until the arduous project of confederation led to a transcontinental railway. Throughout their history railways played important roles in military conflicts, colonial expansion and the development of many nations. Because of their importance in colonialism and resource extraction, historians have developed the notion of 'railway imperialism' as a framework for analysing the development of railways in former colonial countries.[50]

The present situation of railways varies considerably around the planet. In Canada and the US there is much talk about railway improvements, including high-speed corridors; but funding so far appears insufficient to realize such changes. Intercity rail barely plays a role in Mexico, where the government-controlled oil industry maintains artificially low fuel prices. Several European and Asian countries are developing high-speed systems or increments and many have improved and expanded slower but highly comprehensive networks.[51]

Maritime and water travel

The period between the beginnings of ancient civilizations and the development of engine-powered water travel saw significant advances in navigation and manoeuvrability, vessel design and expansion and provisioning for long voyages. These were part of the broader dynamic of the increasing importance of water travel for global exploration, cartography, commerce, warfare, nation- and empire-building and maintenance, colonial settlement and resource exploitation, as well as the use of water networks for travel and trade within countries (Derry and Williams, 1993, pp190–211).

The development of powerful and practical engines and propulsion systems changed the dynamics of water travel. By the early 19th century, as steamships began using coal rather than wood, longer voyages became practical for inland waters, coasts and across oceans. From the middle to the end of the 19th century, the steamship was proving its value for passenger, freight and military applications. By the end of the 19th century newly available oil made transoceanic transport even easier, and the completion of the Suez (1869) and Panama (1914) canals magnified the importance of intercontinental shipping. An enormous expansion of goods and passenger movement occurred as a result of these developments (Derry and Williams, 1993, pp364–377). Naval ships became the principal means of projecting military might and moving troops and materials in a timely fashion around the globe. By World War I new forms of naval warfare, including submarines and aircraft carriers, became factors in interrupting shipping lines and military convoys. Oil tankers and their shipping routes became vital to keeping military and war industry running.

The preparations for World War II and its duration witnessed a vast expansion of ship-building and shipping for battle and cargo. Following World War II the significance of traditional naval combat diminished somewhat due to the growth of military aviation and missile technology. The transport of passengers by ships diminished as the size and speed of airplanes increased. Large ocean liners became luxury tourist conveyances rather than the mode of choice for transoceanic travel. During the same period the importance and magnitude of maritime cargo-carrying grew as containerization, computerization and efficient

Figure 3.7 Puget Sound replica of a brig that would ply inland and coastal waters in past centuries

Source: Eric C. Bruun

intermodal transfer progressed (Gilbert and Perl, 2008, pp99–101). Inland and coastal waters shipping have remained relatively small but important parts of maritime freight and a very small part of passenger travel. Chapters 4 and Chapter 5 discuss aspects of marine modes, especially as they are currently used.

Feat of flying

A long history and mythology surrounds human efforts to overcome the limitations of surface travel through flight. The most famous flight myth is that of Icarus, the son of labyrinth designer Daedalus, whose wax wings melted as he soared too close to the sun. A variety of efforts were made in antiquity and the Middle Ages and beyond to create flying mechanisms: from the floating lanterns and large kites of ancient China to Islamic Spain's experiments with gliding devices, to early rocketry. Birdwatcher Leonardo da Vinci experimented a little with gliders and designed a flying machine in 1487 that never got off the drawing board.

By the late 18th century, humans were floating in balloons and some were gliding back to Earth with the help of early parachutes. During the early decades of the 19th century ballooning spread across Europe and made its presence felt in the US Civil War. The steerable dirigible was developed by the beginning of the 20th century, while interest in aerodynamics aided the development of gliders and early motorized unmanned flights (Derry and Williams, 1993, pp396–402).

The first manned flights between 1900 and 1910 were the culmination of imagination: small lightweight motors, liquid fuels, aerodynamics advances and lightweight durable materials development. The airplane's significance was immediately recognized and development of flying craft quickly advanced, helped by the military of various countries. Military aircraft were used prior to World War I and extensive use of aircraft was made by both sides of that war (Davidson and Sweeney, 2003, pp128–133).

Between World War I and World War II there was a steady pace of technological advance as well as rapid growth of civilian, commercial and military aviation in Europe, the US and Japan. In the US, popular interest in aviation grew rapidly during the 1920s as former military pilots took to 'barnstorming' and 'flying circuses', flying into small towns, rural areas and county fairs to thrill crowds with aerobatics and taking passengers for short rides (Onkst, undated). Airmail took off, rudimentary passenger planes were produced and several airlines served domestic and international markets. Across the planet public imagination was captivated by the flying machines and the heroic pilots who attempted transoceanic and around-the-world adventures. Remote regions in Canada, Africa and Latin America were made accessible by versatile bush pilots.

The 1930s witnessed further development of military and civilian aviation in Europe, Japan and the US. The 1937 blitzkrieg bombing of Guernica, Spain, memorialized in Picasso's monumental painting, demonstrated the great vulnerability of innocent civilian populations to this most modern form of warfare. While civilians had not been much targeted by air attacks in World War I, they have often been targets of aerial assault from World War II to the present.

Commercial passenger, air cargo and military aviation continued to expand after World War II. Commercial and cargo planes – often passenger airliners without seats – and their passenger and freight loads grew and demanded more space.[52] In many parts of the world, but especially in North America, new airports on the periphery of urban areas were constructed and existing ones expanded. New expressways linked airports with urban and suburban centres, although public transportation links were often weak to non-existent, or slow to develop. Office buildings, stores and hotels sprang up around many airports and created instant 'airport cities', often forcing their workers to commute by car because of insufficient transit. Large parking supplies and the taxi–car rental orientation of many airports themselves generate much traffic. In contrast, some regions in Europe

Figure 3.8 Wilbur (or is it Orville?) – the Wright brothers' airplane – flies among the astronauts at the Smithsonian National Air and Space Museum

Source: Preston L. Schiller

and Asia have not allowed excessive development to occur around major airports, and offer extensive transit and intercity travel options to passengers and employees. Chapters 4 and 5 also explore aspects of aviation's rapid growth and implications for sustainable transportation.

Telecommunications and transportation

Telecommunications is the transmission and exchange of information over distance. The origins of modern telecommunications are fairly recent. Its growth has been closely linked to transportation, commercial and military needs. Early usage of the word 'transportation' often made it interchangeable with 'communications'. While some point to early elevated bonfires, crude lighthouses, smoke signals, flags, drums and a variety of horns as the origins of telecommunications, it was the development of semaphores, sometimes called 'optical telegraphs', and telegraph systems that stimulated modern telecommunications. Semaphores assisted military and national governmental communications, early train operations and shipping. The peace symbol was derived from the combination of the semaphore codes for 'N' and 'D', denoting nuclear disarmament.[53] Flag codes were used to communicate between ships as well as in land-based military operations. Rapidly growing electrical telegraph systems became the first modern form of transoceanic communications and played a major role in government, military, postal and railway operations. Telephony had significant implications for all of these institutions, as well as profoundly influencing the ways in which businesses operated and people communicated.

Wireless technologies, beginning with wireless telegraphy and radio through the mobile telephone, also had a strong relation to government, military, commerce, transportation and popular culture. The relation of television to mobility is not clear. Televised educational courses and some programmes may reduce some travel; but television advertising stimulates much more. One of the major sources of broadcast media advertising revenue is transportation: its largest component, the automobile and its accoutrements.[54] Similarly, the rapid rise of computers and various wireless devices for moving information speedily over long distances might substitute for some travel but likely stimulates other forms of mobility. Telecommunications speeds up many processes, especially in the world of business and commerce, and may increase travel as a result of making the pace of these activities more rapid.

The exact nature of the relation between telecommunications and transportation is the subject of lively debate and discussion. Some claim that telecommunications replaces travel, while others assert that it leads to increased travel. Some question whether it is even a mode of transportation. Others point to the 'carbon footprint' of the internet as indicative of some of the often neglected issues embedded in this form.[55]

Lessons for sustainable transportation

Each mode developed in relation to what was perceived as problematic or lacking in previous means of mobility. Early cycling was seen as an extension and improvement upon walking and horse travel. Early railroading was seen as an improvement upon road or canal travel. Early automobility was seen as an improvement upon bicycling, horses and railway travel. 'Good Roads' were championed by bicyclists, farmers, automobile interests, even railroads, and paved the way for the dominance of the automobile. The steamship overcame the limits of sail-powered marine travel. All of the 'modern modes' of travel and goods movement were studied with keen interest by commercial, manufacturing, government and military–imperial interests for their purposes. Some modal innovations and applications improved mobility and accessibility without serious environmental consequences. Many modal innovations were rushed into widespread application without sufficient consideration for long-term consequences, such as fossil-fuel dependency and its impacts or land-use effects.

This brief overview of transportation history offers a few 'lessons' related to topics addressed throughout the remainder of this book:

- Walking is a 'built-in' for humans. This aspect of transportation offers a good basis for sustainable and healthy transportation.
- Walking, bicycling and transit could be the basic building blocks of passenger transportation as they have been in certain periods. These modes have historically demonstrated synergies between humans and their settlements.
- Emerging modes often compete strenuously with dominant modes in ways that are shaped by cultural values and beliefs. Racing, 'conquering space and time' and 'travel as consumption' demonstrate how transportation culture interacts with innovation. Cultural values and beliefs are subject to change; in recent years there has been increased emphasis on co-operation and coordination among modes and recognition of the need to reduce energy-intense travel.
- The basic building blocks of freight transportation have been rail and marine shipping. These are the most energy- and space-efficient modes of freight movement.

- Mobility for the sake of mobility, travel as a 'thing in itself', unrelated to basic human needs, is a relatively late development in the history of transportation.
- An important dimension of the history of transportation was the creation of communities who minimized the necessity of travel for basic needs.

Historically, most travel, even locally, was done out of necessity, mainly for sustenance, commerce and military purposes. Communities were located and shaped to minimize travel and maximize accessibility. Today, personal travel is increasingly discretionary; a smaller percentage of trips reflect necessity and a much larger proportion involve choices of whether, where and how to travel. This offers transportation planning and policy-making many interesting challenges and opportunities that will be addressed in subsequent chapters.

Questions for discussion

- Discuss what you think our cities and countryside might look like today had personal transportation technology development stopped with the bicycle and not proceeded to the automobile and truck?
- Discuss the relationship between telecommunications and transportation. Identify ways in which telecommunications might serve sustainable transportation. Identify ways in which telecommunications works against sustainable transportation.
- At the time of the introduction of the ('free') interstate highway system in the US several states were developing toll roads (turnpikes). Discuss what surface transportation might look like today in the US had major intercity and suburban road systems continued to develop along the lines of toll roads and turnpikes rather than being largely supplanted by freeways.

Notes

1   How many millions are also under debate: the current range is between 3 million and 7 million years ago; for more information see www.pbs.org/wgbh/nova/sciencenow/3209/01-ask.html, www.scribd.com/doc/334778/introduction-to-paleoanthropology, Solnit (2000) and Amato (2004).

2   For more on the development of marine technology, see Derry and Williams (1993, pp14, 19, and Chapter 6) and Falola and Warnock (2007, pp277–278).

3   For more on the development of the wheel, see Hindley (1971), Lay (1992, pp26–41) and Derry and Williams (1993, Chapter 6); for more information on the Inca, see Hyslop (1984) and Box 3.4 in this chapter.

4   Between 1953 and 1964, the person identifying herself only as 'Peace Pilgrim' had logged 25,000 miles (42,000km) and then walked across the US at least seven more times (Pilgrim, 1991).

5   Susanne L. Seales is a freelance editor and writer. She holds an MA in History from Western Washington University and a BA in Liberal Studies from Evergreen State College; her area of specialty is gender and the sense of revival in the art and literature of the Victorian world, with a special focus on the women of the Pre-Raphaelite movement. She lives and works out of her centrally located apartment in Bellingham, Washington, where she can walk everywhere she needs to go.

6   For more information on the pilgrimages of the High Middle Ages, see Sumption (1975), Davies and Davies (1982), Melczer (1993) and Shaver-Crandell et al (1995); for more on the 12th-century Renaissance, see Haskins (1971).

7   The term 'Middle Ages' generally refers to 500 to 1500, 'Early Modern' to 1500 to 1800 and 'Modern' to 1800 to the present.

8   For more on the omnibus, see Lay (1992, p129), Derry and Williams (1993, pp385–388) and Bellis (undated).

9   For more on steam vehicles, see Lay (1992, pp137–138), Derry and Williams (1993, Chapter 6), Goddard (1996, pp6–7) and www.steamindex.com/people/stephen.htm.

10   For more on canals and locks, see Derry and Williams (1993, pp436–446).

11   For more on the Draisine, see Gompertz (1851, pp42–49), Herlihy (2004, pp19–65) and Fletcher (2008, exhibit item 24).

12   For more details and graphics, see Herlihy (1992, 2004, pp138–139, 261–282).

13   For author bio, see endnote 5 of this chapter.

14   This story was first published in *The Strand* as part of the 1904–1905 collection of stories *The Return of Sherlock Holmes*, which has been republished in numerous Conan Doyle anthologies, including the one used for this essay (see Conan Doyle, 1903/1920).

15   According to Herlihy (2004, p266), by 1895 women made up about one third of the bicycle market, when just a few years earlier there was a very small handful of female cyclists.

16   For more on women cyclists during the late 19th and early 20th centuries, see Anonymous (1895) and Herlihy (2004); the author of this case study would also like to thank Lena C. (Schiller) Hanson for sharing her senior history paper (Western Washington University), 'The impact of the bicycle on American life from the late 19th to early 20th centuries', which provided some delightful reading and helpful insights on the subject.

17   Also known as the high wheeler, ordinary, the wheel or penny-farthing in reference to the large difference in size between its front and rear wheels.

18   According to Wilson et al (2004, p19): 'The ordinary was responsible for the third two-wheeler passion, which was concentrated among the younger upper-class men of France, Britain and the United States and was fostered by military-style clubs with uniforms and even buglers.'

19   For Tolstoy, see Troyat (2001, pp510–514); for a photo of Tolstoy with bicycle, see Chesterton et al (1903, p6); for other general bicycle information, see Lay (1992, pp142–145).

20   For 'Good Roads', see Waller (1983, pp243–254), Hamer (1987, pp23–24), Goddard (2000), Gutfreund (2004) and Dobb (undated).

21   See illustrations of several early bicycles and velocipedes in Wikipedia's 'velocipede'. While there is often controversy about the accuracy of many Wikipedia entries because of the 'open' nature of their sites, the graphics are often quite useful.

22   This is the figure for the interstates' linear mileage, as opposed to 'lane mileage', which is the sum of all parallel lanes – which would equal over 200,000 miles (334,000km) of lanes. In the year 2000 the total lane mileage of US intercity highways, federal, state and local lanes was 8,239,625 (13,760,173km) (BTS and US Government, 2002); for more on ancient roads, see Lay (1992) and Friedman et al (2006, p35).

23   For author bio, see endnote 5 of this chapter.

24   There are numerous reliable translations of *The Voyages of Marco Polo* available today, including the one used for this case study, published by Orion Press (1958).

25   For more on the travels of Ibn Battuta, see Dunn (1989).

26   For more on the various routes and histories of the great Silk Road, see Wild (1992), Wilford (1993), Whitfield (1999), Wood (2002) and Manchester (2007).

27   For its extent, see the map in Hyslop (1984, p4).

28   France and Germany, as exceptions, each had centrally directed interests in roads, although Germany's central direction began considerably later than that of France; for more information, see Hindley (1971, pp74–77), Lay (1992, pp60, 70, 101–102, 117) and McShane (1994, pp103–104).

29   For more on transit and recreation, see Schaefer and Sclar (1975), Jackson (1985, p112) and McShane (1994, pp27–30).

30   For roads history in France see Hindley (1971, pp74–77); for roads and the popularity of bicycling in France and the Roads Improvement Association see Flink (1988, pp2–4, 169–171);

for England, see Hamer (1987, pp23–24); see also Herlihy (2004). For a different perspective, see McShane (1994), whose work emphasizes the role played by improved roads in generating interest in bicycle and automobility and conflicts between vehicles and pedestrians.

31   For more about the history, revivals and renaming of LAW to the League of American Bicyclists see LAW (undated); for more about the Good Roads movement and the 'Gospel of Good Roads', see Flink (1988), Goddard (1996, 2000) and Gutfreund (2004).

32   Also the French term for bicycle.

33   For Fordism and the GM response to it, the marketing strategy of 'Sloanism', see Rothschild (1973) and Lay (1992, pp160–161); for the relation between bicycles and early automobile development, see Rae (1965), Flink (1988) and Barker and Gerhold (1995, pp52–53).

34   For more on electric cars, see Flink (1988), Scharf (1991, pp35–50), Goddard (2000), Kirsch (2000), Didik (undated) and Hume (undated).

35   For early automobile clubs and how they shaped automobile culture and politics, see Rae (1965), Flink (1988), Scharf (1991), Sachs (1992), McShane (1994), Barker and Gerhold (1995, p55), Goddard (1996) and Gutfreund (2004).

36   For a discussion of the importance of the truck in cities as a replacement for horse-drawn wagons and the role that it played in reshaping urban transportation and road needs, see McShane (1994).

37   For more on standards, see Eno Transportation Foundation (undated), Blanchard (1919) and Rothschild (1973).

38   The quote popularly attributed to Hoover may be only partially accurate: see Safire (2008, p115); for the Joads road odyssey, see Steinbeck (1939), as well as the film version. For several of Dorothea Lange's photos of Hoovervilles and migrant worker conditions in the 1930s, see http://lcweb2.loc.gov/cgi-bin/query/b?ammem/fsaall:LC-USF34-001774-C:collection=fsa.

39   For the Autostrada, see Hindley (1971, p98); for the Autobahn and Volkswagen, see Sachs (1992) and Schivelbusch (2007).

40   Literally a linear park, 469 miles (780km) in its final form; for more on it, see Schivelbusch (2007).

41   For more, see Jackson (1985, pp168–171) and Klein and Olson (1996); the extent to which US streetcar lines were 'killed' by conspiracy or by neglect is subject to debate; for more, see Bottles (1987), Flink (1988), McShane (1994), Goddard (1996) and Gutfreund (2004).

42   For critiques of US suburban development and its relation to street and road design, see ITE (2006), Kunstler (1996), Kay (1997) and Newman and Kenworthy (1999, p150).

43   Historian James V. Hillegas holds an MA from Portland State University and a BA from Fairhaven College; he specializes in 20th-century urban environmental history in North America and is currently writing a book on early water pollution abatement efforts along Oregon's Willamette River.

44   For more about the construction of Interstate 5 through Bellingham and newspaper citations, see Hillegas (2004); for the national context of interstate highway development, see Rose (1979), Lewis (1997), Gutfreund (2004) and Erlichman (2006); for the current situation, see Port of Bellingham (undated).

45   For a sample of critiques, reactions and rejections of highway expansion, see Jacobs (1961), Nowlan and Nowlan (1970), Plowden (1972), Schneider (1972), Rothschild (1973), Davies (1975), Schaeffer and Sclar (1975), Illich (1976) and Sachs (1983); for a sample of fresh ideas and approaches, see Stone (1971), Richards (1976), Stringer and Wenzel (1976) and Gakenheimer (1978).

46   See Chapter 5 of this book for a discussion of freight transportation and globalization.

47   For European transportation policy changes during this time, see Pucher (1997, 2004), Pucher and Lefevre (1996) and Chapter 7 of this book for more detailed discussion and references; for the spread of pedestrianization and traffic calming, see Wynne (1980), Appleyard et al (1981), Untermann (1984), Moudon (1987), Roberts (1988), Engwicht (1989, 1993) and CNU (undated).

48   See discussions of ISTEA in Chapter 7 of this book.

49   For more on early 19th-century rail systems, see Lay (1992), Derry and Williams (1993), Goddard (1996) and Morlok (2005).

50   For more, see Davis et al (1991), especially Robinson's 'Introduction' and 'Conclusion', as well as Roman's 'Railway imperialism in Canada', Fleming's 'Profits and visions: British capital and railway construction in Argentina, 1854–1886' and French's 'In the path of progress: Railroads and moral reform in Porfirian Mexico'.

51   See Chapter 7 of this book for more discussion of deregulation, privatization, etc., especially for the EU and UK.

52   For discussions of the implications of the vast expansion of passenger and freight aviation in recent decades, see Gilbert and Perl (2008); for some of the popular experiences with aviation, see Davidson and Sweeney (2003, pp277–284).

53   For a picture of the peace symbol, see http://en.wikipedia.org/wiki/Peace_symbol.

54   See Box 2.2 in Chapter 2 of this book.

55   For the history of telephony and telegraphy, including semaphores, see Derry and Williams (1993, pp621–629); a good source of current information is the Telecommunications and Travel Research Program, University of California, Davis, at www.its.ucdavis.edu/telecom/; for a discussion of how telecommunications is not replacing travel, see also Mokhtarian (2003); for technical and timelines information, see Huurdeman (2003); for a discussion about relations between telecommunications and travel, see Niles (2009); for a recent view of teleconferencing as a replacement for travel, see Demerjian (2008) and FHWA and USDOT (undated).

References and further reading

Amato, J. (2004) *On Foot: A History of Walking,* New York University Press, New York, NY

Anonymous (1895) 'Bicycles and bicycle riders', *Public Opinion*, pp342–343

Anonymous (1897) 'Against bloomers and bicycles', *New York Times*

Appleyard, D., Gerson, M. and Lintell, M. (1981) *Livable Streets,* University of California Press, Berkeley, CA

Barker, T. and Gerhold, D. (1995) *The Rise and Rise of Road Transport, 1700–1990*, Cambridge University Press, Cambridge, UK

Bellis, M. (undated) 'Streetcars–cable cars', About.com, http://inventors.about.com/library/inventors/blstreetcars.htm, accessed 14 July 2009

Blanchard, A. (ed) (1919) *American Highway Engineer's Handbook*, J. Wiley, New York, NY

Bottles, S. (1987) *Los Angeles and the Automobile: The Making of the Modern City*, University of California Press, Berkeley, CA

BTS (Bureau of Transportation Statistics), RITA (Research and Innovative Technology Administration) and US Government (2002) 'Table 1–1: System mileage within the United States (statute miles)', www.bts.gov/publications/national_transportation_statistics/2002/html/table_01_01.html, accessed 15 July 2009

Caro, R. (1975) *The Power Broker: Robert Moses and the Fall of New York*, Vintage Books, New York, NY

Chesterton, G., Perris, G. and Garnett, E. (eds) (1903) *Leo Tolstoy*, Hodder and Stoughton, London

CNU (Congress for the New Urbanism) (undated) *Urban Thoroughfares Manual*, www.cnu.org/streets, accessed 11 July 2009

Conan Doyle, A. (1903/1920) 'The adventure of the solitary cyclist', in *The Complete Sherlock Holmes (Volume 2)*, Doubleday & Company, Inc, Garden City, NY

Davidson, J. and Sweeney, M. (2003), *On the Move: Transportation and the American Story*, National Geographic, Washington, DC

Davies, H. and Davies M.-H. (1982) *Holy Days and Holidays: The Medieval Pilgrimage to Compostela*, Bucknell University Press, Lewisburg, PA

Davies, R. (1975) *The Age of Asphalt: The Automobile, the Freeway, and the Condition of Metropolitan America*, Lippincott, Philadelphia, PA

Davis, C., Wilburn, K. and Robinson, R. (eds) (1991) *Railway Imperialism*, Greenwood Press, Westport, CT

Demerjian, D. (2008) 'UN wants us to fly less, teleconference more', *Wired*, www.wired.com/autopia/2008/07/un-wants-us-to/, accessed 6 July 2009

Derry, T. and Williams, T. (1993) *A Short History of Technology: From the Earliest Times to A.D. 1900*, Dover, New York, NY

Didik, F. (undated) 'History and directory of electric cars from 1834–1987', www.didik.com/ev_hist.htm, accessed 6 July 2009

Dobb, K. (undated) 'An alternative form of long distance cycling: The British Roads Records Association', www.randonneurs.bc.ca/history/an-alternative-form-of-long-distance-cycling_part-4.html, accessed 10 July 2009

Dunn, R. (1989) *The Adventures of Ibn Battuta: A Muslim Traveler of the 14th Century*, University of California Press, Berkeley and Los Angeles, CA

Economy-point.org (2006) 'Karl Drais', www.economy-point.org/k/karl-drais.html, accessed 9 July 2009

Engwicht, D. (ed) (1989) *Traffic Calming: The Solution to Urban Traffic and a New Vision for Neighborhood Livability*, CART (Citizens Advocating Responsible Transportation), Ashgrove, Australia, reprinted (1993) STOP (Sensible Transportation Options for People), Tigard, OR

Engwicht, D. (1993) *Reclaiming Our Cities & Towns: Better Living with Less Traffic*, New Society Publishers, Gabriola Island, British Columbia

Eno Transportation Foundation (undated) 'William Phelps Eno', www.enotrans.com/index.asp?Type=B_EV&SEC={59B58976-4BBF-43AF-9CC0-14664D065FD5}, accessed 11 July 2009

Erlichman, H. (2006) *Camino del Norte: How a Series of Watering Holes, Fords, and Dirt Trails Evolved into Interstate 35 in Texas*, Texas A&M Press, College Station, TX

Falola, T. and Warnock, A. (2007) *Encyclopedia of the Middle Passage*, Greenwood, Westport, CT

FHWA (Federal Highway Administration) and USDOT (US Department of Transportation) (undated) 'Teleconferencing', www.fhwa.dot.gov/REPORTS/PITTD/teleconf.htm, accessed 4 July 2009

Fletcher, K. (2008) 'The pre-history of the motor car, 1550–1850', an exhibition at the ABA antiquarian book fair, The Assembly Rooms, George Street, Edinburgh, www.aba.org.uk/edinexhib.pdf (14/15 March 2008 description) and www.aba.org.uk/edinexhibcat1.pdf (full exhibit description), accessed 11 July 2009

Flink, J. (1988) *The Automobile Age*, MIT Press, Cambridge, MA

Friedman, D., Bratvold, D., Mirsky, S., Kaiser, G., Schaudies, P., Bolz, E., Castor, R. and Latham, F. (2006) *A Guide to Transportation's Role in Public Health Disasters*, NCHRP Report 525, Transportation Research Board (TRB.org), Washington, DC, www.trb.org/publications/nchrp/nchrp_rpt_525v10.pdf, accessed 15 July 2009

Gakenheimer, R. (ed) (1978) *The Automobile and the Environment: An International Perspective*, MIT Press, Cambridge, MA

Gilbert, R. and Perl, A. (2008) *Transport Revolutions: Moving People and Freight without Oil*, Earthscan, London

Goddard, S. (1996) *Getting There: The Epic Struggle between Road and Rail in the American Century*, University of Chicago Press, Chicago, IL

Goddard, S. (2000) *Colonel Albert Pope and his American Dream Machine: The Life and Times of a Bicycle Tycoon Turned Automotive Pioneer*, McFarland, Jefferson, NC

Gompertz, L. (1851) *Mechanical Inventions and Suggestions on Land and Water Locomotion, Tooth Machinery, and Various Other Branches of Theoretical and Practical Mechanics*, second edition, W. Horsell, London (Original from the University of Michigan, digitized 8 September 2006), http://books.google.com/books?id=fJQPAAAAMAAJ, accessed 24 May 2009

Gutfreund, O. (2004) *Twentieth-Century Sprawl: Highways and the Reshaping of the American Landscape*, Oxford University Press, New York, NY

Hamer, M. (1987) *Wheels within Wheels: A Study of the Road Lobby*, Routledge and Kegan Paul, London

Hanson, S. and Giuliano, G. (eds) (2004) *The Geography of Urban Transportation*, third edition, Guilford Press, New York, NY

Haskins, C. H. (1971) *The Renaissance of the Twelfth Century*, Harvard University Press, Cambridge, MA

Healey, J. R. (2009) 'Obama's auto faux pas leads to history lesson', *USA TODAY*, 24 February 2009, www.usatoday.com/money/autos/2009-02-25-obama-claim-daimler-differs_N.htm, accessed 8 May 2009

Herlihy, D. (1992) 'The bicycle story', *Invention and Technology*, spring, pp48–59

Herlihy, D. (2004) *Bicycle: The History*, Yale University Press, New Haven, CT, and London

Hillegas, J. V. (2004) '"Pushing forward with the determination of the machine age": Planning and building Interstate 5 Bellingham, WA, 1945–1966', *Journal of the Whatcom County Historical Society*, Special Edition Bellingham Centennial, Bellingham, WA

Hindley, G. (1971) *A History of Roads*, Peter Davies, London

Hume, B. (webmaster) (undated) '"The invention of the modern automobile": Chronology of the history of science', http://campus.udayton.edu/~hume/Automobile/auto.htm, accessed 6 July 2009

Huttman, G. (ed) (2006) 'Karl Drais – the new biography', www.karl-drais.de/en_biography.pdf, accessed 24 May 2009

Huurdeman, A. (2003) *The Worldwide History of Telecommunications*, Wiley Blackwell, New York, NY

Hyslop, J. (1984) *The Inka Road System*, Academic Press, Orlando, FL

Illich, I. (1976) *Energy and Equity*, Marion Boyars, London

imdb.com (1940) *The Grapes of Wrath*, www.imdb.com/title/tt0032551/, accessed 15 July 2009

imdb.com (1988) *Who Framed Roger Rabbit?*, www.imdb.com/title/tt0096438/, accessed 15 July 2009

ITE (Institute of Transportation Engineers) (2006) *Context Sensitive Solutions in Designing Major Urban Thoroughfares for Walkable Communities: An ITE Proposed Recommended Practice*, ITE, Washington, DC

IVCA (International Veteran Cycle Association) (undated) http://ivca-online.org/, accessed 15 July 2009

Jackson, K. (1985) *Crabgrass Frontier: The Suburbanization of the United States*, Oxford University Press, New York, NY

Jacobs, J. (1961) *The Death and Life of Great American Cities*, Random House, New York, NY

Kay, J. H. (1997) *Asphalt Nation: How the Automobile Took Over America, and How We Can Take It Back*, Crown Publishers, New York, NY

Kirsch, D. (2000) *The Electric Vehicle and the Burden of History*, Rutgers University Press, New Brunswick, NJ

Klein, J. and Olson, M. (1996) *Taken for a Ride*, New Day Films, Yellow Springs, OH

Kunstler, J. H. (1996) *Home from Nowhere: Remaking Our Everyday World for the 21st Century*, Simon & Schuster, New York, NY

LAW (League of American Wheelmen, now League of American Bicyclists) (undated) www.bikeleague.org/about/history.php, accessed 15 July 2009

Lay, M. (1992) *Ways of the World : A History of the World's Roads and of the Vehicles That Used Them*, Rutgers University Press, New Brunswick, NJ

Lewis, T. (1997) *Divided Highways: Building the Interstate Highways, Transforming American Life*, Penguin Putnam, New York, NY

Manchester, K. (ed) (2007) *Silk Road and Beyond: Travel, Trade, and Transformation*, Art Institute of Chicago, Yale University Press, New Haven, CT

McShane, C. (1994) *Down the Asphalt Path: The Automobile and the American City*, Columbia University Press, New York, NY

Melczer, W. (1993) *The Pilgrim's Guide to Santiago de Compostela: First English Translation, with Introduction, Commentaries, and Notes*, Italica Press, New York, NY

Merington, M. (1895) 'Woman and the bicycle', *Scribner's Magazine*, vol 17, p703

Mokhtarian, P. (2003) 'Telecommunications and travel: The case for complementarity', *Journal of Industrial Ecology*, vol 6, no 2, pp43–57, www.its.ucdavis.edu/telecom/, accessed 6 July 2009

Morlok, E. (2005) 'First permanent railroad in the US and its connection to the University of Pennsylvania', www.seas.upenn.edu/~morlok/morlokpage/transp_data.html, accessed 6 July 2009

Moudon, A. V. (ed) (1987) *Public Streets for Public Use*, Van Nostrand Reinhold, New York, NY

Mumford, L. (1961) *The City in History: Its Origins, Its Transformations, and Its Prospects*, Harcourt Brace, San Diego, CA

Newman, P. W. G. and Kenworthy, J. R. (1999) *Sustainability and Cities: Overcoming Automobile Dependence*, Island Press, Washington, DC

NIEHS (National Institutes of Health, Department of Health & Human Services) (undated) *Daisy Bell (A Bicycle Built for Two)*, http://kids.niehs.nih.gov/lyrics/daisy.htm, accessed 15 July 2009

Niles, J. (2009) 'Global telematics', www.globaltelematics.com/mediachoice/index.htm, accessed 7 July 2009

Nowlan, D. and Nowlan, N. (1970) *The Bad Trip: The Untold Story of the Spadina Expressway*, New Press, House of Anansi, Toronto, Ontario

Onkst, D. (undated) 'Barnstormers', US Centennial of Flight Commission, www.centennialofflight. gov/essay/Explorers_Record_Setters_and_Daredevils/barnstormers/EX12.htm, accessed 11 July 2009

Pilgrim, P. (1991) *Peace Pilgrim: Her Life and Work in Her Own Words*, Ocean Tree, Santa Fe, NM

Plowden, S. (1972) *Towns against Traffic*, Deutsch, London

Plowden, S. (1980) *Taming Traffic*, Deutsch, London

Polo, M. (1958) *The Travels of Marco Polo* (translator unknown), Orion Press, New York, NY

Port of Bellingham (undated) *Waterfront Redevelopment*, www.portofbellingham.com/content/ ArchivesItem_147_1163_v, accessed 14 June 2009

Pucher, J. (1997) 'Bicycling boom in Germany: A revival engineered by public policy', *Transportation Quarterly*, vol 51, no 4, pp31–46

Pucher, J. (2004) 'Public transportation', in S. Hanson and G. Giuliano (eds) *The Geography of Urban Transportation*, third edition, Guilford Press, New York, NY

Pucher, J. and Lefevre, C. (1996) *The Urban Transport Crisis in Europe and North America*, Macmillan, Basingstoke, UK

Rae, J. B. (1965) *The American Automobile: A Brief History*, University of Chicago Press, Chicago, IL

Richards, B. (1976) *Moving in Cities*, Westview, Boulder, CO

Roberts, J. (1988) *Quality Streets: How Traditional Urban Centers Benefit from Traffic-Calming*, Transport & Environment Studies, TEST report no 75, London

Rose, M. H. (1979) *Interstate: Express Highway Politics, 1941–1956*, The Regents Press of Kansas, Lawrence, KS

Rothschild, E. (1973) *Paradise Lost: The Decline of the Auto-Industrial Age*, Random House, New York, NY

Sachs, W. (1983) 'Are energy intensive life-images fading? The cultural meaning of the automobile in transition', *Journal of Economic Psychology*, vol 3, pp347–365

Sachs, W. (1992) *For Love of the Automobile: Looking Back into the History of Our Desires*, University of California Press, Berkeley, CA

Safire, W. (2008) *Safire's Political Dictionary*, Oxford University Press, New York, NY

Schaeffer, K. and Sclar, E. (1975) *Access for All: Transportation and Urban Growth*, Penguin, Baltimore, MD

Scharf, V. (1991) *Taking the Wheel: Women and the Coming of the Motor Age*, Free Press, New York, NY

Schivelbusch, W. (1986) *The Railway Journey*, University of California Press, Berkeley, CA

Schivelbusch, W. (2007) *Three New Deals: Reflections on Roosevelt's America, Mussolini's Italy, and Hitler's Germany, 1933–1939*, Picador, New York, NY

Schneider, K. (1972) *Autokind vs Mankind: An Analysis of Tyranny, a Proposal for Rebellion, a Plan for Reconstruction*, Schocken, New York, NY

Shaver-Crandell, A., Gerson, P. and Stones, A. (1995) *The Pilgrim's Guide to Santiago de Compostela: A Gazetteer*, Harvey Miller Publishers, London

Solnit, R. (2000) *Wanderlust: A History of Walking*, Penguin, New York, NY

Steinbeck, J. (1939) *The Grapes of Wrath*, Viking Compass, New York, NY

Stone, T. (1971) *Beyond the Automobile: Reshaping the Transportation Environment*, Prentice-Hall, Englewood Cliffs, NJ

Stringer, P. and Wenzel, H. (1976) *Transportation Planning for a Better Environment*, Plenum Press, New York, NY

Sumption, J. (1975) *Pilgrimage: An Image of Mediaeval Religion*, Rowman and Littlefield, Totowa, NJ

Toronto (City) 'Did Toronto have toll gates?', www.toronto.ca/archives/toronto_history_faqs.htm#tollgates, accessed 10 July 2009

Troyat, H. (2001) *Tolstoy*, translated by N. Amphoux, Grove Press, New York, NY

Untermann, R. (1984) *Accommodating the Pedestrian: Adapting Towns and Neighborhoods for Walking and Biking*, Van Nostrand Reinhold Company, New York, NY

Vasconcellos, E. (2001) *Urban Transport, Environment and Equity: The Case for Developing Countries*, Earthscan, London

Waller, P. (1983) *Town, City, and Nation: England 1850–1914*, Oxford University Press, Oxford, UK

Whitfield, S. (1999) *Life along the Silk Road*, University of California Press, Berkeley and Los Angeles, CA

Wikipedia (undated) 'Velocipede', http://en.wikipedia.org/wiki/Velocipede, accessed 9 July 2009

Wild, O. (1992) *The Silk Road*, www.ess.uci.edu/~oliver/silk3.html, accessed 25 June 2009

Wilford, J. (1993) 'New finds suggest even earlier trade on fabled Silk Road', www.nytimes.com/1993/03/16/science/new-finds-suggest-even-earlier-trade-on-fabled-silk-road.html, accessed 25 June 2009

Wilson, D., Papadopoulos, J. and Whitt, F. R. (2004) *Bicycling Science*, MIT Press, Cambridge, MA

Wood, F. (2002) *The Silk Road: Two Thousand Years in the Heart of Asia*, University of California Press, Berkeley and Los Angeles, CA

Wynne, G. (ed) (1980) *Traffic Restraints in Residential Neighborhoods*, Transaction Books, New Brunswick, NJ

4

Modes, Roads and Routes: Technologies, Infrastructure, Functions and Interrelatedness

Introduction

Transportation modes are ways of moving people and freight. Decisions about which modes to invest in and/or emphasize have long-term consequences. Previous chapters have discussed the importance of the relation of history and cultural factors to modal emphases and some of their consequences for the environment and urban life. Modes may be for passengers, freight or both, and some of their operational and infrastructure considerations are interrelated. All passenger modes have some cargo capacity or potential: personal motor vehicles (PMVs) almost always have some cargo storage; airliners carry much cargo along with baggage in their bellies; most trains accommodate luggage and some carry small amounts of freight; and some ocean freighters accommodate a few passengers. Even walking and bicycling have the potential for carrying some cargo: backpacks and wheeled carts or luggage for pedestrians; panniers and trailers for bicycles, as well as bicycles built as small cargo vehicles. Freight modes and related matters will be discussed in depth in Chapter 5. This chapter focuses on passenger modes and matters related to moving transportation in the direction of greater sustainability. It explores the great variety of modes, differences between modes, and the great diversity that can exist even within a modal category. It emphasizes how modes affect or interact with a number of factors, including:

- infrastructure – right(s) of way (RoW), sidewalks, paths, roads, rails, ports and airports;
- land use, urban design and the built environment;
- social, economic and cultural dimensions, including equity;
- travel and trip characteristics – individual, group, purposes such as work or recreation;
- functional characteristics – for peak period, necessity or discretionary, valuation of trip;
- environmental considerations – pollution (including noise), energy and resource consumption, habitat disruption.

Two important concepts about modes that should inform our discussion and analysis of them are:

1   *Multi-modal*: the ability to choose among several modes for a trip. One could travel by foot, bicycle, transit, PMV, or any combination of these.
2   *Intermodal*: the ability to make connections between modes, such as mounting a bicycle on a bus or transferring between bus and rail or between a land mode and a ferry or airport. The convenience of intermodal transfers can be of great value to persons using public modes. Intermodal is also a term that is widely used in freight to denote transfers between trucks and trains, or trucks, trains and ships.

These two concepts increase travel options or allow people to combine modes for more complicated travel in order to reduce the need for automobility.

Modes involve technical and technological matters, which are discussed in this chapter; but modes are more than these and need to be understood in the context of travel situations, the system of modal technology and application, and the interrelationship of modes with the factors enumerated above. The chapter's framework will emphasize the importance of travel contexts and trip characteristics, from in-town to intercontinental.

Figure 4.1 Effective bus and train transfers at light rail transit stations, Portland, Oregon

Source: Tri-Met

In-town modes: Getting to work, school, shopping, services and recreation

Most trips taken and distances travelled generally occur in town or within an urban region. While trips to work, or commuter trips, are very important to individuals and to society, and tend to be the longest of trips taken regularly, they comprise only a small portion of the total number of trips that people make. The majority of travel is for shopping, services, education, recreation and family, and friendship purposes. Most trips, with the exception of those by commuters who live at a substantial distance from their work, are relatively short: in the range of 0.5 to 2 (or 3) miles (1km to 5km) or fairly easy walking and bicycling distances. But the combination of traffic and automobile-oriented urban design – segregating types of uses–have made many short trips difficult, uncomfortable or unsafe under foot power. The same conditions work against attracting riders to public transportation; if one cannot cross the street safely one is unlikely to ride the bus. There is often a lack of good information readily available about walking, bicycling or transit. Some researchers have found that simply providing the public with personalized information about their mobility options can lead to a fair amount of selecting of previously unfamiliar choices, especially for shorter local trips (SocialData America, undated).

Many modes may serve utilitarian purposes, such as forms of transit designed principally for commuters' needs (e.g. regional rail, or RGR, vehicles), while other forms may be designed principally for a non-utilitarian purpose, such as modes that convey tourists up a steep mountain grade so that they can snap photos to send home or post on a website. The array of modes and their different uses have led analysts such as Vuchic (2007) to approach the topic through the useful concept of the 'family of modes', which combines addressing the uniqueness of some modal applications as well as the overlap and interactive phenomenon of intermodalism.[1]

The major in-town modes, in order of importance for sustainable transportation (ST), are:

1   *walking* – including walking assistance and mobility assistance devices such as wheelchairs;
2   *bicycling* – including three-wheeled variations;
3   *public transportation or transit* – including buses, rail modes, shuttle services, taxis and jitneys;
4   *PMVs* – including automobiles, two-wheelers (motorcycles, mopeds), vans and light trucks.

Table 4.1 summarizes and compares selected characteristics of in-town modes, which are then discussed.

Walking

As discussed in Chapter 3, walking is the simplest and most natural form of human mobility. Walking is difficult in most urban regions, and it is especially difficult and uncomfortable in automobile-dependent cities and urban regions. With the combined efforts of policy-makers, planners, engineers and concerned citizens, it can become a safer, easier and more attractive mode.[2] All of the exemplary cities (see Chapter 9) have succeeded in improving pedestrian conditions in many parts of their communities.

Some of the most important factors about walking are:

- *Capacity*: properly designed pedestrian facilities such as wide sidewalks, especially in commercial areas, and car-free zones in either commercial or dense residential areas (see the section on 'Freiburg im Breisgau, Germany: The pin-up sustainable city' in Chapter 9) can accommodate the mobility of large numbers of pedestrians.
- *Function and trip types*: the majority of short trips in urban areas for school, shopping, services and recreation could be done on foot with appropriate infrastructure (sidewalks, separated paths, pedestrian zones) and safety provision (separation, lateral and grade, where necessary, better policing of motorists).
- *Infrastructure needs and costs*: walking can be very cheap; sidewalks and pathways cost very little to build or maintain, about one tenth or even one twentieth the costs of a paved street, especially when included in street construction or reconstruction.

Table 4.1 Selected characteristics of urban in-town modes

Mode	Max hourly capacity (wealthy nation crowding standards)	Key functional and trip characteristics	Infrastructure needs and cost drivers	Average speed and effective range	Environmental, health, safety impacts	Vehicle/operating costs (wealthy nation levels)
Walking	Good facilities; thousands of persons/ hour (pers/hr)	All trip types – lengthen with better facilities	Paths, sidewalks; $50–500,000 per mile	V = 1–4mph R = l/4–4mi	Minimal environmental damage; healthy if safe from motorized	Nothing to minimal
Bicycling	Good facilities; thousands of pers/hr	All trip types – lengthen with better facilities	Paths, lanes, bikeways; $100–700K per mile	V = 8–15mph R = l–15mi up to 100mi for athlete	Minimal environmental damage; healthy if safe from motorized	$100–500 bicycle; $0.1 per mi+/- operating cost
Local bus transit	Right of Way (RoW) C; 3–5K pers/hr	Frequency increases – trips shorten; feeds faster modes	Minimal – shelters, signs, possible signal priority	V = 6–16mph; entire region	Dangerous exhaust from olde-/poorly tuned; safer than PMVs	$100–500K per bus; $60–100 per hr
Streetcar	RoW C; 5–10K pers/hr	Frequency increases – trips shorten; penetrate pedestrian zones	Modest – track, power, shelters, signal priority	V = 6–20mph; entire central city	No local air pollution, noise varies, safe for passengers	$1.5–2.5M per car; $5–10 per car-mi
Bus Rapid Transit (BRT)	RoW B; 5–10K pers/hr	All types of longer trips	Dedicated lanes, signal priority, high cost if RoW A	V = 16–24mph; depends on station spacings, central city, suburbs	Modest noise/air pollution, safe for passengers	$500–1,500K per bus; $80–140 per hr
Light Rail Transit (LRT)	RoW B: 10–20K pers/hr	All types of longer trips; good for peak commute capacity	Dedicated lanes, stations, power, signal priority	V = 16–28mph; depends on station spacings (like BRT)	No local air pollution, safe for passengers	$2.5–3.5M per car; $7–18 per car-mi
Rail Rapid Transit (RRT/ Metro)	RoW A; 15–40K pers/hr	All types of longer trips; good for peak commute capacity	Elevated structures/tunnels, large stations, power, large depots, high average cost	V = 20–35mph; depends on station spacings – entire central city	No local air pollution, noise when overhead, extremely safe	$2–3M per car; $7–13 per car-mi
Mopeds, scooters, motorcycles	2000 pers/hr/lane in poorer countries; no issue in wealthy	All trip types where transit is poor, especially courier	Dedicated lanes rare; need dedicated parking to prevent sidewalk abuse	V = 8–20mph; personal endurance limits daily use	Exhaust/noise extreme hazards, unsafe to users	$2–5K; $0.15–0.25 per mi

Source: Eric C. Bruun

- *Velocity and range*: there is a wide range of pedestrian speeds depending upon the walker and the situation. Children, the elderly and physically constrained people usually walk more slowly than others, which makes the conventional timing of traffic signals for automobile convenience or capacity rather tricky for them. The average pedestrian can probably move comfortably along at a rate of 3 to 4mph (4 to 6kmph) when not interfered with by traffic and its limiting signals and other impediments, which might slow walking to a speed of 1mph (1.6kmph). The effective range of walking trips for everyday purposes is between 0.25 miles (0.4km), which might be the distance to the nearest bus stop, to 4 miles across town to a special destination. One planning guide for ST could be to have bus stops, grocery stores and restaurants with pubs no further than 0.25 to 0.5 miles distant from one's residence or place of work. The accessibility of mixed uses is an important factor in reducing the need to drive for many trips.

Figure 4.2 Portland's Park Blocks connecting the central business district with Portland State University attract pedestrians and people in wheelchairs (top); north-east Portland's residential area sidewalk demonstrates good design – a planter strip for trees and adequate width with fencing recessed at least 1 foot (0.3m) from the sidewalk (bottom left); wide sidewalk in downtown San Francisco leaves room for pedestrians and kiosks (bottom right)

Source: Preston L. Schiller

Figure 4.3 Floating pedestrian and bicycle bridge across the Danube tributary, Vienna, opens at mid-span for boat passage

Source: Eric C. Bruun

- *Environmental, health and safety considerations*: walking, so long as it does not damage habitat, has no negative environmental impacts. It is good for one's health and one's community in that it increases sociability and neighbourhood security. In situations where 'cars rule' it can adversely affect personal well-being due to pollution and safety risk. Motorists kill hundreds of thousands of pedestrians each year (WHO, 2004a, 2004b); Road Safety Foundation, undated, a worldwide problem especially severe in less wealthy countries, which have frequently developed motorized travel without any provision for pedestrians or bicyclists. The situation has become exceptionally grave in Asia and parts of Latin America.[3]
- *Costs*: walking is very inexpensive, if not free, depending upon the type of footwear or gear used. To date, privatization interests have not discovered ways of tolling most sidewalks and pathways.

Bicycling

Bicycling is the most energy-efficient mode of transportation, requiring less input per distance unit than walking. Along with walking, bicycling generates no emissions or noise. While bicycling shares or overlaps many of the attractions, health and cost benefits and hazards of walking, neither is a menace for motorists; the authors know of no instances where motorists were killed as a result of colliding with pedestrians or bicyclists.

Some of the most important factors regarding bicycling are:

- *Capacity*: properly designed bicycle-designated areas, such as widened sidewalks with a portion dedicated to cyclists (available in an increasing number of European cities), car-free zones (especially in commercial or dense residential areas) or lanes protected from traffic facilitate bicycling (see the example of Freiburg in Chapter 9). City-wide and regional bicycling paths or networks of traffic-calmed streets can accommodate the mobility of large numbers of bicyclists. In town, and even for some long-distance trips, special trailers are available for bicycles, and urban cargo bicycles are also being increasingly used for hauling and delivering.

Figure 4.4 Bicycle lanes, such as this one in Rotterdam, can separate and protect riders from traffic

Source: Preston L. Schiller

- *Function and trip types*: the majority of short trips and many of moderate length in urban areas for school, shopping, services and recreation could be done on bicycles with appropriate infrastructure and safety provisions (e.g. separation, lateral and grade, where necessary, and better policing of motorists). Rechargeable battery systems with relatively good range are available at fairly low cost to help riders with tired legs facing steep grades.
- *Infrastructure needs and costs*: bicycling is a bargain; sidewalks and pathways cost very little to build or maintain, about one tenth or less the costs of a paved street, especially when included in street construction or reconstruction, or where existing RoW can be used. Justice and equity would dictate that motorists should pay for bicycling infrastructure costs since most of it is necessitated by roads designed for PMVs and faster than necessary driving.
- *Velocity and range*: there is a wide range of bicycling speeds depending upon the cyclist and the situation. The average cyclist can probably pedal comfortably along a relatively flat route at a rate of 8 to 15mph (12 to 25kmph), when not interfered with by traffic and its limiting signals and other impediments. The effective range of cycling trips for everyday purposes is between 1 to 15 miles (2km to 25km). More athletically inclined cyclists can travel up to 100 miles (160km) at velocities between 20 to 30mph (30 to 50kmph). Recumbent bicycles (person in the reclined position) can achieve impressive speeds, especially when modified with fairings (streamlined shells) and complex gearing (see Box 4.1).
- *Environmental*: bicycling on prepared facilities has no negative environmental impacts. There is, however, some controversy about the level of habitat damage created by off-road or off-trail mountain bicycling and even on-trail mountain bicycling.[4]

- *Health and safety*: bicycling is good for one's health and shares with walking some of the community benefits of sociability and 'eyes on the street'. It also shares with walking many of the pollution exposure and safety risks caused by automobility, albeit at a somewhat lower level. Motorists kill tens of thousands of bicyclists each year (WHO, 2004a, 2004b), a worldwide problem especially severe in less wealthy countries where motorized travel has grown often without adequate (or any) provision for pedestrians or bicyclists.
- *Costs*: operating a bicycle is a bargain compared to driving. Depending upon the type of bicycle, accompanying gear, amount of cycling, and whether the cyclist does his or her own maintenance, bicycling can cost as little as US$0.10 per mile (US$0.06 per kilometre). To date, privatization interests have not discovered ways of tolling bicycle lanes and paths. Along with pedestrians, bicyclists are generally banned from limited-access highways and toll roads.

Some cities have initiated bicycle rentals available at strategic locations around town. Many more are planning to offer the same. While a couple of efforts have experienced problems with vandalism, most seem to be working and are well used. Bicycles are very competitive with PMVs and even transit for many in-town trips. Some cities have staged commuter competitions between various modes between major urban destinations often separated by a few miles. The bicyclists frequently win since traffic congestion often slows motorized modes. A little help from bicycle lanes or paths helps considerably (Mapes, 2009). It is also a reminder to motorists that the tortoise and hare fable applies to many of their trips.

Box 4.1 Recumbent versus diamond frame bicycles

Michael Ferro[5]

The most familiar form of bicycle is the 'diamond frame', named after its shape. It is also referred to as the 'conventional' or 'safety' bicycle for purposes of this discussion. Conventional upright bicycles are quite easy to learn to ride and handle. They are reasonably comfortable for most people to ride primarily because the riding posture is very close to that of a person walking. The usual bicycle seat is designed more for efficiency of movement than for comfort, and larger more comfortable seats are sometimes the target of derision among more athletic bicyclists. Others, less athletically pure, think of the smaller seats as instruments of torture, upon which the rider's most tender, vulnerable and personal parts most surely will weigh heavily and suffer fully. In past decades the conventional bicycle's turned-down handlebars added further postural insults to the back, neck, wrists and hands. Several handlebar options are now available allowing riders a more erect and comfortable posture.

Recumbent bicycles or tricycles allow the rider to be positioned in a reclining posture with legs pushing forward on pedals. The recumbent offers a broad resilient seat not unlike a patio lounger. Handlebars may be placed high or low, but appear not to need to bear any bodily weight. The recumbent's riding position looks up at the whole wide world rather than down at the surface of the road. The recumbent design suggests fun and freedom. In a short wheelbase recumbent, the bicycle's pedals are in front of the front wheel(s). The short wheelbase design is quickly responsive to turning movements. In a long wheelbase recumbent, the pedals are behind the front wheel(s). Long wheelbase recumbents are likely to be slower to respond to steering inputs and somewhat more stable. Recumbent bicycles, because of their different configuration, require a different and, for some people, more demanding set of riding skills to master (Felau, 2006).

There are advantages to both designs. Recumbents offer greater rider comfort with regard to seating, hand positioning, head and neck angles and forward visibility. They have much lower air resistance at speeds above about 15mph and are significantly easier to pedal at higher speeds. On bicycle paths they often leave conventional bicycles 'in the dust'. Because of their superior speeds they dominated bicycle racing for many years until they were made ineligible by the major bicycle racing organizations. Human-powered vehicles (HPVs) based on recumbent designs hold world speed records.

The conventional diamond frame, or 'safety' design, also has its advantages. It is easier to balance since its riding posture is similar to standing. It is easier starting up and climbing hills because the rider's weight is over the pedals. It is more suitable for turning the upper body for looking behind. Viewing of rear gear cluster is possible for checking which gear is engaged. It is more compact and lightweight, facilitating carrying and storage.

Figure 4.5 Todd and Heather Elsworth and their daughter, Violet, are a recumbent family in Bellingham, Washington

Source: Clara Elliott

Figure 4.6 The late Susie Stevens, bicycle advocate, demonstrates a bicycle that folds in and out of a suitcase which can also function as a bicycle trailer (left); ramps such as these at the Stavanger train station assist bicyclists and pedestrians with roller luggage (right)

Source: Preston L. Schiller

Small wheeled luggage, carts, trailers and other auxiliary mobility assistance devices

Walkers and bicyclists can increase their carrying capacity through the use of trailers and other wheeled devices. In wealthier countries, a wide array of bicycle trailers, folding bicycles and freight bicycles is now available to assist people with loads or making intermodal travel connections. Use of small-wheeled devices to assist walkers with loads has increased rapidly in recent decades, including luggage with wheels and two-wheeled shopping carts that fold up compactly when not used. These assist compact mixed-use development and public modes by extending the practical walking range and increase the percentage of trips suitable for walking alone or in conjunction with other modes. Once seen primarily at airports or train stations, small-wheeled luggage or briefcases on wheels are increasingly seen around educational facilities and commercial districts.

Public transportation or transit

Transit can be an extremely space- and energy-efficient urban mode.[6] When done well, it can help to focus and facilitate compact development and obviate the need for private motoring for many or most urban trips. If cities are to reduce auto usage dramatically, as well as space dedicated for their driving and storage, transit must attract a large usage.

The performance of transit is greatly affected by its right of way (RoW) conditions. In fact, they are probably the single largest determinant. Using Vuchic's (2007) terminology, there are three basic types:

1   *RoW A*: a full separation from all other modes and all cross-traffic. The most expensive solution, it also gives the best performance.
2   *RoW B*: a lateral separation such that the mode runs in a fully separated lane, but there are still at-grade conflicts with other traffic at intersections. It is intermediate in cost and performance.
3   *RoW C*: operating in mixed traffic, it requires little investment beyond the existing roadway and is thus the least expensive. It also guarantees that transit will be slower than private automobiles.

The higher the standard of RoW is, in general, the higher the speed and capacity. Large cities need RoW A if they are to maintain liveability. RoW B is increasingly used in medium cities, in particular with the light rail transit (LRT) and bus rapid transit (BRT) modes, in order to 'jump-start' stagnant or overloaded transit systems. A range of techniques, commonly known as 'transit priority', help to speed transit vehicles through intersections and other traffic

Figure 4.7 Electrified trolley bus in Seattle, Washington (top left); electrified mini-bus in Montmartre, Paris (top right); a properly done transit mall in Portland, Oregon, with lanes sufficient for boarding passengers as well as for passing buses (bottom)

Source: Eric C. Bruun and Preston L. Schiller

Figure 4.8 Modern light rail transit (LRT) on the T3 line in right of way (RoW) B in Paris crosses an intersection where traffic has been stopped by a transit priority signal control (top); Vienna's ultra-low floor LRT operates in RoW C and B (bottom)

Source: Eric C. Bruun

bottlenecks, thus improving both speed and reliability of transit operating on RoW B and C. Several telecommunications techniques can provide transit riders with real-time service information and providers with ways of dynamic scheduling and flow adjustments. There is a wide variety of intelligent transportation systems (ITS) that are helping to provide more attractive and reliable services, and to help people plan their trips. This is in line with increased expectations for more information in all aspects of people's daily lives. These same ITS also generate rich data archives that facilitate further improvements in transit planning.[7]

Figure 4.9 Rolling streetcar museum with kerb service in RoW C, Vienna (left); private buses and taxicabs vie for passengers in RoW C, Lima, Peru (right)

Source: Eric C. Bruun and Preston L. Schiller

Figure 4.10 SEPTA's rail rapid transit (RRT) operates in RoW A in Philadelphia, Pennsylvania

Source: Eric C. Bruun

Some of the most important factors regarding public transportation are:

- *Capacity*: as Table 4.1 indicates, the capacity of a transit mode depends on several factors, including vehicle design and size, the acceptance of crowding at times of peak demand (higher in some Asian and South American countries, lower in the US and Canada). It is also important to keep in mind that capacity can be offered at different speeds – people will endure less pleasant conditions if the service is faster and more reliable.
- *Function and trip types*: transit modes can deliver large numbers of people with great efficiency to many important destinations. They can accommodate a broad range of trip types, from neighbourhood services to very speedy services operating in exclusive RoW. Transit is especially space efficient, an important consideration for central business districts (CBDs) and many other facilities that attract large numbers of trips (e.g. sports centres, medical complexes and universities) since it delivers large numbers of people without the need for devoting space or resources to excessive all-day parking (see the section on 'Time–area: An important tool for analysing a transportation investment' in Chapter 6). The same benefit allows roadway systems to manage peak demands without major expansions – a lesson not well learned in many automobile-dependent cities and regions.
- *Infrastructure needs and costs*: these will vary considerably with the technology and RoW applied. As previously mentioned, costs tend to rise as the category of RoW improves. Costs are very site specific. Sometimes RoW must be purchased at astronomical costs; at other times it is already in possession. Bridge-building, and especially tunnelling, can also cause great uncertainty in costs due to unknown soil conditions, utility relocation difficulties and a host of other unanticipated problems.
- *Velocity and range*: transit speeds are a function of technology, vehicle attributes, spacing of stops and RoW characteristics. In mixed traffic (RoW C), the bus may be no faster than a PMV. A typical operating speed (average including stops) in US cities is 12mph (19kmph). In RoW B, with appropriate transit priority measures, LRT or BRT might reach operating speeds between 18mph (29kmph) and 24mph (39kmph). In RoW A, LRT or rail rapid transit (RRT, or Metro) can reach operating speeds ranging from 24mph (39kmph) to as high as 35mph (56kmph). Regional rail (RGR) can attain similar operating speeds as the high end of RRT, up to 50mph (80kmph) when running express or with long station spacings.
- *Environmental, health and safety considerations*: to the extent that transit is fossil-fuelled, it can contribute to air pollution, although transit providers generally work hard to reduce their emissions. New generations of buses often have numerous emission-reducing features and some have adopted hybrid (electric and diesel motors) advances. Electrified transit, trolleybus or rail are much more energy efficient and are emissions free where they operate. Their carbon footprints depend upon the source of their electricity. It should be noted that compressed natural gas (CNG) and some other alternative fuel buses can be cleaner than the older generations of diesel buses, but they actually generate more greenhouse gases (GHGs).
- *Costs*: the operational costs of transit vary greatly depending upon the types of vehicles used, their energy source and their levels of ridership (or

patronage). As indicated elsewhere (see the section on 'The problems of automobile dependence' in Chapter 1), transit services that are well used very often require little or no public subsidy. Costs for transit users (patrons) vary widely depending upon the transit provider, fare and transit pass structure, as well as the distance to be travelled.

Special needs, special populations contribute to large transit subsidies

Even where ridership is high some aspects of transit may require public subsidy. Because of the sprawling and segregated nature of many cities, especially in the US, inner-city and poor residents are often at a disadvantage when commuting to jobs in distant suburbs. Sometimes special 'reverse commute' services need to be offered to help them participate in the workforce. This is one of the costs of sprawl development. In the less wealthy countries this same inability to reach job-rich sites is an impediment to economic development, a serious financial burden to governments to provide such services, or both.

Many of the improvements needed to station and vehicle access for mobility-challenged people, such as low-floor or 'kneeling' buses, benefit the general population as well, through faster and easier boarding and alighting. But the commitment to serve mobility-challenged and transit-disadvantaged individuals sometimes unavoidably adds considerable cost to some services, vehicles and infrastructure. Some of the ways in which transit providers can meet the needs of special populations through innovative services that cost less than the segregated services are made available through free publications.[8]

Personal motor vehicles (PMVs)

PMVs include a number of types: automobiles, small town cars, vans, light trucks and sports utility vehicles (SUVs), and motorized two-wheelers (and, occasionally, three-wheelers) such as motorcycles, scooters and mopeds. Some PMVs are also used as for-hire taxis, shuttles and limousines. Motorized recreational vehicles (RVs) ranging from bus-sized to small off-road vehicles (ORVs) and snowmobiles will not be analysed in this chapter, but are discussed in the section on 'Tourism: The car culture evolves into the fly-drive and recreational vehicle' in Chapter 2. Almost all PMVs are powered by internal combustion engines (ICEs); but an increasing number of hybrid power systems are being introduced for both transit vehicles and PMVs – a smaller ICE motor keeps a battery storage system charged or powers the vehicle when the batteries' energy has been exhausted, or additional peak power is needed. Fully electrified PMVs are slowly being developed and introduced to replace ICE-powered vehicles, but these are likely to remain small and of limited range. Thus, they are unlikely to displace cars that are also used by single PMV households for longer-distance driving.

Some of the most important factors regarding PMVs are:

- *Capacity*: from 1 to 12 individuals, with some cargo possible.
- *Function and trip types*: commuting to work, shopping, services and recreation.

- *Infrastructure needs and costs*: these vary, depending upon type of road, surface and engineering (e.g. separated RoW, bridges, over/underpasses, elevated, tunnel, etc.), from US$1 million per mile for unimproved roads, to $10 million per mile for urban arterials and boulevards, to $100 million per mile for urban expressways, to $6.5 billion per mile, the current estimate for Boston's 'big dig'.
- *Velocity and range*: 30 to 120mph (45 to 200kmph) / 200 to 300 miles (300km to 450km).
- *Environmental*: PMVs are in the forefront of GHGs, smog, acid rain and other urban pollution emissions problems. They are the major source of pollution for bodies of water in or near urban areas and the major source of urban noise.
- *Health and safety*: PMVs and trucks kill over 1 million people each year worldwide. The majority of those killed are 'vulnerable road users' – pedestrians, bicyclists and motorcycle riders. Motor vehicles are the greatest cause of mortality for children and young persons (WHO, 2004a, 2004b). In brief, PMVs are one of the world's greatest environmental, health and safety problems (Newman and Kenworthy, 1989, 1999; Freund and Martin, 1993; Whitelegg 1993, 1997).
- *Costs*: the Automobile Association of America (AAA) estimates the cost of owning and operating an average PMV in the US to be over US$9000 per annum, or at least US$0.55 per mile driven.[9] Costs for SUVs are considerably higher and slightly lower for more fuel-efficient vehicles. Due to higher taxes and fees, the costs of PMVs are higher in most other parts of the world.

PMV ownership, cost-bundling or car-sharing?

Most of the costs of owning and operating a PMV are 'bundled' (see discussion of bundled costs in Chapter 6), meaning that one pays lump sums for purchase, insurance and even storage at work or at some residential buildings regardless of the level of use of the vehicle. After assuming all the upfront bundled costs of vehicle ownership, the costs of operating a PMV are experienced as relatively cheap marginal costs. This is in contrast to public transportation where there may be no upfront costs but the cost of fares or passes may exceed the marginal costs of driving. One possibility for reducing the urban population of PMVs, while still offering their use as an option, is the 'car-share' organization, which allows members to pay an annual fee so that they can use a car as needed for a daily or hourly fee. Some car-share organizations, especially in major European cities, offer a bouquet of fleet vehicles, bicycles and discounted transit passes, and some are affiliated with other cities' car-share organizations so that

Figure 4.11 Minicabs carry two passengers around Havana (top); the Corbin Sparrow one-passenger electric mini-car (legally a motorcycle) was part of the Boulder Car Co-op fleet until their insurance company became nervous (bottom): Such vehicles take up very little space and several can fit into one regular parking space

Source: Preston L. Schiller

members can use vehicles when visiting.[10] The modal characteristics of PMVs are included in Table 4.2.

Regional–metropolitan area modes: Long commutes, regional services, recreation, peak demand

As previously discussed, the majority of trips are in town and most are for relatively short distances. In large metropolitan areas, people may live at a considerable distance from their places of employment. Sometimes this is a matter of choice; sometimes the distance has been created by an employer's decision to locate or relocate in a fringe office park area where land is cheaper than in a town centre. Occasionally households with two employed individuals face the complicated issue of where to live relative to either partner's place of employment.

Some regional trips are for specialized services, such as those at a medical specialty centre. Other regional trips may be to a special recreational attraction, such as a sports centre, zoo or museum. Facilities that either employ large numbers of people, such as regional hospitals, or attract large crowds, such as sports arenas, should be encouraged to locate in areas accessible by transit for the sake of both visitors and employees. There are several considerations relating to modes chosen or promoted for regional trips:

- *Walking*: most regional trips are not amenable to walking, although the pedestrian conditions around transit can be an important factor for choosing that mode.
- *Bicycling*: regions that have created good bicycle networks can attract small but significant percentages of travel by this mode. Where bicycles are facilitated in large numbers, such as the Copenhagen S–Tog transit system, they serve as a feeder/distributor system and their use is increased even further.
- *Public transportation*: many regional trips can be attracted by transit modes when planning and provision is adequate. RRT / Metro, RGT (sometimes inappropriately termed commuter rail), especially when offered at a level of service greater than peak period and peak direction, and regional bus networks (Express Bus or BRT services) and special for-hire services (buses to airports and train stations) can all make significant contributions to attracting commuters and other individuals who need to travel to

Figure 4.12 Sounder commuter train, Seattle, Washington (top); smaller commuter train, Portland, Oregon (bottom)

Source: Eric C. Bruun and Preston L. Schiller

regional centres. In some regions ferries play a significant role in transporting people to and from major centres. All of these services work best with good intermodal connections.

- *PMVs*: many wealthy regions have virtually no option but the PMV, except perhaps in their older traditional parts built earlier in the 20th century that may still have some walkability and transit. Regions should invest in sidewalks, bicycle lanes and good transit in order to lessen their automobile dependence. This is becoming ever more urgent as the population ages and the numbers of transit-dependent workers' jobs relocate to such areas. Less wealthy regions lacking good transit services may need to depend upon PMVs for some purposes. Many already have a traffic mix with high proportions of motorized two-wheelers and shared for-hire services. Some wealthy regions have attempted to improve bus performance as well as attract more commuters to carpools or vanpools through high-occupancy vehicle (HOV) lanes on major roads. This is a questionable practice, as is discussed in Chapter 6 (see, in particular, Box 6.7).

Figure 4.13 Passenger and car ferry, Washington State Ferries, Seattle

Source: Eric C. Bruun

Regional roads in urban areas often face serious congestion during commuter hours and other times of great travel demand, such as sports events and holiday periods. When congestion occurs at predictable periods, usually during the morning and afternoon commuter 'rush' hours, it is referred to as peak period congestion. The hour with the worst congestion is termed the 'peak hour'. A few years after the US began its suburbanization trajectory, major congestion occurred on highways leading into and out of CBDs (or other employment areas) in the morning and late afternoon. This has been termed 'peak direction'. Today, due to some gentrification of inner urban areas, many US cities have peak period congestion; but these are not as marked peak directional flows as in decades past. As more and more driving occurs for all trips, some urban regions experience peak congestion all day, into the evenings and at weekends.

Many regions, such as Washington, DC's Northern Virginia and Maryland suburbs, have been busy expanding highways and bridges rather than expanding transit services. The result? More congestion. Why the strategy of expanding roadways to accommodate peak PMV travel is self-defeating can be easily explained:

- The phenomenon of induced driving or traffic generation, where roadway expansion results in increasing levels of traffic, is well documented and explained elsewhere in the text.
- A general traffic lane for a limited-access highway can only accommodate at most 2000 to 2200 vehicles per hour (less for most urban arterials) before becoming unstable. It can then approach the speed at which an infant crawls before speeding up again in phenomena called 'shock waves'.

- At peak commuter hours, PMVs generally have their lowest passenger occupancy rates, barely averaging more than one person per PMV.
- At peak hours, transit vehicles usually have their highest passenger occupancy rates.
- A roadway lane dedicated to transit only can carry the equivalent of many times the persons occupying one general purpose lane; adding two tracks of rail transit capacity can exceed peak period roadway capacity of an entire multiple lane freeway.
- Diverting PMV traffic to transit also reduces parking demands, an extremely important factor in the overall complexity of moving towards more sustainable transportation and land-use forms.

Rather than 'biggering' the roads, a better strategy is to manage peak period demands through improved transit, non-motorized facilities and incentives for people to work at home at least part of the week. This will be discussed further in Chapter 8.

Box 4.2 Peak hour can last all day in some automobile cities

Bellevue, Washington, is a city that was mostly pastures and farmland before World War II. Then it became a suburb designed for the automobile, both in its exclusively zoned low-density residential neighbourhoods and its commercial and office districts and central business district (CBD), where tall office towers and a large shopping mall are fed by ever widening arterial roads. It has miles of strip mall-style development along many of its arterial roads. Because there is relatively little mixing of residences, offices, shops and services, and a retrograde pedestrian and bicycling environment, residents and employees drive everywhere. Often they drive from one parking lot to another in the CBD because of the car culture, rigidly enforced restrictions in parking lots or both. As a consequence, Bellevue has become a poster child for the midday peak: employees take to their cars to run errands and find a place to meet and eat; residents take to their cars to run errands and find a place to meet and eat; and all become very frustrated by the huge traffic back-ups. Right now it is developing an 'upscale' downtown mall along with expensive condominium towers to try to outdo the existing CBD mall. At least the residents will not have to drive to the mall. They will not have to walk either; it will be in the same building (www.thebravern.com).

Source: Preston L. Schiller

The barrier effects of different rights of way

Virtually all forms of rights of way (RoW) for motorized modes have connectivity and barrier effects. Barrier effects that limit the ability to cross a motorized RoW can seriously affect the ways in which people travel in town, especially by walking and bicycling, and the ways in which buses are routed. Large or busy traffic roads can act as barriers to travel, commerce and sociability within neighbourhoods, as well as making the areas adjacent to them unpleasant through noise and fumes. Streets where transit demand is very high and transit vehicles are so numerous as to create a 'wall of buses' should be considered as corridors for creating RoW A, either in tunnels or elevated structures.

Figure 4.14 Barrier effect of large urban highway, RoW C, Ulsan City, Korea

Source: Eric C. Bruun

Long distance: Modes and types of travel

Long-distance travel can be defined as travel outside the region of one's residence and beyond the reach of local and regional public transportation. Its distance might range from 100 miles to several thousand miles. Long-distance travel occurs for several reasons: business and professional matters; family visits and emergencies; medical needs; and recreation, including international and intra-national tourism. In wealthy countries, most moderate long-distance travel is done by PMV, and very long trips involving hundreds or thousands of miles are usually done by airlines. Japan is one of the few exceptions to this generality, having invested wisely and heavily in a high-performance intercity rail system since the 1960s. It was then able to direct much in-country long-distance travel to this system rather than to highway or aviation expansion for such purposes.

The modes most commonly used for long-distance travel whose characteristics need to be considered are coaches (buses and jitneys), railways, airliners, ships and ferries, and PMVs. Motorcycles account for a relatively small percentage of long-distance travel, even in less wealthy countries where they are much used for much local and regional travel. Table 4.3 summarizes and compares selected characteristics of long-distance modes, which are then discussed.

Table 4.2 Regional–metropolitan area modes

MODE	Max hourly capacity (wealthy nation crowding standards)	Key functional and trip characteristics	Infrastructure needs and cost drivers	Average speed and effective range	Environmental, health, safety impacts	Vehicle/ operating costs (wealthy nation levels)
Bus Rapid Transit (BRT)	BRT same as urban; express capacity up to 50K pers/hr if no stations	Longer trips, especially commuter	Elaborate stations, HOV or high cost dedicated lanes if RoW A	20–50mph; to outer suburbs	Modest noise/air pollution, safe for passengers	Same as local per hr, less per mi
Rail Rapid Transit (RRT / Metro)	Less than local due to higher seating standards	Suburb to city and trans-regional; tends to all-day usage	Stations fewer than local, with expensive intermodal features	Higher speed than local RRT due to longer station spacings	No local air pollution, noise when overheac, extremely safe	Same as local per hr, less per mi
Regional Rail (RGR)	10–25Kpers/hr/track; multiple tracks	Longer trips, especially commuter	Stations modest for lower demand systems	30–50mph depending on stopping patterns; to outer suburbs	No local air pollution if electric; old diesel dangerous	$13–22 per car-mi
Passenger, auto ferries	Site specific, up to 2K persons and 200 cars per ship	Water crossings where no bridges; serves all trip types	Loading slips, gangway, car storage areas	20mph, less than 1 hr trip	Significant pollution with old diesel, unsafe if overcrowded	Very specific to particular application
Motorcycles, medium large	Dedicated lanes rare in wealthy nations, not common in developing	Same as PMVs, and where parking scarce; courier use	Minimal, dedicated parking to avoid sidewalk abuse	Faster than PMVs when filtering is allowed; to outer suburbs	Old designs are highly polluting, least safe motorized mode	$5–20K; $0.25–0.45 per mi
PMVs	2200 per hr per lane or RoW A, but unstable; 1600 on arterials	For all trip purposes; especially inefficient for peak period travel	Extremely space inefficient for lanes/ storage; high infrastructure cost relative to capacity	30–50mph on RoW A (unstable); 20mph on RoW C; suburb-to-suburb, entire region	One vehicle negligible, cumulative very high; less safe than all types of transit	$12–75K; $0.35–0.75 per mi

Table 4.3 Selected characteristics of long-distance modes

MODE	Max hourly capacity (wealthy nation crowding standards)	Key functional and trip characteristics	Infrastructure needs and cost drivers	Average speed and effective range	Environmental, health, safety impacts	Vehicle/operating costs (wealthy nation levels)
Intercity bus/coach	50–70 per bus, depending on size; limited by roadway and terminal capacity	City to city trips for persons w/o PMVs; connect rural to city	Terminals in larger cities; many have no terminals	50mph if few intermediate stops, up to 1K mi per day	Significant air pollution if old diesel; good safety record in wealthy countries.	$400–700K, $60–100 per hr
Intercity rail	2–10Kpers/hr/track	Same as intercity bus/coach; attracts more choice riders	Modest upgrades on freight track, up to $200M per city for urban access improvement	60–120mph, up to 1500 mi per day	No local air pollution if electric; minor diesel pollution relative to passenger load; very safe	$3M per car, operating costs similar to RGR
High-speed rail	5–10Kpers/hr/track	Attracts persons from both PMVs and airliners	Operates on conventional track, but needs very expensive dedicated track for high speeds.	120–160mph, depending on stops; network limited but continually lengthening	No local air pollution; noise significant at higher speeds; extremely safe	$35M per train-set, operating cost higher than intercity per hr, but lower per mi due to high speed
Ferry and oceanic ships	Up to 2000 persons per departure, few per day; oceanic passenger ships very rare	Ferry important part of highway system; ocean freighters carry airplane averse	Large piers, loading ramps and gangways, large terminals, car storage areas	20–24mph for ferries and ocean freighters, 30–36mph for oceanic passenger ships	Significant air pollution if old diesel; very good safety record in wealthy countries	Ferries application specific; oceanic ships – expensive, inefficient
Airliners	Capacity limited by airport capacity; 30 take-offs plus landings per hr per runway typical	Trips of all types; lack of rail = short trips; vital to mountain and island locations.	Runways and terminals at large airports very expensive, land acquisition very difficult	300–560 mph, 100–8000mi	Very high air and noise pollution near large airports; ozone-damaging; very safe	Wide range of purchase costs – up to $250M per plane; wide range of operating costs

Source: Eric C. Bruun

Long-distance mode considerations

- *Walking and bicycling*: very little long-distance travel is on foot or by bicycle due to time constraints and the vicissitudes of using these modes for lengthy trips. Bicycle touring is a very small but slowly growing portion of tourist travel in many countries and holds considerable promise for further growth (see the section on 'Tourism: The car culture evolves into the fly-drive and recreational vehicle culture' in Chapter 2).
- *Public transportation*: the major modes available to the public for long-distance travel are buses (coaches and jitneys), railways, ferries, and ocean vessels and airliners. The role that government plays with regard to these modes varies considerably from country to country. Virtually all governments regulate long-distance transportation to some extent, and international agreements and agencies play a role in international and intercontinental regulation. Some long-distance providers, including many passenger railway and ferry services and a few national airlines, are within the public sector; but most coach services, airlines and ocean passenger vessels are not. In these cases, public transportation generally means public access, but not necessarily control.
- *PMVs*: much long-distance travel is done by PMVs, especially for trips of moderate distance that may be for business, professional or family purposes. These trips may be taken by PMVs in countries where driving is heavily subsidized and rail and coach options are not available or attractive. A fair amount of longer-distance trips may be done by PMVs for recreational and tourism purposes, especially in countries where driving is heavily subsidized and alternatives are scarce or unappealing (see the section on 'Tourism: The car culture evolves into the fly-drive and recreational vehicle culture' in Chapter 2).

Coaches, buses and jitneys

Coach services range from those that are incorporated and scheduled and have a substantial regional, national or international reach, to semi-formal jitney services. Some of these services are available at bus stations or intermodal facilities with good information sources; others are informal, roadside flagging-down or pick-up arrangements with little information available. Some coach and chartered services have buses of substantial size with a variety of amenities aboard, including all of the old martial arts films one never wanted to see. Some provide arranged transportation and accommodation for large groups.

Coach services play an important role in countries that lack adequate passenger rail services and have low rates of PMV ownership. Their quality, reliability and comfort may range from excellent to poor. Crowding can be a serious problem in some countries where passengers may even ride on bus roofs. They tend to be the least comfortable mode, having neither the privacy of the auto nor the space of a train, and often have less personal space than even the airliner, while the duration onboard may meet or exceed that of a very long airliner trip.

Coach services could play an important role as parts of intermodal systems feeding railways in wealthy and not-so-wealthy countries. Under deregulation in North America and the UK this does not seem to have been the case. Coach services there enjoy some of the same subsidies associated with highway modes and often successfully compete with inadequate and often very slow passenger rail. In the car-rich US and Canada, many cities, large and small, have been left with relatively few long-distance travel options, rail or coach, as railway services disappeared and profitability rather than need directs most decisions made by private coach lines. Columbus, Ohio, is an urban area with a population of 1.7 million. Within a radius of 100 to 200 miles are the populous urban areas of Cleveland, Detroit, Cincinnati, Dayton, Toledo and Indianapolis. Chicago is 300 miles away and Washington, DC, is 400 miles distant. Columbus has no passenger rail services. Its long-distance options are to drive, fly, 'ride the dog' (as Greyhound Coach is popularly known) or hitchhike. One could cite numerous examples of this across the US. A recent US trend has been the proliferation of low-priced intercity coach services that operate more like developing nations' jitneys than quality services for a wealthy country. They generally lack much, if any, infrastructure, such as reservations and information systems or terminals. They provide low-cost express services between several major cities, especially in the North-East and Mid-Atlantic regions of the US, undercutting the larger established coach services and Amtrak.

Range of vehicles and facilities

Intercity buses range in size from 12-passenger minivans, to 24-seat minibuses, to 14m long three-axle buses carrying almost 70 seated passengers in luxury. In a few cases, such as South Africa, buses will carry passengers on the lower level typically used for luggage and cargo, with a trailer pulled along behind for the luggage. In poorer countries, old school buses will sometimes see a second life in the intercity role. In some cases, there are no terminals or even stops, simply hailing. At the opposite extreme, there can be air-conditioned and secure waiting facilities at all major stops.

Passenger railways

Well-planned and promoted passenger railways can be an attractive alternative to long-distance driving or flying. Japan's Shinkansen carries intercity passenger volumes similar to metropolitan regional trains elsewhere in the world. Its first line opened in 1964 with a peak speed of 200kmph, medium speed by today's standard. Current trains run 270 to 300kmph, with a few lines now running at 350kmph.

There are corridors in other countries where upgraded train services have also succeeded in making inroads on the airliner mode share on an increasing number of routes. This is especially true for the rapidly increasing high-speed network in Europe where the number of origin–destination pairs for which trains can compete multiplies. High-speed trains are capable of operating on conventional tracks as well, albeit at reduced speeds, such that more cities off the high-speed corridor can also receive direct service.

Projects such as Europe's Railteam (2009) aim to slow or even reverse the trend of increasing reliance on the automobile for intercity and long-distance travel through integrated fares and better connections across national boundaries. Korea has its own high-speed rail system based on French *train à grande vitesse* (TGV), or high-speed train, technology, designed to attract ridership from both autos and airliners. China is making large investments in additional rail capacity, but with less emphasis on attracting people from autos since auto-ownership is still very low. Instead, it aims to decrease overcrowding on existing trains, reduce the need for airport expansion and improve the economies of rural regions through better connectivity.

These examples, along with many others, suggest that a high-speed train is probably the most dynamic intercity mode in wealthier nations, as well as some of the fast-growing nations in Asia, such as Taiwan, China and South Korea. But the very high construction cost of true high-speed rail (usually defined as greater than 250kmph) means that compromise solutions must also play a large part. The European high-speed trains are all designed to approach stations in large or small cities on branch lines using existing tracks. One of the serious flaws in the magnetic levitation (MagLev) technologies, which has no doubt contributed to their failure to attract many implementations, is the need for completely separate infrastructure, even in highly built-up areas (see 'Futuristic modes' for further details on MagLev).

Passenger services that run at mid-range speeds are also playing an increased role. They often share track with freight trains, but run at speeds faster than the automobile, up to speeds approaching genuine high-speed trains, with peak speeds between 140 to 250kmph. They use newer generation train designs that are lighter and more energy efficient, and some tilt to take curves at higher speeds. These new designs, combined with targeted additions of track at key locations, provide significant reductions in travel time and reduced operating costs for relatively modest investment. This is the approach that the Nordic countries have been taking due to challenging terrain.

The examples of Amtrak in the US and ViaRail in Canada show that relatively slow traditional services can attract more passengers. Both are experiencing ridership growth and increased demand; but both suffer from speed and capacity limitations due to decades of underfunding and conflicts with freight operations. At issue in both countries is whether additional capacity will be added to freight networks, or whether entirely separated lines will be built. Recent developments in the US indicate a great deal of interest in creating higher-speed rail corridors in several regions. The Quebec–Windsor corridor in Canada has been discussed for many years as a promising higher-speed corridor. Funding and political will to undertake this project have been lacking, although an extremely costly and controversial new freeway and bridge connecting Detroit and Windsor is under construction, while an interesting railway tunnel renovation option under the Detroit River was ignored. Similar decisions about railway infrastructure need to be taken in developing countries such as India.

Successful railway programmes benefit from good marketing strategies. Information at stations and websites is generally of high quality. Pricing, fare integration and reduced-cost pass programmes reflect an intention to utilize off-peak capacity fully, as well as serve goals such as competing with both automobility and flying. The French TGV is a good example, using a two-tier pricing structure, with the departures most convenient to business travellers costing more (SNCF, 2009) (see the discussion of pricing in Chapter 6). Many European countries, with Germany in the lead, offer an abundance of regional, national and seasonal pass programmes to attract riders. Some European countries have yet to develop a coherent railway pricing structure aimed at attracting motorists and airline passengers for moderate and long-distance travel. Unfortunately, some of the better efforts are undermined by low-fare air services benefiting from public subsidies like untaxed fuel.

Figure 4.15 Intercity express trains serve a very different purpose than mountain tourist trains

Source: Jeffrey R. Kenworthy and Eric C. Bruun

Range of passenger rail vehicles and facilities

Services of limited frequency tend to be operated with diesel locomotive-pulled units and they are subject to regular delays due to conflicts with freight trains. Stations and terminals tend to be modest. At the opposite end are the dedicated RoW high-speed lines where only trains of similar speed operate and reliability is very high. Stations and terminals are designed to be attractive and comfortable. The current trend is to replace medium-speed trains of traditional locomotive-pulled designs with electric multiple unit (EMU) designs that are substantially more energy efficient.

Ferries and ocean-going ships

For transoceanic travel, the main alternative to airliners is an ocean freighter, many of which have a limited number of passenger compartments. Cruise ships should not be confused with true ocean liners, of which there are but a handful left in operation. Cruise ships are very slow vessels better characterized as floating hotels (or even cities) that meander from port to port.

There are a large number of ships that travel overnight or a maximum of one day that are usually defined as 'ferries', but they bear little resemblance to the ferries crossing inland waterways. They can carry walk-on passengers, private autos and motorcycles, and even passenger trains when rails are installed in the deck. Typical examples are those that operate in the Baltic and Mediterranean seas and in archipelago regions such as Indonesia and the Philippines.

Figure 4.16 The Alaska Marine Highway passenger/vehicle ferry, south-east Alaska to Bellingham, Washington

Source: Eric C. Bruun

Range of ferry vehicles and facilities

Ferries can range from vessels carrying a few hundred foot passengers and a handful of motorized vehicles (such as between Indonesian islands) to ships that hold a few hundred cars, buses and trucks and over 1000 passengers (such as ships that cross the Baltic and Mediterranean). There are also special variants that can carry entire trains, as tracks are built into the car deck, and that have icebreaking hulls. In the case of Northern Europe, the ferries can be part of the highway system.

Aircraft and airliners

Direct travel by air is generally limited to travel between relatively large metropolitan destinations or as a feeder from a smaller city to a larger city with a major airport. Otherwise, connecting flights are usually required. Unlike ground modes, intermediate stops at smaller towns along the way are not possible. Commercial airports for turbofan-powered airliners require significant land and noise buffer space, and are typically very limited in number within a region.

As distances became longer, the commercial airlines became dominant in the wealthy countries. When crossing the continent of North America, it takes five to six hours versus two to three days by ground-based modes. The crossover distance when an individual is likely to select the air mode becomes shorter when there are geographic obstacles such as mountain ranges or bodies of water, as these further slow the competing water or ground transport relative to air travel. It becomes longer when there is a frequent train service, automobile driving conditions are favourable or the airport is in an inconvenient location. The distance of crossover from airliners to trains will also decrease in corridors where frequent and higher-speed rail is available.

Figure 4.17 Airliners combine cargo and passenger functions

Source: Eric C. Bruun

Due to the paucity and poor performance of most rail services in the US and Canada, the public subsidization of commercial aviation and the marketing strategies of airlines, much air travel occurs between cities less than 500 miles apart. Between 25 and 50 per cent of a regional airport's operations may be given over to relatively short flights whose passenger loads are generally lower than longer-distance flights. This inefficiency and environmental damage could be corrected by promoting and providing better intercity rail and coach options.[11]

For transoceanic travel, the jet airliner has taken a position of extreme dominance. Its productivity and time saving over the piston propeller airplane quickly caused the displacement of the latter. While ocean liners could do well from an efficiency standpoint due to passenger loads in the thousands, they had another drawback in addition to the extra days relative to an airliner (five days at least to cross the Atlantic). They had the extra expense of the hotel services to support people with food, lodging and entertainment. Ocean liner trips are now very limited in number and are, essentially, luxury cruises for vacationers. People with an aversion to, or medical restriction against, flying can occupy one of the limited number of cabins on many ocean freighters.

Range of vehicles and facilities

Long-range aircraft range from 150 to 350 seats of mixed classes, with ranges from 7000 to 10,000 nautical miles. Service tends to be concentrated from very large airports with major hub-and-spoke operations that feed and distribute passengers to smaller cities, although even medium-sized cities will sometimes have a few long-distance services. The new A380 is far larger than the previous largest aircraft, the 747-400; but its popularity remains to be proven. There is also a trend towards aircraft with extremely long ranges, up to 14,000 nautical miles.

In terms of range of vehicles and facilities, turboprop aircraft are the most efficient for shorter distances and range up to 50 to 70 seats. A more recent trend is to go to 'regional jets' of 50 to 100 seats in size; but analogous to the trend from auto to SUV, they consume more fuel. Larger airliners range from about 100 seats to up to 250 or 300 for trunk routes between major cities.

Airports require large amounts of land, including noise perimeters around the airport where types of development are restricted. It is perhaps fortuitous for proponents of alternative modes that suitable quantities of land are increasingly difficult to assemble and new airports are rare.

Sustainability considerations

In addition to modal and trip characteristics, there are several issues and discussions around modes relevant to sustainable transportation that are not always well understood in media coverage or public discourse, and which tend to focus too narrowly on the technical and technological aspects of modes. Issues that benefit from broader analysis and discussion include energy and environmental factors; the relation of modes to land use, urban form and urban economy; and health, safety, equity and social justice concerns. Aspects of these are discussed in various sections of this text and a brief summary and overview is included here.

Energy and environmental factors: Tailpipe and fuelish fixes

A holistic approach to the issues of transportation's environmental effects and energy consumption is needed. The discussion of these matters often focuses narrowly on end-of-the pipe or tailpipe factors for which technological fixes are usually proposed. Transportation pollution is too often seen as a localized matter, one of reducing the levels of certain pollutants such as carbon monoxide or the oxides of nitrogen, or providing special catchment basins for road runoff, rather than a systemic problem that needs to be addressed first at the level of policy and planning, and then with technology when and where appropriate. The examples of vehicle pollution control devices and the efforts to increase motor vehicle energy efficiency, including the US Corporate Average Fuel Efficiency (CAFE) standards, serve as examples of problems with tailpipe approaches. The desirability of lowered pollution and improved energy efficiency is not at question, but the sufficiency of technological approaches is open to question and reconsideration in light of a broader understanding of the way in which transportation interacts with a wide array of non-technical, non-technological factors.

Emissions controls

A variety of pollution control devices, most notable among them the catalytic converter, have been developed to reduce or eliminate certain harmful ICE emissions. Among the several issues with having pollution control devices at the centre of clean air efforts are the following:

- Only a handful of pollutants are targeted and monitored for control – generally, carbon monoxide, certain oxides of nitrogen and some hydrocarbons. Carbon dioxide, the greatest global emissions threat, is not controlled by these devices. The great majority of pollutants emitted by motor vehicles, numbering in hundreds, are unknown, unanalysed or uncontrolled. The mix of tailpipe pollutants can vary with batch-specific refining and whether or not vehicle owners use fuel additives or even maintain pollution control devices properly. In many developing countries, there is the further problem of adulteration of fuel, such as the cutting of diesel fuel with kerosene.
- Some aspects of pollution control devices have undesirable impacts. Some pollution control devices reduce the fuel efficiency of vehicles, and the technologies involved might create pollution elsewhere in the vehicle's life cycle through increased mining, energy use, industrial impacts or disposal impacts.

Alternative fuels and carbon sequestration

Alternative fuels are much in the media and public discussion. The fact that so much attention and so little thorough analysis and critique is afforded them is, perhaps, a function of the optimism of those who hope for a technological fix to the problems of transportation and its enormous dependence upon petroleum-based and GHG-producing fuels. There are several issues with which ST should be concerned in terms of alternative fuels:

- The quest for lowering GHG atmospheric loadings through alternative fuels or carbon sequestration may lead nowhere. It may also divert attention away from the difficult task of reorganizing urban development and transportation systems to reduce overall levels of PMV and freight transportation.
- The production of agriculturally derived alternative fuels may divert needed croplands from feeding people to feeding vehicles. The equity and social justice implications of this orientation are self-evident. After only a few years of US ethanol subsidies, world food prices for corn have risen as a result. Increased demand for palm oil for biodiesel fuel has led to destruction of rainforests.

Fuel and energy efficiency: Vehicles, fuels or cities?

Developing and spreading the use of fuel and energy-efficient vehicles is a laudable goal. But there are several issues around the ways in which such efforts have been defined or shaped:

- Fuel efficiency may be a vehicular attribute, but the nature of the fuel itself may be inefficient when the whole production and life cycle of fuel production and distribution is considered. Chapter 5 discusses the interesting phenomenon of how a major portion of transoceanic shipment is devoted to the transport of fuels and related products. Energy efficiency should be assessed in the context of life-cycle analysis and the prospects of renewability. Currently, the worldwide transportation system is approximately 95 per cent dependent upon fossil fuels.
- There is a certain irony with recent concern about fuel efficiency after decades of neglect or retrograde movement in this area. For decades, the major PMV manufacturers have been using mechanical improvements to foster performance, especially acceleration, rather than efficiency. In recent decades, the US has seen highway speed limits increased and tax incentives promoting the purchase of SUVs while fuel efficiency declined overall. Recently, the federal government has begun to discuss efficiency as a policy goal, although what effective action will be taken is unclear.
- In the absence of reductions in driving and the rapidly growing motor vehicle population, tailpipe and fuel efficiency efforts may not be very effective. In most countries there is very little in the way of formal policy or planning mechanisms to direct development into patterns that reduce driving, facilitate transit and non-motorized travel, and consequently significantly reduce the impacts of PMVs. Northern Europe is the area where the most concerted efforts are being made.

Much of the promotion of pollution control and energy-efficient vehicles unfortunately misses the point: a city could be filled up with fuel-efficient automobiles and yet be consuming energy in the extreme. As the discussions of automobile dependency (Chapter 1) and the space consumption of various vehicles (see 'Time–area: An important tool for analysing a transportation investment' in Chapter 6) indicate, it is the urban pattern and the availability

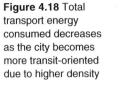

Figure 4.18 Total transport energy consumed decreases as the city becomes more transit-oriented due to higher density

Note: data from energy use in 58 higher-income cities

Source: Jeffrey R. Kenworthy

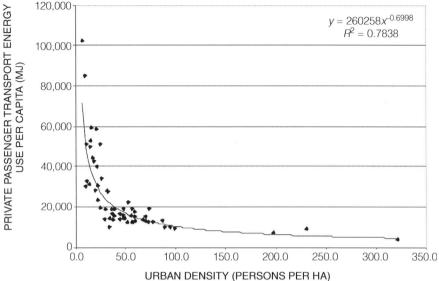

and promotion of quality transit, walking and bicycling provisions that shape whether a city is efficient or inefficient, extremely polluted or less polluted. The true test of reduction in energy consumption isn't on an individual vehicle basis, but on the total basis for the entire city. Figure 4.18 shows a very strong relationship between energy use per capita and density in higher-income cities. This density is only physically possible with a supportive high-capacity transit system. This not only reduces the amount of private car use, it also enables a much higher percentage of non-motorized trips.

The business as usual (BAU) discussion of modes generally avoids such considerations and finds it easier to keep alive hopes that a 'green' automobile or 'clean' fuel is just around the corner. It also generally avoids discussions of modal and social inequities: the disadvantaging of certain modes and certain sectors of society through automobile dependency and limiting access to affordable alternatives either through planning and policy or pricing. But it must also be said that the current generation of individuals educated in transportation engineering, city planning and other fields related to modes and urban development are making this generalization less true every day.

Despite the above criticisms about simplistic tailpipe fixations and fuelishness in transportation energy thinking, the matter of modal energy efficiency is very important. To the extent that people will move around in motor vehicles and own some forms of PMVs, it is better that energy efficiency is considered. To the extent that people will move around cities, regions and nations, and travel between nations, it is important to consider the energy efficiencies of various modes. Tables 4.4 and 4.5 compare several land, air and water passenger modes. The commercial vehicle types are based on actual duty and are quite accurate. Those for private use are generally less reliable since individual driving habits, driving conditions and maintenance habits vary considerably. It is important to note that energy consumption is affected greatly by passenger loads and capacities.

Table 4.4 Energy efficiency of land passenger modes

Mode	Average energy usage in miles per gallon (litres per 100km)	Typical passenger load		Capacity load[b] All seated = (s) Crush = (c)	
		Passengers	Miles per gallon/ passenger	Passengers	Miles per gallon/ passenger
Land					
Scooter (WASP)	75.0 (3.13)	1	75	2 (s)	150
Medium motorcycle (Suzuki GS500)	60 (3.9)	1	60	2 (s)	120
Gas–electric hybrid auto – city + highway (Toyota Prius)	47.6 (4.94)	1.5	72	5 (s)	238
Very small auto – highway (Smart Car for two)	41[c] (5.73)	1.5	62	2 (s)	
Very small auto – city (Smart Car for two)	33[c] (7.12)	1.2d	40	2 (s)	
SUV – highway (Ford Explorer V8)	21.6[c] (10.9)	2	43	7 (s)	151
SUV – city (Ford Explorer V8)	14.1[c] (16.7)	1.2[d]	17	7 (s)	98
40 foot diesel transit bus (BC Transit – city and express average)	3.1 (76.0)	25	78	90 (c)	279
40 foot trolley bus (New Flyer low floor)	9.77 (24.06)	30	293	77 (c)	752
Light rail transit (LRT) (Siemens Combino)	13.6 (17.2)	65	887	180 (c)	2460
Rapid transit (Bombardier T-1)	8.0 (29.4)	100[a]	800[a]	315 (c)	2520
London Underground (Hybrid rapid transit/ regional rail)	7.4 (31.9)	19	141	152 (c)	1125
Regional rail (GO Transit loco-powered 10 bi-level cars)	0.26 (940)	1000	260	3600 (c)	936
Intercity rail (Swedish Railways Regina EMU)	3.35 (70.3)	34	114	167 (s)	560
High-speed rail (TGV Atlantique train-set)	1.58 (149)	291	460	485 (s)	767

Notes: a = ridership varies a great deal; busy lines will average more passengers than seats over the course of a day.
b = crush load varies, typically assumed at four people per square metre in Europe and North America.
c = official US Environmental Protection Agency figures, higher than seen in practice.
d = average passenger load in US for PMVs during commuting hours.

Source: Strickland (2009), unless otherwise noted

Table 4.5 Energy efficiency of air and water passenger modes

Mode	Average energy usage in miles per gallon (litres per 100km)	Typical passenger load[c]		Capacity load[a]	
		Passengers	Miles per gallon/ passenger	Passengers	Miles per gallon/ passenger
Air					
Private small airplane (Cessna 172)	12.6 (18.7)	1	12.6	4	50.4
Regional turboprop (DHC 8-300)	1.19 (198)	35[c]	41.7	50	59.3
Short- to medium-range airliner (Boeing 737 'Next Generation' mixed fleet – 607 mile average flight length)	0.43 (547)	96[c]	41.3	137	58.9
Medium- to long-distance airliner (Airbus 320 – 1358 mile average flight length)	0.447 (526)	109[c]	48.7	156	69.7
Very long-distance airliner (Boeing 777-200ER – 6818 mile flight length)	0.252 (933)[b]	211[c]	53.1	301	75.8
Water					
Passenger-only double-ended ferry (Vancouver SeaBus)	0.25 (944)	140	35	400	100
Passenger + car ferry ship (BC Ferries Spirit Class)	0.0246 (9572)	1000	24.6	2100	51.7
Transoceanic luxury ship (Queen Mary 2–25 knots)	0.00753 (31,250)	2000	15.0	3090	23.2

Notes: a = legal safe capacity of ferries is typically far exceeded in developing countries.
b = Boeing Company, www.boeing.com/commercial/777family/pdf/777environ_1.pdf.
c = 70 per cent load factor used for typical load factor for all commercial airliners for comparison.

Source: Strickland (2009), unless otherwise noted

Futuristic modes

There are some modes that could be discussed as futuristic: they have yet to have had a successful or replicable application, or there are serious limitations to their applicability at this time. Among these are the following:

- *MagLev*: there are two technologies – magnetic repulsion, where the vehicle is pushed away from the track, and magnetic attraction, where the vehicle is pulled towards it. In either case, there is no physical contact between track and vehicle except at very slow speeds. Once under way, it operates on the same principle as a linear motor. Japanese and German industries have developed competing systems. It is telling that there has been no large-scale implementation in either country; both continue conventional rail technology expansions.

- *Personal rapid transit (PRT)*: the concept is that a network of small vehicles holding two to four people operating on separated guideways will deliver individuals around the town with even more convenience than a private auto. This concept has been around since the 1960s and there is still no successful implementation.[12] It is perhaps inherently unusable, as it combines the high cost of rail infrastructure with the low capacity of automobiles. It will be very interesting to see how or whether the system proposed for Heathrow Airport materializes.

- *Jetsonmobile*: appropriately named after a TV cartoon series, the idea of using a private levitating bubble car is more interesting as a sociological statement than as a possible or feasible mode.

- *Vertical take-off (VTO) or short take-off and landing (STOL)*: an airport in every backyard or, at least, neighbourhood. Some have proposed variations of small or personal aircraft either for bypassing crowded highways or large airports. Frank Lloyd Wright toyed with the idea of individual aircraft serving sprawled exurban developments, and James Fallows has proposed developing personal aviation options that would allow individuals or small groups in small aircraft to gain access to small airports outside urban centres, bypassing the security and runway queues common to larger airports. Variations of small VTO or STOL vehicles have been published in popular mechanical and scientific magazines. There have been a few airplane-cars and gyrocopters that one could buy. But the idea of mass use is preposterous. The safety implications would be frightening, as would the air and noise pollution impacts.

Figure 4.19 Translohr rubber-tyred single-guide rail vehicle (a bus rapid transit vehicle that is otherwise like a light rail transit vehicle) blurs modal distinctions in Padua, Italy

Source: Edward A. Beimborn

Figure 4.20 The Segway Personal Transporter is a vehicle increasingly used for police patrolling in cities across the world, as seen here in one of the ubiquitous counter-flow bicycle lanes in Frankfurt, Germany

Source: Jeffrey R. Kenworthy

Conclusions

This chapter has given an overview of the numerous considerations that must be addressed when studying transportation modes. This is a complex matter because often there are no hard and fast distinctions between or within modal categories. Issues of policy, economics and cultural preferences also enter into discussions of modes. Some of the more interesting technical and planning considerations and innovations around transit are presented in a transit primer in Appendix 1 at the end of the book. The next chapter addresses freight modes and logistics, an extremely important and often neglected area needing more attention in ST discussions.

Questions for discussion

- Discuss whether one could draw accurate conclusions about the future energy efficiency of cities based primarily on the anticipated future fuel efficiency of vehicles? What are the limitations of a fuel efficiency emphasis in transportation and energy planning?
- What else gets considered in the decision to make a trip on a particular mode besides the out-of-pocket costs? Of these concerns, identify and discuss those that are inexpensive and quick to accommodate compared to those which are expensive or take a long time to accommodate.
- What else is needed to define a mode besides the physical characteristics of the vehicle?

Notes

1   For a somewhat less technical introduction to the family of modes, see Grava (2003).

2   For more information about how to retrofit existing streets with non-motorized facilities in the US, Fruin (1971) and the National Complete Streets Coalition (2009) are good sources.

3   For more, see WHO (2004a, 2004b); for dangerous conditions in Bogotá, see Bogotá city profile at www.urban-age.net/04_publications/city_profiles.html and Càmara de Comercio de Bogotá, *Observatorio de movilidad: la demanda de transporte en Bogotá* at http://camara.ccb.org.co/contenido/contenido.aspx?catID=434&conID=2294.

4   For more on the impact of off-road/trail activities, see www.americantrails.org/resources/ManageMaintain/SprungImpacts.html and www.wildlandscpr.org/ecological-impacts-mountain-biking-critical-literature-review.

5   Michael Ferro of Oakland, California, has been a rider and owner of both conventional bicycles and recumbent bicycles and tricycles.

6   See discussion of transportation energy below in this chapter, as well as the section on 'Time–area: An important tool for analysing a transportation investment' in Chapter 6.

7   For a primer on the role of ITS in both passenger service and planning, see Bruun (2007) and the transit primer in Appendix 1 of this text.

8   For example, see the Transit Cooperative Research Programme, Project Action and EU CONNECT.

9   See www.aaaexchange.com/main/Default.asp?CategoryID=16&SubCategoryID=76&ContentID=353.

10   For example, STATTAUTO in several German cities, and Carsharing.net for other worldwide resources. See also PhillyCarShare (undated).

11   For a discussion of planes versus trains in the Cascades Corridor of British Columbia, Washington and Oregon, see Schiller (2008).

12   The oft-mentioned Morgantown, Virginia, system is really an automated people mover using larger vehicles with few stops.

References and further reading

Bruun, E. (2007) 'The role of intelligent transportation systems', Chapter 4, *Better Public Transit Systems: Analyzing Investments and Performance,* APA Press, Chicago, IL

Carsharing.net (undated) www.carsharing.net/library/index.html, accessed 15 September 2009

Felau, G. (2006) *The Recumbent Bicycle*, Out Your Backdoor Press, Williamston, MI

Freund, P. and Martin, G. (1993) *The Ecology of the Automobile*, Black Rose Books, Montreal, Quebec

Fruin, J. J. (1971) *Pedestrian Planning and Design*, Metropolitan Association of Urban Designers and Environmental Planners, New York, NY

Grava, S. (2003) *Urban Transportation Systems: Choices for Communities*, McGraw Hill, New York, NY

Mapes, J. (2009) *Pedaling Revolution: How Cyclists Are Changing American Cities*, Oregon State University Press, Eugene, OR

National Complete Streets Coalition (2009) *Frequently Asked Questions*, www.completestreets.org/complete-streets-fundamentals/complete-streets-faq/, accessed 15 September 2009

Newman, P. W. G. and Kenworthy, J. R. (1989) *Cities and Automobile Dependence: A Sourcebook*, Gower Technical, Aldershot, UK, and Brookfield, VT

Newman, P. W. G. and Kenworthy, J. R. (1999) *Sustainability and Cities: Overcoming Automobile Dependence*, Island Press, Washington, DC

PhillyCarShare (undated) www.phillycarshare.org, accessed 15 September 2009

Railteam (2009) 'Welcome to railteam: Seamless high speed travel across Europe', www.railteam.co.uk, accessed 15 August 2009

Road Safety Foundation (undated) 'Too many children die on our roads', www.roadsafetyfoundation.co.za/RoadSafety/tabid/56/Default.aspx, accessed 5 September 2009

Schiller, P. L. (2008) 'Connections within the western U.S.–Canada border region: Toward more sustainable transportation practices', in J. Loucky, D. K. Alper and J. C. Day (eds) *Transboundary Policy Challenges in the Pacific Border Regions of North America*, University of Calgary Press, Calgary, Alberta, Chapter 5

SNCF (2009) 'TGV reservations', www.tgv.com/EN/index_HD.html, accessed 15 September 2009

Socialdata America (undated) http://socialdata.us/index.php, accessed 10 September 2009

STATTAUTO (undated) www.eaue.de/winuwd/86.htm, accessed 15 August 2009

Strickland, J. (2009) 'Energy efficiency of different modes of transportation', http://strickland.ca/efficiency.html, accessed 20 June 2009

Vuchic, V. R. (2007) 'Urban passenger transport modes', in V. R. Vuchic (ed) *Urban Transit: Systems and Technology*, John Wiley and Sons, Somerset, NJ

Whitelegg, J. (1993) *Transport for a Sustainable Future: The Case for Europe*, Belhaven Press, London

Whitelegg, J. (1997) *Critical Mass: Transport Environment and Society in the Twenty-First Century*, Pluto Press, London

WHO (World Health Organization) (2004a) *World Report on Road Traffic Injury Prevention*, http://whqlibdoc.who.int/publications/2004/9241562609.pdf, accessed 30 May 2009

WHO (2004b) *WHO Warns of Mounting Death Toll on Asian Roads*, www.wpro.who.int/media_centre/press_releases/pr_20040405.htm, accessed 30 May 2009

5

Moving Freight, Logistics and Supply Chains in a More Sustainable Direction

Introduction and overview

The extent and nature of freight movement around the planet presents a number of challenges for sustainable transportation – and for sustainability itself. There is increasing recognition that the freight transport system has been growing in size, complexity and the externalization of its social and environmental impacts, and is less sustainable (see Box 1.1 in Chapter 1 for a snapshot of the magnitude of freight mobility). The growth in volume of raw materials and goods puts an ever increasing strain on infrastructure and pressure to provide new facilities in a manner analogous to passenger transportation. Coupled with this volume growth is an increase in the distances that raw materials and goods get moved, which increases the amount of energy that must be expended and the pollution generated by our economic system. Figures 5.1a and 5.1b show the tremendous growth in tonne kilometres (tkm) (the product of weight of goods multiplied by the distance travelled) for both the US and the European Union since 1970. Note that despite the smaller population, the US has over double the volume of movement by all modes combined, part of which can be explained by longer transport distances. Note also the ominous decline in usage of the railroad within the European Union.

Freight hasn't received the same attention as passenger transport by environmentally oriented institutions and elected officials. This chapter intends to increase awareness of how the worldwide freight transportation system functions, and how it might be moved in a more sustainable direction. Its principal focus is the US because of its role as the largest consumer of transportation and goods. The history and trends of supply chains are reviewed and the concept of total logistics cost (TLC) is introduced. TLC is central to understanding how businesses make decisions about structuring supply chains. Suggestions about how particular elements of the system can be improved are included and a discussion of public policies that can promote sustainability concludes the chapter.

Freight logistical systems are complex and do not lend themselves to simple interventions or quick redirection. Transportation itself is but one of several factors comprising this larger logistical system. Thus, it is best to understand

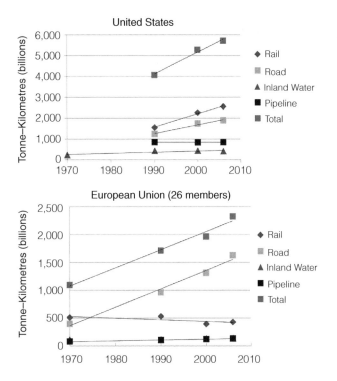

Figure 5.1 (a) Trend of freight movement, US; (b) trend of freight movement, European Union

Source: International Transport Forum (2007)

freight movement in the broader context of supply chains and the logistical considerations shaping shipping strategies. The conventional or business as usual (BAU) functioning of some logistical systems will be presented and then compared with a more sustainable orientation.

Some freight movement has been global in nature for several centuries. Some regions simply depended upon fuel and certain foods that were impossible to obtain nearby, and the wealthy always had a taste for the exotic. But contemporary globalization has added to the size, complexity and reach of freight transport so that logistical support systems and worldwide transport networks are needed. Now, even things that were previously available locally are often obtained from sources that are across continents and oceans.

Most short-term to medium-term decision-making about freight logistics is done within the private sector. A typical freight movement, or shipment, might involve several private- and public-sector interests. The public-sector role is usually limited to regulatory functions. In the longer term, there is some involvement with infrastructure planning, development and operation. The levels at which public-sector involvement and its extent and effectiveness in shaping freight logistics occur may vary from one society to another and from one mode or product sector to another. As with passenger transport, there is continuing pressure on governments to support the capacity expansion needs of private interests, largely for private benefit. At the same time, there is pressure from the public to mitigate the negative impacts, which include truck traffic congestion, excessive road damages, the severity of crash incidents involving trucks in comparison to smaller motor vehicles, large amounts of land devoted to freight facilities, and pollution from all motorized freight modes.

BAU logistics, and the freight movement part, in particular, affect social and environmental sustainability in several ways:

- energy consumption and pollution;
- social equity: artificially cheap transportation creates market and wage and labour distortions;
- accessibility equity: the accessibility needs of disadvantaged people are neglected;
- overdependence upon trucking leads to emphasis on, and expansion pressures for, roads;

- infrastructure demands, especially for highway freight modes, are very land consuming;
- overdependence upon a limited number of major ports and intermodal transfer locations leads to severe impacts in select locations and abandonment of others.

Background to current freight movement factors

Freight and trade considerations have shaped the location and development of cities for millennia. Centuries ago, shipping across large bodies of water or along coasts, rivers and canals was one of the only ways to transport substantial volumes of heavy goods for long distances. Many, if not most, cities evolved at trans-shipment points and their fortunes ebbed and waned with changes in the types of goods shipped and the modes and techniques used for shipping. Chicago has been an important freight hub since its inception. Philadelphia and New York developed on rivers fed by major canal systems and had natural sea harbours; their domestic and international trade thrived. The canals were later superseded, first by rail and then by truck networks. The London Docklands area was once the transfer hub at the centre of the British Empire, but it has been superseded by dispersion to ports in other cities in the UK. Such evolution is ongoing.

As industries diversified and populations grew quickly, cities such as these hubs became major generators of freight demand in themselves. The convenience of the locations for many manufacturing and process industries made them logical industrial centres. Their use of ever greater volumes of raw materials stimulated the warehousing and financial sectors that supported them. As wealth began to increase, demand expanded into purchases of luxury goods and foods from a worldwide market. Logistical systems have continually grown to support trans-shipment, industry and local consumption. As they have grown, communities have seen dramatic changes, both positive and negative.

Over time, improved technologies and vehicle designs lowered transport costs. During the late 19th and early 20th centuries, motorization increased the speed and capacity of ocean-going vessels considerably, while the speed and cargo capacity of land-based modes, especially trains, similarly increased. Trains using boxcars and flatcars for solid cargo, and tanker cars for liquid and gaseous cargoes, could move huge quantities to many more places faster than 19th-century canal barges. Large quantities of liquids and gases could be inexpensively moved by pipelines over long distances. These improvements joined with several nation-specific, as well as international economic and policy, factors to engender a vast expansion of freight movement in recent decades. In order to understand this development, as well as how freight movement can become more sustainable, it is necessary to review its conventions.

Factors that shape freight movement: Supply chains, logistical systems and shipping strategies

Freight transport is best discussed in the context of supply chains. The concept can be understood with Figure 5.2, a typical retailing supply chain. Numerous raw materials and subassemblies of a bigger product can flow down this supply

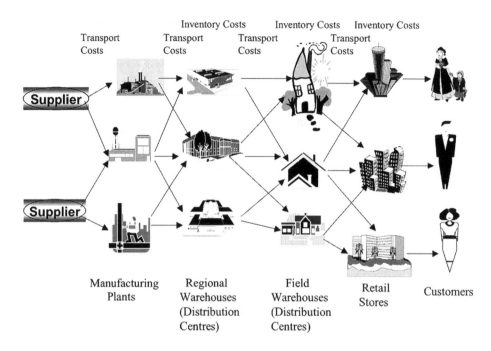

Figure 5.2 Typical supply chain for consumer goods figure

Source: Danny Cho

chain, entering and exiting at different points. A variety of transportation modes may be used and materials may be stored at multiple locations before the final product reaches the end user. The major components of this relatively simple supply chain are:

- suppliers who may produce a variety of works in progress, raw materials from resource extraction, fuels, etc. (manufacturers and process industries);
- manufacturing plants that generate materials and fuels used in manufacturing, agriculture, heating, etc.;
- storage, loading and trans-shipment facilities (regional and field warehouses);
- end users (retail stores, customers).

In addition to these major physical components there are several other factors that influence the development of shipping strategies, each of which needs to be considered along with the interplay between them, making this a very complex matter:

- the quantities and type(s) of freight to be transported, whether bulk (liquid or solid), break bulk (items that are neither bulk nor containerized), outsized items (e.g. large construction girders or beams, large turbines, etc.), containerized, perishable or time-sensitive items (foods, live animals, etc.);

- distance(s) between origins, processing, transfer and storage points and final destinations;
- distribution considerations and availability of storage facilities;
- geographical, topological and climate characteristic of distances to be transported: ocean, inland waters, land, air, weather;
- modes and infrastructure characteristics and availability: ports, railways (rail lines and rolling stock), intermodal facilities, storage facilities, highways;
- relative shipping rates for the various modal options;
- economic, policy and governance factors: whether or to what extent aspects of the supply chain are subsidized, regulated, subject to taxation, whether there is competition or monopolistic control, whether all costs are internalized or externalized (see Chapter 6 for further detail);
- business and market factors: market demands and expectations of customers, seasonality.

The concept of supply chain management (SCM) can be understood as the sum total of this decision-making environment in which the professional staffs of shipping companies develop their supply chains and shipping strategies and policy-makers make their investment and pricing decisions. In order to understand how the key logistical system elements work together to influence supply chains and shipping strategies, it is first necessary to review freight transport infrastructure and modes.

Freight transport infrastructure and fleets

The major forms of US freight transport infrastructure and some of the types within each are as follows:

- roads: limited access, interstate, urban, rural, paved, unpaved (the US Interstate System is also a limited-access road system, but distinctly separate);
- rail lines: Class 1 – major freight and passenger, short lines (Class 1 railroads are very large railroads with networks spanning significant portions of the continent, while short lines operate only locally with connections to larger railroads; in the US, Amtrak is the only national passenger railroad, operating on Class 1 railroads, with the exception of the Northeast Corridor);
- inland waterways (major canals and locks, navigable channels);
- seaports (large containerized; special ports for bulk such as coal, minerals, lumber, steel products, grains, etc.; and special, sometimes offshore, oil and oil products ports);
- airports (commercial, shared military–commercial, private non-commercial);
- pipelines (mostly for oil and gas).

Table 5.1 presents a snapshot of the size and extent of freight infrastructure in the US in 2002. Table 5.2 shows the trend in infrastructure extension over 45

Table 5.1 Major elements of the US freight transportation system, 2002

Mode	System extent
Highway	**Public roads** 46,769 miles of Interstate highway 115,032 miles of other National Highway System roads 3,828,046 miles of other roads
Air	**Public-use airports** 5286 airports
Rail	**Miles of railroad operated** 98,944 miles by Class I freight railroads in the United States 15,648 miles by regional freight railroads
Water	26,347 miles by local freight railroads 26,000 miles of navigable waterways **Commercial waterway facilities** Great Lakes: 600 deep-draft, 154 shallow-draft Inland: 2361 shallow-draft Ocean: 4284 deep-draft, 1765 shallow-draft Locks: 275
Pipeline	**Oil** Crude lines: 64,336 miles of pipe Product lines: 75,565 miles of pipe **Gas** Transmission: 309,503 miles of pipe Distribution: 1,079,565 miles of pipe

Note: 1 mile = 1.67km.
Source: Freight in America (2006, Table 2a), www.bts.gov/publications/freight_in_america/

Table 5.2 System mileage by year within the US

	1960	1970	1980	1990	2000	2005
Highway	3,545,693	3,730,082	3,859,837	3,866,926	3,936,222	3,995,635
Class 1 rail	207,334	196,479	164,822	119,758	99,250	95,830
Navigable channels	25,000	26,000	26,000	26,000	26,000	26,000
Oil pipeline	190,944	218,671	218,393	208,752	176,996	162,829
Gas pipeline	630,950	913,267	1,051,774	1,189,200	1,369,300	1,437,500

Note: 1 mile = 1.67km. Refer to original table source (below) for detailed notes on sources of data.
Source: US Bureau of Transportation Statistics (2007), Table 1-1, www.bts.gov/publications/national_transportation_statistics/2007/html/table_01_01.html

years. Note that there has been only a rather small change in road length (linear) of less than 13 per cent between 1960 and 2005. While the linear expanse of roads has not increased significantly, other data indicate that there has been considerable road widening during this time period so that the total number of lane miles has actually grown substantially, especially on major urban arterials and freeways. This was generally done primarily to accommodate peak-hour automobile traffic and suburban commutes, as new facilities

Table 5.3 Number of vehicles, aircraft, railcars and vessels

	1980	1990	2000	2002
Highway				
Passenger cars plus other 2-axle 4-tyre vehicles	149,186,777	181,975,051	212,706,399	220,931,982
Truck, single-unit 2-axle 6-tyre or more	4,373,784	4,486,981	5,926,030	5,650,619
Truck, combination	1,416,869	1,708,895	2,096,619	2,276,661
Truck, total	5,790,653	6,195,876	8,022,649	7,927,280
Air				
Air carriers	3808	6083	8055	8194
Rail				
Class 1, locomotive	28,094	18,835	20,028	20,506
Class 1, freight cars[1]	1,168,114	658,902	560,154	477,751
Non-class I freight cars[1]	102,161	103,527	132,448	130,590
Railcar companies and shippers' freight cars[1]	440,552	449,832	688,194	691,329
Water	**38,788**	**39,445**	**41,354**	**41,002**
Non-self-propelled vessels[2]	31,662	31,209	33,152	32,381
Self-propelled vessels[3]	7126	8236	8202	8621
Ocean-going steam and motor ships[4]	864	636	454	426

[1] Beginning with 2001 data, Canadian-owned US railroads are excluded. This accounted for about 47,000 cars in 2000.

[2] Non-self-propelled vessels include dry-cargo barges, tank barges and railroad-car floats.

[3] Self-propelled vessels include dry cargo, passenger, off-shore support, tankers and towboats.

[4] 1000 gross tons and over.

Sources: US Bureau of Transportation Statistics (2006b), Table 9, www.bts.gov/publications/freight_in_america/);
US Bureau of Transportation Statistics (2007, Table 1-11, www.bts.gov/publications/national_transportation_statistics/2007/html/
table_01_11.html)

primarily for the benefit of trucks are rare – although trucking interests have generally been very active in supporting road expansions.

Table 5.3 shows the trend in various US modal fleet sizes in the 22 years from 1980 leading up to 2002. The year 1980 is significant as it was the year that railroads were deregulated under the Staggers Act. Over this time period, the truck fleet size increased by about 37 per cent. During this same period, there was a substantial decrease in railroad track length, as the major (Class 1) railroads abandoned track, much of which was reduction of double track into single track. But the reduction in locomotives cannot be assumed to be due to a reduction in traffic. Larger locomotives of higher horsepower supplanted older ones. The large increase in airliner fleet size was mostly due to passenger transport deregulation, and largely of airplanes of smaller sizes. But it did add substantially to the airfreight lift capacity available. The relatively small number of US Flag ocean-going ships is due to the registering of vessels in other nations under 'flags of convenience'. This issue will be discussed in the section on 'Ocean shipping reforms' in this chapter.

Freight fleets and their usage

Table 5.4 summarizes the vehicle miles (vmi) travelled by the land-based fleets, with personal vehicles added for comparison. Air cargo conveyances are

Table 5.4 US vehicle miles of selected modes (millions)

	1960	1970	1980	1990	2000	2002	2005
Highway, total	**718,762**	**1,102,201**	**1,529,022**	**2,129,079**	**2,746,925**	**2,855,508**	[R] **2,949,578**
Passenger car plus other 2-axle 4-tyre vehicles	587,012	1,039,986	1,420,531	1,982,837	2,523,346	2,624,508	[R] 2,727,054
Truck, single-unit 2-axle 6-tyre or more	98,551	27,081	39,813	51,901	70,500	75,866	[R] 78,496
Truck, combination	28,854	35,134	68,678	94,341	135,020	138,737	[R] 144,028
Truck, total	127,405	62,215	108,491	146,242	205,520	214,603	[R] 222,524
Rail							
Class 1 freight, train-miles	404	427	428	380	504	500	548
Class 1 freight, car-miles	28,170	29,890	29,277	26,159	34,590	34,680	37,712
Intercity/Amtrak1, train-miles	209	93	30	33	35	38	36
Total train-miles1	**613**	**520**	**458**	**413**	**539**	**537**	**584**

Note: 1 mile = 1.67km. [R] = Revised. See original source for notes on data.

Source: US Bureau of Transportation Statistics (2008a), Table 1-32, www.bts.gov/publications/national_transportation_statistics/2007/html/table_01_32.html

excluded from the fleet data because of the complicating factor of freight carried by dedicated cargo planes, as well as in the bellies of commercial flights. The number of personal vehicles (passenger cars, SUVs, light trucks) and freight vehicles both increased greatly between 1980 and 2002, although the ratio of trucks to personal vehicles decreased slightly from 3.9 to 3.6 per cent of the total. But trucks, especially larger (combination or tractor-trailer) trucks annually log many more vehicle miles (vehicle kilometres) than do personal vehicles. Indeed, the ratio increased somewhat during this time period, from 7.6 to 8.1 per cent of annual vehicle miles travelled (vmt), indicating that use has been intensifying.

Trucks and highways expand; rail shrinks

Interactions between freight modes and infrastructure also merit attention. Trucks obtained increasing advantage as more roads were built. Underinvestment in rail infrastructure paralleled highway expansion in the US after World War II. As highways expanded more grade separations were needed so that roads could pass under or over rail lines and not create conflicts or force trains to operate at lower speeds. While such grade separations were often provided along interstate highways, their needs in urban and rural areas were not adequately met.

Compounding the intensity of competition was the subsidization of trucking. In comparison, the railroads remained tightly regulated by the Interstate Commerce Commission (ICC) regarding tariffs and service requirements. They were responsible for the maintenance of their own rights of way, unlike trucking companies that could externalize substantial portions of their operating costs. Fuel taxes and registration fees were not even sufficient to cover the cost of maintaining roads, especially given that trucks do disproportionate damage relative to automobiles due to their much higher axle loadings. This subsidy remains in effect even in modern times. A thorough study performed by Delucchi (1996–1997) estimated that motor vehicles in the US cover only about 60 per cent of their direct costs, with trucks covering less and autos more. Since the federal fuel taxes have not increased since 1993 and they are a per-gallon rather than per-dollar assessment, this percentage continues to drop.

Figure 5.3 Truck-to-truck transfer facilities require much space, inside and outside, and a location near a major highway

Source: Eric C. Bruun

As a result of this uneven competition, during the same post-World War II period there was substantial consolidation among railroads and the abandonment of many rail lines that were not deemed profitable. Many of the remaining lines deteriorated as maintenance was reduced. European rail networks had an additional disadvantage: incompatible locomotives between national networks and border delays. Consequently, in most of the more industrialized nations, trucking gained more advantage over rail: truck speeds increased while rail speeds decreased, and highways and many areas formerly served by railroads could now only be served by trucks. Higher speed also enabled truck shipment of perishable goods over a wider range.

In general, almost all of the more developed nations in this same period saw a continued densification of the network of paved roads. Indeed, trucks and other delivery vehicles specialized to the size needed for the given payload and access requirements make them ubiquitous from the smallest town to the biggest city, and from remote resource extraction sites to ports connected to the entire world.

Freight modes, network and transfers

If a truck can be entirely filled by one shipper it has the advantage of being able to go directly from one loading dock to another. If a single shipper can't fill an entire container or trailer, a common situation for smaller businesses, then it can hire firms that do less-than-truckload (LTL) operations. These involve consolidating pallets of cargo moving in the same direction at warehousing and distribution centres. LTL comes with a trade-off of lower cost, but also longer time than direct shipping of a full truck. The shipment can either be picked up at the nearest distribution centre or it can be delivered directly to the end user at extra cost.

The rail mode provides a more limited network. A factory or warehouse with rail sidings could directly receive railcars, or a factory might be co-located with a seaport. Other interregional movements not so conveniently located eventually required some form of local distribution by truck in time-consuming loading and unloading processes. Matson Lines of Hawaii designed a solution to this recurring problem of multiple transfers and applied it to their sea operations.

Since unified currency and open borders became a reality, the European Union has removed a lot of the power of what were previously national railway monopolies or near monopolies. It has mandated 'open access' such that any prospective private operator wishing to run trains must be permitted to do so at a reasonable price. There are already a few companies that are running their own trains, and this is expected to increase in the future. This opens up new possibilities of multiple freight operators on the same line, something that has historically been rare. The longer-term implications remain to be seen.

Containerization and intermodal transfer

During the 1950s, Matson's solution quickly transformed the industry with its standardized intermodal containers. These containers are either 20 foot or 40 foot in length, and ships, trailers and railcars are all designed to accept them. Capacity of vehicles and vessels is now defined by 20 foot equivalent units (teu). Thus, a slot will be designed to hold two 20 foot containers or one 40 foot container, both of which constitute 2 teu.

Using containers lowered transportation costs and increased average speed across the supply chain. Containers can be loaded and offloaded from ships with large cranes in a fraction of the time of the older more labour-intensive methods. They can also be relatively quickly stacked for storage, and shifted on and off trucks and trains. Specialized refrigerated containers have enabled movement of perishables over long distances. Bulk cargoes such as grain and oil continue to move by bulk freighters and tankers when water crossings are required.

Figure 5.4 Container ships can carry several thousands of 20 foot equivalent units

Source: Eric C. Bruun

Truck and train intermodalism

There are some situations where containers can be directly transferred between ships and trains, thus taking advantage of the energy efficiencies of each mode. Containers can be double-stacked on rail cars where tunnels and underpasses allow sufficient clearance. In the US and Europe most intercontinental freight transfer is between ship and truck; but a significant amount also moves between ship and train at ports with train access. There has been marked success in shifting interregional movements of trailers and containers from truck to intermodal truck/train in the US and Canada, where distances are long. Since the 1980s, productivity increased with the introduction of the aforementioned double-stacked container trains. But a 40 foot container moving under about 1000km (600 miles) would most likely still go solely by truck in most regions. Reducing this distance remains a high priority in both academia and in railroad-operating companies. Techniques for doing this are discussed in a later section.

The most common intermodal transfer of containers in the US occurs between trucks and trains, where trains haul the container for distances over 600 miles. A variant that has existed for some time is 'piggybacking', also known as trailer on flatcar (TOFC). The mounting of wagons or trailer-like conveyances on a rail car began with the pre-truck era needs of Barnum & Bailey's Circus during the late 19th century. Another variant gaining in popularity is trucks on trains (TOT) or roll on, roll off (RORO), where a truck and trailer are driven onto a flatcar and transported together as a unit. Because of the weight and space implications of carrying a tractor on the train along with a trailer, these were historically mostly used across mountains and in other applications where trucks did not perform well. More recently, special facilities have been developed to efficiently drive trucks and trailers onto and off flatcars so that the many advantages of long-distance conveyance by train can be combined with the need to use trucks and trailers for the beginnings and ends of many freight trips. This will be discussed further in connection with shortening the breakeven distance of intermodal truck–rail services.

Airfreight

In the early days of aviation, not much more than mail and military-related cargo was carried by plane. The world's airlines mostly developed as a regulated industry, and cargo was usually carried in the belly, along with a limited fleet of pure air-freighters. The airfreight market was deregulated in 1977 in the US and quickly expanded across the globe. The rapid growth of FedEx, UPS and DHL and similar couriers was a reflection of large pent-up demand to send certain documents and high-value hardware quickly. Couriers and almost all other airfreight providers are heavily dependent upon trucks for pick-up and drop-off and are thus inherently intermodal operators.

Cargoes of very high value-to-weight ratio or cargoes that need to be delivered quickly over medium to long distances tend to go by air, and their volume had increased at a rapid pace for decades. But the use of the internet and electronic signatures has begun to reduce the need for courier services. Internet shopping and direct-to-consumer sales are replacing them. As with the rest of the logistical system, the airfreight sector continually evolves.

Inequities and contrasts between wealthy and less wealthy countries

In the less developed world, the contrast can be quite stark to the sophisticated supply chain infrastructure and vehicles of the richer countries. In many countries, infrastructure investments during the 20th century were targeted primarily at assisting export industries. This would mean the construction of roads and railways connecting to ports, port facilities, free-trade zones and so on. As a result, the road network and support infrastructure did not extend towards much of the interior, and small businesspeople and farmers may still have difficulty getting to the market in the nearest town due to poor roads. Reliance upon pack animals and women carrying backbreaking loads is still common in many developing countries.

Poor roads often become impassable at certain times of the year. Compounding the problem is the lack of suitable vehicles. Lack of purchasing power by rural people has meant that few manufacturers build vehicles, un-motorized or motorized, to meet their needs. Rural areas often stagnate due to lack of links to the larger logistical systems, and even to local and regional destinations.

Some important trends: 'Biggering' the modes and infrastructure

Maritime modes

The worldwide trend has been towards ever larger vehicles for the longer-distance or 'line haul' movements. It has been especially dramatic in the oceanic shipping business. The tremendous increase in exports from East Asia to Europe and North America has been accompanied by a huge increase in container ships plying the world's trade routes. Container ships that carry as many as 8000 teu are becoming common. Oil tankers now displace up to four times what a US Navy 'super carrier' displaces, but with only a tiny fraction of the horsepower. Associated with the increased size are public investments in deeper ports, more waterfront acquisitions, larger cranes, and more congestion from trucks entering and exiting ever expanding ports. Indeed, in some cities, the seaport has come to dominate the waterfront, leaving limited public access for other uses.

Rail

Trains have become larger and longer while reducing crew. In North America, trains can reach up to 1.6km (1 mile) in length with several locomotives and only two crewmembers. Boxcars have become wider and taller and test the limits of operating envelopes. Unit trains carry containers on double-stack railcars between mega-terminals with no intermediate stops for dropping or adding cars in order to beat truck transit times. Although not as large as in North America, rolling stock has become larger in Europe as well, while locomotives that are compatible with infrastructure in multiple countries are reducing transit times by eliminating switching of equipment at borders.

Figure 5.5 Double-stack container trains can be up to 1 mile (1.6km) long

Source: Eric C. Bruun

Airliners

Airliners have become larger and the productivity of vehicles and crews has increased substantially. As the volume of global trade has increased, the concentration of traffic along certain air corridors has multiplied as well, justifying capacity increases through large dedicated air-freighters. These supplement greater belly capacity and increasing commercial flights. Airfreight is typically moved through hub-and-spoke terminals, which has required investment in very large facilities at key airports and generated significant night-time air and truck traffic.

Recently, the number of smaller cities being served by airlines has reduced as a cost-cutting measure. This is leaving many towns without a means for high-priority shipments such as repair supplies for industry and surgical supplies and pharmaceuticals. Filling this gap is perhaps an opportunity to use public policy to encourage more sustainable replacement options.

Trucks

Trucks have not increased in size to the same extent as other modes. They have basically stayed for decades in the 40 tonne range for a semi-trailer configuration, otherwise known as an '18-wheeler'. However, longer trailers in the range of 53 feet (16m) have been allowed in many places and are commonly used if the contents don't need to be intermodally connected. There are many exceptions, such as the truck-trains that operate in the outback of Australia, and permits to exceed weight and dimension restrictions for outsized cargo are regularly granted elsewhere. There are periodic attempts to get regulations changed to permit larger trucks in both North America and Europe; but these are usually defeated by coalitions of railroad, environmental and safety interests.

In the less developed countries, trucks tend to be older and less specialized for their particular tasks. They also tend to be in poorer condition due to lack of regulatory enforcement and insufficient profitability to afford new equipment. Highly polluting engines are a health hazard, while overloaded trucks with poorly maintained brakes and worn tyres are a safety hazard.

Shipment size and speed considerations

In general, the slower the mode, the lower the transport cost on a per unit distance basis. But slower modes have less area coverage of a nation or region; rail isn't as ubiquitous as roads, while ships and barges are limited to ports and rivers. Trans-shipment to a road-based mode may well be necessary from the origination point and to the final destination. The slowness may also represent a significant cost of capital tied-up holding assets in 'moving warehouses'. Trans-shipment and asset ownership costs will often offset some or all cost savings from using slow modes. Therefore, in general, only low to moderate value items are moved in slow modes, such as boxcars, when faster options such as trucking are available. The values can range much higher for ocean shipping as the only alternative is often very costly airfreight.

Larger shipment quantities cost less on a per unit distance basis than do smaller ones. But the shipment quantities that yield significant shipping cost reductions may be far more than is immediately needed, thus introducing the need for committing capital to inventory ownership, plus ownership, leasing, operation and maintenance of storage facilities. Consequently, there may be trade-offs between sending large shipments infrequently with slower, less expensive modes and smaller shipments more frequently with faster, more expensive modes.

From haul to mall to home

The sector of customer or end user of consumer goods supply chains has grown considerably. Before urban form was adapted to the use of private automobiles, shopping was done locally, often daily, due to the limited amount that one person could carry and the convenient co-locating of stores with residential areas. Large items were delivered as a service by the selling company or by couriers. UPS began as a company focused on department store home deliveries.

The externalities generated by 'haul to mall' are generally not included in the design of most supply chains since private firms generally don't concern themselves with this part of the supply chain unless the retail store is bypassed by use of direct-to-consumer sales. Given the reality of the urban form that is already extant, the question needs to be asked whether it is better for consumers to come to the store, or the store to deliver to consumers. The limited research to date tends to be either inconclusive or difficult to generalize. Whether home delivery can be more efficient depends upon many factors, such as who else in the area needs deliveries, how tight the delivery window must be, whether someone needs to be available to receive the goods, how much the consumer would otherwise buy on one shopping trip, and other complications. Moreover, shopping is often linked to recreational activities and the trip might occur anyway. What is known for certain is that stores in closer proximity to end users are better than farther away, so future developments can be built to reduce these externalities from the outset and existing communities might possibly be retrofitted.

Logistics of systems integrators

The subject of 'logistics' refers to designing and managing supply chains such that numerous trade-offs are given due consideration. Many firms are 'systems integrators', incorporating materials and subassemblies from all over the world. The current state of professional practice is to consider the entire supply chain within the production planning process and sales and marketing strategies. The locations of facilities, the ordering of supplies and the scheduling and sizing of the production batches should be coordinated at one end with marketing and sales efforts, and at the other end with transportation and distribution efforts. The result is a reduction in undue inventory-holding costs and production costs and delays. Much effort goes into establishing the right amount of 'safety stock' to avoid production shutdowns and losses of sales due to 'stocking out'. One of the techniques is to try to receive deliveries just in time (JIT); but this is often impeded by increasing congestion in the transportation network, which decreases the predictability of delivery times. JIT also implies increased

Box 5.1 Yogurt on wheels

Stefanie Böge's 'The well-travelled yogurt pot' (Böge, 1995) demonstrates the extensiveness of supply chains and their externalization of costs and pollution for a taken-for-granted product such as a small jar of yogurt. The complex map of product flows, from raw materials through production to the retail shelf, is shown in Figure 5.6, followed by explanatory text.

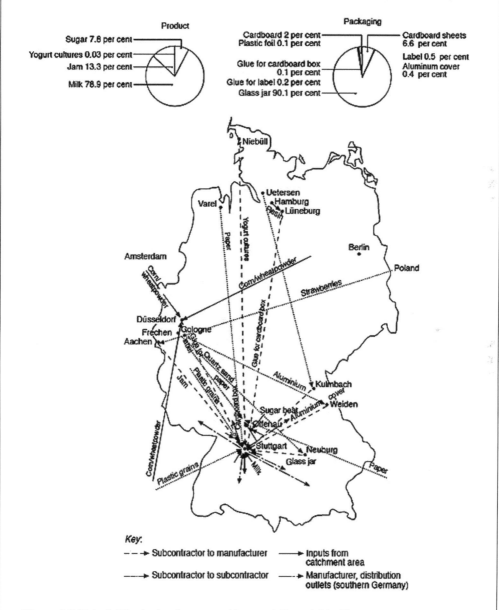

Figure 5.6 Stefanie Böge's strawberry yogurt transportation relationships

Source: Stefanie Böge, Wuppertal Institut, 1993

Strawberries from Stefanie:

- To bring one truckload of product to a distribution outlet in southern Germany, one 'theoretical' truck (including all examined relationships) must be moved 1005km. In 1992, theoretically, 24 fully packed lorries with 150g pots of strawberry yogurt had to be moved each over this distance to supply the southern German area with this product (Böge, 1995, p8).
- Higher transportation costs, which depend largely on higher petrol or diesel costs, have considerable impacts on the internal cost structures of manufacturers. With the increase of diesel costs in which the external costs are internalized so far as possible, the total transport costs of the yogurt manufacturer would increase by about 21 to 65 per cent (Böge, 1995, p8).
- On the basis of the specific distance covered, one 150g strawberry yogurt has used 0.004 litres of diesel if it is distributed in southern Germany. To sell the sales quantities for 1992, 24 lorries had to be used, and for them 10,200 litres of diesel (Böge, 1995, p8).
- But, at the same time, it is remarkable, that so-called 'environmental' products are not environmental if the distances travelled are included. Specifically, the greater distances are from the manufacturer to the supermarket. The longer the distances are for a product, the more environmental impacts result. The demand of the consumers to buy everything everywhere and at any time has direct consequences [for] freight shipment. Increasing demands in this direction increase the effects on the environment and on lifestyle. The existing production system based on the externalization of costs is supported. Consumer behaviour plays a part in forming production and distribution systems. Last, but not least, there is no detailed information for consumers on the connections between production and consumption (Böge, 1995, p10).
- The strawberry yogurt included a new ingredient: a distance of approximately 10m of lorry movement. This does not seem a lot, but it is enough to make looking in your own trolley [shopping cart] or refrigerator worthwhile. In it there is a great sum of distances, which mostly result from [the] distant manufacturing of these products. Besides the consumption of these products, distances are consumed, which have, because of the means of transportation (the lorry), considerable effects on the natural and human environment (Böge, 1995, p11).
- Those negative effects of products that are the result of their transportation processes can be reduced by paying attention to buying regional and seasonal products. 'Ecological' products are regionally and seasonally differentiated products. If food is purchased which has been grown in the neighbourhood and in the appropriate season, long distances of freight shipment are also avoided (Böge, 1995, p11).

Source: Böge (1995), with permission

externalization of warehousing costs: rather than making large shipments to a warehouse, there are many smaller 'warehouses' that are on wheels with concomitant trucking pollution, highway damage and congestion.

Problems of global supply chains

Longer supply chains imply more energy consumption and pollution generation. Because many transportation costs are not fully internalized, the prices paid at all steps in the chain by shippers fail to reflect the full cost. Of particular concern is the consumption of non-renewable resources and the long-term environmental damage to ecosystems. Prices for consumption and extraction of input material are based on their short-term costs, as the discount rate used by commercial firms to express the time value of money devalues anything to almost zero within 15 to 30 years (see Chapter 6). Such discounting works against sustainable development in all facets of society, including transportation. Daly and Cobb's (1989) work was an early critique of BAU in all facets of society, including transportation.

Supply chains have become increasingly imbalanced, often with very large differences in flow in opposite directions. This results in poor use of available capacity and much larger fleets than would be required if trading volumes in both directions were more equal. The imbalance of shipping between the US and China, in particular, has become extreme, as is shown in Figure 5.7. Furthermore, this imbalance is characterized by raw or scrap materials moving West and then returning East as finished products. Examples include shipping raw logs that return as furniture and used paper that is recycled via a trip back and forth to China. Why such clearly energy wasteful moves occur is explained by the concept of total logistics cost.

Total logistics cost: Widgets near or widgets far?

The basic method taught to supply chain professionals for deciding upon shipment size and suitable price/performance package for transportation is based on trading off the annual cost of ordering product versus the annual cost of holding product. Ordering cost is largely independent of how much is ordered, so it is cheaper to order in large quantities. But then one has to pay the cost of owning and storing larger quantities of product until it is needed. There is an optimal order size that is a trade-off between the two known as the economic order quantity (EOQ).[1] Added to this is the cost of transportation, since one source of product might be much closer than another, or it might have better shipping service options. Together, these three costs – ordering, owning and storing – form the total logistics cost (TLC) when the product costs the same from all sources. One should then order from the source with the lowest TLC. The following is a simple example that will then be extended to a case where the product cost is not the same from all sources.

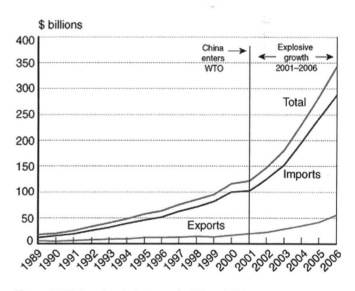

Figure 5.7 Value of trade between the US and China per year

Source: reprinted from US Bureau of Transportation Statistics (2008b); primary source: US Census Bureau (2008)

Assume a widget costs US$100 per unit and a factory needs 1250 per year, as it consumes five every weekday. An administrative cost of US$6.25 is imposed every time an order is placed. The annual holding cost of inventory is 25 per cent of the annual purchase cost. The EOQ can be computed to be 25 units. Thus, orders should be placed 50 times per year. The transportation or shipping cost is another US$50 per shipment for a total of $2500 per year. The winning candidate from the domestic market then has a TLC of US$3125.

However, when widget prices are different from different suppliers, one needs to take this into account by adding the total annual purchase cost onto the TLC. Let us now assume that the product costs only US$10 from overseas in comparison to $100 domestically. The EOQ is now computed as 79 units and orders should be placed 15.8 (say 16) times per year. As a result of the source being overseas, the transportation cost is now ten times as much, or US$500 per shipment, for a total annual cost of $8000. The TLC subtotal for this option is US$8197.50, substantially higher than the domestic option. But when the total annual purchase cost is added to each, a very different picture emerges. For the nearby option, this annual purchase cost is 1250 x $100 = $125,000. For the faraway option, the cost is only 1250 x $10 = $12,500. Adding these onto their respective subtotals, the faraway option is vastly cheaper, less than one fifth the total cost. In fact, it is so much cheaper that there really isn't any point in even doing the TLC calculation as the far lower purchase cost dominates the decision (see Tables 5.5 and 5.6).

This example is typical for most, but not all, categories of manufactured products. For most categories, the significant decrease in production cost far outweighs the increase in shipping costs. In the example shown here, even if transportation costs were to quadruple, it still would not persuade companies to buy locally when the purchase price difference is so large. For such products, even large increases in fuel taxes are unlikely to encourage local purchase.

Table 5.5 Total logistics cost for widget available nearby

Ordering costs		$312.50
+ Holding costs		$312.50
+ Transportation costs		$2500.00
	Subtotal:	$3125.00
+ Nearby purchase cost		$125,000.00
	Total:	$128,125.00

Table 5.6 Total logistics cost for widget available far away

Ordering costs		$98.80
+ Holding costs		$98.80
+ Transportation costs		$8000.00
	Subtotal:	$8197.60
+ Faraway purchase costs		$12,500.00
	Total:	$20,697.50

Elements aimed at increasing freight sustainability

There are several ways to move supply chains in a more sustainable direction, some of which are more germane to supply chains involving heavy reliance on one particular mode than to all modes. These include:

- increasing the efficiency of freight vehicles;
- differentiation of the fleet, especially at the level of smaller and non-motorized vehicles;
- more efficient scheduling and vehicle use;
- improved intermodal services and facilities;
- policy efforts to promote shifting the truck–train breakeven point towards rail;
- ocean shipping reforms;

- shifting some airfreight to higher speed rail services;
- reverse logistics;
- redistribution of sourcing;
- shortening supply chains;
- policies to promote shortening distances and reducing volumes of freight.

Increasing the efficiency of freight vehicles

Road goods transport vehicles, especially heavier trucks and tractors for semi-trailer configurations, have generally become more efficient and lighter for any given payload range. Until recently, European vehicles tended to be more efficient than North American vehicles, as higher fuel prices justified more efficient and expensive engines and other efficiency components. For urban stop-and-go operations, such as delivery trucks and vans, hybrid vehicles are beginning to displace traditional internal combustion engine (ICE) fleets, as their pollution and energy consumption reductions are significant. Nevertheless, more efficient vehicles will not be sufficient, as demonstrated by the earlier example of the relatively small role played by fuel in freight cost structure for many products.

Differentiation and equitability of the fleet: Smaller motorized and non-motorized vehicles

There is a need for a more differentiated freight fleet, especially at the level of smaller and in-town vehicles. There are many small freight deliveries or consumer trips in developed countries that can be made with smaller, more efficient motorized or non-motorized vehicles, such as cargo motorcycles (sometimes three-wheelers) or cargo bicycles or bicycle trailers, if infrastructure and protective measures are put in place to promote such a change.

This is especially needed in developing countries where freight vehicles tend to be of obsolete design and poorly maintained, making their replacement even more urgent. Poorer economies face higher operating costs for their supply chains as well as higher externalities, such as pollution and accidents. Vehicles tend to be less tailored to their task as the owner-operators' narrow profit margins only allow them to have trucks that can serve multiple purposes. There are also compelling needs for better freight motorcycles and bicycles in developing countries; but apparently the profit margin isn't sufficient to attract enough manufacturers' interest. This is in stark contrast to the situation of the richest countries where some people drive a large SUV to carry a payload consisting of a package of cigarettes or a yogurt jar. In the poorest countries, women often carry heavy loads on their heads or backs to market. This is an area that should be considered for a large increase in developmental aid; greater variety of appropriate vehicles and infrastructure could bolster efforts to promote micro-economic betterment.[2]

There is a general rule to consider when judging policies that promote or discourage a particular type of vehicle purchase. If the policy promotes downward migration, it is positive. Examples would be replacement of delivery vans with a small motorcycle or three-wheeled variant and a guarantee of parking, replacement of a moped with a lightweight and strong bicycle, and guarantee of an uncongested bicycle lane network. Exceptions where upward migration should be accepted would be for those currently suffering from excessive reliance on their own strength or on beasts of burden for freight transport.

More efficient scheduling and vehicle use

There is considerable potential for reducing the empty movements and waiting times of long-distance trucks, improving both the profitability of a chronically distressed sector and sustainability. Internet sites already provide load matching services enabling carriers to seek shippers near their last drop-off location. A more advanced and effective concept revolves around providing even the smallest operators with tour planning and scheduling services available to large corporations for managing their fleets. The European Union funded the development of one such system that would be available for a monthly fee, similar to the way in which taxis belong to a co-operative (GIFTS, undated).

Improved truck–rail intermodal services

In most of the more developed countries, the truck is the dominant freight transport mode and the single largest cost of the entire supply chain. Table 5.7 provides a breakdown of costs in the US.

The truck is probably the most important mode to concentrate upon for efficiency gains and pollution reductions. An alternative that consumes substantially less energy, and generates considerably less pollution, is the placement of containers on trains for the long haul, using trucks for the local moves at one or both ends. While the quantity of such intermodal service has been steadily increasing over the years, even further shifts are needed in order to reduce energy consumption and externalities. Placement of trailers (piggyback

Table 5.7 Logistics spending in the US, 2006

Transportation		
Trucks	US$635 billion	($432 billion intercity; $203 billion local)
Railroads	$54 billion	
Water	$37 billion	($32 billion international; $5 billion domestic)
Oil pipelines	$10 billion	
Airlines	$38 billion	($15 billion international; $23 billion domestic)
Freight forwarders	$27 billion	
Inventory carrying costs		
	US$446 billion	($93 billion interest; $101 billion warehousing; $252 billion taxes, insurance, etc.)
Shipper-incurred plus administration costs		
	US$56 billion	($50 billion logistics administration; $6 billion shipper incurred)

Source: Logistics Management (2007)

or TOFC) and even trucks and TOT can also reduce the distance of trucking while still accommodating the need for trucks at each end of the rail trip.

One transportation engineer who has studied the matter found pent-up demand for TOT service between western Canada and central and southern California; several truckers indicated that they would be highly interested in a service that allowed them to load their trucks, often carrying finished wood products such as plywood and lumber, onto trains destined for California deliveries, sleeping or enjoying the scenery along the route. The railway from Mumbai to Mlore offers such a service and Indian officials are interested in expanding it to several other rail lines.[3] As part of a broad effort to encourage the transfer of more travel to walking, bicycling and rail, the region of Provence–Alpes–Côte d'Azur in the south of France is working to 'transfer part of the heavy goods traffic to the railway network ... [by] developing multimodal platforms dedicated to 'rail-routing' [trucks on trains]' (Region Provence–Alpes–Côte d'Azur, undated).

Shifting the truck versus rail / truck intermodal breakeven point

The cost structures of intermodal truck–train service and trucking service alone are quite different. Intermodal requires investment in a transfer terminal, including tracks, truck waiting areas, trailer and container storage areas, and cranes. These represent the intermodal fixed cost in Figure 5.8. By comparison, the truck fixed cost is much smaller. But once under way on a train, the cost of moving the trailer or container per unit distance is much lower. This is shown by lower slope of the variable cost curve for the intermodal service than for the truck service. At some distance, the two cost curves intersect, which signifies the *breakeven distance*. This is roughly 600 miles in the US, less in some markets with special conditions.

There is a variety of ways in which this breakeven distance can be reduced. When the price of fuel increases, the steepness of the variable cost curves increases, but the truck service goes up faster than intermodal, as fuel is a larger component of this cost. Hence, increased fuel prices will cause a shift to the left of the breakeven point. But it is also possible to shift the entire variable cost curve for intermodal service downwards by making terminal facilities and terminal processing more efficient. This includes shorter waiting times for loading and unloading, more frequent and reliable services to again reduce waiting times, and better information and better technology for improved matching of feeder trucks to trains. The afore-mentioned GIFTS system is an example of better technology, an

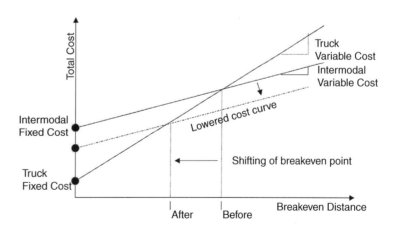

Figure 5.8 Intermodal breakeven distance

Source: Eric C. Bruun

intelligent transportation systems (ITS) application that combines hardware and software into comprehensive solutions. Another very important reducer of intermodal costs is faster or cheaper loading techniques. Currently, most operations involve a crane fee and a wait during sequential loading. But there are designs such as Modalohr (Lohr Industries, undated) that allow simultaneous loading of many trailers and containers at once. It is also helpful to increase the numbers of such intermodal terminals to reduce the access distance; but this can be resisted by communities who wish to avoid the spectre of increased truck and train traffic, so this option is often restricted.

In Europe some public capital assistance is made available for tunnelling, acquiring land and building terminal facilities for intermodal freight. In the US, freight railroads have essentially shunned public investment since the Staggers Act of 1980 brought deregulation to the US. Railroads have feared a repeat of over-regulation of their fares. Public financing of the raising of bridges or lowering of track beds to accommodate double-stack trains was a notable exception, prompted by the concern of port authorities that they would lose much of their business. In the US, at least, accelerating the shift to truck/rail intermodal will require more such public investment and planning.

Ocean shipping reforms

As one of the first industries to undergo globalization, competitive pressure created cargo ships of very large size that have a very small staff in order to maximize productivity. They also have minimal safety and environmental protection features. They tend to fly 'flags of convenience', meaning that the ship-owning firms shop around for certification authorities that maintain lax standards. As a result, these enormous ships tend to have low power and a single propeller. This reduces manoeuvrability when engines fail, an especially serious situation for oil tankers. Environmental standards are low; engines usually run on Bunker C or other low-grade diesel fuels with extremely high sulphur content from near the bottom of the distilling pyramid. The low-quality fuel generates enormous amounts of particulate matter and ozone-creating compounds and is a significant health hazard (Corbett et al, 2007). There has recently been some recognition of this under-regulated pollution and a few countries have begun to issue higher standards as a requirement for entry into their waters (Vidal, 2009). Some ports are providing electrical hook-ups to power ships when docked so that polluting engines need not idle. Similar measures are being applied to trucking to reduce pollution from idling.

More must be done. In particular, cleaner and, thus, more expensive fuels and more cleanly combusting engines must be mandated. Increased fuel costs and higher engine standards will modestly raise the cost of ocean shipping, but probably not enough to significantly alter trade patterns, as ocean shipping will still be relatively inexpensive. Other measures taken to increase sustainability that serve to decrease the length of supply chains and improve trade imbalances would also lead to an eventual decline in shipping growth, and possibly even reversal. In light of this possibility, further expansion of port capacity should probably be discouraged in the more developed countries.

Oil and petroleum products constitute a very large percentage of ocean shipping: approximately one third today and as much as half before the huge surge in global trade.[4] This ratio can be a little misleading in that the absolute amount of oil and oil-related shipping has increased as a result of dramatically increased global trade. In effect, a major portion of ocean shipping consists of huge tankers moving oil and fuel great distances and creating significant emissions and spill hazards. A certain portion of the oil is being transported across oceans to refineries and then shipped again by tanker as refined product. This clearly is one of the least sustainable and most environmentally threatening aspects of oceanic shipping. In recent years, perhaps as an anticipation of oil depletion, the rate of manufacture of new oil tankers has slowed (Marshall, 2007). This could also mean that the less safe single-hulled tankers may continue to dominate the fleet for many years unless intervention occurs, forcing their replacement.

Shifting some airfreight to higher-speed rail services

Only a very small portion of all cargo moves by air when measured by weight or volume. But a very large portion is carried when viewed by cargo value. Figure 5.9 indicates that total US international air cargo in 2003 was only 0.4 per cent by weight, but 26.4 per cent by value. This high-cost choice often appears compelling when using the TLC analysis; the cost of holding high-value inventory in slow-moving modes is too great. Furthermore, if the purchase cost is far lower, the much higher transportation cost may still be outweighed.

Similar estimates for worldwide international trade are given in Table 5.8. The figures are not totally comparable to US international statistics as trade within groups such as the North American Free Trade Agreement (NAFTA) or the European Union (EU) is considered domestic. The dominance of trade via ships by weight and dominance of trade by value of airplanes can again be seen.

While some of the transoceanic smaller item, parcel and high-value demand freight would be difficult to attract to ocean shipping, the situation for long-distance land freight might be amenable to shifting to rail. A

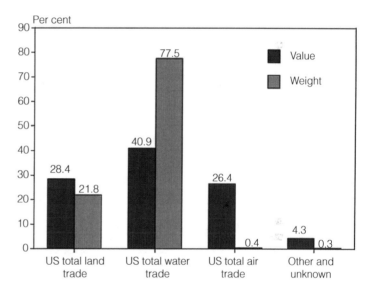

Figure 5.9 US international trade by weight and volume, 2003

Note: see original source for notes on data.
Source: US Bureau of Transportation Statistics (2005)

Table 5.8 All international trade by weight and volume

Mode	Weight in tonne kilometres (percentage)	Shipment value (percentage)
Water	96.7	49
Road	1.5	11
Rail	1.0	3
Air	0.3	35
Pipeline (other)	0.5	2

Source: Gilbert and Perl (2008, p96)

large portion of intra-national and intra-continental airfreight is moved by global courier/express operators and large airlines, all using a trunk-feeder system of airliners. Some of these feeder lines have great promise for eventual conversion to high-speed trains. Already, one courier company has ordered TGV trains of comparable performance to their passenger counterparts to deliver high-value cargo to their hub at Charles De Gaulle Airport outside Paris.

Reverse logistics

Reverse logistics is defined as returning of the leftover materials, spent material and packaging for reuse or recycling. The 'reverse' refers to moving in the opposite direction of the delivery supply chain. In reality, this is not necessarily the way in which the process works. Instead, a largely independent chain may be used. A good example is newspaper – individuals return these to collection points that are not co-located at the newspaper stand and are in no way associated with the newspaper firm.

The placing of deposits on beverage containers was intended to incentivize the reuse of bottles. Over the years, refilling of bottles has decreased, but recycling of them continues. The requirement to accept containers back has probably contributed to efficiency advances such as lighter plastic bottles shipped with shrink wrap. Both the outbound and reverse direction shipment weights are reduced. This example illustrates that producers can incorporate consideration of waste materials within the forward production cycle, thereby reducing the waste generated in the first place. As an example from Germany, larger food stores must accept packaging that their customers consider excessive after they leave the checkout counter. This is probably an effective way to reduce excessive packaging as it pits large firms, such as supermarkets and other retail chains that must dispose of the excess, against the companies that generate it, a more even power relationship than consumer against producer.

Purchasing products with lower virgin material content is a growing consumer trend. But prices for reusable and recyclable materials have fluctuated widely, thereby continually changing the economic appeal for both recyclable material collectors and potential reusers of the materials to participate in these markets. Policies should be promoted that attempt to promote more stability in these markets and even increase their flow by expanding recycling to a wider range of manufacturers beyond those making containers and packaging. There are already limited cases such as Germany where heavy and complex products such as automobiles must be recycled. This can be expanded further.

In developing countries, deposits aren't always necessary, as there is likely to be an industry based on collecting and returning recyclables, although it still deserves public-sector encouragement and support. Developing countries can avoid much of the need for reverse logistics by not shaping their cities and economies in the lower-density, auto-dependent manner of many of the richest countries.

Redistribution of sourcing

The late comedian George Carlin observed how one could be on a highway in the middle of nowhere and see truckloads of potatoes going in each direction.

Clearly, if buyers could buy product of exchangeable quality at the same cost but closer by, shipping costs would be reduced. However, this can be problematic as firms tend to want longer-term contracts to hedge for price stability and availability. They also don't like to discuss their sourcing with competitors. There may even be competition-law violations associated with excessively detailed negotiations between multiple buyers and producers. Nevertheless, advanced technological means such as internet-based load matching have the potential to provide more local sourcing and should be explored further.

Shorten supply chains

The most direct way to increase sustainability of the freight transport system is to reduce the length of travel of moving materials. Decreasing travel has a larger impact than just reducing energy consumption of vehicles. It has a cascading effect across the network, reducing the number of vehicles and the size and number of logistics-related facilities needed. The situation is analogous to passenger transportation: much of the built environment has evolved over decades and it can't be reversed overnight, but some facilities could be converted to other uses over time. Unfortunately, this can't be done by mandate, so various shorter-term incentives and longer-term logistical system changes, and infrastructure/urban form changes must be considered.

Promote increased efficiency and sustainability

As explained in connection with the discussion of TLC, there are economic drivers behind the BAU supply chain structures. It will be unrealistic to expect individual companies to take measures voluntarily when their competitors do not. Thus, policies that 'keep a level playing field' need to be employed. The most obvious policy is to increase the cost of fuel through taxes in order to incentivize efforts of firms to modify or redesign their supply chains.

Unfortunately, in most sectors, transportation is such a small part of the TLC that even a large increase in fuel prices might have little effect. Vanek and Morlok's (2000) commodity-based research approach demonstrates that in many products, manufacturing consumes far more energy than its transportation supply chain. Even more importantly, the labour costs and environmental compliance costs may be far more dominant than energy costs. It would be hard to influence such manufacturers through higher energy prices alone. But there are a few commodity groups where transportation energy is a substantial part of the total:

- food and food by-products;
- lumber and paper products;
- apparel.

These are industries that would have other major environmental and social benefits if they were to be strengthened and made more regionally self-sufficient. An increase in fuel taxes will help to encourage shorter supply chains for these and other commodities where transport is a high part of the cost. As yet it is unclear whether cap-and-trade systems, especially the relatively weak system currently under development in the US, will reduce GHG emissions as much as higher fuel taxes.

Because of the damage that trucks do, an even better tax than a simple fuel tax would be a weight–distance tax. As the name implies, it also takes into account how heavy the vehicle is. It reduces or eliminates the subsidy to the heaviest vehicles that cause most of the damage to the roads. In the longer run, it incentivizes firms to change their supply chains such that heavier loads are shifted to rail. The weight–distance tax is already in force in Germany through a nationwide onboard truck tolling system that replaced the tax on diesel fuel. The European Union is developing a technological solution that would facilitate use of similar onboard equipment in all member countries.

Considerations of policy change

Restricting two-wheelers and pedestrians

During recent years, several major rapidly growing Chinese cities have joined some of their counterparts in highly motorized cities around the globe in banning or disadvantaging bicyclists on key corridors in favour of more motor vehicle traffic. Many North American cities restrict or make it very difficult for pedestrians to circulate; most traffic signals allow little crossing time for pedestrians and often channel them into crowded crosswalks at widely spaced intersections, further denying them easy access to intermediate destinations. Efforts to ban or widely restrict bicycles and other non-motorized modes, especially walking, are contrary to efforts to promote sustainability.[5]

It probably is not realistic to attempt a ban on motorcycles or any particular vehicle type. The existence of any mode in large numbers is a reflection of an otherwise unmet need in the society. The 'motoboys', motorcycle couriers of São Paulo, are generally considered a public nuisance (Rohter, 2004). But if they were forcibly eliminated, important documents and materials would be stuck in traffic jams. A wiser approach might be to improve the alternatives and then reduce the numbers of motorized couriers over time as substitute options become available. Better regulation of motorized couriers and occasional pedestrian-menacing bicycle couriers in some cities, along with improved enforcement protecting pedestrians, might also be advisable. There are ethical and political considerations associated with banning motorcycles when wealthy businesspersons and merchants operate automobiles and trucks at their convenience.

Trucks, trains, yogurt pots, farmers' markets and environmental education

In countries where the freight companies are largely without public assistance, they may need to accept public planning and participation, again to some extent. It is in the public interest to hasten the development of supply chains that are less reliant on trucks. This overlaps with the promotion of passenger rail, as capacity needs to be expanded in corridors where freight and passenger transportation run on the same tracks. Reinstatement of some abandoned rail lines, strengthening of existing short lines and preservation of rights of way for

Figure 5.10 Moving day on bicycles: Amsterdam (top) and Boulder, Colorado (bottom)

Source: Preston L. Schiller (Amsterdam photo); GO Boulder (Boulder, Colorado, photo)

future rail corridors should also be considered as conflicts between passenger and freight use of rail lines over available capacity already abound, and can be expected to increase.

Increasing vehicle efficiency, while a laudable goal, will not shorten supply chain transport distances or decrease the total quantity of shipment. The 'claw-back' phenomenon associated with fuel efficiency can lead to longer hauls and greater quantities shipped. The concept is simply that higher fuel efficiency at a

Figure 5.11 Swedish postal delivery bicycle

Source: Eric C. Bruun

given price level is equivalent to cutting the shipping rate – hence there will be more use of shipping services.

Public education of the environmental consequences of long supply chains might promote buying more locally. As evidence of public concern, farmers' markets are successfully returning to many cities in the US and Canada. Böge (1995) also suggests some consumer and producer educational measures that can be taken around freight transport (see Box 5.1).

De-globalization of freight?

Globalization, with its heavy dependence upon long-distance supply chains, works against sustainable development. Even though it is anathema to many BAU economists, tariffs or other restrictions might need to be reinstated for several reasons:

- It is possible that GHGs simply won't reduce quickly enough through market mechanisms, current regulatory mechanisms or even with higher taxes.
- Low prices of globalized goods don't reflect their externalities. There is no consensus between trading partners on how to internalize costs; in fact, many actors plan to maintain their price advantage by not internalizing costs.
- Long supply chains imply vulnerability to world events, while more local production increases self-reliance and security.

The next chapter will examine aspects of economics and investment strategies for passenger and freight transportation that can inform sustainability efforts.

Questions for discussion

- How do international agreements such as the European Union (EU) Common Market, North American Free Trade Agreement (NAFTA) and, especially, the World Trade Organization (WTO) affect the length of supply chains?
- How can it make business sense to send scrap material all the way across the Pacific Ocean and then back again as finished product when it seems so wasteful?
- Why are there so many trucks on the highways? Why isn't more freight being shifted to the railroads?

Notes

1   See Bowersox et al (1996) for a mathematical exposition of how the EOQ is derived.
2   See the work of the Institute for Transportation and Development Policy (ITDP: www.itdp. org), the International Bicycle Fund (IBF: www.ibike.org) and Bikes not Bombs (http:// bikesnotbombs.org/) as examples.

3   For graphics of piggybacking and double-stacked containers, see Rodrigue (2009b), http://
     people.hofstra.edu/geotrans/eng/ch3en/conc3en/pbdblstk.html; for the pent-up demand in
     western North America, information was derived through pers comm with consulting
     engineer Hal B. H. Cooper, Jr., Kirkland, Washington; for India TOT, see http://www.team-
     bhp.com/forum/shifting-gears/38141-trucks-train.html. See also Anonymous (undated),
     Bjornstad (2003) and Rodrigue et al (2009).
4   See the highly informative discussion in Gilbert and Perl (2008, pp97–98), as well as their
     source, www.unctad.org/en/docs/rmt2006_en.pdf (Table 5); for general information about
     the oil industry and petroleum shipping, see Rodrigue (2009a), http://people.hofstra.edu/
     geotrans/eng/ch5en/appl5en/ch5a1en.html.
5   Of course, bicycles may not fit into a completely pedestrianized zone, although they can be
     allowed where their speed is limited; see examples discussed in other chapters.

References and further reading

Anonymous (undated) *Trucks on a Train (Konkan Railway; Mumbai to Mlore)*, www.team-bhp.
   com/forum/shifting-gears/38141-trucks-train.html, accessed 30 August 2009
Bjornstad, R. (2003) 'Inventor envisions trucks on trains', *The Register–Guard*, 12 March, ppD1,
   D3, Eugene, OR, http://news.google.com/newspapers?nid=1310&dat=20030312&id=Tn0VA
   AAAIBAJ&sjid=_-sDAAAAIBAJ&pg=3277,2760469, accessed 30 August 2009
Böge, S. (1995) 'The well-travelled yogurt pot: Lessons for new freight transport policies and
   regional production', *World Transport Policy and Practice*, vol 1, no 1, pp7–11, www.ecoplan.
   org/wtpp/wt_index.htm, accessed 6 July 2009
Bowersox, D. J., Closs, D. J. and Helferich, O. K. (1996) *Logistical Management*, Macmillan,
   New York, NY
Corbett J. J., Winebrake, J. J., Green, E. H., Kasibhatla, P., Eyring, V. and Lauer, A. (2007)
   'Mortality from ship emissions: A global assessment', *Environ Science Technology*, vol 41, no 24,
   pp8512–8518
Daly, H. and Cobb, J. C. (1989) *For the Common Good*, Beacon Press, Boston, MA
Delucchi, M. (1996–1997) 'Report UCD–ITS–RR–96–3', in M. Delucchi (ed) *The Annualized
   Social Cost of Motor Vehicle Use in the United States*, vols 1–23, Institute of Transportation
   Studies, University of California at Davis, Davis, CA
GIFTS (Global Intermodal Freight Transport System) (undated) http://gifts.newapplication.it/
   gifts/project_deliverables/public/GIFTS_BROCHURE.pdf, accessed 14 February 2009
Gilbert, R. and Perl, A. (2008) *Transport Revolutions: Moving People and Freight without Oil*,
   Earthscan, London
International Transport Forum (2007) *Transport Trends 2007*, Organisation for Economic
   Co-operation and Development, www.internationaltransportforum.org/statistics/trends/index.
   html#Freight_Transport, accessed 4 September 2009
Logistics Management (2007) 'Annual report', *Logistics Management*, July
Lohr Industries (undated) 'Modalohr', www.modalohr.com/gb.htm, accessed 10 June 2009
Marshall, G. (2007) 'The outlook for oil tanker new construction', TSCF (Tanker Structure
   Cooperative Forum) Shipbuilders Meeting, www.krs.co.kr/kor/file/14Outlook%20for%20
   Oil%20Tanker.PDF, accessed 5 July 2009
Region Provence–Alpes–Côte d'Azur (undated) 'Multimodal platforms', www.regionpaca.fr/index.
   php?id=12094&L=1, accessed 30 August 2009
Rodrigue, J.-P. (2009a) *International Oil Transportation*, http://people.hofstra.edu/geotrans/eng/
   ch5en/appl5en/ch5a1en.html, accessed 30 August 2009
Rodrigue, J.-P. (2009b) *Piggyback and Doublestack Train Cars*, http://people.hofstra.edu/geotrans/
   eng/ch3en/conc3en/pbdblstk.html, accessed 30 August 2009
Rodrigue, J.-P., Comtois, C. and Slack, B. (2009) *The Geography of Transport Systems*, Routledge,
   New York, NY

Rohter, L. (2004) 'Pedestrians and drivers beware: Motoboys are in a hurry', *New York Times*, 30 November

US Bureau of Transportation Statistics (2005) *Pocket Guide to Transportation*, Tables 23 and 24, www.bts.gov/publications/pocket_guide_to_transportation/2005/, accessed 5 August 2009

US Bureau of Transportation Statistics (2006a) *Freight in America*, Table 2, www.bts.gov/publications/freight_in_america, accessed 5 August 2009

US Bureau of Transportation Statistics (2006b) *Freight in America*, Table 9, www.bts.gov/publications/freight_in_america, accessed 5 August 2009

US Bureau of Transportation Statistics (2007) *National Transportation Statistics*, Table1-1, www.bts.gov/publications/national_transportation_statistics/2007/html/table_01_01.html, accessed 5 August 2009

US Bureau of Transportation Statistics (2008a) *National Transportation Statistics*, www.bts.gov/publications/national_transportation_statistics/excel/table_01_32.xls, accessed 5 August 2009

US Bureau of Transportation Statistics (2008b) *BTS Special Report: US–China Trade Growth and America's Transportation System*, April SR-007, www.bts.gov/publications/bts_special_report/2008_007/index.html, accessed 5 August 2009

US Bureau of Transportation Statistics (2009) *National Transportation Statistics*, Table 1–11, www.bts.gov/publications/national_transportation_statistics/html/table_01_11.html, accessed 5 August 2009

US Census Bureau (2008) *FT 920 US Merchandise Trade Selected Highlights*, www.census.gov/foreign-trade/balance/c5700.html#2009, accessed 5 August 2009

Vanek, F. M. and Morlok, E. K. (2000) 'Improving the energy efficiency of freight in the United States through commodity based analysis: Justification and implementation', *Transportation Research Part D*, vol 5, no 1, pp11–29

Vidal, J. (2009) 'Health risks of shipping pollution have been "underestimated"', *The Guardian*, London, 10 April

6

Transportation Economics and Investment: Improving Analysis and Investment Strategies

Introduction

Previous chapters have explored transportation modes and aspects of how they move people and goods. Economics and strategies for investment are two important factors that need to be taken into account in policy and planning for sustainable transportation (ST). This chapter reviews basic economic analysis methods in common usage, critiques of the methods used with respect to their potential role in promoting more ST systems, and suggests ways of integrating improved economic analysis methods within public policy, project evaluation and investment decisions.

There are two basic purposes for applying economic analysis to transportation questions:

1   Inform public policies in the interest of wise and equitable use of resources.
2   Inform the evaluation of individual projects.

The word 'inform' is chosen carefully to emphasize that economics is not the sole discipline or lens through which public policy and projects should be analysed. There is often pressure through business as usual (BAU) procedures to do just that. It is worthwhile to understand the basic economic arguments and tools in order to be able to challenge and defend against inappropriate and incomplete economic arguments and to promote an understanding of how to attain sustainable transportation.

Many of the inefficiencies of conventional approaches, services and programmes in the transportation arena stem from public policies whose shortcomings can be understood in large part by using economic analysis. Three issues familiar to most people that can be illuminated by economic analysis are:

1   pollution generated by motorists without compensation or regard for the consequences to those affected (see the discussion on the polluter pays principle in 'Regulation versus pricing');

2   traffic congestion created in large part by overly low pricing or subsidies for private motor vehicles, such that demand strains available supply;
3   land development based on a policy of low pricing or subsidies, which in turn reinforces the reliance upon private motor vehicles.

Over time BAU has reflected the concerns of institutions with a vested interest in maintaining such reinforcing cycles, rather than more dispassionate analysis or public expression of their collective will.

Basic concepts and principles

Externalities

One of the most basic principles of neo-classical economics, the prevailing school of thought, is that prices for products and services should reflect the full cost of their production. If the price is too low, more goods will be produced than is necessary. This low price is enabled by the fact that the individual, firm or agency providing this product or service is imposing undesired impacts or 'externalities' on others. Instead, the costs should be absorbed by the producer, or 'internalized' and reflected in the cost of a product or activity. In this instance there is an atypical 'happy convergence' between neo-classical economists and environmentalists. In the longer run, this not only serves the cause of fairness by not shifting the cost to others, it incentivizes the search for ways of reducing or even eliminating externalities. Externalities such as air and water pollution, land and soil degradation, non-renewable resource consumption and greenhouse gas generation are all very important in the context of sustainability.

Marginal or incremental social costs

More specifically, the price for most (but not all) products and services should be set, such that it equals the full social cost of producing the last increment of production, also known as the 'incremental social cost' or 'marginal social cost'. Full cost means that the price should include sufficient charges to cover all externalities. The exceptions are products and services for which costs decrease with increased quantity, instead of increasing with each unit, creating the conditions for a 'natural monopoly'. This is historically the reason for the creation of major public utilities and transit systems – having more users of the same system could lower the cost for all. Some countries, including most in Europe, levy high taxes on fuels in order to help fund more fuel-efficient transport alternatives and an array of social and health care programmes, many of which are necessitated by the current highly mobility-dependent lifestyles.

Congestion delay

One of the most important components of the marginal social costs in transportation is the cost of congestion. Each additional vehicle adds delay not only to the occupants themselves, but to all other people in the traffic stream by increasing the density of traffic, hence slowing it down. This delay externality is actually far larger than the cost imposed to oneself, so it cannot be argued that everyone's imposition of delay simply cancels one another out. Congestion caused by private vehicles often slows public transportation considerably, especially when bus lanes and other transit priority measures are not in place. Transit delay can be viewed as a doubling of traffic congestion's externalities: it adds delay to each of the bus passengers as well as increasing costs, such as driver time and fleet size requirements, to the public agency itself.

Monetization

Placing an actual monetary value on the delay requires providing a value to individuals for the time lost. To do this, total time delay to users is multiplied by a value of time to obtain a monetary value. It is not practical to assign a value for every individual, so averaged values are used based on aggregated characteristics of subpopulations. Similarly, other costs, such as air and noise pollution, are converted from one set of physical emission units into monetary units that are purported to express health system expenses, property value reduction and other costs.

The process of putting additional costs and benefits that are not already directly expressed as monetary expenditures and receipts onto the same monetary scale is called monetization. As will be explained shortly, this is necessary in preparation for using the most popular economic evaluation methods. It can be problematic; the value of time, for example, is often simply placed at one half the average hourly income of people living or working in an area, even though it is clear that income levels vary a great deal and the purposes of trips change the value of time. As another example, part of the monetized cost of air pollution of a particular type and quantity can be traced indirectly through statistical means to reduced crop yield and extra medical expenses. Reasonable people can question the appropriateness of monetizing reduced visibility, shortened lives or the uprooting of communities caused by rising sea levels. Then there are items that defy even quantification, let alone monetization, such as the quality of life.

The conversion factors used for monetization can be a subject of contention, with estimates varying as widely as those making them. Less frequently recognized are the other items that should be included but cannot be in strictly monetary-based methods. Additional evaluation approaches designed to take them into consideration are also sometimes used.

Current evaluation methods

A few basic methods are currently used to conduct economic assessments. This pertains both to proposed changes in public policies as well to evaluation of individual projects. In some nations, and in some regions, these methods are mandated for projects for which public funds are sought and are a primary determinant. In other cases, these methods are only one input to the decision.

Net present value

From an economic perspective, a project can be viewed as incurring a series of costs and benefits over its useful life. Therefore, it is an important step in a

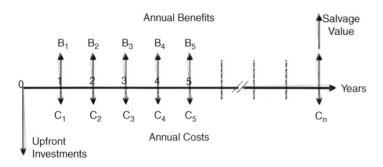

Figure 6.1 Typical diagram used to compute net present value (NPV) of a project

Source: Eric C. Bruun

project proposal to estimate the investment costs, operating costs and externality costs on an annual basis. Similarly, the revenues, monetized time savings to users and other identified benefits are assigned on an annual basis. A generic stream of costs and benefits for a project is shown in Figure 6.1. The salvage value at n years reflects the possibility that the remaining assets may have a residual value that can be recaptured, known as the salvage value.[1]

For a project to be worthwhile, its benefits should exceed its costs over its lifetime. Net present value (NPV) is the mathematical expression of the idea that the sum of all monetary and monetized benefits over a certain number of years minus the sum of all monetary and monetized costs has to be greater than zero. Furthermore, the subtotal for each future year must be discounted back to the present. This is done by using an annual discount rate. It is a rate that compounds each year. As a result, all costs and benefits for a given future year are multiplied by a factor that is less than the one that preceded it.

The discount rate reflects the fact that money today is worth more than the nominal amount of money tomorrow. Another conceptualization is that for deferring the use of money today, one needs to be compensated by an increase in the amount of money that will be available tomorrow.

The amount by which the value is reduced is shown for two different discount rates in Figure 6.2. The selected discount rate is known as the minimum allowable rate of return (MARR). The actual value of the MARR is set by government for publicly funded projects and by private firms for privately funded projects. Private companies almost always demand a higher MARR than public agencies. In Figure 6.2, the 15 per cent rate was selected since it is typical for a private firm, and the 7 per cent was selected since it is typical for a public agency. In general, it can also be stated that the MARR for public agencies tends to be higher in developing countries than in the richer countries in order to reduce the number of feasible projects in line with the available funding.

A project that has an NPV greater than or equal to zero at the given MARR is said to be economically feasible. If there are multiple policy or project alternatives, then the one with the highest NPV should be selected.

The concept of internal rate of return (IRR) is sometimes referenced, but it is

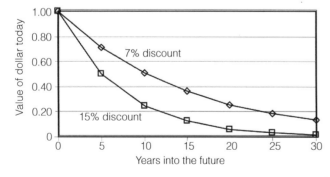

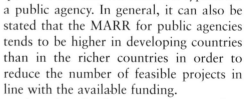

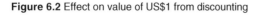

Figure 6.2 Effect on value of US$1 from discounting

Source: Eric C. Bruun

obsolescent and should be avoided. It has technical problems, such as the possibility of generating negative values of interest rates. The MARR serves to replace it and represents the minimum value that the IRR must be in order for the project to be feasible. When a project has been evaluated using the IRR concept, it is generally advisable to redo it with the NPV method if the data is available, before comparing it to other projects.

Benefit–cost ratio

The benefit–cost ratio (BCR) method is based on the exact same inputs as the NPV method. But instead of subtracting the discounted sum of costs from the discounted sum of benefits, it is the ratio of discounted sum of benefits over the discounted sum of costs. This is an oft-cited value; but, like the IRR, it should generally be avoided. It has a technical problem: it is not always clear whether a change in a particular monetary or monetized item is an increase in benefits or a decrease in costs. Depending upon how it is interpreted, the ratio will be different. More fundamentally, this ratio implies a completeness of analysis that may not be justified if there are some costs and benefits that were not included since they were not monetary or could not be monetized.

One very important limitation of both the NPV and BCR methods is that they make no distinction about who receives benefits and who incurs costs. It is quite possible that one segment of society or locale receives virtually all the benefit while others incur virtually all of the costs. Thus, the incidence of the costs and benefits must also be discussed in any evaluation.

Lack of concern for the incidence of costs was a common complaint in the 1950s and 1960s during the planning and construction of the US Interstate System, which severed urban communities and forced the relocation of many residents. Once completed, freeways would permanently generate noise and air pollution, affecting people living nearby, some of whom did not use the facilities. Compensation was directed to the relocation of individuals within the right of way, but not for the disruption and degradation of whole affected communities.

Since then, communities in the US who feel that they will receive an excessive burden from a project have learned to put up more effective resistance. In general, this can be said for most of the richer countries, empowered by legal requirements for public participation and 'environmental justice'. Although it is often vaguely defined in the law, the term 'environmental justice' can be interpreted as addressing the imbalances between the incidence of environmental costs and the incidence of benefits. If the perspective is widened from environmental impacts to all negative impacts, the term 'social justice' is used instead.

Mitigation

It is sometimes necessary for the good of the many to impose costs on some elements of society. Costs and impacts should then be mitigated and aggrieved parties should be compensated. Identified monetary costs for proposed mitigations and compensation are increasingly factored into the economic analysis, often mandated by law or required by funding sources. A common example of mitigation is a sound wall along a motorway. An example of compensation would be replacement of infilled wetlands with newly created wetlands nearby. There is often controversy about the effectiveness of such strategies. Although many mitigation practices are imperfect, they do demonstrate the principle of redress for harmful effects.[2]

Mitigation and compensation are good practices because they serve the causes of environmental and social justice, and also reduce the time to achieve the desired goals since lawsuits, litigation and general community resistance will all decline. Moreover, the give and take of negotiation and any redesign attempts all serve to push projects in a more sustainable direction.

Cui bono?

Just as those incurring excessive costs should be compensated, it is equitable to ask those non-users receiving benefits to make financial contributions. It is often the case that users of other transportation modes are beneficiaries. When auto drivers have better driving conditions because of the diversion of many previous drivers to public transport, it reduces their travel time and the total pollution emitted. Charging some of the cost to them is equitable. There may also be windfall beneficiaries, a subject which will be discussed further in connection with subsidies.

Multi-criteria evaluation

Multi-criteria evaluation (MCE) is a broader approach used when it is recognized that there are significant non-monetary and non-monetizable benefit-and-cost components to a proposed policy or project. This is typical of major transportation works. In fact, some of the major reasons for public works projects involve the stimulation or creation of non-monetizable benefits and reduction of non-monetizable costs. In order to emphasize that not all costs and benefits are monetary or monetizable in nature, the broader term 'impacts' is sometimes used instead.

There is a variety of MCE methods, and they are all designed to allow inclusion to the cost-benefit analysis of various impacts that are not expressed on a monetary scale. Examples would be emission or concentration levels of particular pollutants, community preference study results and miscellaneous survey data. Some of these methods are quite sophisticated mathematically and can provide insights to the professional analyst. But due to their complexity they would not be suitable politically for decision-making since laypeople would be suspicious of such 'black box' results. Other methods are too simple and unrealistic (but sometimes used nevertheless). Officially sanctioned methods need to be somewhere in between.

Methods commonly used typically involve the creation of other categories of impacts. Examples of categories might include environmental impacts, social impacts and long-term economic development impacts. The non-monetizable costs and benefits are assigned to these other categories, while those on the monetary scale might still be summarized by indicators such as NPV. Some of the more contentious monetized values may be reassigned to one of these other categories as well. In the most straightforward methods, each project alternative is then scored on comparative scales for each item within a category. A scale could be from 1 to 10; from 1 to 4; from −5 to +5, etc. The scale might signify a range from best to worst, least effective to most effective, very unsightly to very beautiful, and so on. Picking the scale requires some consideration, as it must be the same for all impacts within the same category. The intermediate result is an overall averaged score of all impacts within this same category. The end result is an averaged overall score across all categories. The project alternative with the best overall score should be selected.

The analytic hierarchy process (AHP) is a promising multi-criteria method not yet in widespread use, and is discussed in detail in connection with public participation (see Chapter 7).

Muddled models

Conventional or BAU planning uses complex transportation and land-use models that have been termed 'black boxes' because they complicate and render opaque processes that should be straightforward and subject to public and policy-maker deliberation. Some experts who have analysed black box modelling processes have found them to be open to considerable questioning and challenge. Such muddled models often have enormous influence in guiding highway expansions and sprawl generation. Box 6.1 presents an analysis of black box modelling.

Hidden and intentional subsidies and externalities

Any costs or portions of costs imposed by elements of the transportation system that are not covered by the users and other beneficiaries may somewhat loosely be called 'subsidies'. The historical failure to include particularly significant subsidies that benefit one mode while including those that benefit competing modes has warped economic analyses for both policy-making and project evaluation. Sometimes this neglect is encouraged by existence of modal trust funds or dedicated revenue streams that do not allow for the consideration of alternatives outside the particular mode. Such dedicated funds can also seem to suggest that a mode is paying its way. In this case, the neglect stems from a lack of periodic reflection about long-held beliefs by the analysts in question.

An example of lack of reflection would be the oft-stated position that roads and the provision for autos is a basic cost of a modern society that should be borne by all, while public transport is primarily of benefit for its users and should be financed primarily by its users. A more fair and thorough economic analysis would dictate inclusion of all identifiable subsidies for all modes. In the real world of policy formation, defenders of BAU try to skew the formal economic evaluation process with the result that there are deliberate inconsistencies that favour certain outcomes. The analyst concerned with sustainable development must always try to highlight these and find ways of removing them to the maximum extent possible.

Box 6.1 Muddles in the models

In the more developed countries, and increasingly in developing and newly industrializing countries, mathematical models are used to forecast future usage of existing roads and transit facilities and to predict the impact of adding new roads or transit facilities. These changes in transportation arise out of changes in land use, and in a typical planning process, a number of different future land-use scenarios are tested. Such models were first created and implemented in the US in support of the highway-building boom during the 1950s and 1960s after the seminal work of Mitchell and Rapkin (1954). Their basic structure is important to understand so that their limitations can also be understood. A danger with such tools is that they can lend a seemingly scientific justification to a project where it is not warranted. Their complexity can also intimidate those outside the privileged planning circles from questioning the project.

These models represent a region simplified down to nodes and links connecting single points within areas known as transportation analysis zones (TAZs) or origin–destination zones. A region might consist of hundreds of TAZs. Each node concentrates all of the trips that originate within this zone or are destined for this zone. Connecting the nodes, the links have capacity and speed characteristics that reflect the sizes and types of road or transit facilities that connect them.

Creating and executing such a model consists of a four-step process:

1   *Trip generation*: each type of activity has a different rate at which it generates trips. For example, a shopping mall will be different than an office building, both in the hourly rate and the times of day at which these trips are generated. Adding up the total generation based on the composition of activities within a TAZ gives the total generated trips for a time period.
2   *Trip distribution*: each of the generated trips in one TAZ has to be distributed to other TAZs within the region and the trips destined to this TAZ must be attracted from another TAZ. The typical methods to determine this distribution are based on analogies to gravitational attraction or entropy, and are, in fact, termed gravity models, which are calibrated by actual empirical evidence of observed traffic flows.
3   *Modal choice*: based on the availability of discrete modes (simplified list of choices) between any two TAZs and the demographic information about people travelling between them, a probability is established for their choice of mode. It would be impossible to study each traveller separately, so travellers are aggregated into groups with similar demographic characteristics. The percentages within each of the classes are then calculated to get the total demand on each mode between these two TAZs.
4   *Trip assignment*: the last step is to choose the particular paths that travellers will take using each mode. Sometimes there are numerous possible paths. The principle used is to assign travellers such that all possible paths have the same travel time, but with some correction for additional factors such as auto tolls that might exist on some links and for different fares, if there is more than one transit option.

The limitations of such models are a subject in their own right (Kenworthy, 1990; Beimborn et al, 1996; Bruun, 2007; also see Chapter 7 of this text). It is sufficient here to give a few basic categories of criticisms. First, these models are not theoretically sound, as people do not make travel choices in the sequence suggested. Furthermore, they require feedback to ensure that assumptions in each of the four steps are consistent; but this feedback is not always done. Second, the modelling of congestion and performance of automobiles along links is usually much more detailed and accurate than it is for transit. Third, they do not have any ability to predict non-motorized trip behaviour because these are mostly short intra-zonal trips, which the models do not handle well, making the models useless for study of local improvements. Perhaps most importantly, there are two critical flaws. Typically, 75 to 80 per cent of predicted economic benefits from such models arise from small increments of travel time savings multiplied by large numbers of vehicles. Such time savings from road widenings or new roads are thus assigned large economic values; but the time savings are at best ephemeral (unlike new fully segregated rail links, which provide permanent travel time savings), and the road improvements are typically used to just travel further. The models are also used to justify capacity expansions along certain links (e.g. highway widenings). But this just creates induced demand that eventually causes other links in the network to become congested. Thus, these models generally lead a region to a non-converging process of infinite road expansion. In simple terms, these models typically produce self-fulfilling prophecies of more roads, more congestion and more sprawl, which neither saves time, nor reduces fuel use or emissions.

The negative impacts upon cities in the developed world of relying on such BAU models for transportation planning have been increasingly realized so that the models have somewhat lost their gloss and their prescriptions are increasingly scrutinized. Therefore, such 'predict-and-provide' approaches are progressively being replaced by a visioning process of how the broader community want their city to look in the future – a 'debate-and-decide' process (see discussion of these in Chapters 7 and 8 of this text). This only happens, however, where urban governance is reasonably strong and civil society is active. Thus, many parts of the developing world are excluded from such sustainability-oriented approaches and are the passive recipients of this BAU transportation planning approach, in much the same way as they became the new market for DDT after it was banned in developed countries. Dramatically increasing motorization and automobile dependence in developing and newly industrializing countries is underpinned by these now limited and outdated approaches. Their prescriptions are generally not subjected to rigorous sustainability-oriented analysis.

Source: Mitchell and Rapkin (1954); Kenworthy (1990)

Perverse subsidies

The fact that many subsidies support practices that are economically and environmentally harmful has been a happy instance of agreement between many neo-classical economists and those whose principal concerns lie with reducing environmental damage, especially in the transportation sector. Box 6.2 discusses what many economists and environmentalists term 'perverse subsidies': subsidies that harm or provide results in conflict with intended purposes.

The types and amounts of subsidy for transport vary from mode to mode, nation to nation, province to province and even city to city. Some basic categories can be identified to facilitate the aforementioned thorough evaluation.

Box 6.2 The no-win madness of Catch-22 subsidies

Norman Myers and Crispin Tickell[3]

Economists and environmentalists are not always best friends. But on one issue they can, and should, unite: that is to oppose the propensity of governments to misuse fiscal instruments.

Few contest that such instruments ... should be designed to promote good policies and discourage bad ones. Instead, almost every government has created ... an encrusted apparatus of subsidies, which, once established, proves almost irremovable. Worse, many of these subsidies are harmful to our economies as well as our environments. In different ways, such perverse subsidies bedevil all our economics. The public interest, which was their justification, has been lost ...

Worldwide, perverse subsidies are prominent in six main sectors: agriculture, fossil fuels, road transport, water, forestry and fisheries. In all cases, the subsidies serve to undermine national economies as well as environments ... Subsidies for fossil fuels are a prime source of pollution. Subsidies for road transport also promote pollution ...

It is hard to calculate the value of such subsidies worldwide, but they probably amount to at least US$2000 [billion] a year. On both economic and environmental grounds, they defer the time when we can achieve the holy grail of sustainable development. The total of US$2000 [billion] is 3.5 times as large as the Rio Earth Summit's proposed budget for sustainable development, a sum that governments then dismissed as simply not available. The Organisation for Economic Co-operation and Development countries account for two thirds of perverse subsidies, and the US over one fifth.

A typical British taxpayer pays at least UK£1000 a year to fund perverse subsidies, then pays another £500 through increased prices for consumer goods and through environmental degradation. Yet, perverse subsidies persist virtually untouched. This is because subsidies tend to create powerful interest groups and political lobbies. Were just half of these perverse subsidies to be phased out, the funds released would help many governments [to] reduce or abolish their budget deficits, reorder their fiscal priorities in the true public interest, and repair environmental damage ...

Our present mode of exploiting the Earth and its environmental resources – unsustainable exploitation for the most part – suggests we view our planet as a business liquidating its capital, rather than one profiting from the interest on it. Should we not live on our planet as if we intended to stay, rather than as if we were visiting for a weekend?

Infrastructure construction subsidies

Infrastructure construction is perhaps the most physically obvious cost of transport. In many cases it appears to be fully covered by a trust fund based on user fees, but this can be misleading. Until recently, the US Interstate System was financed by federal gasoline taxes; but this did not really make it subsidy free. In reality, the connecting roads were often covered by non-user taxes, making the road transportation network, as a whole, subsidized. In some countries, motorways are financed by private investors who charge tolls that are sufficiently high to recover investments, but not externalities borne by society. Airports and seaports will often be built using revenue bonds issued by a public authority who eventually recovers the costs through facility user charges. Freight railroads in some countries receive construction subsidies, while others, as is typical in North America, receive almost nothing. Passenger railroads and public transport systems typically receive construction subsidies almost everywhere they are built. Without these construction subsidies, the fares would have to be prohibitively high, and projects would likely not be built.

Infrastructure operation and maintenance costs

Infrastructure operation and maintenance costs are distinguished from construction costs by their recurring nature. In most of the developed countries, road user charges, such as registration fees and gasoline taxes, exceed these costs, allowing some repayment of the construction cost and compensation for other externalities. In the case of Canada, the charges roughly equal these costs. In the case of the US, the road user charges covered only about 60 per cent of operation and maintenance of roads from about 1980 to 2003, the rest being generally covered by other non-transportation revenues such as local property taxes, general state revenues and other sources. More recently, the percentage has dropped further to only about 50 per cent. As this is being written, the fuel taxes in the national Highway Trust Fund have been fully expended. The incoming revenue is now being supplemented by non-user sources, including general tax revenues from the federal government (Hanson, 1992; Delucchi, 1996–1997; Pew Charitable Trust, 2009).

Airport and seaport operating and maintenance costs tend to be covered by user charges, but not necessarily in an equitable fashion. For example, very high parking charges can cross-subsidize airside operations at airports, but are generally not applied to public transportation or even automobile access from public roads. Railroads and urban transport systems in the more developed countries almost universally receive operating and maintenance subsidies. On the other hand, in less developed countries, public transport might well be required to be self-sufficient.

Congestion costs

Traffic congestion generates a cost to everyone who uses the affected transportation system and indirectly raises costs through much of the economic system. It is especially burdensome for public transportation systems because it reduces operating speeds. This simultaneously reduces its attractiveness to potential users and raises operating costs since the fleet can make fewer productive trips through the course of a day.

The cost of congestion delay is of increasing importance not only in urban areas; even many rural highways routinely experience delay. The reason is that in most of the richer countries there has been expansion of travel over the years without a corresponding increase in infrastructure capacity. This pertains to road, rail and air modes, and to passenger as well as freight modes. Delays to freight movement raise the direct costs of products through a less efficient supply chain. The externalities also tend to be more pronounced than with passenger travel due to the size and types of vehicles that are used.

In the poorer countries, the problem is often exacerbated. There tends to be far less available infrastructure capacity, much less delineation between transport and non-transport land uses along urban streets, less traffic enforcement, and more mixing of slower non-motorized modes with higher speed modes. Furthermore, older and more polluting vehicles are often prevalent in the traffic stream, which translates into worse air quality than in richer countries.

Free parking exists only in Monopoly®

Parking pricing can be very inconsistent, ranging from 'free' to rates that some motorists find excessive. Sometimes the charge on a per unit time basis might be very low for long periods of time and very high for short periods of time. This practice often benefits parking lot owners, who face lower management costs, and commuters, who take advantage of all-day or 'early bird' pricing, but reduces parking turnover and prevents short-term visitors to stores or medical centres from finding parking. The cost of parking can also be bundled, meaning that it is indirectly included in the purchase prices of residential and office buildings, included as an employee benefit or included in the cost of purchases at a retail store. These arrangements are often experienced as 'free parking' by users because the costs associated with them have been accounted for elsewhere – sometimes at public expense. 'Free parking' on public streets and at transit Park & Ride facilities costs taxpayers money and is generally not paid for directly by those who benefit from its use. There can be unequal tax status of different modes, such that giving parking to employees is a legitimate business expense while public transport is a private expense. Don Shoup, in his seminal book *The High Cost of Free Parking* (2005), asserts that there really hasn't been any widespread and agreed upon economic theory of parking (see Figure 6.3 and Box 6.3).

Transportation-generated pollution

Transportation-generated pollution is a clear example of uncompensated externalities. This includes more than the immediately obvious noise and air emissions caused by the act of transport. There are also indirect effects, such as flooding and soil erosion from excessive paving. Following the life cycle of transport systems, one can also identify pollution from the industrial processes associated with infrastructure construction, vehicle manufacturing and from maintenance. Even equipment retirement often generates pollution due to hazardous materials, such as lead acid batteries. Of special importance for a sustainable future is the reduction of greenhouse gas (GHG) emissions. They do not have the immediate health and aesthetic impacts of other pollutants, but they indirectly impose increasing costs to future generations.

Some analysts have also included a portion of military expenditures as a subsidy on the basis that one of the functions of militaries is to safeguard the flow of oil from the Middle East. Related to this is the issue of the cost to future generations from the current and past extraction and use of non-renewable resources such as oil. Extraction both damages the environment and denies future generations the use of these same resources.

Land taxation

Land taxation is strongly affected by the amount of land that is rateable. Wide public roads represent a large portion of land that cannot be taxed and is of benefit only to private motorists. Private lands typically will also be taxed at a lower rate when they are parking lots than for higher valued uses. As a result, property taxes on the remaining non-transportation lands must be higher in regions with highly auto-supportive urban forms. An urban layout that is convenient for private motorists is generally detrimental to transit and non-motorized mode users, making the land subsidy an additional burden. This is why many advocates of transportation reform justify requesting compensation, such as construction of bike and pedestrian paths and transit-operating support through property taxes.

Another subsidy is introduced when the fuel taxes are too low to cover construction and maintenance of roads; taxation forms considered by economists to be regressive (affecting lower-income people more than the wealthy), such as property, sales or general tax revenues, are used instead. This puts the needs of motorists in direct competition with transit, schools, parks, fire departments and police. In many automobile-dependent countries a substantial portion of fire and police budgets, a significant percentage in most US jurisdictions, is spent in response to motorist-related events.

Figure 6.3 Prices have increased since this photo was taken; but the early bird reduced parking pricing inversion, lower pricing for longer use, higher pricing for shorter periods, still encourages commuters to drive and park all day, while leading to less parking turnover and availability for short-term users such as shoppers and service-seekers

Source: Preston L. Schiller

Land value

Land value is strongly affected by the transport infrastructure and services that are available nearby. Land at a highly accessible location such as a freeway

Figure 6.4 Highway subsidies twist language: 'Public investment, wasteful subsidy'

Source: Andy Singer (www.andysinger.com)

interchange will be more attractive for a shopping mall or office park. It is an external benefit conferred on landowners, and can therefore be said to be a subsidy to them. As another example, land along a streetcar line will have a higher value for retail use or for apartment buildings. In the present day, the owners of the land typically contribute very little to the cost of constructing or maintaining the transportation facilities. In the past, the opposite occurred. Property (and utility) owners themselves built transportation facilities and services in order to promote their primary businesses.

Specialized transport services

Specialized transport services are those that the general population must support due to the impracticality or impossibility of certain sections of society to participate in society without them. A very significant example in the US is school bussing. It consumes a major portion of school budgets and is necessitated by distances that are too long to walk, by lack of facilities for walking and lack of regular transit options. Other examples are buses that carry people to medical appointments and to senior centres.

Subsidies: When are they justified?

If subsidies can cause excess consumption and burdens to non-users of transportation, when are they justified? This is an extremely important question and the reasoning used should be clear, while public policy decisions should be made consciously rather than by default. Some possible reasons for subsidies follow:

- Subsidies may be given when they help society as a whole without serious negative externalities. Education is subsidized because it helps individuals and improves quality of life and the economic competitiveness of society without pollution or physical harm to others. Automobility subsidization benefits individuals, while many costs are imposed on others and the ecosystem.
- When one transportation alternative, such as automobility, is subsidized, it might be necessary to subsidize others so that they can compete or even survive. In automobile-oriented regions, public transport may need subsidization in order to have a basic service and presence. This is justifiable since those who do not have access to an automobile have had their mobility options greatly diminished.
- Regions that can support substantial public transport because of strong core areas designed in an earlier era might still be strongly auto dependent outside the core, requiring higher transit subsidies, perhaps as high as 80 per cent of operating costs. Cities with larger public transport networks

and older urban forms are more likely to cover about 50 per cent or more from the fare box at similar fare levels. When driving becomes extremely unattractive due to severe congestion and very high parking charges, such as exist in London, higher transit fares and patronage reduce the need for subsidy and may even create an operating surplus.

- Covering the full cost of a service or infrastructure provision from fees can make use prohibitively high for lower-income users. When there is extreme income inequality, it becomes necessary to transfer income from the wealthy to support basic services. Democratic societies are compelled to do this by the electorate. Even undemocratic countries must often do this to maintain social stability. As income levels improve, subsidies can be reduced if targeted properly.[4]

- Charging schemes have to be practical. Clearly, it would be preposterous to charge people every time they used a sidewalk or entered their neighbourhood park. Collecting transit fares in systems where they cover only 10 per cent of operating costs is questionable, especially since collecting and managing money itself contributes to increased overhead. Tolls may be reasonably easy to collect on major highways, but cannot be practically collected on small roads and streets.

- A subsidy may be a statement of democratic values and may not need to have an economic justification, although it might be wise to use economic analysis to inform decisions.

Opportunity costs

The value of something that is forgone because resources are applied to something else instead is known as the 'opportunity cost'. Evaluation processes often require a 'do nothing' alternative so that opportunity costs can be evaluated and compared. This requires some extrapolation about future outcomes if the present course proceeds, and can be prone to error, so caution is needed.

If the investments and resources involved in various project alternatives result in only marginal improvements, the investment might be better placed elsewhere. If economic analysis of the 'do nothing' scenario reveals a very negative future (sometimes it reveals a very negative present, itself a very valuable result), it strengthens the case to execute one of the project alternatives.

In theory, the best project alternative should be selected based on a fair and thoroughly inclusive analysis of all impacts for all project alternatives, regardless of the modes involved. In practice, there are institutional constraints. Money might be dedicated to one mode: the mandated evaluation processes are not mode neutral and powerful interests can insert themselves into the process on behalf of a certain alternative. This raises the question of whether the winning alternative should be supported as the best possible

Figure 6.5 The 'good old days' before the 1973 oil embargo with price in US cents per gallon

Source: Richard Untermann

outcome under the circumstances, or whether it should be opposed as the product of a flawed process. The latter would mean that benefits from the project are delayed, perhaps indefinitely. In the context of sustainable development, the need for progress is often urgent.

Box 6.3 Parking pricing and investment: Opportunity costs and opportunities

Preston L. Schiller

Parking may be the single most important factor shaping the decision whether and when to drive to a destination or use an alternative mode for a trip – or whether to make the trip at all. The availability, direct cost and placement of parking are powerful shapers of urban transportation behaviour in countries with high rates of automobile ownership. Free, cheap or plentiful parking has a magnetic attraction for automobile trips. Merchants, businesses and service providers located in commercial districts that choose to limit and price parking worry about placing themselves at a disadvantage relative to sprawled developments that entice motorists with 'free' parking.

Parking is never really free or cheap, although it may be heavily subsidized, with its cost hidden from motorists, or 'bundled' with other costs, as in its automatic provision with office or residential rentals. Zoning codes that mandate large amounts of parking for such uses appear to be at cross-purposes to fostering sustainability in cities. A few of the ways in which free parking is not free include the following:

- The opportunity cost of space consumed for public parking, whether on or off streets, is rarely paid directly by motorists. Occasionally, parking fees and fines generate a small revenue surplus for some cities; but most of the time they barely meet or lower the costs associated with enforcement.
- Tax assessments for parking lots and structures, and parking associated with commercial buildings, are often at lower rates than those for other commercial building space and generate less tax revenue than other uses.

Contrary to the beliefs of many merchants and motorists, parking is oversupplied in most urban areas, even in many central business districts (CBDs). Improved management and pricing could lead to a better match between supply, demand and spatial distribution. In order to lessen the overconsumption of urban space by motor vehicle storage, manage traffic better, reduce emissions and promote walking, bicycling and public transportation, cities need to engage in several strategies in addition to educating the public about the un-free nature of parking. These include:

- Better management of parking pricing and supply. Parking management and pricing should serve policy goals such as traffic reduction and the enhancement of alternatives to driving. As much as possible, parking should be under a unified management and pricing structure in order to discourage motorists from driving around searching for the best price. Effective pricing and intelligent transportation systems (ITS) that supply monitoring with electronic signage directing motorists to available parking, such as that pioneered in Stuttgart's CBD and now in use in many other cities, can also reduce motorists' excessive 'parking search'.

- Unbundle parking from both residential and commercial rental agreements and from zoning requirements. Zoning requirements that mandate minimum parking provision lead to overbuilding of parking that is generally not available to the public and to the perverse phenomenon of lessening density and housing affordability (Shoup, 1992, 1993). A better strategy would be to remove these requirements from building development and make parking more of a public utility (Shoup, 2005). Charging separately for parking in a residential complex would lower construction costs and thus allow for lower rents for people with no or few automobiles. Charging separately for parking in commercial office developments provides a basis for 'parking cash-out' whereby people who drive to work pay for parking and a portion of those revenues can go to paying for passes and bonuses for those who take transit, bicycle or walk to work.

The construction costs of parking are substantial. The US price for a surface parking lot is in the range of US$5000 to $10,000 per stall and between US$30,000 and $70,000 per stall for structured parking. There are also substantial ongoing maintenance and management costs for parking. These translate into a substantial opportunity cost for parking when compared to the much lower costs associated with the non-driving options of transit, bicycling and walking. One strategy has been to justify parking structure costs if associated with surface parking removal related to the creation of a pedestrian mall: such was the case for Boulder's Pearl Street mall (see Chapter 9). Toor and Havlick (2004) discuss many ways in which campus transportation demand management (TDM) programmes can outperform parking construction and provision strategies.

The assumption that more people will come just because there is more parking should be questioned. Tourists do not flock to car-congested downtowns in Los Angeles or Houston as they do to downtowns with less parking provision, such as those of San Francisco or Manhattan. The blank walls caused by large numbers of parking garages and the unpleasantness of parking driveways cutting sidewalks every few yards create unfriendly pedestrian environments in automobile-dominated downtowns.

When a transit strategy is promoted, even non-CBD and outlying shopping malls can benefit. Portland's Lloyd Center, Vancouver's Metrotown and Toronto's Scarborough Town Center are examples of large shopping centres that have been able to attract substantial numbers of transit riders and reduce parking demand. Good connections between rail transit, buses and the shopping centre itself also add to the attraction of transit riders. In contrast, many US shopping malls do not encourage, and sometimes do not allow, transit access. Over time, malls are increasingly recognizing that their own workers need transit.

Figure 6.6 This parking garage consumes a square block of some of the most valuable real estate in the heart of San Francisco's central business district (CBD)

Source: Preston L. Schiller

Considering what the real world choices are could help in deciding whether the selected project alternative still merits support despite reservations about it as 'ideal'. Opposing a project when the BAU has a far worse economic evaluation, and no other realistic alternative seems overwhelmingly superior, might be counterproductive. To inform the decision, it can be very helpful to do additional analysis that addresses the flaws in the official decision-making process. The official method for evaluating proposed new rail transit projects used by the US Federal Transit Administration was revamped as a result of legislatively mandated changes enacted in 1991 as a result of pressures to address flaws in decision-making processes, although it took until 1999 before the new method was fully developed and ready for implementation (US Government Accountability Office, 1999).

Opportunity cost consideration also exists between spending on transportation and other societal needs. It might be easy to say that building medical clinics and schools would be more urgent than building a metro in a large developing city, if that is the real choice, although funding for one may not be fungible for the other. But if the real choice is between building a metro or building a motorway, the non-transport opportunity costs of forgone schools and clinics is not relevant. Opportunity costs can also be used to justify a project. Some needed facilities, such as transit tunnels or rights-of-way acquisition, may be much more difficult or costly to achieve in the future, making investment a wise choice now.

Figure 6.7 Donkey parking lot in a Berber village, Atlas Mountains, Morocco

Source: Preston L. Schiller

Critique of current methods with respect to sustainable outcomes

Discounting the future

The concept of using a discount rate in NPV analysis to reflect the time value of money is deeply ingrained in public policy and in officially sanctioned evaluation methods. The NPV approach does make sense for private profit-seeking firms that are concerning themselves only with actual monetary intakes and expenditures in the short- to medium-term planning horizon. But it becomes highly problematic when one tries to seriously promote sustainable development in a public investment context. Many sustainability advocates argue that one should consider the next seven generations. Yet, the discounting concept biases evaluation towards considering only short-term impacts. As was shown in Figure 6.2, the value of future cost benefits is almost zero within 30 years – not much more than one generation.

Some important practical consequences of discounting are that pollution and other environmental impacts endured by future generations and depletion of non-renewable resources are simply not important. Similarly, any positive impacts that could be of lasting value to future generations are also not important. Referring back to Figure 6.2, the value of the impacts after only 30 years is almost zero using a 15 per cent discount rate. Even with a lower 7 per cent rate, more typical for public agencies, the impact value is only about 15 per cent of its initial value. Thus, the NPV method as currently practised is not suitable for public projects when there are wide-ranging and long-lasting impacts.

It would have a profound impact upon public policy and project selection to revise the officially sanctioned methods and procedures to remove the short-term bias from discounting. It is clear that actual money streams such as construction and operating expenditures and revenues have less value in the future, so it would be appropriate to maintain these discounts for such entries to the cost-benefit ledger. But there are other costs and benefits that do not consist of actual money transactions. Some examples are reduced health care or personal transportation spending for future generations. Then there are others such as the natural water cleaning by wetlands or reduction in traffic deaths where monetization is merely a proxy to allow these impacts to be added or subtracted on the same monetary scale as the actual money streams. For all such impacts that persist in perpetuity and do not represent actual money streams, it might make sense to eliminate discounting.

Depreciation of assets is another type of discounting that is also permitted in the conventional NPV evaluation approach and thus also bears mention. The concept of depreciation is that assets wear out, and the continually decreasing value of them needs to be taken into account. While this is certainly true of assets with fixed lives, such as buses, it is not true of many major public works. As an example, the construction cost of a tunnel may be borne by one generation through bond payments until it is paid off, but future generations might benefit for the next 100 years. Indeed, many of the subway and railway tunnels built in the 19th century are still in use. Rather than allow the decrease in value of such assets towards zero, a much more modest, yet more realistic, provision would be to assign future costs for periodic repair and modernization.

Regulation versus pricing

Most economists will agree, regardless of their personal ideology, that costs that were previously externalized should be internalized. Up the chain, each company or public agency that provided products or services to the transport system should pay the full cost of production – not just their direct monetary costs, but all additional socio-economic costs as well. The intent is that the price the end user pays should reflect all costs to society, otherwise known as the user pays principle. When the specific type of cost under consideration is pollution, this is known as the polluter pays principle.

The alternative method to limit externalized costs is through 'command-and-control' measures. A typical example would be a regulation that specifies the legal emissions from an engine type. Another, in the US context, was the corporate average fuel efficiency (CAFE) standard, which mandated the fuel consumption across the automobile fleet mix of a manufacturer. While these types of measures are sometimes effective, they can also be inadequate and hard to adjust due to resistance. They may also be 'blunt instruments' that, unlike the user pays principle, do not assign costs to the perpetrator, and they can fail to incentivize a culture of continuous improvement.

Internalizing externalities

In order to overcome these failings, externalities can be internalized through pricing policies. In theory, the 'right price' to try to set is the marginal social cost (MSC). It includes the entire array of socio-economic costs such as public investment costs, congestion delays, pollution and whatever other negative impacts are created in a specific context. The cost of each impact should be measured at the last unit of production. The last unit is decisive for most costs. The level of congestion is dictated by the last car added to the traffic stream; capacity that is felt necessary to add is dictated by the last load of passengers that must be carried, and so on.[5]

Getting the prices right

Nations with fuel taxes that are much higher than the direct costs of building, maintaining and operating roads are already closer to the MSC; but there are studies that show that they should be higher.[6] The US, in particular, would benefit from much higher fuel- and driving-related taxes, since current forms of taxation generate revenues considerably below the direct costs of the highway system, as the recent shortfall of the Highway Trust Fund revealed. The CAFE standard proved ineffective in reducing fuel consumption as most technological improvements went into making the new automobiles faster and more powerful, rather than more efficient. Getting the aviation prices right could also reduce some flying while creating incentives for improved railways. Airlines around the world pay very low taxes on fuel relative to ground modes. Getting prices right remains as unfinished business to a lesser or greater extent everywhere.

Limitations on the use of pricing

While the MSC is certainly a benchmark that can be used to help evaluate whether the levels of taxes, fees, tolls and fares are appropriate, there are limits to its usefulness. As a practical matter, it is not really possible to measure all cost components under all conditions, let alone to administer finely honed prices that would vary with the conditions. While 'getting the prices right' can do much to correct many economic distortions and perversities, there are interactive effects between the transportation system and other aspects of the economy and society that simply cannot be easily included under economic paradigms.

The limitation of economic paradigms can be illustrated by an example. The relationship of the urban form to the passenger modal composition within the urban area is complex and important to the long-term sustainability of a city, but not fully captured by an MSC. Delucchi (2000) computed an MSC for rail transit that was averaged across peak and off-peak conditions. It appeared to be higher than for the auto, largely because of the huge infrastructure investments and operating support required. He then pointed out that the other offsetting benefits from building rail transit perhaps make it worthwhile anyway. In the end, he concedes that the MSC might not be a guide to action.

Instead of trying to draw conclusions using the economic cost versus benefit paradigm, it should be recognized that one of the underlying assumptions is not valid. Specifically, there is no realistic possibility for substitution between modes to meet the peak-hour demands and density requirements of CBDs (see the following section on 'Time–area: An important tool for analysing a transportation investment'). Thus, there is limited meaning to a comparison between their MSCs for the purposes of deciding which mode(s) to favour by public policy or for investments.

What is missing is an understanding of the physical relationship between modes and urban form. It is not possible to achieve a quality urban density city based primarily on automobiles. The capacity and space required for effective CBD density is based on peak period conditions, not on average conditions. Rail is far more space efficient than the automobile, which had the lower MSC in Delucchi's example. When rail transit is largely in tunnels and elevated structures instead of the street, even higher density can be supported. Thus, averaged values of MSC over the course of the day cannot be used for comparison. The range of realistic capacities for modes is not the same, nor is the quality of the service.

The higher density facilitated by transit has multiple impacts, some of which are not usually attributed to transportation and, hence, not considered in the cost versus benefit analysis. Higher density creates the possibility for a high percentage of non-motorized trips and reduces the average trip length for any given population size. Both these impacts reduce energy consumption. Furthermore, higher density also translates into more energy-efficient buildings and reduces the demand to consume land on the periphery, with all of its attendant negative effects on agriculture supply chains and the environment. Moreover, the lifestyle of a lower-density city is different than a higher-density city, a factor that resists attempts at quantification, let alone monetization.

Figure 6.8 Consumption of street space by people: People in their cars (top); same number of people without cars (centre); same number of individuals on one streetcar (bottom)

Source: Toronto Transit Commission

To summarize, while the MSC can give some insights, it is not conclusive. Picking the mode that should be promoted through public policy or that should receive public investment, based on the lowest MSC, or, indeed, using any method of selection that purports to be based on identifying the 'least cost', might be a mistake. There are likely to be invalid assumptions and important impacts that are left out.

Time–area: An important tool for analysing a transportation investment

Sustainable transportation will need a variety of analytic tools in order to overcome the deficiencies of BAU analyses and models. One promising approach described in Box 6.4 is time–area analysis, which considers the immediate and cumulative spatial impacts of motor vehicles upon the urban setting.

Moving public policy and investment evaluation towards promoting sustainability

Removing the discount factor from costs and benefits that do not correspond to actual monetary transfers would do more than any other single change in economic evaluation methods towards promoting a long-term outlook. The mobility benefits (or lack thereof), environmental costs, depletion of non-renewable resources and many other impacts to future generations are currently all discounted in most evaluation processes. Even if laws or regulations cannot be readily changed, it should still be possible to point out double standards and inconsistencies in current evaluations, which could lead to better informed public discussion. As an example, the oft-stated assertion that continuing highway construction is essential to future economic competitiveness is a way of saying that there should be no discount to the mobility benefit. If that is the assumption, then for consistency the environmental and resource-depletion consequences should not be discounted either.

In the US, there is often a double standard between modal evaluations. Most highway projects avoid any economic analysis at all – they are merely deemed necessary based on level-of-service criteria. By comparison, public transport projects are subjected to intense scrutiny at federal and local governmental levels. All monetized costs and benefits are subjected to discounting. In a more objective process, all modes would be subject to similar requirements.

Economic evaluation of transportation involves selection between choices. The trick is to apply the notion of economic efficiency to transportation policy and investment decisions to all modes in a fair way without falling into the trap of a simplistic 'least cost' approach. Holistic approaches such as life-cycle analysis (i.e. cradle-to-grave costs of automobiles versus public transit), inclusion of the energy and materials consumed to build infrastructure, etc. are all steps in the right direction. There is an increasing amount of published research that can inform the analyst.

The best test of whether particular investments will push a city or nation in the direction of increasing sustainability is to compare the cumulative effect of decades of investment, rather than at the level of the individual project. This tends to cancel out the effect of projects that are far less or far more effective than average. More importantly, it is the total quantity that counts for many sustainability indicators, not the individual parts. Urban areas developed with an emphasis on transit and transit-oriented development (TOD) rather than highways show better results for several environmental factors, including overall emission levels and land consumption (Kenworthy et al, 1997; Newman and Kenworthy, 1999).

The economic model of consumer choice that is applied to retail consumer goods is not necessarily applicable to transportation. A free market from which the 'sovereign consumer', whether individual or corporate, picks an ideal option does not appear to exist in transportation. A person or company cannot use an option that does not exist. Nor can one predict what will happen if an option should become available. There are too many factors that influence decisions that are outside the transportation arena, such as economic downturns or unforeseen changes in regional master development plans. Forecasting models that predict mode split and land development patterns have some uncertainty, but their results are essential inputs to any economic evaluation. Thus, a range of outcomes based on different scenarios can be quite helpful in accessing the consequences of this uncertainty and evaluations should be reported in terms of a range of results.

Because of all the uncertainties, project alternatives should be designed that are 'robust', meaning that they can be adapted to changing conditions. In addition to their economic efficiency and effectiveness, they should also be designed to promote the achievement of equity and social justice goals. Sustainable development will be impossible without it. For instance, the dispersion of the population of large US cities into the farmlands of the surrounding countryside and the simultaneous abandonment of large parts of these same cities was largely a consequence of racially discriminatory politics. In the developing world, abandonment of rural villages and migration to informal settlements on the edge of cities is driven by extreme income inequality.

In general, financing strategies that respect the user pays and polluter pays principle are preferable to use of general revenues. These strategies promote equity and social justice as well as economic efficiency. This does not mean that subsidies should never be given, only that they should be given as a result of a considered decision. There should be either an economic justification, or the subsidy should reflect a public interest and willingness to promote or facilitate

Box 6.4 How automobiles devour urban space and time[7]

The huge amount of space needed to accommodate cars is a perennial source of frustration to people trying to maintain the amenities and efficiencies possible in cities. It has long been recognized that transit is tremendously more space efficient than cars. The Toronto Transit Commission produced a useful graphic illustrating this several years ago (see Figure 6.8).

The amount of space consumed by various modes when combined with the duration of that consumption may be analysed with the time–area concept. This quantitative tool can help to advance the discussion of urban transportation policy, which is so often centred on monetary costs of investment and operational characteristics of various modes, to include insights about the physical and spatial implications of various modes and investment strategies.

Time–area is the product of the time and the area consumed by a vehicle within a chosen timeframe and location. This is a valuable measure because time and area can be equally important determinants in facility sizing and in capacity computations. An automobile commuter to the central city occupies a large amount of area while driving, but only for a short period of time. The driver then parks and consumes a lesser immediate area than while driving, but for a much longer duration. The total time–area expresses the entire resource demand as one unit, typically in square metre seconds (m^2 s) or square metre hours (m^2 h). Conventional methods analyse driving and parking separately.

The time–area concept has several advantages:

- It represents a common measure for evaluation of area and time consumption by any transportation unit (pedestrian, road vehicle, train), rather than for each mode separately.
- It allows joint measurement of consumption by moving and stationary transport units (either vehicles or persons).
- It unifies the two usually different concepts of static and dynamic components of a transportation system.
- It can provide a common variable for the comparison of different transportation modes.

Using this concept, it is possible to do an informative analysis of relative land-use and congestion effects of the various modal combinations urban travellers can select. In order to understand time–area, a few aspects of vehicle motion must be reviewed. As a vehicle moves along its right of way, it may be visualized as travelling with an open area attached to the front of it, an area referred to as its 'shadow'. The purpose of the shadow is to maintain adequate reaction and braking distance from the preceding vehicle. The minimum shadow depends upon the 'safety regime': the vehicle-following rule which determines the degree of safety offered under various circumstances.

The length of the vehicle plus its shadow, multiplied by the width of the lane or right of way, represents the 'instantaneous area' or 'module' that the vehicle occupies. Multiplied together with the amount of time during which it occupies it, the result is the amount of time–area consumed. Another very useful comparison is on a 'per unit of transportation work performed' basis (i.e. the time–area consumed per passenger kilometre, found by dividing by the average occupancy of the type of vehicle in question). The complex calculation method is described in Bruun and Vuchic (1996), where examples of typical commute trip components by foot, transit and automobile were compared. Their analysis showed the following:

- The automobile had a time advantage over the combined walk and transit trip, but it consumed considerably more time–area due to its area consumption and low vehicular load.
- Transit is much more time–area efficient than automobiles because its loadings at peak times are at their greatest and it does not consume the great amount of time–area that automobiles consume while parked at the worksite all day.

Even more telling is the graphical presentation of the cumulative time–area consumed by various modes. Figure 6.9 represents time–area by the vertical axis and elapsed time over the course of the day on the horizontal axis. Such a format shows both the rate of consumption and the total time–area consumed by each type of user as the day proceeds. This conveniently depicts not only the total consumption up to any given time, but the slope of the curve shows the rate of consumption; a horizontal line represents no consumption. One can see at a glance that the bus rider uses a very small fraction of the time–area of the car rider, and that the latter continues to consume during the entire day as a result of parking requirements. The need to have parking nearby is an inevitable major cause of time–area consumption by automobile users.

This same figure also compares the effects from increasing car occupancy from the peak-period average of 1.2 to 2, the level which qualifies automobiles for entry into many high-occupancy vehicle (HOV) lanes in the US, to 4 persons per vehicle, the level which carpool advocates would consider a highly successful outcome. While increases in car occupancy reduce time–area consumption, the rate for a full automobile is still far above the consumption for even a quarter-full bus.

Some of the important characteristics of commuting that can be observed using the time–area concept include the following:

- The automobile offers time savings and convenience of not having to transfer; but these advantages are traded off against the much higher land area requirements needed for driving it.
- Parking all day is the predominant component of time–area consumption of a car commuter if travel speeds are slow (as they are at peak periods) because the somewhat smaller area requirement while parked than while driving is far offset by the long duration of parking.
- Passengers in a fully loaded automobile consume far more time–area than a person in even a partially filled bus, both while driving and while parked. This argues powerfully against providing the same priority as buses to even four-person carpools. Bus lanes are far more space efficient than HOV lanes, especially when consideration is given for parking requirements at the destination.
- These findings are important for decision-makers. As environmental concerns focus more and more on the necessity of reducing consumption, one hopes that the promotion of efficient transit and the limiting of the automobile's overconsumption of urban space and time will find their way into the lexicon of green planning and policy-making.

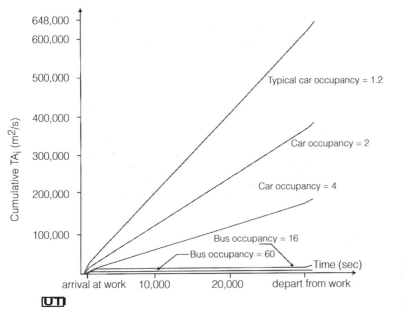

Figure 6.9 Cumulative time–area graph

Source: Bruun and Schiller (1996)

a desired outcome from the transportation system. This is particularly true in the interim period as financing strategies are being revised. Subsidies to automobile driving, for example, will strengthen the case for public transport subsidies and under-priced truck driving will strengthen the case for freight rail investments from the public purse.

Taxes, tolls and tax increment financing

Revenue sources for new projects should be broadened to improve the match of incidence of financial responsibility versus the incidence of benefits received. Fuel taxes and registration fees, when they are high enough, are a primary source of operating and investment capital. Toll roads and toll bridges are also typically paid off by selling revenue bonds. These focus on the user; but it is also possible to try to recapture some of the external benefits that are internalized as windfalls to property owners. Tax increment financing (TIF), a surcharge on property taxes within a major transport infrastructure benefit area, is also increasingly used to defray costs of construction.[8]

Land value taxation

Land value taxation (LVT) is a concept that was pioneered by Henry George in the 19th century that deserves greater attention. It asserts that much of the value of land is due to its proximity to particular infrastructure, including transportation. Thus, the property tax collected should be based primarily on location, not on the value of the buildings and structures. 'Georgians' argue that the current dominant system rewards landowners who let buildings decay or convert property into low-value uses such as parking lots, and punishes landowners who invest in higher-density residential and commercial buildings.[9]

Public–private partnership

A commonly discussed strategy in financing public works today is the public–private partnership (PPP). This covers a wide array of possible financial schemes ostensibly founded on the recognition that it can be mutually beneficial to share financial responsibilities and rewards. It can provide the means to execute projects much faster than with only public resources. PPP can promote equity by requiring that private interests who will benefit also contribute; but caution is advised. In the US, at least one of the main reasons that PPPs have become necessary is that taxes on high-income individuals have decreased and wealth concentration has increased. The PPPs are a way of attracting investors. Private firms need a higher MARR than public agencies and this may increase the overall cost, in which case it would be better to simply tax the beneficiaries directly.

Depending upon how they are crafted and overseen, PPPs could work to enhance public services or could work against sustainable development. Cash-strapped governments can be tempted with upfront money from the sale or leasing of assets, or from granting permission to build new infrastructure. Later on, future politicians and public agencies may find that they have been deprived of their own abilities to programme future revenues. In order to avoid raising taxes in the present, an unscrupulous or short-sighted government can shift the costs to future administrations. As with all major planning and project efforts, PPP proposals should be analysed in detail with an eye to the impact upon future generations. Two examples follow.

The Dulles Toll Road serving the suburban area between Interstate 495 (the Beltway) and Dulles Airport was extended past the airport and on to Leesburg, Virginia. It was made possible through a concession to a private firm. While it may pay for its own construction and operating cost, its very existence has contributed to low-density development over 30 miles (50km) from Washington, DC, and has thus created many externalities for a long time to come. A more positive example can be seen in Helsinki, where its outdoor suburban bus terminal, which at one time exposed riders to the harshest of winter conditions, was transformed into the Kampii, a multi-storey shopping mall with an indoor facility that includes loading terminals for both suburban and intercity buses. This was made possible through a joint development effort by regional authorities, and includes a reclaimed public area in front of the mall.

Figure 6.10 Victorian house transformed into transit station, Toronto, Ontario

Note: Rather than disrupt the neighbourhood, the Toronto Transit Commission recycled a Victorian building into the entrance of the Spadina Subway Station and bus transfer location. The 1960s–1970s proposed Spadina freeway would have destroyed this building and much of its neighbourhood – the citizens' movement Stop Spadina successfully promoted a rail transit line instead.

Source: Preston L. Schiller

Case studies

Three case studies about important investment and economic analysis are presented below. Two illuminate the ways in which economic analyses can be used to further ST goals and one illustrates how a poorly conceptualized and under-analysed highway investment can be costly to taxpayers and harmful to the environment. The first case study discusses how joint development around transit can benefit developers, cities, and transit providers and users.

A significant issue in many parts of the world is the overuse of trucking for freight transport and the underdevelopment of freight railways and intermodal facilities. This can lead to congestion in major highway corridors and considerable pressure to expand roads and bridges. This issue is discussed in Chapter 5. Box 6.6 discusses how economic analysis might be applied to this problem.

High-occupancy vehicle lanes:
A questionable transportation investment

Around the highway world, and through some of the more tired minds of the transit world, the peculiar notion of high-occupancy vehicle (HOV) lanes has

Box 6.5 Investment around transit: Joint development and value capture

Jeffrey R. Kenworthy[10]

Joint development and value capture are the means by which the community is able to share in the broader economic benefits of a major public investment in rapid transit. Joint development specifically refers to the shared or multiple use of transport corridors, particularly station areas, to the benefit of both the transit agency and private parties. A study by Cervero et al (1992) of more than 100 projects and 24 cities states that:

> The idea behind joint development is simple and appealing. In exchange for the right to develop a private project at, above, below or adjacent to a mass transit facility, the developer either assumes some of the cost of developing (or renovating) the facility, or makes a direct payment to the transit operator.

Vuchic (1981) provides insight into why rail is the favoured mode for concentrated urban development and, hence, the most common mode involved in private–public joint development:

> The most significant single impact of rail transit is its strong influence on land use and the form of cities. The permanence of rail transit lines and stations generates the developments of land use which interact with and depend on the high-quality transit service ... in time stations generate their own patronage and 'anchor' themselves ... With good planning and urban design, this interaction can be used for the creation of attractive urban environments.

For rail to be more effective than buses in concentrating land uses it must be more attractive in the minds of development decision-makers. Transit is seen by developers as offering excellent land-use opportunities in that it 'conserves the use of prime real estate for greater commercial and economic activity, rather than for the storage of automobiles' (Elms, 1989).

A major survey of key real estate decision-making positions in eight US and three Canadian cities with comparatively new light rail transit (LRT) and bus-way facilities (Henry, 1989) found that there were several key factors that made development around LRT attractive, including:

- Residential development potential received a higher rating for LRT than busway stations.
- There was better understanding of LRT routes and services when compared with most bus systems.
- More favourable land-use regulations were in existence, including a more attractive environment around LRT stations.

The most common form of joint development is the sale or lease of air rights over transit rights of way. Joint development seeks to gain the greatest economic return to the government on the transit investment and to achieve a more environmentally attractive and integrated relationship between the rail system and adjacent land uses. It can be a key tool in ensuring that land use and public transport are more mutually supportive.

Value capture

Value capture, in the context of funding public transport, specifically refers to the taking of some, or all, of the enhanced value of property, which is attributable to the government's investment in a transit system. There are many potential mechanisms for doing this, some direct and others less direct. Different cities use different approaches according to local political, administrative and legal situations. Some examples of value capture methods that have been used include:

- capturing the improved value of resumed land adjacent to stations;
- joint venture agreements with private developers;
- *ad valorem* taxation (an agency taxes the assessed market value of land or improvements);
- station cost-sharing or direct contribution of the private sector towards aspects of the rail system;
- connector fees;
- leasing of advertising space;
- special transit tax districts, such as special benefit assessment districts in the US;
- sharing the increased tax base from higher-density/value land use between the public transport operator and local authority.

The single most effective method of value capture is the taking of the component of increased land value (windfall profits) resulting from public planning decisions, and specifically capturing land value increases that result from planning approval for higher-value, more intensive land uses as a result of a public works investment (e.g. a new railway).

It is important to note that the provision of rail or any high-quality transit service cannot of itself generate development where the general economic climate is not conducive. In other words, 'transit cannot turn a sow's ear into a silk purse. Transit can influence location decisions within a market, but it cannot generate a market where none exists' (Elms, 1989).

Joint development/value capture and bus systems

The principles of joint development can be applied to bus stations, as in Ottawa (Cervero, 1986) and in Cedar Rapids, Iowa (2008 population: 128,000; Lundberg and Aller, 1984). The US$31 million development in Cedar Rapids involved the city's main downtown bus station, an intercity bus terminal, a major private office building and parking garage, plus pedestrian concourses to the

CBD and a housing project for the elderly and handicapped. It has stimulated further adjacent redevelopment.

Conditions for successful joint development

Cervero et al (1992) conclude that there are four major conditions necessary for successful joint development projects:

1   The local real estate market must be active and healthy.
2   The agency with primary responsibility must have an entrepreneurial bent.
3   Sound coordination is essential when projects involve more than one public agency.
4   Sponsors need to understand the long-term benefits of joint development that go beyond generating revenues. The best joint development projects are those that encourage transit use, create more interesting station environments and reinforce other planning and development goals, such as a more efficient and desirable urban form, reduced congestion and a better jobs/housing balance.

Box 6.6 Moving truck freight onto tracks: A hypothetical example of a policy-directed economic analysis

If a goal were to be set to reduce intercity truck use in North America by a certain percentage, this could be translated into the cost reduction that would be needed for intermodal truck/rail services in order to make them attractive to shippers at shorter breakeven distances. A mode split model could estimate the cost reduction needed specific to particular corridors. Depending upon the cost reduction needed, a capital subsidy to private freight railroads to build infrastructure and to install equipment that would reduce loading/unloading times might be sufficient. Or it might require even more investment to acquire land to build additional terminals. In some corridors it might prove infeasible, unless fuel costs to truckers increased dramatically. Once the investment amounts are known, these can be compared to the known monetary and monetized cost reductions to be expected from eliminating this certain percentage of trucks. If discounting were removed from non-renewable resources and pollution, the cost reductions would be higher yet and the public investment that could be justified would increase.

been spreading in recent decades. When knocked down as an inefficient or ineffective way to spend transportation or transit funds, it rebounds in the form of proposals for high-occupancy toll (HOT) lanes, a sexier title more in keeping with auto-eroticism and the privatization fad, but no less muddled in its thinking than HOV. The US alone has built thousands of miles of HOV lanes. Some European and Asian countries, who should know better through their

Box 6.7 High-occupancy vehicles (HOVs): A date is not a carpool!

Preston L. Schiller [11]

In the US, carpools (or vanpools) are generally defined as arrangements where two or more people share a ride from one destination to another, ostensibly reducing the number of vehicles that might otherwise be used for such travel. HOV lanes are often financed with transit funds (many transit agencies in the US also operate vanpool programmes) or federal funds for pollution reduction since it is believed that they reduce emissions, although this assumption has been strenuously challenged (Johnston, 1991; Replogle, 1993). They are expected to increase the proportion of individuals riding transit or carpooling by allowing better and more reliable travel times. Some of the earliest HOV lanes were bus-only lanes that were opened, or downgraded, to carpool lanes for three or more people ('3+') to a vehicle. Since many newly constructed HOV lanes were not necessarily built in areas where there were job concentrations or carpool programmes, this criterion was generally lowered across the US to 2+ in order to have any appreciable use made of the lanes. Many of these lanes are HOV only during peak traffic periods.

There are several problems inherent in these assumptions about carpool criteria and motivation for ride-sharing. First, the travel time savings while in a vehicle must be significant in order to overcome the time penalty paid by participants in carpools. In other words, most car-poolers must either wait for the carpool to arrive or spend some time in travel (often by car) to a rendezvous location, which undermines the time saved travelling in the HOV lane. Second, just as there are some 'inconveniences' associated with transit travel, compared to personal vehicular travel, there are inconveniences associated with carpooling – adhering to a fixed schedule when work hours may vary, inability to change plans or run errands, or even disdain for the type of music preferred by the driver have been cited as objections to carpooling.

The assumption that, given the right environment and incentives, single-occupant vehicles (SOVs) would evolve into two-person carpools (HOVs), which would further evolve into three-person carpools over time, is a curious instance of Darwinian thought applied to urban transport. Upon examination, it turns out that anywhere from almost 50 to 80 per cent of 2+ vehicles in HOV lanes are occupied by members of the same household, leading to the term 'fampool' (Fielding and Klein, 1997; Pisarski, 1997; Poole, 2007). Others may be friends on an outing or a date. The extent to which these vehicles move out of a general lane into a newly provided HOV lane is merely a matter of rearranging the furniture on the freeway. It is not a triumph of shift from one modal status to another. The fact that the designation 'high-occupancy vehicle' is given to two-person cars is yet another example of how far down the road past Orwell's *1984* double-think language American highway planners have gone. That a date is not a carpool should have been obvious to policy-makers long ago. The ultimate mixing of American transportation and political values occurred when a pregnant woman cited for driving solo in a 2+ HOV lane contested her Seattle area traffic citation. Asserting that a foetus is a person, she claimed status as a carpool. The court found otherwise.

When the person-moving peak-hour performance of bus-only and HOV lanes is analysed, it becomes clear that bus-only lanes far outperform general lanes and HOV lanes. Among the best performing bus lanes are those on New Jersey's I-495, serving New York's Lincoln Tunnel and carrying the passenger equivalent of at least 14 general lanes, and the O–C Transitway in Ottawa, Ontario, carrying the equivalent of at least five general lanes or 70 per cent of all peak-hour traffic into downtown. In most HOV lanes, buses are carrying many more people than automobiles in either HOV or adjacent general lanes. When the best performing bus-only and HOV lanes in North America were compared, it was found that buses carried 67 per cent of the traffic of the combined HOV and bus-only lanes. In lanes open to buses and carpools, buses still carried 48 per cent of all passengers (Schiller, 1998, p4).

One might ask promoters: 'If HOV is so good, why not just convert some existing general lanes to HOV – especially given the drawbacks and expense of constructing new HOV lanes?' While recent years have seen more construction of bus-only lanes, most were conversions from traffic or parking lanes. Very few freeway lanes have been converted for bus or carpool use. But generally, the planning of HOV lanes ignores the conversion alternative and the cost-benefits associated with such a strategy, and labels it with the pejorative term 'take a lane'. 'Optimize a lane' would be a more fair term.

The question needs to be asked whether HOV is a belief desperately seeking validation – a highway expansion in search of meaning? Meanwhile, the difficult details of improving transit and land use, and reducing pollution and global greenhouse gases, are being overlooked in the rush to build more lanes to nowhere.

Figure 6.11 'And tow'ring o'er his head in triumph ride': The Trojan priest Laocoön and his sons are attacked by poisonous highway serpents

Source: Andy Singer (www.andysinger. com); quote from the Dryden translation of Virgil's *Aeneid*

experience with quality public transportation, have also been bitten by the HOV bug. Some Canadian regions, including transit-savvy Vancouver and Toronto, have similarly been afflicted. A wide-ranging body of researchers and policy analysts have criticized these efforts as cloaked forms of highway expansion that weaken transit, promote sprawl through the facilitation of longer commutes and damage air quality. Box 6.7 reports on this critique.

Questions for discussion

- Which costs and benefits from proposed transport projects are the most difficult to include when governments insist on using monetary evaluation to make funding decisions?
- Discuss the prospects for creating more sustainable public transport systems primarily through market mechanisms such as re-regulation or deregulation – that is, without major street redesigns, legal restrictions on lane use, major public investments, etc.
- Using the concept of time–area, discuss the physical limitations to the numbers of personal motor vehicles (PMVs) that a city can support? Discuss this in light of investing in road expansions (including high-occupancy vehicles, or HOVs) or transit and non-motorized infrastructure.

Notes

1   It can, in fact, be negative, as is the case with nuclear power plants.
2   Sound walls tend to redistribute rather than eliminate noise; new wetlands generally need to be created on a much larger scale than those they have replaced in order to equal the productivity of those destroyed.
3   Adapted from the *Financial Times*, FT.com site, 27 July 2003, accessed 15 September 2009. Professor Norman Myers is honorary visiting fellow of Green College, Oxford and has acted as scientific consultant to the White House, the United Nations and the European Commission. Sir Crispin Tickell is chancellor of the University of Kent at Canterbury and chairman of the Climate Institute of Washington, DC.
4   Subsidies also exist that aggravate inequality and unsustainability. As an example, urban bus companies in most Indian cities are not subsidized, but taxed instead, with the taxes used to build roads for the benefit of the small minority who own cars. See also Litman (1998).
5   Positive externalities, by comparison, need no government intervention in order to be recognized and internalized – there are always parties willing to accept a windfall. Instead, the problem becomes recapturing them as a possible means of financing projects.
6   For more, see Kageson (1993, 1996), Komanoff (1994), US Congress (1994) and Liechti (2003).
7   This item is based upon Bruun and Schiller (1996); excerpts and figures are used with the permission of the publisher. The notion of analysing time–area had been discussed by Louis Marchand of the Régie Autonome des Transports Parisiens (RATP) and his colleagues as early as 1977, but has not received the attention and application that it deserves. The original articles are now obscure; more recent articles are by Marchand (1985, 1989) and Delucchi (2000).
8   For more, see Smith and Gihring (2003) for a bibliography of land value capture schemes that have been used to fund transit.

9   For more, see Metalitz (2004) for a description of how this might work to fully fund transit in the Chicago area.

10   Jeffrey R. Kenworthy is professor of sustainable cities at the Curtin University Sustainability Policy Institute (CUSP) at Curtin University in Perth, Western Australia.

11   Excerpted from Schiller (1998), with permission of the publisher. See also Leman et al (1994).

References and further reading

Beimborn, E., Kennedy, R. and Schaefer, W. (1996) *Inside the Blackbox: Making Transportation Models Work for Livable Communities*, http://www.environmentaldefense.org/documents/1859_InsideBlackBox.pdf, accessed 13 December 2009

Bruun, E. (2007) *Better Public Transit Systems: Analyzing Investments and Performance*, Planners Press, Chicago, IL

Bruun, E. and Schiller, P. (1996) 'How cars devour urban space and time', *Urban Transport International*, Paris, Groupe Actis, no 5, pp38–39

Bruun, E. and Vuchic, V. (1996) 'Time–area concept: Development, meaning, and application', in *Transportation Research Record* 1499, Transportation Research Board, Washington, DC, pp95–104

Cervero, R. (1986) 'Urban transit in Canada: Integration and innovation at its best', *Transportation Quarterly*, vol 40, no 3, pp293–315

Cervero, R., Hall, P. and Landis, J. D. (1992) *Transit Joint Development in the United States*, Monograph 42, National Transit Access Center, Institute of Urban and Regional Development, University of Berkeley, CA

Delucchi, M. A. (1996–1997) *The Annualized Social Cost of Motor Vehicle Use in the United States*, vols 1–23, Report UCD–ITS–RR–96–3, Institute of Transportation Studies, University of California at Davis, Davis, CA

Delucchi, M. A. (2000) 'Should we try to get the prices right?', *Access 16*, Institute for Transportation Studies, University of California at Davis, www.its.ucdavis.edu/publications/2000/UCD-ITS-RP-00-08.pdf, accessed 15 July 2009

Elms, C. P. (1989) 'Issues and requirements of real estate developers', in *Light Rail Transit: New System Successes at Affordable Prices*, Special Report 221, Transportation Research Board, Washington, DC, pp113–120

Fielding, G. J. and Klein, D. B. (1997) 'Hot lanes: Introducing congestion pricing one lane at a time', *Access*, no 11, pp10–15.

Hanson, M. (1992) 'Automobile subsidies and land use: Estimates and policy response', *Journal of the American Planning Association*, vol 58, no 1, pp60–71

Henry, L. (1989) 'Ridership forecasting considerations in comparisons of light rail and motor bus modes', in *Light Rail Transit: New System Successes at Affordable Prices*, Special Report 221, Transportation Research Board, Washington, DC, pp163–189

Johnston, R. A. (1991) 'Comments on the California Air Resources Board document on HOV systems plans as air pollution control measures', Division of Environmental Studies, University of California at Davis, Davis, CA

Kageson, P. (1993) *Getting the Prices Right, A European Scheme for Making Transport Pay its True Costs*, European Federation for Transport and Environment, Stockholm and Brussels

Kageson, P. (1996) 'Effects of internalisation on transport demand and modal split', Chapter 3, in *Internalising the Social Costs of Transport*, OECD, www.internationaltransportforum.org/europe/ecmt/taxes/pdf/94socCosts4e.pdf, accessed 25 August 2009

Kenworthy, J. R. (1990) 'Do not shoot me I'm only the transport planner (apologies to Elton John)', in P. Newman, J. R. Kenworthy and T. Lyons (eds) *Transport Energy Conservation Policies for Australian Cities: Strategies for Reducing Automobile Dependence*, Final report on National Energy Research, Development and Demonstration Council project no 1050, ISTP, Murdoch University, Perth, Australia

Kenworthy, J. F., Laube, F. B., Newman, P. W. G. and Barter, P. (1997) *Indicators of Transport Efficiency in 37 Global Cities: A Report for the World Bank*, Institute for Science and Technology Policy, Murdoch University, Perth, Australia

Komanoff, C. (1994) 'Pollution taxes for roadway transportation', *Pace Environmental Law Review*, vol 12, no 1, pp121–184

Leman, C. K., Schiller, P. L. and Pauly, K. (1994) *Rethinking HOV: High Occupancy Vehicle Lanes and the Public Interest*, Chesapeake Bay Foundation, Annapolis, MD, http://ntl.bts.gov/DOCS/retk.html, accessed 15 September 2009

Liechti, M. (2003) *Getting the Prices Right + 10: Towards Target Oriented Pricing*, European Federation for Transport and Environment (T&E), www.transportenvironment.org/Publications/prep_hand_out/lid:54, accessed 25 August 2009

Litman, T. (1998) 'Driving out subsidies: How better pricing of transportation options would help protect our environment and benefit consumers', *Alternatives Journal*, vol 24, no 1, pp36–42

Lundberg, B. D. and Aller, T. L. (1984) 'Joint development in Cedar Rapids', *Planning*, American Planning Association, June, pp11–14

Marchand, L. A. (1985) 'A fruitful concept in town planning: Space–time consumption', in *Régie Autonome des Transports Parisiens*, RATP, Paris, pp3–6

Marchand, L. A. (1989) 'How to allocate road space in urban places', Presentation at Congress of the Union International des Transports Publiques (UITP), Singapore

Metalitz, C. (2004) 'Paying for transit only once, and other advantages of a transit benefit tax based on land value', Research Note 5, Henry George School, Chicago, IL

Mitchell, R. B. and Rapkin, C. (1954) *Urban Traffic: A Function of Land Use*, Columbia University Press, New York, NY

Myers, N. and Tickell, C. (2003) 'The no-win madness of Catch-22 subsidies', *Financial Times*, 27 July, www.ft.com, accessed 15 September 2009

Newman, P. W. G. and Kenworthy, J. R. (1999) *Sustainability and Cities: Overcoming Automobile Dependence*, Island Press, Washington, DC

Pew Charitable Trust (2009) 'Analysis finds shifting trends in highway funding: User fees make up decreasing share', *Subsidyscope*, 24 November 2009 (update), www.subsidyscope.com/, accessed 23 December 2009

Pisarski, A. E. (1997) 'Testimony before the Senate Subcommittee on Transportation and Infrastructure', 13 February, http://epw.senate.gov/105th/pisarski.htm, accessed 16 September 2009

Poole, R. (2007) 'It's time to replace HOV lanes: Employer-certified HOT-3 lanes offer a solution to the problems plaguing many HOV lanes', Reason Foundation, http://reason.org/news/show/its-time-to-replace-hov-lanes, accessed 15 September 2009

Replogle, M. (1993) *Transportation Conformity and Demand Management: Vital Strategies for Clean Air Attainment*, Environmental Defense Fund, Washington, DC

Schiller, P. L. (1998) 'High occupancy vehicle (HOV) lanes: Highway expansions in search of meaning', *World Transport Policy & Practice*, vol 4, no 2, pp32–38, www.eco-logica.co.uk/WTPPdownloads.html (then select <wtpp04.2.pdf>), accessed 15 September 2009

Shoup, D. (1992) *Cashing Out Employer Paid Parking*, Report No FTA–CA–11–0035–92–1, Federal Transit Administration, available from NTIS, USDOT, Washington, DC

Shoup, D. (1993) *Cashing Out Employer Paid Parking: A Precedent for Congestion Pricing?*, Working Paper UCTC No 205, University of California Transportation Center, Berkeley, CA, www.uctc.net/papers/205.pdf, accessed 15 September 2009

Shoup, D. (2005) *The High Cost of Free Parking*, APA Planners Press, Chicago, IL

Small, K. A. (1997) 'Economics and urban transportation policy in the United States', *Regional Science and Urban Economics*, vol 27, pp671–691

Smith, J. J. and Gihring, T. A. (2003) *Financing Transit Through Value Capture: An Annotated Bibliography*, Victoria Transport Policy Institute, Victoria, British Columbia, www.vtpi.org, accessed 15 July 2009

Toor, W. and Havlick, S. (2004) *Transportation and Sustainable Campus Communities: Issues, Examples, Solutions*, Island Press, Washington, DC

US Congress (1994) *Saving Energy in US Transportation*, OTA–ETI–589, Office of Technology Assessment, US Congress, US Government Printing Office, Washington, DC, www.fas.org/ota/reports/9432.pdf, accessed 24 August 2009

US Government Accountability Office (1999) *FTA's Progress in Developing and Implementing a New Starts Evaluation Process*, Report RCED–99–113, US Government Printing Office, Washington, DC

Vuchic, V. R. (1981) *Urban Public Transportation: Systems and Technology*, Prentice Hall, Inc., Englewood Cliffs, NJ

7

Public Policy and Effective Citizen Participation: Leadership, Deliberation, Back-Casting, Scenarios, Visualization and Visioning

The public, policy and participation

This chapter examines the areas of transportation policy and public participation with a view towards how each of these areas can interact with and help sustainable transportation (ST) efforts. Policy-making, planning and participation can be viewed as intimately entwined processes. Defining what makes for good policy-making and effective public participation is neither an easy matter nor one about which there is much consensus. Both may be viewed as areas of 'wicked problems' (areas that do not lend themselves to simple and 'scientific' solutions) (Rittel and Webber, 1973), as well as of 'contested definitions' (matters about which there is often little agreement as to how an issue or problem is defined) (Day, 1997; Roberts, 2004). It is important to understand much of transportation policy-making and participation in the context of process rather than product because of their complex and multifaceted nature. Policy-making and participation for ST emphasize processes informed by a vision for a preferred future. Because they are so closely interrelated they are treated together here rather than in separate chapters.

Who is the 'public', what is 'public'?

The 'public' generally refers to a large body of individuals, the 'people', sharing or united in some broad common characteristic such as citizenship in the same nation. That which is 'public' (open to use or access by citizens) is often best understood in contrast to its opposite, 'private' – that which is owned by individuals or corporations and not subject to access or use by a people at large. But these meanings often become blurred when one considers real-life situations. Most streets and roads are 'public', open to the people at large and usually built at public expense. But most vehicles are privately owned, serving private purposes. Many other facilities, such as shipping ports, terminals and airports, are financed by public funds but operated for the benefit of private entities such as shipping lines and airlines. The public may have access to such facilities but the facilities benefit private interests.

Public policy

Public policy as a field developed as part of the movement towards improved planning, rationalization of governmental processes, and greater accountability and transparency to the public and its officials. While there are many excellent and competing attempts at defining public policy by scholars (Gerston, 1997; Cochran and Malone, 1999; Anderson, 2000; Birkland 2005), public policy can be defined for the purposes of this chapter as the creation and institutionalization of government plans of action, the definition of terms and concepts involved in such policies, and the body of discussion and discourse that surrounds and emerges from policy formulation and deliberation. Dimensions and differentiations within public policy include:

- the locus of policy-making, as well as its geographical target and locus of implementation – local, regional, state–provincial, national or international;
- types of policy that include 'substantive' (addressing what government wants to do), 'procedural' (addressing how government should accomplish its goals and objectives), 'promoting' change, control/regulation, or distributing/redistributing certain goods or services (Cochran and Malone, 1999, pp12–14; Anderson, 2000, pp7–18; Birkland, 2005, pp139–149);
- policy scope, which refers to whether policy is intended to be narrow or far reaching, long enduring or of a delimited timeframe.

Scholars of public policy also categorize policy as to whether it is administrative, within a legislative framework or whether it is action oriented, such as a mandate to create a large number of new jobs within a short period of time to resolve an economic crisis. They also pay close attention to the cast of 'actors' in policy 'dramas', as well as how a policy agenda is developed and executed.

Transportation policy: From mobility promotion to mobility management and sustainability

Transportation policy is a domain of public policy, and ST policy is a fairly recent area that has developed out of dissatisfaction with business as usual (BAU). It is a challenging area because it involves the environment, the economy, the spatial form of cities and personal behaviour and values. At present, while BAU still dominates much policy, there are many efforts under way to develop and promote ST policy. These range from broad policy studies to localized efforts to reduce the domination of private motor vehicles. Some governments are actively developing ST policies, while some of those that are lagging behind are being prodded by non-governmental organizations (NGOs) to develop better policies.[1]

Prior to the 20th century, most transportation planning and policy-making was formulated in response to technological developments and innovations, such as the newly emerging railroad, steamship, bicycle or automobile and improved road surfaces and engineering. Strategic developments involving decades or centuries of comprehensive planning and resource commitments, such as the Roman ports and roads networks and Inca roads system, were exceptions. Much policy was *ad hoc*, developing around specific projects. Some policy-making in the 19th and early 20th centuries was oriented towards 'grand visions', such as the Erie Canal linking the Hudson River with the Great Lakes in North America, or France's vision of an improved road network linking Paris with the most far-flung of provinces. With France and Germany as exceptions, most policy was oriented towards a lesser scale – a small canal, a few miles of turnpike or an improved port facility. Rarely were these linked to a national plan or policy, systematized, or even seen as in need of broad-ranging intervention (Akaha, 1990; Stevens, 2004).

The complexity of transportation issues

The locus of transportation policy-making ranges from local and regional to national and international. From the point of view of ST, some of the most interesting and exciting initiatives are occurring at the local and regional levels. This section surveys this range broadly, with more detail about exemplary efforts included in the case studies. Part of the complexity that policy-makers face is trying to sort through and address the many issues posed to them, including:

- Whose trips are most valuable and to whom: individual citizens, freight interests, tourists?
- Which trips are most valuable and for whom: commute to work, local goods distribution, long-distance freight, farm to market, leisure- or service-seeking?
- How can one manage the conflicts among these competing interests, levels of society and broader issues, such as economy and the environment?
- Which services and investments should be supported from public funding and which should be left to individuals and private-sector interests?

These questions are often in the minds of policy-makers and policy-shapers at all levels of transportation decision-making.

Transportation policy in the 20th century: A global perspective

A survey of the greatly varied terrain of transportation policy around the globe captures the great differences between what occurs in the wealthier nations and cities and the situation of the poorer nations and cities. Many wealthy countries seem to have an oversupply of roads, while many less wealthy countries seem to suffer from an undersupply of good roads and few mobility options in town or countryside. Many nations are giving much attention to the facilitation of global freight movement, which is seen by some as contradicting efforts to address climate change and greenhouse gas production (Curtis, undated). The national and international emphasis on freight mobility contrasts with 'stage centre': concerns about personal or passenger transportation in most cities and urban regions, wealthy or impoverished. The great variation in response to urban transportation issues across the spectrum of wealth and poverty is striking. Some cities, rich or poor, are investing significantly in transit, walking and bicycling, while many, rich or poor, are investing in roads and private vehicle expansions. Many nations are directing policy efforts towards deregulation, liberalization and expansion of transportation to facilitate global trade, while some cities within these same nations are struggling to better manage personal mobility and promote localization. Hence, any generalizations must be taken with caution since so much variability is involved.

After World War II, large-scale development of transportation policy began to occur (Stevens, 2004, pp15–16; Gifford, 2003). The post-war period may be viewed as three somewhat different periods: 1945 to 1970, 1970 to 1990 and 1990 to the present.

1945–1970: Reconstruction and expansion American style and its discontents

Some of the important elements of transportation history in the post-World War II period have been summarized in Chapter 3. In general, the most important policy issues of the period from 1945 to 1970 centred on developing policies, plans and resources for rebuilding or expanding transportation infrastructure, and refurbishing, replacing and modernizing transportation material such as buses, trains, shipping and aviation fleets damaged, destroyed or simply worn out in the war years.

There were wide-ranging differences as well as some convergences in policy and investment emphases among nations and regions during this period. At one end of the spectrum was the US policy and investment emphasis on highway expansion that culminated in the 45,000 linear miles (72,000km) of an interstate highway system. At the other end was Japan, which began planning for major rail improvements in the 1950s and opened its first high-speed rail line, the Shinkansen, connecting Tokyo and Osaka on 1 October 1964, in time for the Tokyo Olympics. Most other industrial countries were in between, contenting themselves with modest improvements to existing railways, or allowing railways to shrink, while some highway expansion was undertaken.

Decolonization began in several developing parts of the planet. There was a fair amount of variability as to whether the colonial transportation systems, roads and railways, designed for resource extraction and military and administrative movements, were maintained, abandoned or, in a few cases, improved. Some countries, such as Senegal and Zimbabwe, have maintained the good road systems that have been one of their few useful legacies from the colonial era. Others, such as Cameroon, have not maintained their roads well.[2] Commercial aviation services, generally affordable only by business and government officials, replaced some of the former colonial surface transportation services leading to the deterioration of some surface networks and services. This period also saw the beginnings of trade liberalization, deregulation and privatization that were to significantly affect several aspects of national and international policy and practice, especially in freight and air services over the next several decades (Pucher and Lefevre, 1996; Stevens, 2004; Button and Hensher, 2005).

1970–1990: Rethinking cities and highways; beginnings of global 'liberalization'

The period from 1970 to 1990 saw many public and political reactions against the policy emphasis on roadway expansion in many places, especially in cities, as well as their continued expansion in other places. In some countries, including the US, Canada and the UK, both occurred.[3] Some reactions against pro-highway policy led to innovations aimed at improving the overall quality of urban life. The movement towards traffic calming in cities began in the 1970s and 1980s, spreading in the 1990s across the globe from Europe to Australia, Japan and, eventually, the US and Canada.[4] A few Latin American cities re-examined their planning policies. The city of Curitiba, Brazil, led the way in planning for future growth and environmental and transportation needs, and influenced changes for transit, walking and bicycling that have taken place in Bogotá, Colombia, in recent years.

At the national and international levels a few countries began railway improvements; but most policy energy was directed towards liberalization, deregulation and privatization.[6] Such efforts resulted in the lowering of barriers

---

Box 7.1 Curitiba and Bogotá: Political leadership makes a big difference

Curitiba, Brazil, and Bogotá, Colombia, exemplify how political leadership can influence urban planning and investment in a sustainable direction. Theirs are two very different stories. Curitiba was able to plan a concentration of population along developing corridors to be served by a busway. Bogotá made planning and investment changes within the context of an already built environment to improve equity through bicycle and pedestrian amenities. Both opted for the lower-cost bus rapid transit (BRT). But as ridership grows, the limits of BRT become evident – and when politics changes, as it has in Bogotá, some of the recent accomplishments are at risk.

Curitiba has attracted much global attention to its accomplishments. During the 1960s this Brazilian city with approximately 1.8 million residents began to transform its planning: environmental, land use, social and transportation. Architect, planner and later Mayor Jaime Lerner was in the forefront of this transformation. The result has been linear dense development served well by a BRT that has brought many innovations to that transit form. Daily transit ridership is approximately 2 million.

In the mid to late 1990s and early 2000s, under the political leadership of Mayors Antanas Mockus and Enrique Penalosa (1995 to 2003), Bogotá (population 7 million) moved in a more progressive transportation direction. It created a *ciclovia* bicycle–pedestrian way, expanded parks, reclaimed some street space from cars for larger pedestrian and public spaces, cleared some slums to create public spaces, improved housing in other areas for its poor, and introduced the TransMillenio BRT, whose daily ridership currently is approximately 1 million, providing a much needed efficient and affordable transportation option for all citizens. The city became safer and municipal government became more honest and transparent. Now some of that progress may be at risk from political change as the current administration appears to be reversing some of the progressive changes in parking controls and pedestrianization; a demonstration of the fragility of some urban transportation reform efforts.[5]

to long-distance transportation services – whether on land, sea or air – as well as significant movement in the direction of promoting competitiveness among providers. Privatization of services previously in the public sector and deregulation took several forms and varied considerably from country to country. In some cases, private-sector expertise in management and personnel preparation assisted in the modernization of public services. In other cases, such as that of Thatcher's England, the manner in which privatization and deregulation occurred served to weaken and undermine many public services (Pucher and Lefevre, 1996; Bruun, 2007).

1990s to present: Transportation policy moves in various directions at different levels

At the international level, the Kyoto Climate Change Protocol, commonly referred to as the 'Kyoto Accords' (Boisson de Chazournes, undated), spurred an interest in moving transportation in a more sustainable direction. The extent to which the goals of Kyoto have been met is controversial since progress in meeting these goals can be confounded by the effects of global recession. It is not controversial to assert that, despite the Kyoto efforts, transportation-related greenhouse gas emissions (GHGs) continue to rise.[7]

More than a few countries have developed policy and planning discussions that show some promise in terms of ST, including pricing reforms, carbon taxes and other measures that might lead to reduced transportation emissions, although the thrust of investment has not always been matched by results. Many countries in Europe and Asia have expanded and improved performance of railways with better intermodal integration for freight and passengers, and a few have begun programmes aimed at moving some freight off rubber wheels and onto steel wheels. A few nations are promoting bicycling at city and intercity levels. However, as in the 1970s and 1980s, much national and international effort has gone into the transportation side of trade liberalization, deregulation and other factors facilitating globalization and the '3000 mile Caesar salad'.[8,9] There are also several promising discussions, but little in the way of concrete enactment.

Box 7.2 The unfulfilled promise of the US Intermodal Surface Transportation Efficiency Act reform

Although the US did not join in the Kyoto Accords, it did open the door to a new policy direction with its passage of the Intermodal Surface Transportation Efficiency Act (ISTEA) in 1991, when Congress decided that the old way of building highways, without regard to the negative consequences for communities, had to change. The federal government provides a large amount of transportation funding to state and local government, and its funding and guidelines influence and leverage a great deal of planning and projects construction at those levels. The 1991 bill had several remarkable departures from previous BAU bills: it improved funding for walking, bicycling and transit, but was unable to comprehensively change the overall direction of transportation policy and investment. Highway investments and planning continued to dominate, and highway interests weakened the next two iterations, 'TEA–21' (1998) and 'SAFETEA–LU' (2005).[10]

More progress towards ST has been achieved at the level of cities and urban regions than at state, national or international levels. Many cities in Europe and several in Asia have been working for greater traffic restraint, more pedestrianized commercial streets and public spaces, and improved transit and cycling networks (see Chapter 9). A few national and international alliances of cities have formed around the goals put forward in the Kyoto Accords. In the European Union the CIVITAS Initiative promotes ST projects among its many members, from Ploesti to Preston and Toulouse to Tallinn. The US Conference of Mayors sponsors the Mayors Climate Protection Center to administer and track a Mayor's Kyoto Accords agreement, as well as to promote energy efficiency and more sustainable transportation at the urban level, although only Portland, Oregon, appears to be making much progress in that direction. The growth in pedestrianized zones in many cities, especially in Europe, coupled with a transportation policy emphasis on walking, bicycling and transit as the modes of choice, has encouraged a small but influential movement towards car-free cities.[11]

Box 7.3 Germany: Bicycle policy transformation at federal, state and city levels

Over several decades a policy transformation that promotes bicycling has been occurring at national, state and city levels in Germany. The transformation is the result of interactions and synergy between these levels of society and government. Some of the transformation is due to policy changes in road transportation thinking, such as reduction of speed limits in cities and the promotion of traffic calming, while some policy change has been specifically targeted at bicycle promotion. Two prominent researchers see the improvements in bicycling conditions and gains in riding as the result of an overall transformation of German transportation policy that coordinates efforts between local, regional, state and national levels. According to Pucher and Buehler (2009, p17):

> There are five categories of government policies that have been particularly important for transport sustainability in Germany. First, taxes and restrictions on car use help to limit car use and mitigate its harmful impacts. Second, the provision of high-quality, attractively priced, well-coordinated public transport services offers a viable alternative to the car for many trips, especially in large cities. Third, infrastructure for non-motorized travel has been vastly improved to increase the safety and convenience of walking and cycling. Fourth, urban development policies and land-use planning have encouraged compact mixed-use development, discouraged low-density suburban sprawl, and thus kept many trips short enough to make by walking or cycling. Fifth, all of these policies have been fully coordinated to ensure their mutually reinforcing impact.

At the national level, the promotion of traffic calming and pedestrian zones began as early as 1961 and became widespread, including bicycle promotion, by the 1970s and 1980s. During the same time period the federal government began to modify its motor vehicle-oriented road standards in the direction of allowing more flexibility at the local level, which has facilitated walking, bicycling and neighbourhood safety through the lowering of urban speed limits. It began providing research, analysis and encouragement, including some funding, for bicycle improvements. Several states actively supported this transformation with the North Rhein–Westphalia (Nordrhein–Westfalen) in the lead. This has resulted in regional bicycling programmes from paths to planning and information provision that have encouraged cycling between towns and for tourism.

The transformation has been most dramatic at the level of cities, small to large. Münster (population circa 280,000) has won wide acclaim for its bicycling achievements, including plaudits from Minnesota

Congressman Oberstar, chair of the House Transportation and Infrastructure Committee. Heavily bombed in 1944, it rejected the automobile–suburban orientation common to many rebuilding plans and chose to restore itself along traditional lines, but with greater building heights and densities, on average, than before. Bicycling grew and became an important mode, achieving a 35 per cent modal share. By the 1980s a combination of bicycle-promoting policies, including counter-flow bicycle lanes on one-way streets, street redesign, provision of facilities (from bicycle paths and promenades to parking), and bicycle priority in traffic, had made Münster an international leader. Freiburg, one of the cities featured in Chapter 9, focuses on improving all 'green modes', as well as creating highly effective synergies between land use, transportation and other key planning and policy areas.[12]

A few of the many cities making significant progress towards sustainable transportation through reorientations of policy are listed in Table 7.1.

Policy conclusions

There is quite a bit of variation between and within nations and regions in the extent to which transportation policy is moving in the direction of sustainability or remaining stuck in BAU. While much transportation policy remains oriented towards preserving the status quo, there are promising signs that some countries and cities are moving in the direction of sustainability. Programmes such as the Transport, Health and Environment Pan-European Programme (THE PEP) and similar programmes of integrated policy are examples of current ST efforts (Schwedler, 2007). Table 7.2 summarizes some major differences between BAU and ST.

The next section considers the crucial role of public participation in transportation planning and policy-making and its implications for sustainability.

The public and participation

The issue of public participation is an important and complex one for democratic societies. Participation, when and where it occurs, is generally in institutions and processes defined as public or governmental: elections, planning, projects, schools and neighbourhood issues. There are few ways in which the average citizen can participate in private-sector decision-making. The public is rarely invited to participate in the governance of corporations or in the planning of privately controlled projects unless they affect the public realm – and even then public participation or scrutiny is often at the end of private processes. Because of this exclusion a great deal of public energy is exercised in influencing the public side of the public–private relationship.

One problem in discussing public participation is defining who the 'public' is, what 'public participation' is and what is 'successful'. One of the original leaders in this field, Sherry Arnstein (1969, p216), stated that 'the idea of citizen participation is a little like eating spinach; no one is against it in principle because it is good for you'. Whether it is analogous to eating spinach or not, there is general consensus that citizens should participate in one form or another in the governance of a democratic society.

Figure 7.1 Skaters in the pedestrian square, Haarlem, The Netherlands (top); child and bicyclist on older street, Stavanger, Norway (middle); antique cannon and cannonball bollards, Old Havana, Cuba, are authenticated by Latin American Colonial historian Nancy Elena van Deusen (bottom)

Source: Preston L. Schiller

Table 7.1 Cities moving towards sustainable transportation: A selection

City (Country)	Selected accomplishments
Bogotá (Colombia)	Ciclovia bicycle–pedestrian–greenway and bus rapid transit (BRT); quality transportation options to poor neighbourhoods, car-free celebrations
Boulder (Colorado, US)*	Integrated planning, community transit network – eco-passes, bicycle emphasis, pedestrianization of central business district (CBD), university–city co-operation
Copenhagen (Denmark)	Early leader in pedestrianization, public spaces, emphasis on bicycling
Curitiba (Brazil)	Integrated planning – ecological emphasis, BRT and urban intensification – emphasis on lower-income housing
Freiburg (Germany)*	Integrated planning – ecological emphasis, integration of all transportation modes, pedestrianization, traffic calming
Groningen (The Netherlands)	Early leader in greening of transportation policy and planning, motor vehicle restraint, pedestrianization and bicycling emphasis
Lund (Sweden)	Leader in moving from vision to implementation, outreach to households
Münster (Germany)	Early leader in greening of transportation policy and planning, extremely successful bicycling–bicycle streets emphasis
Paris (France)	Ubiquitous transit–intermodal leader, reclaiming automobile space for transit, bicycling and pedestrians
Portland (Oregon, US)*	Transportation policy public participation, successful light rail transit (LRT) and transit-oriented development (TOD) integration, public space development in CBD, new bicycling emphasis
Seoul (South Korea)*	Elimination of major highway; major transit improvements
Stockholm (Sweden)	Early leader in rethinking pedestrianization and pedestrian safety, passenger intermodalism, development along rail lines
Surubaya (Indonesia)*	Kampung Improvement Programme
Vancouver (British Columbia, Canada)*	Transit–walkability-oriented development; passenger intermodalism
Zurich (Switzerland)	Passenger intermodal integration, maximizing existing streets for transit

Note: * Cities featured and explored in greater depth in Chapter 9.
Source: Preston L. Schiller

Until recent decades most governments practised top-down (or 'one to many') 'consultation' with the public about major programmes or projects, mainly through carefully controlled informational meetings or public hearings (Campbell and Marshall, 2000). A new emphasis on bottom-up participation began to emerge by the 1960s. In the US a 'War on Poverty' invited 'maximum feasible participation'. Growing awareness of the consequences of pollution, industrial

Table 7.2 Policy characteristics: Business as usual (BAU) versus sustainable transportation (ST)

Dimension	Business as usual (BAU)	Sustainable transportation (ST)
Process	Predict (forecast) and provide	Build scenarios, backcast, deliberate, decide
Data analysis	Accepts current trends, forecasts	Uses analysis to interrupt harmful trends
Funding–investing	Supports current situation and trends	Reflects and shapes desired outcomes
Feedback–evaluation	Not generally built into planning	Ongoing feedback and evaluation: all phases
Benchmarking	Not always included or heeded	Serious part of planning, feedback, evaluation
Planning	Usually in separated 'silos'	Maximizes integration of planning and policy

Source: Preston L. Schiller

Figure 7.2 Vehicles blocking or encroaching upon pedestrian space signify a failure of policy and law enforcement: The wide sidewalk in San Francisco's Russian Hill neighbourhood is blocked by a selfish resident (top); motorcycles are taking over Parisian sidewalks after the city finally succeeded in removing parked cars from sidewalks (bottom)

Source: Preston L. Schiller (top); Eric C. Bruun (bottom)

and vehicular, led to the creation of environmental legislation and regulatory agencies in many countries during the 1960s and 1970s with a concomitant increase of public participation in their processes. A recent large-scale US study has attempted to sort through the various levels and venues of public participation, especially in environmental review processes where some form of public participation is mandated. The study includes many useful observations and recommendations and concluded that: 'When done well, public participation improves the quality and legitimacy of a decision and builds the capacity of all involved to engage in the policy process. It also can enhance trust and understanding among parties' (Dietz and Stern, 2008, pp1–5). The insufficiencies of conventional public participation have also been noted in discussions of the preparation of Canadian planners (Hodge and Gordon, 2008, Chapter 12).

Discussions about public participation have been the subject of many efforts focused on sustainable development issues. The United Nations 1992 Rio Declaration on Environment and Development, Principle 10, includes a strong statement about public participation:

- public access to information;
- public participation in decision-making processes;
- public access to judicial and administrative redress – often termed 'access to justice' (Bruch, 2002, p2).

It recommends that the public be involved early in the decision-making process, 'when options are still open'.[13] The work of the Rio Declaration was built upon through the work of the United Nations Aarhus Convention (UN Aarhus Convention on Access to Information, 1998). Clearly, there is broad agreement of the importance of public participation and its relation to policy-making. Public participation in transportation will now be examined in order to assess what might be needed to advance the goals of ST.

Public participation in transportation

Much early citizen participation was in opposition to major projects, technologies or developments felt to be injurious to their interests. Beyond the occasional protest or political campaign, there was little organized citizen effort to participate and relatively little welcoming of the public before the era following World War II. As citizens, government and private interests interacted more around transportation issues, a multifaceted 'transportation public' emerged in many countries, which includes:

- individuals directly affected by a project or proposal or new policy or plan or need;
- users, consumers, employees, providers and employers;
- interested citizen(s), sometimes as community members, sometimes as taxpayers;
- commercial interests, businesses, professionals;
- stakeholders and interest groups; professional/business/labour associations, lobbies, environmental and other NGOs (Hook, 2005, Chapter 4).

Despite the comprehensive nature of the transportation public, there are many groups and interests often left out of participation and policy-making in transportation because they are insufficiently organized, socially marginal or without voice unless championed by an interest group. These include:

- children (rarely allowed to represent themselves; have mobility and safety concerns);
- guest workers and recent immigrants (legal or illegal);
- socially marginal individuals (homeless, discriminated-against sectors);
- wildlife often at risk of becoming 'road kill' or endangered by highway construction or new development and, some might assert, nature itself!

Box 7.4 Dr Seuss: 'Who speaks for the trees?'

'I am the Lorax. I speak for the trees.
I speak for the trees, for the trees have no tongues ...

I'm the Lorax who speaks for the trees
which you seem to be chopping as fast as you please.'

'I, the Once-ler, felt sad
as I watched them all go.
BUT ...
business is business!
And business must grow ...

I meant no harm. I most truly did not.
But I had to grow bigger. So bigger I got.
I biggered my factory. I biggered my roads.
I biggered my wagons. I biggered the loads
of the Thneeds I shipped out. I was shipping them forth
to the South! To the East! To the West! To the North!
I went right on biggering ... selling more Thneeds.
And I biggered my money, which everyone needs.'
(Geisel, 1971)[14]

How the transportation public participates

Since the 1960s many countries have made some form of public participation mandatory for major transportation projects and policies.[15] Forms of public participation and their effectiveness vary from one level of government to another and within civil society. This section describes a number of public participation types, techniques, venues and effects and attempts to evaluate them in terms of their relevance for achieving changes in policy in the direction of ST.

There are many forms, venues and degrees of structure and organization of public participation:

- *Media communications*: include information from transportation agencies; citizens' responses include letters to editors, letters or petitions, calling in to talk shows, televising of public meetings, web blogs, postings and networking.
- *Town meetings*: public forums open to all citizens where pressing issues can be debated and deliberated upon.
- *Public consultations* and *public hearings*: examples of top-down formats; informational conveyances usually organized by government. These venues typically present developed plans and record reactions; there is little depth discussion of the plan or alternatives. Improvements could include having alternative viewpoints as part of a roundtable discussion and small group discussions.
- *Committees and commissions*: governments at various levels, including transit providers, may create special committees or commissions for advice or even assistance in developing policies and plans.

Figure 7.3 This attractive north-east Seattle, Washington, traffic circle slows motor vehicles, makes the intersection safer and is maintained by the neighbourhood; the flag indicates that traffic calming can be patriotic

Source: City of Seattle Transportation Department

- *Study circles:* formed by people with an interest in an area or issue that they hope to influence or shape. It is a 'bottom-up' approach to learning and preparation for effective participation.[16]
- *Social movements:* citizens' concerns about a transportation-related matter may be addressed through an existing social movement, as when environmental movements include transportation matters in their agenda or when parent associations include safe walking routes to school or 'walking school buses' as a major concern.
- *Politically oriented participation:* includes 'watch-dogging', coalitions, lobbying, litigation and political contest. Citizen 'watchdogs' might closely follow an issue or inspire media investigations. Some NGOs undertake lobbying or litigation. Electing or un-electing officials is the most widespread form of public participation in government. While it makes clear who is accountable for government decisions, participation rates vary and major reform may be slow. In some countries or regions within countries, the law permits citizens to launch initiatives, referenda or recall elected officials.

The two mini case studies that follow (see Boxes 7.5 and 7.6) illustrate some ways in which citizens and policy-makers can work together to change the direction of ST.

Techniques and processes of participation for sustainable transport

Several techniques, processes and venues can be used to enhance citizen participation in transportation. Some are visually oriented or incorporate visualizations. Among these are the following:

- *Analytic hierarchy process (AHP):* a planning technique that attempts to incorporate a variety of evaluation techniques and information sources within

Box 7.5 City–community collaboration: Seattle neighbourhood traffic circles

Many cities around the world suffer from speeding motorists and too much traffic. When urban traffic grows without control, it spills over from major thoroughfares into and through residential neighbourhoods or around school districts. Speeding or 'rat-running' (sometimes termed 'maze-running') motorists become a problem.

One way to slow local traffic down and increase street safety is the neighbourhood traffic circle, usually constructed at an intersection or at mid-block. This device is very popular in Seattle (Washington), Portland (Oregon) and many other US cities. The traffic circle needs to be of sufficient radius so that motor vehicles slow considerably as they manoeuvre around it, but allow width sufficient for delivery trucks and emergency vehicles. A well-done traffic circle is landscaped to add aesthetic value to the neighbourhood and has a sign explaining how to manoeuvre around it. In order to be effective, traffic circles need to be installed at multiple intersections in a neighbourhood, especially along those streets that are subject to rat-running motorists. If successful, traffic circles slow and inconvenience through motorists sufficiently so that they remain on major thoroughfares.

The City of Seattle has a highly effective programme. Neighbourhood residents are invited to analyse their street problems and then submit a proposal to the Seattle Department of Transportation. If neighbourhood residents volunteer to maintain the traffic circle as a garden spot, the city will provide soil and plantings; otherwise asphalt will cover it.[17]

Box 7.6 Boulder, Colorado: Political leadership and effective citizen participation[18]

During the 1980s, Boulder's political and community leadership decided that a new transportation direction was needed. The city sponsored a series of pedestrian conferences and learned much from invited experts such as Jan Gehl, Peter Newman and Jane Holtz Kay. It then launched a series of efforts:

- GO Boulder, a special transportation demand management (TDM) unit, was established and charged with planning transit, bicycling and walking and intermodal improvements.
- A community transit network (CTN) was designed to augment or replace several underperforming services provided by the regional transit district (RTD). The first few routes were designed with input from large year-long committees of citizens, planners, university students, faculty, merchants and employers. Frequent user-friendly services were carefully planned and marketed, one per year for several years, and became overnight successes with large annual ridership growth rates. Recent routes reach out to provide service to nearby communities with substantial numbers of Boulder-bound commuters.
- A highly successful eco-pass was developed for students, employees and neighbourhoods.
- An extensive non-motorized network, currently at 300 miles (500km) with 74 underpasses, was developed and continues to expand; linking neighbourhoods, downtown, the university, parts of the greenbelt and many major employment sites.
- A significant portion of Pearl Street was transformed into a downtown pedestrian mall. It is a highly successful commercial zone and popular gathering place.
- A citizens' advisory committee was formed in the mid 1990s to review plans and policies and transportation needs.
- Funding for many of these efforts was expanded and made stable over time. Recently, the city added a carbon tax to its transportation funding mix.[18,19]

Figure 7.4 Community participation helped to plan the community transit network, Boulder, Colorado: Routes are given catchy names, buses are decorated and passengers are made to feel welcome

Source: GO Boulder

a coherent framework for analysis and decision-making. It may incorporate information from essentially qualitative sources (preference surveys, expert panels, visualizations, etc.) and information from quantitative sources (project costs, returns on investments, modelling, etc.) into a framework whereby scaled values representing weights of importance for aspects of the project or proposal under analysis may be applied and used to arrive at rankings. It weights the importance of goals and the effectiveness of each proposed project alternative towards meeting that goal. Similarly, it weights the importance of negative impacts or costs and the severity of each proposed project alternative with respect to that impact or cost. The end result is a set of benefit-to-cost ratios more realistic and inclusive than the traditional net present value analysis based primarily on monetary or monetized values. It also lends itself to further sub-analyses and reiterations of the decision-making process.[20]

- *Charrette (or charette)*: A technique often used in planning and urban design where small groups are involved in an intensive process with the goal of arriving at consensus about a plan, policy or project design. Typically one or more specialists present information, including graphics about the issue under review, some of which may be spontaneously developed. The group may consist of other planners or designers, government officials, people who represent special interests related to the matter under review – sometimes known as 'stakeholders', – members of the public, or a combination of these (Schommer, 2003).

- *Visualizations and simulations*: computerized techniques allow comparisons of alternatives and multiple perspectives and simulations to test ideas about traffic and transit. These may be combined with other techniques described in this section (Batty et al, 2000; Levy, 2006).

- *Visioning*: a process through which a community or a government agency, or both, may develop a consensus of a preferred future and then begin to shape policies and plans in order to attain it (Okubo, 2000; also see the following point on 'Scenarios and backcasting').

- *Visual preference survey*: a technique that records citizen, planner and developer reactions to a variety of street, building and community-design possibilities. Participants record their reaction, usually along a positive-to-negative numeric scale.[21]

- *Scenarios and backcasting*: when forecasting and trends indicate an undesirable outcome, possible outcome scenarios could be constructed and the most desirable and least harmful chosen. The group could then turn its attention to 'How do we get there from here?' It could engage in a backcasting exercise and identify planning and policy measures necessary to attain the desired future.[22]

- *Hybrid and comprehensive approaches*: agencies, developers and citizens' groups may incorporate several of the techniques described above. An excellent source describing several successful TOD and context-sensitive solutions (CSS) efforts using multiple participation techniques, including visualizations, simulations and a variety of types of community outreach, concluded that: 'One of the most compelling findings in these cases is how in each project, those involved challenged conventional approaches to transportation planning and design'(Schively, 2007, p2).[23]
- *Citizens' juries*: a group of citizens is convened by a governmental entity or an NGO to deliberate upon the merits of a plan, project proposal or policy. When this form of deliberative democracy has considerable influence with public officials, its findings may gain considerable media coverage and encourage its participants as well as other citizens that participation can be meaningful.[24]

The potential for public participation

There is considerable potential for incorporating effective public participation within ST efforts. A study of several European cities indicates that citizen activity played a major role in redirecting policies, planning and investments towards sustainable transportation. Table 7.3 illustrates that, by the 1990s, through great and prolonged effort commencing in the 1960s and 1970s, the five cities studied were able to slow or reverse the growth of automobile transportation and enhance and increase travel by transit and non-motorized modes.

To put the accomplishments of these cities in perspective, most US cities would have an automobile share between 80 and 90 per cent (or more), a transit share between 1 and 5 per cent and a walk–bicycle share between 1 and 5 per cent.[25] Canadian cities, on average, do better than their US counterparts with a few approaching European transit mode levels. Vancouver (British Columbia), Portland (Oregon) and Boulder (Colorado) have been making

Table 7.3 Modal split (for all residents' trips), 1990*

City (Country)	Automobile	Transit	Walk–bicycle
Zurich (Switzerland)	28	37	35
Basle (Switzerland)	38	30	32
Amsterdam (The Netherlands)	31	23	46
Groningen (The Netherlands)	36	6	65
Freiburg (Germany)**	42	18	40

Notes: * Or latest available year prior to 1999; figures are percentages of total trips.
** Freiburg is explored in depth as an exemplary city in Chapter 9.

Source: adapted from Bratzel (1999, p183)

policy and citizen-led efforts to change their modal splits over the past 30 years; their experiences are presented in Chapter 9 of this volume.

A cautionary note is in order: while greater participation is generally a welcome phenomenon, and many citizen initiatives lead to outcomes in the direction of ST, some move away from a sustainable outcome. Such was the case of a 1999 citizen initiative in Washington State (see Box 7.7).

The Initiative 695 case study illustrates the confusion surrounding some issues. Motorist resentment, weak public understanding of the issues and policy-maker lack of fortitude combined to deal public transportation a major setback. Subsequent voter support for local transit tax increases indicates that the I-695 vote was not anti-transit *per se*. In the absence of effective public participation and deliberation, policy-makers might misperceive public intent. A comprehensive critique of public participation in transportation found that important factors inhibiting progress include the tendency for many government officials to underestimate the extent of public support for ST solutions. As a response to such inhibiting factors, the author called for engaging citizens in

---

Box 7.7 Initiative 695:
A citizen participation and policy-maker failure

In 1995, self-styled Seattle populist Tim Eyman began a lucrative and controversial career of soliciting donations and organizing citizen initiatives in Washington State – one of a number of US states that allows citizens to initiate legislation (initiative), nullify an existing law (referendum, which also allows the legislature to refer measures to citizens for a vote), or even recall elected officials (recall). Some of these options exist in several other US states, parts of Canada and a few other countries such as Switzerland. Annually, Eyman and his organization, Permanent Offense, challenge transportation and property taxes, affirmative action laws, high-occupancy vehicle (HOV) lanes and public projects that they dislike. They win some, they lose some.

In 1999, the Eyman-organized Initiative 695 (I-695), repealing the Motor Vehicle Excise Tax (MVET), passed by a margin of 56 to 44 per cent. MVET was a tax levied on the value of a motor vehicle. It imposed an annual fee ranging from very little for older cars to hundreds of dollars or more for newer, more expensive models. While most transportation taxes are unpopular with motorists, MVET was especially unpopular since it assessed a vehicle's tax value somewhat higher than standard estimates. Washington's state constitution dedicates all revenues from fuel taxes to highway purposes. MVET was not encumbered in this way. Its revenues were applied to public transportation and a variety of social and educational programmes. Washington State is considered by many experts to be somewhat backward and regressive in its tax policies; it has no state income tax, relies heavily on sales tax and MVET was one of its few progressive taxes.

Opponents of I-695 waged a weak battle against it. The legislature chose not to reform MVET. When I-695 passed, it was immediately challenged in court. While the case was being litigated, then Governor Gary Locke called the legislature into a special session to lower the MVET to a fixed US$30 per year fee – in effect, ratifying Eyman's victory. When a few months later the state Supreme Court found I-695 to be unconstitutional, neither the governor nor the legislature reversed their hasty action.

Many transit agencies were able to recoup some of their funding losses through local voter-approved tax increases. But most of these measures took years to pass and some agencies have not been able to regain the level of funding that they had before 1999. The state's rail programme is now several years behind in its efforts to improve passenger rail, despite greatly increased ridership and demand.[26]

Box 7.8 Participative democracy: Deliberative decision-making and social learning

Eric Manners[27]

As a cyclist, activist and student in Australia, I watched traditional 'top-down' transportation planning fail to make any significant progress towards safer streets and more sustainable transportation. All levels of government had adopted policies to reduce car use and air pollution, but seemed to lose their nerve whenever it came time to prioritize walking, cycling and public transportation. Officials insisted that the public was not ready for a serious move towards sustainability, so business would continue as usual, mainly consisting of greater investment in roads.

Like Australian cities, many Western cities have adopted policies to work towards more sustainable transportation, but very few cities are successfully implementing these policies. I decided to focus my MSc on this phenomenon (Manners, 2002), and realized early in the literature review that the key question was not how to technically design a sustainable city, but how the policy development process itself could aid successful implementation of the eventual policy.

Essentially, I concluded that more 'deliberative' forms of democratic decision-making help increase the level of responsibility citizens take for their own actions and behaviours. Participation also gives citizens an opportunity for 'social learning' – hearing the views of other citizens, talking through the range of possible solutions, and comparing the impacts of various alternatives in terms of their own and others' short-term and long-term interests.

Good decision-making begins at the democratic foundation. Barber (1984) and Dryzek (1990) suggest that the 'representative' or 'liberal' form of democracy, where public influence rarely transcends the election process, is unlikely to facilitate any significant social change, such as a shift towards sustainability. They advocate a more 'participatory', 'direct', 'discursive' or 'deliberative' form of democracy, where the public is allowed to influence individual policy decisions.

For deliberative democracy to work at the practical level, proposals must be genuinely up for discussion, rather than being pushed through with minimal fine-tuning, as is too often the case. Forester (1989) and Innes (1995) focus on the importance of a planner being able to facilitate a negotiation between diverse stakeholders with the goal of reaching a consensus decision. Gunderson (1995) suggests that environmental decision-making grounded in deliberation and discussion results in more 'collective, holistic and long-term thinking'.

In practice, 'participation' and 'involvement' in decision-making often fall far short of true deliberative democracy. Arnstein's (1969) 'ladder of citizen participation' was one framework developed to help address this shortcoming. According to Arnstein's ladder, only the top three of eight rungs ('citizen control', 'delegated power' and 'partnership') represent true citizen participation. The other five rungs, including the popular techniques of 'placation' and 'consultation', represent 'degrees of tokenism' or, worse, 'non-participation'.

Many politicians and planners seem to resist true citizen participation, possibly because they feel that citizens are not qualified to make important decisions. But Fischer (1990) criticizes this 'technocratic' view of planning. Planners do not always know what is best for society, and planning outcomes could be improved substantially through consideration of local knowledge, or what Irwin (1995) calls 'citizen science'.

Deliberative democracy is about giving people the opportunity to discuss and better understand decisions affecting them so that they are better able to support decisions that will benefit themselves and others in the longer term. But in good deliberative processes, politicians and planners can also learn from citizens. This two-way learning process is what many authors, such as Dewey (1920/1950) and Mumford (1938), have called 'social learning'. Milbrath (1989) and Lee (1993) suggest that decision-making must provide more opportunities for social learning if we are to tackle global environmental challenges such as climate change.

Based on this research, I concluded that in order to be successful in moving towards sustainability, deliberative planning processes should be:

- broad scale;
- consensual/collaborative;
- discursive/dialogical;
- empowered/independent;
- local;
- multi-scale; and
- ongoing/continuous.

Such a process would clearly cost more than most traditional methods of consultation, but the benefits are also far greater.

I was also pleased to encounter a variety of inspiring case studies illustrating a number of successful approaches to deliberative planning and democracy from around the world. For instance, the Brazilian city of Porto Alegre involves thousands of its citizens in setting annual local 'participatory budgets', with local representatives contributing towards regional budgets (Abers, 1998, 2000; Sandercock, 1998). Elected 'neighbourhood councils' in Mexico (Flores, 2002) and Norway (Aarsæther et al, 2002) provide citizens with more direct influence over local decisions. The Vision 2020 process in Hamilton–Wentworth, Ontario, Canada, allowed 1000 citizens to help set out a community vision for sustainability over which they then felt a greater sense of ownership (Region of Hamilton–Wentworth, circa 1996, 1999). And the TravelSmart travel demand management and dialogue marketing programme in Perth, Western Australia, although a more top-down approach, was a broad-scale process bringing information to every household in the city on how they could change their travel behaviour (Transport WA, 1999), and could be expanded to include a two-way dialogue on transport improvements and policy development.

Successful deliberative planning processes are clearly possible. The main challenge in my own experience, working in local government since graduation, has been finding the necessary time and funding to run meaningful, ongoing engagement processes. But as long as the dominant voice is still the motorist, implementation of ST policy will be challenging. Deliberative planning and social learning through genuine citizen involvement in decision-making may be our best chance to beat the climate change clock.

significant roles in deliberative decision-making as continuously and inclusively as possible (Manners, 2002, pp9–11, 32–35, 45–69).

Box 7.9 provides another successful example of a broad public participation effort that used several visioning and deliberative techniques and effectively influenced policy-makers in Perth, Western Australia.

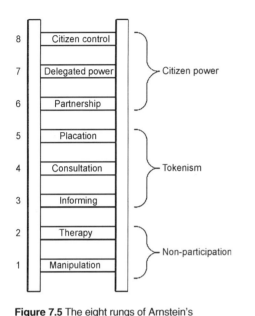

Figure 7.5 The eight rungs of Arnstein's 'Ladder of Citizen Participation'

Source: Arnstein (1969, p217)

Figure 7.6 Residents help to shape a new walking and cycling route in Islington, London

Source: Feilden Clegg Bradley Studios

Box 7.9 Visioning, dialogue and deliberation in Perth, Western Australia

Jeffrey R. Kenworthy [28]

Perth, Western Australia, engaged in a community visioning process in 2003 called Dialogue With the City, which evolved out of a broader state sustainability strategy involving 42 areas of government, together with business and civil society. The human settlements part of this strategy emphasizes innovative and efficient use of resources, less waste output, enhanced equity and liveability, and a greater sense of place in local communities.

Faced with a huge increase in urban sprawl and car dependence, the state government decided to involve the community on an unprecedented scale to develop a future vision for Perth for 2030. The process involved a community survey of over 1700 households and a one-day forum involving 1000 participants. A critical part of the forum was a game that each group of ten people played to plan for the expected increase in population. Each decision taken had a flow-on effect, which was either positive or negative. People were thus forced to confront the dilemmas of urban planning, trading-off personal lifestyle preferences with systems effects, such as loss of bushland, traffic congestion and other implications.[29]

> The next phase of the exercise is an action plan called The Network City, which calls for around 60 per cent of new dwelling construction within existing built-up areas to reduce car dependence and sprawl. The process forced participants to consider the social, economic and environmental considerations wrapped up in all urban planning (i.e. to adopt sustainability-based thinking).
>
> *Source:* Kenworthy (2006)

From business as usual (BAU) to sustainability in transportation

Because transportation is a very complex field, touching many aspects of everyday life and activity, it offers many challenges to policy-makers, planners and citizens wishing to move it away from BAU. But there are many fine examples of how transportation policy is breaking out of the confinements of conventionality and giving us glimpses of how sustainability can be attained in this domain. Public participation, too, is a difficult and complicated area; but there are many examples of how it can be an effective ingredient of planning and policy-making. In the next chapter the ways in which a new paradigm of planning can build upon policy leadership and effective citizen participation will be explored.

Questions for discussion

- Identify and discuss some of the ways in which the forms of policy-making and public participation in your community are supporting business as usual (BAU) or sustainable transportation (ST).
- Discuss and evaluate whether and to what extent technology is changing the ways in which public participation occurs. What are some positive aspects of this? What are some negative aspects of this?
- Discuss Arnstein's Ladder of Citizen Participation and the various public participation and deliberation–decision-making techniques described in this chapter to their applicability in planning, policy-making and public participation processes in your community.

Notes

1   Scandinavian countries, The Netherlands and Germany are among the leaders in developing ST policies; the US, the UK and Canada are examples of countries lagging behind. For an international sampling see Whitelegg and Haq (2003).

2   For more information on the road systems in these countries, consult http://travel.state.gov/travel/cis_pa_tw/cis/cis_1013.html, www.1uptravel.com/travelwarnings/zimbabwe.html or http://travel.state.gov/travel/cis_pa_tw/cis/cis_1081.html.

3   For more on the history of these issues, see Chapter 3 of this volume.

4   See the pioneering work of the late John Roberts (1989) and his organization, Transport & Environment Studies (TEST), especially *Quality Streets*.

5   For more information on recent Bogotá reversal, see Margolis (1992), Hyatt (2005) and Pardo (2008); for more information on the role of Gil (Guillermo) Penalosa, whose important

work on walking, bicycling, parks and other public spaces preceded his brother Enrique's mayorship, see Parasram (2003), Penalosa (2005), McManus (2006), Cohen (2008) and www.walkandbikeforlife.org.

6   Consult the Glossary for definitions of these terms; see also Button and Hensher (2005).

7   For more information about the Kyoto goals, see Doyle (2007), Kanter (2009) and Pincas Jawetz's 2009 post on SustainabiliTank.

8   Including China, Spain, Germany and France, among many others.

9   For more on the future of these transportation goals, see Brown (2008, especially Chapter 2) and Jim Kunstler's report *Clusterfuck Nation: A Glimpse into the Future* at www.kunstler.com/mags_ure.htm.

10   For more information about acts, see Schiller and DeLille (1997), Schiller (2002, pp11–12) and Gifford (2003). More information is also available at www.tpl.org/tier3_cd.cfm?content_item_id=10863& folder_id=188 and http://ntl.bts.gov/DOCS/424MTP.html and Slater and Linton (2003).

11   CIVITAS stands for CIty–VITAlity–Sustainability; see www.civitas-initiative.org/main.phtml?lan=en; for US mayors' efforts and critiques, see www.seattle.gov/mayor/climate/default.htm#what and www.eukn.org/netherlands/news/2007/01/climate-change-us-cities_1015.html; for car-free cities, see www.worldcarfree.net/. See also Low and Gleeson (2003) and Koppenjan (undated).

12   For a chronology, see pp46–47 of GTZ (2003, pp46–47); also see Schley (2001) and Pucher and Buelher (2007, 2008, 2009), www.geo.sunysb.edu/bicycle-muenster/index.html, www.muenster.de/stadt/tourismus/en/city-of-bikes.html and www.bmvbs.de/Anlage/original_11696/Ride-your-bike-Information-in-englischer-Sprache.pdf; for more information on the Münster–Minneapolis connection, see Moore (2006). See also Pucher (1997).

13   For more, see Bruch (2002, pp9–12), although, curiously, transportation issues are not included in this very valuable discussion. See also Transportation Research Board (2002).

14   Excerpt from *The Lorax*, a children's fable by Dr Seuss (Geisel, 1971). The Once-ler is the greedy chopper of trees. A Thneed is a useless item made by destroying Truffula trees.

15   See discussion of ISTEA and Arnstein's Ladder in this chapter; there were other early FHWA/NEPA-inspired studies and handbooks from the 1960s and 1970s with contributions from Arnstein, Julie Hoover and Alan Altshuler (Arnstein and Metcalf, 1976). See also Warburton et al (undated) and Wassenhoven (2008).

16   Sometimes called Swedish study circles after their country of origin; for more information, see Haines (2006) and Warner (undated).

17   For more information on traffic circles, see Johnson (2008) and the following websites: www.seattle.gov/transportation/trafficcircles.htm and www.trafficlogix.com/traffic-calming-history.asp.

18   Boulder, Colorado, will be explored further in Chapter 9 of this volume.

19   See www.bouldercolorado.gov/index.php?option=com_content&task=view&id=8774&Itemid=2973.

20   See Bruun (2007, pp269–276); see also Chapter 6 of this volume.

21   Since the 1990s the originator Anton Nelessen has been working to refine this technique and a number of others have developed their own variations; see also www.lgc.org/freepub.

22   The term 'backcasting', as used here, refers to the process that follows scenario-building and is directed towards achieving visioned goals; see Gilbert and Wiederkehr (2002), especially Chapter 1. Another form of backcasting, not used here, assesses the effects of projects after their construction or implementation and compares these with their intended effects.

23   See Schively (2007, p3) and her sources for excellent graphic examples and general references on public participation techniques; another good source is the International Association for Public Participation (IAP2), www.iap2.org/, especially the 'Public Participation Toolbox'.

24   An NGO that specializes in citizens' juries is the Jefferson Center, www.jefferson-center.org/. For a discussion of the merits of including this form of deliberative democracy, see Smith and Wales (2003).

25   New York City has the highest transit share of 27 per cent, with a handful of cities between 10 and 15 per cent; a few cities have a slightly higher rate than 1 to 5 per cent for non-motorized.

26   For Eyman's financial improprieties, see www.permanent-offense.org/; see also Washington State Attorney General's 2002 press release, *State Reaches Settlement with Eyman and Permanent Offense*, www.atg.wa.gov/pressrelease.aspx?&id=5798 and www.seattlepi.com/local/65900_eyman10.shtml; for information on Washington State Supreme Court decision, see *I-695 Declared Unconstitutional by State Supreme Court*, www.mrsc.org/subjects/finance/695/i-695.aspx; and additional information on Eyman, see www.mrsc.org/mc/courts/supreme/142wn2d/142wn2d0183.htm and http://portfolio.washington.edu/tarabl/495/25293.html.

27   Transport Policy and Planning, London Borough of Islington.

28   Jeffrey R. Kenworthy is professor of sustainable cities at the Curtin University Sustainability Policy Institute (CUSP) at Curtin University in Perth, Western Australia.

29   All results were recorded and a final report can be found at www.dpi.wa.gov.au/dialogue/finalproc.pdf.

References and further reading

Aarsæther, N., Nyseth, T. and Røiseland, A. (2002) 'Neighbourhood councils – municipal instruments or grass-roots movement? Some reflections on results from two Norwegian surveys', in P. McLaverty (ed) *Public Participation and Innovations in Community Governance*, Ashgate, Aldershot, UK

Abers, R. N. (1998) 'Learning democratic practice: Distributing government resources through popular participation in Porto Alegre, Brazil', in M. Douglass and J. Friedmann (eds) *Cities for Citizens: Planning and the Rise of Civil Society in the Global Age*, John Wiley & Sons, New York, NY

Abers, R. N. (2000) *Inventing Local Democracy: Grassroots Politics in Brazil*, Lynne Rienner Publishers, Boulder, CO

Akaha, T. (ed) (1990) *International Handbook of Transportation Policy*, Greenwood, Westport, CN

Anderson, J. E. (2000) *Public Policymaking: An Introduction*, Houghton Mifflin, Boston, MA

Arnstein, S. R. (1969) 'A ladder of citizen participation', *Journal of the American Institute of Planners*, vol 35, no 4, pp216–224

Arnstein, S. R. and Metcalf, E. I. (1976) *Effective Participation in Transportation Planning, Volume II, A Catalog of Techniques*, USDOT, Washington, DC

Barber, B. R. (1984) *Strong Democracy: Participatory Politics for a New Age*, University of California Press, Berkeley, CA

Batty, M., Chapman D., Evans, S., Haklay, M., Kueppers, S., Shiode, N., Smith, A. and Torrens, P. (2000) 'Visualizing the city: Communicating urban design to planners and decision-makers', *CASA Working Papers*, vol 26, Centre for Advanced Spatial Analysis, London, www.casa.ucl.ac.uk/publications/workingPaperDetail.asp?ID=26, accessed 15 June 2009

Birkland, T. A. (2005) *An Introduction to the Policy Process: Theories, Concepts, and Models of Public Policy Making*, ME Sharpe, Armonk, NY

Boisson de Chazournes, L. (undated) *The Kyoto Protocol to the United Nations Framework Convention on Climate Change: Kyoto, 11 December 1997*, http://untreaty.un.org/cod/avl/ha/kpccc/kpccc.html, accessed 16 June 2009

Bratzel, S. (1999) 'Conditions of success in sustainable urban transport policy – Policy change in relatively successful European cities', *Transport Reviews*, vol 19, no 2, pp177–190

Brown, L. R. (2008) *Plan B 3.0: Mobilizing to Save Civilization (Substantially Revised)*, W. W. Norton & Company, New York, NY

Bruch, C. (ed) (2002) *The New 'Public': The Globalization of Public Participation*, Environmental Law Institute, Washington, DC, www.eli.org, accessed 13 June 2009

Bruun, E. (2007) *Better Public Transit Systems: Analyzing Investments and Performance*, Planners Press, Chicago, IL

Button, K. J. and Hensher, D. A. (eds) (2005) *Handbook of Transport Strategy, Policy and Institutions*, Elsevier, Oxford, UK

Campbell, H. and Marshall, R. (2000) 'Public involvement and planning: Looking beyond the one to the many', *International Planning Studies*, vol 5, no 3, pp321–344

Cochran, C. L. and Malone, E. F. (1999) *Public Policy: Perspectives and Choices*, McGraw–Hill, New York, NY

Cohen, J. (2008) 'Calming traffic on Bogotá's killing streets', *Science*, vol 319, no 5864, pp742–743

Curtis, F. (undated) 'Climate change in the context of peak oil', www.e3network.org/Curtis_9.pdf, accessed 15 June 2009

Day, D. (1997) 'Citizen participation in the planning process: An essentially contested concept?', *Journal of Planning Literature*, vol 11, no 3, pp412–434

Dewey, J. (1920/1950) *Reconstruction in Philosophy*, New American Library, New York, NY

Dietz, T. and Stern, P. C. (eds) (2008) *Public Participation in Environmental Assessment and Decision Making: Panel on Public Participation in Environmental Assessment and Decision Making*, National Academies Press, Washington, DC, www.nap.edu/catalog.php?record_id=12434, accessed 17 June 2009

Doyle, A. (2007) 'Surging transport threatens EU Kyoto goals report', www.reuters.com/article/environmentNews/idUSL2669609620070227, accessed 16 June 2009

Dryzek, J. S. (1990) *Discursive Democracy: Politics, Policy, and Political Science*, Cambridge University Press, Cambridge, UK

Fischer, F. (1990) *Technocracy and the Politics of Expertise*, Sage Publications, Newbury Park, CA

Flores, A. (2002) 'Tlalpan neighbourhood committees: A true participatory option', in P. McLaverty (ed) *Public Participation and Innovations in Community Governance*, Ashgate, Aldershot, UK

Forester, J. (1989) *Planning in the Face of Power*, University of California Press, Berkeley, CA

Geisel, T. S. (a.k.a. Dr Seuss) (1971) *The Lorax*, Random House, New York, NY

Gerston, L. N. (1997) *Public Policy Making: Process and Principles*, M. E. Sharpe, Armonk, NY

Gifford, J. (2003) *Flexible Urban Transportation*, Elsevier, Oxford, UK

Gilbert, R. and Wiederkehr, P. (eds) (2002) *Policy Instruments for Achieving Environmentally Sustainable Transport*, Organisation for Economic Co-operation and Development, Paris

GTZ (2003) *Sustainable Transportation: A Sourcebook for Policy-Makers in Developing Countries*, Sustainable Urban Transport Project, www.sutp.org, www.vtpi.org/gtz_module.pdf, accessed 15 September 2009

Gunderson, A. G. (1995) *The Environmental Promise of Democratic Deliberation*, University of Wisconsin Press, Madison, WI

Haines, A. (2006) 'Sustainable communities: Lessons from Wisconsin and Sweden', *Land Use Tracker*, vol 6, no 2, Center for Land Use Education, www.sustaindane.org/Pages/ecomunicipality_where.htm, accessed 13 June 2009

Hodge, G. and Gordon, D. L. A. (2008) *Planning Canadian Communities: An Introduction to the Principles, Practices, and Participants*, fifth edition, Nelson, Toronto, Ontario

Hook, W. (2005) *Training Course on Non-Motorized Transport*, GTZ, Eschborn, Germany

Hyatt, J. (2005) 'Post-event narrative: Towards car-free cities VI – Bogotá, Columbia', http://carfreeBogotá.blogspot.com/2006/10/post-event-narrative.html, accessed 23 June 2009

Innes, J. (1995) 'Planning theory's emerging paradigm: Communicative action and interactive practice', *Journal of Planning Education and Research*, vol 14, no 3, pp183–189

Irwin, A. (1995) *Citizen Science: A Study of People, Expertise, and Sustainable Development*, Routledge, London

Jawetz, P. (2009) 'The Kyoto Protocol, signed in 1997, was widely viewed as badly flawed; President Obama will place the United States at the forefront of the international climate effort raising hopes that an effective international accord is possible', www.sustainabilitank.info/2009/03/02/the-kyoto-protocol-signed-in-1997-was-widely-viewed-as-badly-flawed-president-obama-will-place-the-united-states-at-the-forefront-of-the-international-climate-effort-raising-hopes-that-an-effective/, accessed 10 June 2009

Johnson, J. M. (2008) 'Gardens in the round: In Seattle, traffic circles have become bonus open space', *Planning*, www.entrepreneur.com/tradejournals/article/176651969.html, accessed 10 June 2009

Kanter, J. (2009) 'Europe expected to outperform Kyoto goals', http://greeninc.blogs.nytimes.com/2009/05/29/dimas-europe-will-outperform-kyoto-goals/, accessed 17 June 2009

Kenworthy, J. R. (2006) 'The eco-city: Ten key transport and planning dimensions for sustainable city development', *Environment & Urbanization*, vol 18, no 1, pp67–85

Koppenjan, J. (undated) 'Involving politicians in interactive policy making processes: Theoretical considerations and practical experiences', in *Papers for the International Conference on Democratic Network Governance*, Copenhagen, 21–22 October 2004, www.ruc.dk/demnetgov_en/Conferences_and_Seminars/int_conf/papers/, accessed 12 June 2009

Lee, K. (1993) *Compass and Gyroscope: Integrating Science and Politics for the Environment*, Island Press, Washington, DC

Levy, R. M. (2006) 'Urban design and computer visualization: Applications in community planning', in S. Tsenkova (ed) *People and Places: Planning New Communities*, www.ucalgary.ca/cities/Places_and_People/Chapter%209%20-%20Urban%20Design%20and%20Computer%20Visualization%20-%20Applications%20in%20Community%20Planning.pdf, accessed 17 June 2009

Low, N. and Gleeson, B. (2003) *Making Urban Transport Sustainable*, Palgrave Macmillan, New York, NY

Manners, E. (2002) *The Role of Participatory Democracy in Achieving Environmental Sustainability*, MA thesis, Griffith University, Australia

Margolis, M. (1992) 'A third world city that works', *World Monitor*, March, pp42–50

McManus, R. (2006) 'Imagine a city with 30 percent fewer cars: Low-tech transit is the fastest route to a great city, says a Brazilian architect', www.sierraclub.org/sierra/200601/interview.asp, accessed 10 June 2009

Milbrath, L. W. (1989) *Envisioning a Sustainable Society: Learning our Way Out*, State University of New York Press, Albany, NY

Moore, R. (2006) 'A drive for more biking and walking options: 2006 Oberstar Forum addresses the role of non-motorized modes of transportation', *University of Minnesota News*, 11 April, www1.umn.edu/umnnews/Feature_Stories/A_drive_for_more_biking_and_walking_options.html

Mumford, L. (1938) *The Culture of Cities*, Harcourt Brace and Company, New York, NY

Okubo, D. (2000) *The Community Visioning and Strategic Planning Handbook*, National Civic League Press Denver, Colorado, third edition, www.ncl.org/publications/online/VSPHandbook.pdf, accessed 20 August 2009

Parasram, V. (2003) 'Efficient transportation for successful urban planning in Curitiba', www.solutions-site.org/artman/publish/printer_62.shtml, accessed 16 January 2008

Pardo, C. F. (2008) 'Bogotá's time machine', http://list.jca.apc.org/public/sustran-discuss/2008-April/006120.html, accessed 23 June 2009

Penalosa, E. (2005) 'The role of transport in urban development policy', *Sustainable Transport: A Sourcebook for Policy-Makers in Developing Cities*, Module 1a, Deutsche Gessellschaft für Technische Zusammenarbeit (GTZ), Eschborn, Germany, www.gtz.de, accessed 12 June 2009

Pucher, J. (1997) 'Bicycling boom in Germany: a revival engineered by public policy', *Transportation Quarterly*, vol 51, no 4, fall, pp31–46

Pucher, J. and Buehler, R. (2007) 'At the frontiers of cycling: Policy innovations in the Netherlands, Denmark and Germany', *World Transport Policy & Practice*, vol 13, no 3, December, pp8–56

Pucher, J. and Buehler, R. (2008) 'Making cycling irresistible: Lessons from the Netherlands, Denmark and Germany', *Transport Reviews*, vol 28, no 4, July, pp495–528, http://dx.doi.org/10.1080/01441640701806612, accessed 17 June 2009

Pucher, J. and Buehler, R. (2009) 'Sustainable transport that works: Lessons from Germany', *World Transport Policy and Practice*, vol 15, no 1, pp13–46, www.eco-logica.co.uk/pdf/wtpp15.1.pdf, accessed 17 June 2009.

Pucher, J. and Lefevre, C. (1996) *The Urban Transport Crisis in Europe and North America*, Macmillan, Basingstoke, UK

Region of Hamilton–Wentworth (circa 1996) *Creating a Sustainable Community: Hamilton–Wentworth's VISION 2020 – Canada*, www.vcn.bc.ca/citizenshandbook/unesco/most/usa4.html, accessed 13 August 2009

Region of Hamilton–Wentworth (1999) *Summary of the Sustainable Community Planning Process, 1990 to 1999*, Region of Hamilton–Wentworth, Hamilton, Ontario, Canada

Rittel, H. and Webber, M. (1973) 'Dilemmas in a general theory of planning', *Policy Sciences*, vol 4, no 2, June, pp155–169

Roberts, J. (1989) *Quality Streets: How Traditional Urban Centres Benefit from Traffic Calming*, Transport and Environment Studies (TEST), London

Roberts, N. (2004) 'Public deliberation in an age of direct citizen participation', *American Review of Public Administration*, vol 34, no 4, pp315–353

Sandercock, L. (1998) *Towards Cosmopolis: Planning for Multicultural Cities*, John Wiley & Sons, Chichester, UK

Schiller, P. L. (2002) *Taking the High Road*, Trust for Public Land, Washington, DC, www.tpl.org/tier3_cd.cfm?content_item_id=10863&folder_id=188, accessed 15 August 2009

Schiller, P. L. and DeLille, B. (1997) *Green Streets*, STTP, Washington, DC

Schively, C. (2007) *Enhancing Transportation: The Effects of Public Involvement in Planning and Design Processes*, Humphrey Institute of Public Affairs, University of Minnesota, FHWA Report No CTS 07–10, Minneapolis, www.cts.umn.edu/Publications/ResearchReports/pdfdownload.pl?id=824, accessed 18 June 2009

Schley, F. (2001) 'Urban transport strategy review: Experiences from Germany and Zurich', Deutsche Gesellschaft für Technische Zusammenarbeit (GTZ) GmbH, Division 44, Environmental Management, Water, Energy, Transport, Postfach 5180, 65726 Eschborn, Federal Republic of Germany

Schommer, J. (2003) 'A *charrette* is the center of the urban design process', www.charrettecenter.net/charrettecenter.asp?a=spf&pfk=7&gk=261, accessed 18 June 2009

Schwedler, H.-U. (2007) 'Supportive institutional conditions for policy integration of transport, environment and health', European Academy of the Urban Environment, Berlin, www.eaue.de/PUBS.HTM, accessed 17 June 2009

Slater, R. E. and Linton, G. J. (eds) (2003) *A Guide to Metropolitan Transportation Planning under ISTEA – How the Pieces Fit Together*, http://ntl.bts.gov/DOCS/424MTP.html, accessed 10 June 2009

Smith, G. and Wales, C. (2000) 'Citizens' juries and deliberative democracy', *Political Studies*, vol 48, no 1, pp51–65

Stevens, H. (2004) *Transport Policy in the European Union,* Palgrave Macmillan, Basingstoke, UK

Transport WA (1999) *TravelSmart 2010: A 10 Year Plan*, Transport WA, Perth, Australia

Transportation Research Board (2002) 'Going public: Involving communities in transportation decisions', *TR News*, no 220, May–June 2002, http://trb.org/publications/trnews/trnews220toc.pdf, accessed 20 August 2009

UN Aarhus Convention on access to Information (1998) 'Public participation in decision-making and access to justice in environmental matters', www.unece.org/env/pp/, accessed 12 June 2009

United Nations (1992) 'Rio Declaration on Environment and Development', in *Report of the United Nations Conference on the Human Environment*, www.unep.org/Documents.Multilingual/Default.asp?documentid=78&articleid=1163, 5–16 July, accessed 17 June 2009

Warburton, D., Wilson, R. and Rainbow, E. (undated) 'Making a difference: A guide to evaluating public participation in central government', www.involve.org.uk/making_a_difference/, accessed 15 June 2009

Warner, P. (undated) 'Organising the study circle process: A brief introduction', Worker Education Association in Sweden, www.adulteduc.gr/001/pdfs/Oganising_the_study_circle_process.pdf, accessed 15 June 2009

Wassenhoven, L. (2008) 'Territorial governance, participation, cooperation and partnership: A matter of national culture?', *Boletin de la A.G.E.*, no 46, pp53–76

Whitelegg, J. and Haq, G. (eds) (2003) *The Earthscan Reader on World Transport Policy and Practice*, Earthscan, London

8

A New Planning Paradigm: From Integrated Planning, Policy and Mobility Management to Repair, Regeneration and Renewal

Lessons learned from preceding chapters

This chapter builds upon current ideas based on conclusions reached in preceding chapters in order to develop a model incorporating their findings within planning and implementing sustainable transportation (ST). We call this approach the 'new paradigm' because it offers a clear distinction from the old paradigm of business as usual (BAU). The new paradigm is based upon the interaction of:

- integrated policy and planning and mobility management (or transportation demand management: TDM);
- several important 'background' factors that need to inform policy and planning;
- the development of appropriate infrastructure, techniques and technology.

Interest in developing a new paradigm in transportation is not necessarily new. Many researchers and analysts have been pointing to the shortcomings of the BAU paradigm and the need for its replacement for many years. Significant names in previous work to create a new paradigm for transportation include John Adams, Terence Bendixson, Eric Britton, Werner Brög, Robert Cervero, Jan Gehl, Carmen Hass-Klau, Mayer Hillman, Rolf Monheim, Peter Newman, Anthony Perl, Stephen Plowden, John Pucher, Richard Register, John Roberts, Kenneth Schneider, Eduardo Vasconcellos, Vukan Vuchic and John Whitelegg. Such a list can never be exhaustive and there are many more; but all those cited above have in one way or another attempted to draw attention to the need to rein in the dominance of the private automobile in the setting of transportation and urban planning policy and, in particular, the future sustainability of cities.

The new paradigm understands ST not as an end state or static product, but as a dynamic ongoing process (see also Litman, 2003). It builds on feedback, reiteration, revisiting of original visions and a long-term perspective. It is constantly making adjustments and is informed by new information. This chapter also reviews the major 'lessons learned' and findings from previous chapters.

Chapter 1 lessons

This chapter introduced a working definition of ST and provided an overview of some of the thorniest issues confronting the field, especially automobile dependence and equity–inequity issues related to transportation provision and locational disadvantage. The major lesson learned was that automobile dependence creates a host of problems, as well as exacerbating equity issues.

Chapter 2 lessons

This chapter followed on the discussions of automobile dependence and equity–inequity by exploring the differences between walking, transit and automobile cities, as well as the hold that the 'car culture' has on many aspects of life in automobile cities. One lesson is that these cities do not have to remain fixed as such. Another lesson is that the car culture needs to be recognized in its many forms, confronted and superseded.

Chapter 3 lessons

This chapter highlighted a series of important lessons:

- The long, profound and central role of walking in shaping human physical development, cognition and the formation of pre-automobile communities. The lesson here is to put walking at the centre of transportation planning. The pedestrian environment defines the quality of the public realm and its capacity to support human community.
- With regard to the bicycle's history, it is important to deliberate carefully before abandoning a practical, inexpensive and environmentally friendly mode. This lesson needs to be learned in many parts of the rapidly industrializing world as traditional non-motorized modes (bicycles, rickshaws and others) are cast aside to make space for cars and motorcycles.
- Communities over thousands of years were formed in ways that aimed to minimize travel and maximize accessibility to important resources, such as water, food, public realms and trade routes. The lesson here is that transportation and land-use planning need to respect accessibility as one of their first planning mandates. BAU transportation has displaced accessibility with mobility as the key axiom of the land-use transportation system. In simple terms, a 200m walk to a corner shop to buy 1 litre of milk has been replaced by a 4 km drive to a major supermarket to achieve the same end.
- Respect the wisdom of the past in the development of travel modes appropriate to compact communities.

- Another key lesson, especially for cities in developing countries that have been shaped around non-motorized transportation, with only rudimentary development of transit systems, is that attempting to accommodate vast and rapidly growing fleets of motorcycles, personal motor vehicles (PMVs) and trucks in dense urban forms previously oriented towards mixed uses and non-motorized transportation is a recipe for serious congestion, air pollution, traffic danger and mortality.

Chapter 4 lessons

Before the hegemony of the drive-fly culture in wealthy nations, and its domination of the planning and transportation investment activities of many not so wealthy ones, new technologies and modes were used to shape community development and travel patterns in fairly orderly and predictable ways. Certain modes work together very effectively to strengthen compact development patterns and lessen environmental and economic impacts. For instance, walking, bicycling and transit create synergies that strengthen compact urban form. Other lessons learned from Chapter 4 include:

- Technology–technical factors, such as modal and intermodal fit, applications, design criteria, etc., need to be interactive with and inform policy and planning processes.
- Be suspicious of the one 'best' mode; beware of 'silver bullet' or 'alternative fuelishness' approaches. Problems such as sprawl, global pollution and oil depletion will only be solved by reductions in the factors that create automobile dependency and reduce the total demand for PMVs.
- Be aware of the long-term consequences of modal investments.
- Modes may serve unique or diverse purposes.
- Walking is important as a mode in itself as well as in conjunction with other modes.
- There is great potential for increasing bicycling for a variety of trips in wealthy countries.
- There is a complex interplay between modes, rights of way and modal capacities. Some rights-of-way configurations create advantages for some modes, while creating serious barriers for others.

Chapter 5 lessons

One of the most significant lessons learned from Chapter 5 on freight and logistics is that there is moderate to considerable

Figure 8.1 'Alternative fuel vehicles'

Source: Andy Singer (www. andysinger.com)

freight capacity with almost all passenger modes, including non-motorized, as well as for shared loads, such as passenger rail carrying mail and parcels and passenger aviation carrying considerable amounts of high-value freight. This could potentially include the piggybacking of, for example, specially designed freight trams on a regular streetcar or a light rail transit (LRT) network for delivery of goods, especially during the times when passenger services are closed. Non-motorized modes in developing countries (bicycles, rickshaws, etc.) still carry out a considerable freight-carrying role, from the transportation of livestock and food to quite bulky building materials.

Other lessons include:

- Freight logistics are very sensitive to pricing and time issues.
- Much of freight policy and practice is driven by global considerations with little or no concern for localities, regions and, often, nations.

Chapter 6 lessons

Lessons learned from Chapter 6 include the following:

- Several facets of transportation economics, such as pricing, incentives–disincentives, capture of externalities and investment strategies, including transportation demand management (TDM)–mobility management (MM) programmes, need to be subject to intense analysis and fit well with policy and planning objectives.
- Accounting for externalities, such as pollution, inequity, loss of amenity, etc., should be an important part of economic planning and policy; conversely, the unaccounted-for benefits in these areas of seemingly loss-making or subsidized transit systems should also be properly factored in.
- 'Getting the prices right' is important so that distortions are minimized and marginal costs are clarified in order to avoid bias.

Consumers need more options and diversity from which to make choices. Many cities, as will be shown in Chapter 9, have demonstrated that the seemingly irresistible allure and love affair with the automobile can be broken where sustainable modes are carefully and thoughtfully provided against the trend of automobile-based planning.

Chapter 7 lessons

There were several lessons in Chapter 7 about the need for public policy to lead, with strong support and involvement from an enlightened public, in pointing the way towards and providing the resources for ST. Specifically we learned that:

- Much policy has served to promote narrow and often short-term modal interests. The lesson here would be to take a longer-term perspective from the outset. One could argue, for example, that Los Angeles did not evolve into the giant freeway city that it is today from some grand vision in the past to create the city it is now (few would want to say that this was actually planned). Rather, it has developed through a long string of unfortunate narrow, incremental decisions, such as pulling out the extensive electric rail system and building and widening freeways, one by one, over decades in the interests of the automobile.

Most transportation issues are very complex and need the attention of devoted officials and public participants. This requires good knowledge and information so that officials and community members are properly informed about the implications of various decisions and directions. Everyone considers themselves to be 'experts' in transportation; but much of the time popular views are shaped by things that no longer work, such as the belief that widening and building new roads can reduce the overall congestion problem or reduce fuel use and emissions. Chapter 7 also pointed out that:

- Policy and meaningful public participation precede and set the stage for effective planning.
- Transportation policy should reflect the integration of various domains that are generally not incorporated within BAU, including health, economic and financial–fiscal matters, land use, pollution and energy de-intensification.
- Policy and planning need to be informed by public processes, early on or at the outset of significant processes, in order to benefit from the creativity that can potentially flow from public process as well as the creation of support (if not consensus) about desired outcomes. Participation should not become mired in too many details and should be informed by visualization processes and other advanced simulation techniques.
- Different forms of participation are appropriate at different levels, from citizen forums and *ad hoc* committees at the local level to the programmatic efforts of non-governmental organizations (NGOs) for more complex issues at higher levels of society.
- Most of the advances we would characterize under the rubric of ST seem to be occurring at the city and urban-area levels of society. Larger social and governmental units seem to be having greater difficulty in charting and maintaining the course of ST.
- Some participation techniques, such as visioning, scenario-building and backcasting, are much more amenable to ST than passive information-dispensing approaches.

The recognition of the need for a new paradigm: The Buchanan Report and its critics

As early as the 1960s, some in the profession of traffic engineering[1] and planning were beginning to question BAU. Stephen Plowden (1972) offered a prescient critique of conventional transportation planning in *Towns against Traffic*, his response to the influential British government report *Traffic in Towns* (Buchanan, 1963), also popularly known as the Buchanan Report after its principal author Colin Buchanan. The Buchanan Report has shaped much of UK transportation planning between towns, in towns, around towns and through towns since that time. For the most part, the Buchanan Report reflected conventional traffic planning with a slightly greater emphasis on protecting town centres and neighbourhoods from the excesses of traffic, through rigorous traffic separation schemes that separated local from through traffic, than was the standard practice of the 1940s and 1950s.

Plowden's critique begins with a rejection of the traffic engineer's tenet that 'all traffic demands should be met' (Plowden, 1972, pp14–15), and proceeds to the understanding that increasing road supply simply increased demand for driving: 'Very broadly speaking, the amount of traffic is governed by what is regarded as a tolerable level of congestion' (Plowden, 1972, p15). Early in his critique, Plowden cites a prominent American traffic engineer's observation that travel demand and traffic congestion were directly related to road supply:

> As traffic engineering measures and new streets and highways have added capacity to road systems, more motor vehicles have been put into use almost immediately. New roads and more motor vehicle miles of travel have gone hand in hand in the United States. (Plowden, 1972, p16)[2]

Plowden then brought attention to the fact that while traffic congestion was rampant in most cities, it never reached the level of 'gridlock' predicted in many forecasts. He then linked road expansion to urban sprawl: 'New roads will also encourage people to live further from their work or other places of activity' (Plowden, 1972, p18). Plowden was one of the earliest, if not the first, to characterize conventional transportation planning and traffic engineering as a 'predict and provide' (p19) enterprise.

Plowden's critique of 'predict and provide' has been echoed in years since by a series of prominent scholars and analysts (Newman and Kenworthy, 1984, 1989, 1999; Newman et al, 1988; Goodwin et al, 1991). This has helped to establish the basis for a new paradigm for ST.

Box 8.1 Problems and shortcomings of the business as usual paradigm

The business as usual (BAU) paradigm:

- largely ignores environmental and social equity impacts that are associated with capacity-oriented transportation planning, or, at best, attempts to mitigate its damages after the fact or far from where the capacity expansion occurred;
- is largely oblivious to the ways in which it promotes longer-distance urban area travel and facilitates low-density sprawled development;
- allows pricing distortions that promote motoring at the expense of walking, bicycling and public transportation;
- lends itself to a 'build its way out of congestion' approach rather than managing demand;
- highlights the fact that the main economic benefits of a congestion mitigation strategy are purported time savings, which are illusory because new roads just allow people to travel further, not to save time;
- tends to almost always favour one mode (motoring) and one technology (the private vehicle) over a balanced menu of modes and technologies;
- is usually resistant to effective public participation;
- often develops standards for urban roads that are fit only for intercity expressways;
- defines 'safety' very narrowly, usually as motorist safety.

Overview of the new paradigm: Integrated policy-making, planning and mobility management

Integrated policy-making

Integrated policy-making is a key factor in the creation of a new paradigm. Currently, many policy efforts in the domains of transportation, environment, health and general social well-being pursue parallel but usually uncoordinated trajectories. An important effort to integrate these separate policy 'silos' is under way with the Transport, Health and Environment Pan-European Programme (THE PEP) and a valuable definition is offered:

> Policy integration concerns management of cross-cutting issues in policy-making that transcend the boundaries of established policy fields. It also includes management of policy responsibility within a single organization or sector. Integrated policy-making refers both to horizontal integration between policy sectors (different departments and/or professions in public authorities) and vertical intergovernmental integration in policy-making (between different tiers of government), or combinations of both.[3]

Towards better management of existing transportation features

A key ingredient of a new paradigm is better management and maximization of the benefits of current transportation programmes, services and infrastructure. The critique of conventional transportation planning by Plowden (1972) and others from the 1970s and 1980s to the present call for managing transportation systems better, rather than embarking on reflex road and highway expansions. This approach is known as transportation demand management (TDM), as well as 'mobility management'.[4] Mobility management refers to a range of policies, programmes and planning strategies intended to make existing transportation resources function more efficiently, as well as directing users of those resources towards more efficient use of them (see Table 8.1).

While forms of mobility management have been used for many years in parts of Europe and Asia, where transportation planning has been more progressive, it is still in the early stages of recognition as a valuable general tool in other parts of Europe and Asia, as well as North America and Australia–New Zealand. In much of North America and Australia–New Zealand, until recently, mobility management was considered a special response to be implemented in certain situations where conventional solutions were infeasible; parking management and pricing used to be considered appropriate only in major downtowns, where the land and financial costs of providing abundant free parking are infeasible. Elsewhere, generous minimum parking requirements and direct public subsidies have often resulted in abundant subsidized parking at most destinations. Perverse tax incentives still exist in Australia where it is possible to 'salary package' a car with pre-tax dollars, and the fringe benefits tax on the driving done in a salary package car gets less and less the more kilometres that are driven in a year.[5] Meanwhile, it is impossible to salary package (or gain tax benefit from) the costs of public transit fares or a new bicycle. Similarly, in more automobile-dependent places, public transit used to be considered for only a small role, serving non-drivers and special events.

During recent years a combination of trends have increased the importance of mobility management and positioned it as a more valued solution to a variety of problems, including road and parking congestion, increasing facility costs, excessive consumer costs, high accident rates, energy dependency, inadequate mobility for non-drivers, inefficient land-use development and inadequate public fitness and health. Until recently, most traffic safety experts assumed that the total amount of mobility is unchangeable, their efforts focused on reducing crash rates per vehicle kilometre. New research indicates that mobility management can significantly reduce per capita crash rates and therefore can be considered as a traffic safety strategy. Similarly, mobility management is now recognized as an important component of congestion reduction, energy conservation, emissions reduction, public health and community redevelopment programmes. As more of these objectives are recognized, the justification for integrated mobility management increases.

Types and strategies of mobility management

Mobility management includes a variety of specific strategies that tend to fall into four major categories:

1   improving and expanding travel options;
2   incentives to use efficient modes;
3   land-use solutions to transportation problems: 'smart growth' and multi-modal land-use development;
4   implementation programmes.

These strategies are discussed in the following sections.

Improving and expanding travel options

Mobility management often involves improvements, including performance, security, information and user comfort, for public transportation, as well as improved connections between modes (intermodalism). It promotes the expansion of mobility options, such as walking, bicycling, ride-sharing, car-sharing and taxi services. It also supports trip reduction strategies, such as telework (use of telecommunications to substitute for physical travel), teleconferencing and videoconferencing and delivery services.

One mobility management strategy involves asking motorists to identify the alternative mode that they are most likely to consider using for certain trips and other factors which affect their decisions, such as incentives and land-use conditions. One method that has proven to be effective in a number of places globally, including Perth in Western Australia, is Socialdata's individualized or direct marketing method (Socialdata.org: Brög and Erl, 2003). Here participants who show an interest in altering their current car-based travel are taken through a programme where they are provided with details about the transit system in

Figure 8.2 Some cities are facilitating bicycling with counter-flow bicycle lanes on one-way streets, as in this Amsterdam, The Netherlands, example (left); bicycle rentals strategically located around town, such as the Sevici rental rack near the downtown river path in Seville, Spain (right), are proving popular in many cities and reintroducing many residents to this pleasant form of mobility

Source: Preston L. Schiller

their area and are given free tickets to try it. Behavioural change resulting from this programme has been shown to have a high rate of retention.

Part of the suite of new options appearing in mobility management schemes is a wide range of innovative schemes to help people avoid the need to use or own their own car. These include car-sharing schemes, which are increasingly popular in some European countries as an alternative to car ownership, and bike-sharing schemes, such as the much publicized Velib scheme in Paris and Copenhagen's system. In Germany, Deutsche Bahn, the national railway company, has a large fleet of rental bikes that can be reserved with a mobile or regular phone call and provision of credit card details, and picked up anywhere throughout the city. The bikes can be parked and locked anywhere when finished and the rental contract terminated by phone. Customers are charged on the basis of time. In the San Francisco Bay area some BART stations have electric 'station cars' for use by rail passengers.

Incentives to use efficient modes

Incentives to encourage use of efficient modes include bus lanes and transit priority, and various types of pricing and financial incentives and disincentives. Some bus lanes lend themselves to being shared with other vehicles. Depending upon the roadway and the volume of bus service, some bus lanes can be shared with ride-share vehicles and taxis, and in some situations buses can co-exist with bicycles. On freeways and major arterials, and in transit-rich CBD areas, transit should be afforded bus-only lanes and transit priority measures that create greater speed and reliability than driving on congested roadways.[6] Urban highway traffic congestion tends to maintain equilibrium – traffic volumes increase until congestion delays discourage additional growth. Public transit service quality can affect the point of equilibrium: if transit is relatively fast, reliable and comfortable, potential motorists will be more willing to shift, reducing the congestion delay experienced by people who continue to drive; but if transit service is poor, motorists will be reluctant to change modes even if congestion is severe, increasing delay to all users.

Table 8.1 Summary of transportation demand management (TDM) strategies and tools[7]

General strategy	Tools or components
Improve options	Better, faster, more reliable, frequent and prioritized transit; better walking and bicycling facilities and priorities; ride-/car-share, taxis; better travel information and trip planner websites
Trip avoidance	Flextime, telework, teleconferencing, videoconferencing
Incentives/disincentives	Road pricing; congestion and distance-based fees; commuter benefits; transit passes, worksite amenities; parking; pricing, regulation and 'cash-out'; fuel and vehicle de-subsidization, 'pay-as-you-drive' insurance, driving and vehicle restrictions
Land-use management, smart growth	Transit-oriented (and location-efficient) development (TOD); parking management; traffic calming; car-free planning; reducing parking requirements; mixed-use development and retrofit; more residential options near major employment centres
Implementation and management programmes	Commute trip reduction (CTR); school/campus transportation programmes; mobility management and individualized marketing; tourist transportation management; freight transport management

Source: derived from various sources at www.vtpi.org

Figure 8.3 Poorly located freeway transit stop near the University of Washington, Seattle

Note: Difficult-to-reach bus stops can be a disincentive to transit use – this person would have to wait for three traffic signals to cross three busy streets and highway ramps to reach the steps leading down to a freeway transit stop near the University of Washington.
Source: Preston L. Schiller

Pricing disincentives can include PMV ownership reduction strategies, such as those in Singapore and Shanghai, which have been quite effective at suppressing the growth of PMV ownership and use. Through certificate of entitlements, would-be car owners have to bid at an auction to purchase the right to own a car, which can amount to many thousands of dollars. They must then pay for the actual car. The schemes are designed to try to keep the incoming rate of new cars roughly equal to the attrition rate in order to achieve a relatively flat growth in car ownership. It should be noted that pricing incentives and disincentives are among the most potent of the measures available to mobility management (Komanoff, 1994). Table 8.1 presents information about TDM strategies and tools.

Land-use solutions to transportation problems

Since land-use patterns and urban form affect transportation, policies and programmes that help to create more accessible and multi-modal communities are an important part of mobility management. Often the solution to a transportation problem is found in land use. David Nowlan and Greg Stewart (1991) found that adding residential units in Toronto's core significantly reduced automobile trips. Adding 100 residential units to a central area reduced the number of peak period trips to the centre by 120. If a city wants less PMV traffic, it needs to add housing close to employment centres. Forms of development that foster traffic reduction may be called 'smart growth', 'new urbanism', 'transit-oriented development (TOD)', 'walkable communities' or 'location-efficient development'. These all include the features listed in Box 8.2, which are intended to improve accessibility and reduce per capita automobile travel.

In addition to the above approaches, another increasingly popular land-use response in Europe is car-free housing developments, or developments, such as

---

Box 8.2 New urbanism neighbourhood design features

- Development is compact and mixed, with residential density averaging at least six units per acre (15 units per ha), a variety of building types, including small-lot single-family, multi-family, residential over retail, and various commercial and institutional structures close together.
- The community has a discernible activity centre with a transit station. This is often a plaza, square or green, and sometimes a busy or memorable intersection.
- Most dwellings are within a five-minute walk from the centre. Streets are designed for walking and cycling, with sidewalks on both sides, bike lanes where needed, good crossings, traffic calming features used to control motor vehicle traffic speeds, and other features to encourage non-motorized travel.
- Special attention is paid to protecting the public realm and creating quality public spaces, including sidewalks and paths, parks, streetscapes and public buildings.
- Buildings at the centre are placed close to the sidewalk and to each other, creating an urban sense of spatial definition. Buildings towards the edges are placed further away and further apart from each other, creating a more rural environment.
- There are shops and services sufficient to meet common household needs, such as convenience stores, a post office, a bank machine and a gym.
- There should be an elementary school close enough so that most children can walk from their dwellings. This distance should not be more than 1 mile (1.6km).
- There are parks, trails and playgrounds not more than one eighth of a mile (200m) from each dwelling.
- Thoroughfares are relatively narrow and shaded by rows of trees that slow traffic and create an appropriate environment for pedestrians and bicyclists.
- Networks of highly connected roads and paths provide multiple routes between destinations, increasing accessibility and reducing problems if one route is closed.
- Parking supply is minimized and managed for maximum efficiency.

Source: Swift (undated)

Vauban in Freiburg (see Chapter 9), which require that people owning a car park it in a separate multilevel parking garage at the edge of the community in order to keep most of the public space within the community traffic free. Many places are now also introducing the idea of decoupling the purchase or rental of a dwelling from a car parking place. Purchasers can choose to buy a dwelling without a car park, thus saving tens of thousands of dollars in the purchase price, or they can save a significant sum in monthly rent by renting without a car park. If this is also backed up with strict on-street residential parking regulations, it can be a big disincentive to car ownership and use. In Tokyo, where there is simply no room for cars in the dense built-up parts of the city, it is not possible to purchase a car unless you can provide certification that you have an off-street bay to park the car. This severely limits car ownership while keeping streets much freer of parked cars. In the context of the excellent transit systems in Japanese cities, and the very good walking and cycling conditions, such an approach seems fair and equitable.

Implementation programmes

Mobility management programmes may be found in, or organized by, local governments, large employers, campuses, business associations, transportation agencies and NGOs, such as transportation management associations (TMAs). Public transit both supports and is supported by mobility management. As a result, transit planning, funding and programme development are often the basis for comprehensive mobility management programme development. TDM programmes require a combination of resources and professional skills, including planning and evaluation, programme management, appreciation of facility and community design principles, understanding of transit planning and marketing skills.

Mobility management planning can produce a variety of benefits for individuals and society. Specific strategies have fairly specifiable effects linked to specific benefits. A car-share programme or co-operative could lead to lower per capita vehicle ownership, which relieves parking demands, as well as encouraging car-share co-op members to consider walking, bicycling or taking transit before driving. In European cities, people wishing to join a car-sharing scheme who can show that they also have an annual transit pass receive the cars for a significantly lower rate than non-committed transit users. Similarly, some smart growth strategies encourage more walking and bicycling and, therefore, are more health promoting than strategies that encourage driving.

Integrated planning

Because BAU is reductionist and tends to treat modes and facilities in isolation rather than in an integrated manner, it is necessary for sustainable transportation to adopt a multifaceted and integrated approach. Planning needs to be informed and directed by good policy products and processes. It can be most effective when it reflects enlightened policy decision-making rather than when it attempts to circumvent policy processes – however understandable and well-intended that strategy is at times. And planning must inform policy-making, especially through its research and implementation–evaluative/feedback dimensions. The seemingly intrinsic and irresistible internal logic of computer-based transportation modelling that has prescribed more roads as a solution to congestion is a classic case of reductionist planning. It failed to examine the feedback effects between transportation and land use, and the holistic implications for the whole city of building more and more roads (see the section on 'Muddled models' in Chapter 6). Through an integrated approach, ST planning, as described in the model elaborated upon in the next section, will be able to better address several issues, including:

- Stressing accessibility over mobility – this is an almost complete reversal of the BAU paradigm of substituting accessibility with mobility, which has been in operation for many decades.
- Social equity is an important and realizable planning goal. Planning needs to be informed about, and sensitive to, a range of societal and cultural issues.
- Land-use strategies and impacts need to be addressed and accounted for in all planning processes.
- Market and pricing distortions that, for example, fail to take into account the real costs of automobile use, fail to acknowledge the many benefits of transit systems to non-users (most evident during a strike) and do not appear in balance sheets of transit operators, complicate transportation planning and work against ST.

Description of the new paradigm of integrated planning

The new paradigm of ST can be understood as the intersection of three major domains:

1 planning and policy factors;
2 background factors;
3 technical and infrastructure factors.

Each of these domains is made up of numerous factors representing issues or questions that policy-makers, citizens and planners should address. Each of these is listed and then briefly described, drawing on material in the preceding chapters.

Circle 1: Planning and policy factors

Critical event

A critical event is often triggered by a serious problem or threat that creates great concern or crisis, which can be directed into a positive and creative solution. A road expansion plan, 'Route 20', for the inner-western suburbs of Brisbane was the critical event that triggered a citizens' reaction, leading to an exemplary traffic calming proposal for the whole community (Engwicht, 1989, 1993). Some other critical events in cities are described in Chapter 9, such as the City of Vancouver's banning of freeway development, Freiburg's decision to

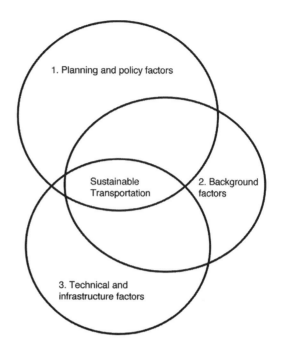

The new paradigm of integrated planning can be graphically understood as a Venn diagram depicting the intersection of three circles: background factors; planning and policy factors; and technical and infrastructure factors.

Circle 1: Planning and policy factors

- Critical event
- Policymakers, integrated policy making, policy adequacy
- Citizens and community leaders
- Careful analysis, economic evaluation, impacts
- Scenario building, evaluation of all options
- Vision of a preferred future, backcasting to inform planning
- Appropriate planning structure, motivated staff
- Deliberative planning
- Good data, evaluation
- Soft path / mobility management orientation
- Effective communications

Circle 2: Background factors

- History, heritage, culture and values
- Geography–topology
- Accountable governance systems
- Social organization
- Existing transportation and land-use systems

Circle 3: Technical and infrastructure factors

- Appropriate infrastructure and energy sources
- Availability of appropriate hardware
- Appropriate standards and measurements
- Orientation and skill sets of technical personnel
- Existing built environment
- Technical aspects of environmental impacts assessment

Figure 8.4 Sustainable transportation as the intersection of three major domains

Source: Preston L. Schiller

drop plans for nuclear energy, Portland's opposition to a particular freeway and the watershed event of deciding to build light rail. One of Curitiba's most celebrated events is the 'over the weekend' conversion of one of its main streets in the central city to a pedestrian mall. Such events can change the entire course of a city because of their symbolic and practical value. Other critical events can be hallmark experiences, such as hosting of the Olympic Games. Some European cities, such as Munich, achieved major upgrading of public transit ahead of the Olympics.

Policy-makers, integrated policy-making and policy adequacy

Are policy-makers informed of the issues? Are they engaged in and supportive of a sustainable solution? Does the existing policy making framework sufficiently integrate the relevant policy domains? For example, are policies about promoting walking, bicycling and walk-to transit in synchrony with investment priorities favouring sidewalks, bicycling and local transit improvements? Is current policy adequate for planning needs (Penalosa, 2003)?

Citizens and community leaders

Are community leaders and citizens well informed about and engaged in the issue at hand? Are they supportive of a sustainable solution? Are there effective channels of communication between citizens, policy-makers and planners? Are leaders prepared to lead and take bold courses of action? The successes of innumerable mayors in changing the course of cities are very illustrative. Curitiba, Brazil, had Mayor Jaime Lerner; Bogotá, Colombia, had Mayor Enrique Penalosa and his commitment to the TransMilenio BRT system; major European cities, such as Munich and Grenoble, had mayors who fought for large pedestrian schemes, often against the advice of their own bureaucracy; London had Ken Livingstone and his central area congestion charge. The list could be expanded to include other elected representatives, such as a number of ministers of transport and ministers of planning in Perth, who fought for a new electric rail system.

Careful analysis of problems, economic evaluation and impacts

Has the problem or issue been properly analysed and subject to research, including economic evaluation? Have the social and environmental impacts been assessed? Is the economic analysis a broad enough one to incorporate the economic, social, environmental and cultural dimensions of sustainability for the particular issue being studied? Is transit evaluated for its widespread community benefits and benefits to non-users, or is it limited to the traditional balance sheets of the operators?

Scenario-building and evaluation of all options

Has analysis and research informed the development of possible future scenarios? Have all reasonable options been considered and by whom?

Vision of a preferred future: Backcasting to inform planning

Has a visioning process been undertaken, incorporating research and analysis findings within scenario-building? Has backcasting been used to inform planning for that future?

Appropriate planning structure

Are current decision-making bodies, procedures and codes adequate to the tasks of responding to policy changes and planning ST? In other words, are the statutory planning framework and the machinery of planning geared towards producing paradigm change developments or BAU developments? It is one thing to change policy and quite another to have mechanisms that allow it to be implemented.

Deliberative planning

There are several issues around deliberative planning that should be considered. Do planning processes involve effective interaction with policy-makers, stakeholders and involved citizens? Is it 'deliberate and decide' rather than 'predict and provide'? Is there trust and confidence in the planning system and political decision-making processes that, once engaged in deliberative democracy processes, the results will be honoured? Are citizens actually empowered to participate in deliberative democracy processes? Involvement has costs, such as child care, and needs direct support for the individuals who want to be involved.

Good data and effective evaluation

There are several issues involving good data and evaluation that should be considered. Has data sufficiently accurate for the planning process been gathered? Is there an effective and ongoing evaluation process in place to provide feedback to the policy and planning processes? Is there a reliable set of regularly monitored and reported sustainability indicators by which to determine if things are getting better or worse? For example, which way is per capita car and transit use headed? Are urban densities increasing? What is happening to walking and cycling rates? The results of such quantification help to determine the effectiveness of policy and implementation strategies.

Soft path and mobility management orientation

Are soft path and mobility management approaches favoured when feasible in plan and programme development?

Effective communications

Are there good forms of multidirectional communication and information-sharing in place around policy and planning processes, including web-based capacities and media outreach?

Circle 2: Background factors

History, heritage, culture and values

Are these factors, both in their general and local expressions, acknowledged and taken into consideration and built upon in efforts to move towards ST? Conversely, are the limitations of cultural strait-jackets addressed, such as stereotypes that certain nationalities will not walk, or certain people are simply wedded to their cars? Culture and history and values can cut both ways. They can be exploited constructively to help forge change and they can be used as a reason for not changing in certain directions.

Geography, topology and climate

Are the natural physical characteristics of the locality taken into consideration and accommodated in ST efforts? Again, the accounting of these factors needs to be positive in the direction of change. They can equally be used as an excuse for not changing. For example, it is sometimes said that people in cold climates in North America will not use transit, walk or cycle, without accounting for widespread exceptions to that rule (e.g. the whole of Scandinavia). Similarly, it is sometimes said that only cold places are ever densely populated, whereas in warm climates people want space and open lifestyles to enjoy the sun. This assertion ignores hundreds of very dense cities in hot climates and tropical zones and countless low-density cities in cold climates. In Switzerland, where topographical factors often work strongly against non-motorized transport, the rate of use of these modes is still high.

Legal and political systems

Are local or societal notions of polity, privilege and justice taken into account in ST efforts? Are systems of governance reliable and accountable, or are they supportive of the vested interests and nepotism?

Social organization

Is the organization of family, work, neighbourhood and friendship networks taken into account and built upon in ST efforts? Is the built environment, through its treatment of the public realm, supportive of the development of loose social networks, or does it make it very hard for this to develop by eliminating the possibilities of 'accidental interactions'?

Existing transportation and land-use systems

Are existing systems scrutinized for improvement, including changes to make them more amenable to ST efforts, before costly changes or expansions are proposed?

Circle 3: Technical and infrastructure factors

Appropriate infrastructure and energy sources

Sustainable transportation depends upon the provision of walking, bicycling and public transportation infrastructure. Good telecommunications resources also help. Attention should also be paid to energy efficiency, as well as the generation of 'green energy'. In many parts of the world, it might be possible to directly link a source, such as local wind power or another renewable energy form, to a transit project, such as an electrified trolley or tram, as a demonstration project. In 2001 a decision was made to run Calgary's LRT system on wind energy. The programme is called Ride the Wind.[8]

Availability of appropriate hardware

Sturdy bicycles, plenty of buses in good repair and attractive trains are the building blocks of ST. This largely depends upon funding for sustainable modes of transportation and, in particular, the relative funding treatment of infrastructure for private transportation relative to the 'green modes'.

Appropriate standards and measurements

Attention should be given to applying the appropriate standards and measurements. For example, it makes no sense to measure traffic mortality and morbidity (especially pedestrian and bicyclist deaths/injuries) in terms of miles/kilometres driven by motor vehicles, as is the practice in some automobile-dependent countries. In the UK, claims were made that road 'improvements' (i.e. usually expansions) led to reduced traffic crash and death rates per kilometre, especially for pedestrians. Further examination determined that lower crash and death rates were caused by people, especially children, walking and cycling less and thus reducing their exposure to the road system and the dangerous conditions for walking and bicycling.

Orientation and skill sets of technical personnel

It is important that staff be interested in and enthusiastic about ST. Their skills sets should be broad and multifaceted, and include the ability to gather and analyse data well. Staff morale, especially within transit agencies, is dramatically affected by how much importance is placed on transit as a valued service, whether funds are being made available to expand the system, and how many new major projects are being undertaken. If transit agencies perceive themselves as Cinderellas to road-building agencies, morale can be very low.

Existing built environment

Wherever possible, the existing built environment should be adapted and maximized to benefit ST, further the goals of compact development and reduce environmental harms. This applies to neighbourhoods as well as streets. For example, are there programmes to change the nature of streets to 'liveable' or 'complete' streets through support for the development of social space and not just movement space?

Technical aspects of environmental impact assessments

The role of the environmental impact assessment (EIA) can be crucial to whether a project is understood or well presented to the public. Some of the issues that need to be considered involve the quality of its preparations and dissemination. Has the EIA been properly done? Is it adequately understood by all those involved? Do the media understand the EIA?

Factors summary

The above sections provide an overview of several of the many ingredients involved in creating sustainable transportation. The process of introducing ST may vary depending upon the locality, population and problems addressed; there is not a set recipe. Taking advantage of critical events when they occur, and ensuring that policy-making is incorporated and informed by effective citizen participation, are likely to be important in all ST efforts. When the above listed factors are combined with appropriate visioning, scenario-building, problem analysis and backcasting to determine the steps and processes needed to attain the preferred future derived from these efforts, the stage will be set for deliberative planning.

Appraisal of preliminary processes

From integrated policy-making, effective citizen participation and the various dimensions of visioning, the new paradigm approach moves to integrated planning and begins with an appraisal of:

- better management or maximization of existing resources (mobility management or TDM);
- an assessment of pertinent background factors, such as local history, the legal system, existing facilities, geography or culture that might affect the plan or its implementation;
- specifying and developing a plan around what has been learned from visioning, backcasting and other co-operative efforts between policy-makers, planners and citizen interests that have led to a vision of a desirable outcome or future.

Appropriate infrastructure and environmental assessments

The planning process then moves on to assess whether or when the limits of mobility management would indicate that new technology or infrastructure is needed in order to attain the goals developed in the visioning and backcasting processes. This part of the planning process necessitates consideration of:

- evaluation of all options;
- economic evaluation;
- environmental impact assessments.

These points are discussed in the following sections.

Evaluation of all options

Modes, technologies, routes and other factors should be evaluated for appropriateness of the plan or project under consideration at present, as well as for its future appropriateness. Assessment of technologies should ensure that it is sensitive to human aspects. For example, people have shown preferences for electrically powered transit modes over diesel ones, sometimes termed the 'sparks effect', and easy to navigate and understand fixed-track systems over flexible bus systems, whose organization is sometimes opaque to the user.

Economic evaluation

Proposal costs and benefits, investment strategies, financing and pricing should all be carefully reviewed and analysed.

Environmental impact assessments

In some cases, ST projects, if done well, can have environmental benefits and actually reverse harms done before a project's implementation, as when paved space that was the province of motor vehicles is converted to pedestrian–bicyclist space or planted with trees, or when transportation energy consumption is reduced. This is very important since the sustainability agenda demands not just a cessation of damage to environments, but actual regeneration and repair of distressed places.

As this brief overview indicates, the development of ST has many important components and dimensions. The next steps in planning involve the development of timetables, benchmarks and milestones, terms that originate in geographical surveying or transportation scheduling, but are used somewhat differently in planning.

Timeliness and timelines

- Timetables establish a calendar or schedule indicating expectations of when certain tasks or goals are to be accomplished.
- Benchmarks and benchmarking refer to the development of standards against which activities, such as the implementation of a plan, can be judged or measured. Cities, in particular, can benchmark against each other and set goals based on achievements in cities that are looked to as models of particular ST factors.
- Milestones are significant points that define the progress that a plan is making.

The extent to which a plan meets these expectations should form part of a comprehensive and ongoing evaluation that provides feedback to the whole process where the trends in sustainability indicators can feature prominently.

Moving from planning and policy to regeneration, repair and renewal

The implications of implementing a new planning paradigm and mobility management are enormous. They have within themselves the capacity to not only stop bad transportation and planning practice, in order to avoid further damage, but also the capacity to begin a process of regeneration, repair and renewal. It is clear from the preceding chapters of this book that transportation systems, especially those based excessively around private transportation and the land-use planning practices that have gone with them, have already done enormous damage. They have threatened the integrity of physical systems, ruined many aspects of the public realm that constitute the interstitial spaces of society and the natural environment, and changed for the worse many of the relationships that exist between people. Human institutions, their professional praxis and guiding paradigms have to varying degrees aided and abetted much of this damage, not because it was their goal, but because the underlying pillars, beliefs and assumptions of those governance and decision-making systems were never fundamentally challenged and not sufficiently reviewed to see where they were leading over a long period of time.

During the 21st century, which bears the cumulative debt of decades of many poor policies and practices in transportation and planning, it is no longer enough just to stop further damage. We must actually regenerate, repair and renew what is already degraded.

This can happen in three ways:

1   regeneration, repair and renewal of the physical environment;
2   regeneration, repair and renewal of the social and cultural environment;
3   regeneration, repair and renewal of governance and decision-making institutions and the economic assumptions underpinning them.

These points are discussed in the following sections.

Regeneration, repair and renewal of the physical environment

This entails the physical transformation of all aspects of the human environment with which people are familiar. This includes all the movement and vehicle storage space that provides the mobility and accessibility needs of people and the greening of the environment in the broadest sense of the word. It also includes the restoration of public spaces, regeneration of transit systems and all their rights of way, stops and vehicles, the renewal of the private systems of transportation, the types of vehicles, the fuels they use, and the emissions that they produce and so on.

Specific examples of physical regeneration, repair and renewal would include:

- car-free zones;
- traffic calming and street and highway reductions;
- complete streets;
- freeway removal;
- restoration of environments destroyed or seriously damaged by auto-based transportation.

These specific examples are discussed in the following sections.

Car-free zones

The most radical way to regenerate or repair city environments from a transportation perspective is to simply exclude cars from them. The pedestrianization schemes in the central cities of Freiburg, Copenhagen, Munich, Barcelona (Las Ramblas) and countless other cities around the world, have transformed these centres into dynamic, beautiful and highly liveable spaces. The success of such areas of course depends upon maintaining access by alternative modes and ensuring that there is the right mix and intensity of land uses to guarantee vitality for most hours of the day. Good transit systems, especially rail systems, often provide the alternative accessibility needed to support car-free centres, along with excellent access by foot and bicycle to ensure that all the land uses located in centres remain on the 'movement economy'.

Car-free zones can also apply to sub-centres around the city that have a sufficient critical mass of activity and alternative accessibility to support

Figure 8.5 Even small cities such as Schwabisch-Gmund in southern Germany had pedestrianized their centres by 1989 (top); the town square of St Valery-en-Caux in Normandy, France, serves as a pedestrianized farmers' market several days of the week, and as a church parking lot for automobiles on Sundays (bottom)

Source: Preston L. Schiller

car-free operation. Excellent examples of these are the Bogenhausen District Centre (or Arabella Park) in Munich. This centre is home to about 10,000 residents and 18,000 jobs and is connected to the rest of Munich by the U4 U-Bahn line and a variety of buses. The centre also has excellent access for pedestrians and cyclists from surrounding areas. The new Messestadt Riem Centre in Munich, situated on the site of the old Munich airport and built on a U-Bahn extension, also has very extensive car-free zones around the main commercial centre and extending right into surrounding medium-density housing areas. Sub-centres on Stockholm's metro system (Tunnelbana), such as Valingby, also boast car-free zones at their heart and extending into the housing areas (Newman and Kenworthy, 1999).

Car-free zones can also operate on a temporal basis, such as at weekends or after hours in certain quarters of cities, as with some main roads in central Tokyo at weekends, some streets in Istanbul that turn into outdoor dining areas in the evening, or areas in many cities that are turned into farmers' markets at particular times. Obviously, such approaches do not provide permanent repair to areas, but do provide relief from traffic at certain times.

Traffic calming and street and highway reductions

The history of human environments since the automobile has been one of devoting more and more space to cars on streets. The original function of the street as both movement and social space has been lost. Traffic calming aims to rectify this situation by reclaiming space away from the car by fundamentally redesigning streets with the purpose of:

- reducing the severity and number of accidents in urban areas by reducing speed and calming drivers;
- reducing local air and noise pollution and vehicle fuel consumption by slowing and smoothing traffic flow;
- improving and greening the urban street environment for non-motorcar users by adding street furniture, widening sidewalks, and planting gardens and trees;
- reducing the automobile's dominance on roads by reclaiming road space for living space and the ability of people to meet and feel comfortable in streets;
- reducing the barrier effects of motor traffic on pedestrian and cycle movement; and
- enhancing local economic activity by creating a greener, better environment, which attracts and holds people for qualitative reasons compared to more auto-based environments (Newman and Kenworthy, 1999).

Traffic calming is not just a traffic management tool. The first traffic calming was the Dutch *woonerf*, or 'living yard', where the street was seen as an extension of private living space and streets were redesigned to limit cars to walking pace. Certainly, traffic calming does use changes in the vertical and horizontal geometry of the road to slow traffic (chicanes, mid-block neck downs, street width reductions, entry statements, rumble strips and so on); but good traffic calming does this in the context of enhancing neighbourhood design through beautification with trees and gardens and quality street furniture, such as new light poles, bollards, benches and bike racks. In cases where traffic calming involves street closures in a grid network, the closed blocks are turned into pocket parks with usable green space and even room for table tennis tables and other games. Traffic calming, done well, can thus have multiple beneficial results. It enhances the desirability of whole neighbourhoods; along with urban reforestation, it greens the city and adds carbon sinks; it can reduce the urban heat island effect; and, of course, it can enhance social interactions in neighbourhoods. Traffic calming repairs neighbourhoods and city environments hurt by traffic.

Traffic calming can be applied to residential streets, shopping and mixed-use streets, as well as larger arterial roads. In the case of arterial roads, traffic calming is a street and highway reduction strategy where sections of six-lane roads are reduced to four lanes or four-lane roads to two lanes. The reclaimed space is used for providing bicycle lanes on both sides of the road, widening sidewalks, providing streetcar alignments and making space for vegetation. One of the repair benefits is that the reclaimed surface is often a more permeable green or vegetative one, allowing better infiltration of rain into the ground and greening the city streets. There are many examples of this in action around the world – for example, in Frankfurt (Germany), Copenhagen (Denmark) and Barcelona (Spain).

Complete streets

Linked with the concept of traffic calming is the movement within the transportation and planning professions in the US known variously as 'great streets', 'liveable streets' and 'complete streets'. These efforts are focused on re-conceptualizing the whole nature of streets from 'traffic sewers' to streets that are multipurpose in nature. 'Such streets are not only tasked to accommodate private motor vehicles, but also pedestrians, cyclists, transit and nature in the form of more trees and gardens or other green space. They are multi-modal transport links as well as places for social life and active living' (Joseph Kott, pers comm, 2010). The push for changing streets in this way can come from initiatives that experiment for a day with new

Figure 8.6 The Netherlands' 'woonerf', or shared traffic-slowed and parking-limited streets

Source: Preston L. Schiller

Figure 8.7 In 2008 Beth Beyers inaugurated a 'Park-ing Day' when she covered over a parking space in downtown Bellingham, Washington, with sod, placed a sign informing passers-by of the burden excessive parking space places on its central business district, and invited them to enjoy a bench, picnic or make music

Source: Jack Weiss

street design, such as in Bellingham, Washington, where a 'Park-ing Day' turned many parking spaces along a main street into strips of green grass where people picnicked, played games and met in a community atmosphere reminiscent of the social vitality of pre-automobile streets. Complete streets restore the balance in the public environment in favour of non-auto users and the social function of city spaces.[9]

Freeway removal

A radical form of city repair and regeneration is to tear down whole sections of freeway. It has been found, as discussed in previous chapters, that traffic tends to expand to fill the space provided for it and likewise behaves more like a gas than a liquid when space is removed, shrinking so as not to 'overflow' its container. A high proportion of traffic simply disappears. Chapter 9 explains how this principle has been used to remove nearly 6km of freeway in central Seoul to bring back to the surface a previously highly polluted river buried under the asphalt and to provide the city with a green linear heart, full of promenading pedestrians and playing children. Other cities have successfully removed freeways, such as in Portland, in order to provide the Tom McCall Park downtown, the Embarcadero freeway in downtown San Francisco in order to regenerate the waterfront, and Milwaukee's removal of the 1.6km long Park East freeway. All such projects have had a positive effect on the city's land values, and new development nearby has occurred, while the physical and social environments of the city have improved.[10]

Restoration of environments destroyed or seriously damaged by auto-based transportation

There are many opportunities to regenerate and renew parts of cities or aspects of cities that have been damaged by auto-based transportation. These include:

- rehabilitation of the visual environment;
- converting shopping malls to more compact mixed-use TODs;
- redeveloping auto strip malls into Main Street-type environments;
- converting parking lots (including Park & Ride lots) and parking structures into parks, residences, natural areas and mixed-use developments.
- constructing new transit systems integrated with a more human- and ecologically oriented public realm;
- shrinking and greening the city;
- new vehicle technology.

These opportunities for urban regeneration are covered in the following sections.

Rehabilitation of the visual environment

Much of the visual environment in cities today is geared towards the automobile. Signs are frequent, large and designed to be read at automobile speed. The architecture of many buildings caters to the car, rather than appreciation by pedestrians. The visual environment is also dominated by the paraphernalia of traffic management systems, such as signs and lights. All of these visual elements make it very hard to have attractive and consistent human-scale urban design qualities. In The Netherlands, a traffic engineer, Hans Monderman, introduced a system where all traffic signs and traffic devices for everything were removed, as well as the marked parking bays for cars, the idea being that the 'social world' of cities should have precedence over the 'traffic world' and people would have to just work things out for themselves and resolve conflicts. The small urban environments treated using this approach were surprisingly successful and had a palpable quality of peace that was not present in the frenetic traffic-oriented environments outside the treated areas (Engwicht, 2005). Much, of course, can be done to regulate the use of oversize signs in cities in order to restore the visual environment, and planning can regulate the design of the built environment so that many of its lost visual qualities are restored.

Converting shopping malls to more compact mixed-use TODs

If urban environments are to be significantly renewed, then finding enough land that can be redeveloped into new forms with fundamentally different qualities is essential. One of the biggest land resources, certainly in the US and also significant in other auto-based cultures, are the shopping malls with their vast car parks. Many of these malls are economically marginal and there are now many examples of the conversion of these places into compact mixed-use centres. The aim is to create developments with more sustainable features, including sustainable water management, use of renewable energy and linking to the transit system. The basic planning principle is 'place-making' where people feel they belong, and the environment is of a human scale. Specifically, the techniques include:

- adding stores that open to the outdoors;
- placing housing above some of the retail;
- replacing open parking lots with structured parking;
- creating street and pedestrian connections to nearby neighbourhoods.[11]

These efforts can knit these places back together and into surrounding communities, and result in travel patterns based on transit, walking and bicycling.

Redeveloping auto strip malls into 'Main Street'-type environments

Another type of land use in great supply in the US and other auto-dominated societies is the 'strip mall' of endless businesses, offices and commercial developments set back along wide multilane streets and separated from streets by huge parking lots. The street environment is dominated by huge auto-oriented signs and architecture and usually has little housing and even less greenery. However, over a period of time such damaged environments can also be turned into more sustainable ones with much lower car use. The Sierra Club has a series of step-by-step images showing how such places in California, Florida and Colorado can be gradually renewed.[12]

The process is essentially one of constructing new higher-density, mixed-use buildings for businesses, shops and residential uses to the edge of the sidewalk in order to create active frontages and 'sleeving' (squeezing in) a reduced amount of parking behind the buildings. Sidewalks are widened, bicycle lanes are added, trees are planted, and light rail transit lines are constructed in the centre of the roads.

Converting parking lots (including Park & Ride lots) and parking structures into parks, residences, natural areas and mixed-use developments

In automobile cities, parking constitutes a high proportion of land. The potential to repair cities by building out parking lots and structures with land uses that promote ST is quite large. Cities such as Portland, Oregon, have already demonstrated the improvements that can occur when this happens. Pioneer Courthouse Square, the main central city square, was constructed on a former parking lot. River Place, a large and attractive mixed-use, high-density development overlooking the river, also replaced parking areas in Portland. Portland has a rather unique approach to downtown parking lots by taking a continuous row of parking spaces around the perimeter to install a continuous line of food trailers that add an active edge to the empty blocks, creating a much richer and more visually attractive pedestrian experience.

Park & Ride lots around transit stations are a form of land banking in cities. These can be built out in the future with attractive mixed-use higher-density developments, perhaps with some Park & Ride bays retained under the developments. Such developments can include some soft surfaces to increase water infiltration. Very often, Park & Ride lots and other parking facilities in cities are the biggest 'holes' in the urban fabric, creating visual blight and making the pedestrian experience less attractive. Parking build-out strategies are a key way, therefore, of helping to repair urban environments.

Constructing new transit systems integrated with a more human- and ecologically oriented public realm

All efforts towards fundamental change in transportation systems and patterns of use must involve adding new transit systems and improving existing ones. Years of marginalization of transit systems in automobile-oriented cities, and now in developing cities, means there is a monumental legacy of neglect that must be overcome with significant investment in new systems. Research has shown that fixed-track systems, especially rail systems, have the biggest positive systemic effect on urban systems. When cities are classed and analysed in the framework of strong rail, weak rail and no rail cities, it has been demonstrated that the more significant the rail system, the higher is the use of the transit system service, as well as the occurrence of walking and bicycling, the less parking there is in the city, and the city has lower energy use, transportation deaths, emissions, costs for transportation and so on (Kenworthy, 2008).

It is not just a matter, though, of building the transit systems themselves. It is important that these new systems have excellent waiting environments and that the vehicles be powered as much as possible from renewable energy sources. The systems also need to be integrated within environments that are greener, more human in scale and have attractive public spaces, which encourage a more public culture. The case of Portland, Oregon, discussed in the next chapter, shows how (concurrently with the implementation of the new LRT and streetcar system), the whole central and inner suburban environments, as well as the more distant suburbs near stations, were renewed into more sustainable and liveable patterns.

Shrinking and greening the city

In the US, there are many cities that are no longer able to economically maintain the vast areas of suburban sprawl, which, due to a variety of factors, including de-industrialization, now have very few people left living in them. There appears to be a new move in the US to actually buy up and demolish vast tracts of abandoned suburbia and return it to nature (meadows and forest) or perhaps use it for farming. This is inspired by the response of Flint, Michigan, the home of General Motors before it moved to Detroit, to the problem of a drastically declining economic situation in the city. It is aiming to shrink its urban area by 40 per cent, concentrating the dwindling population and services into a more compact viable area. This would mean more people having direct access to nature, and the city would be a much better candidate for quality transit and could potentially be more suitable for walking and bicycling. The suggestion is that this programme will be examined for 50 declining cities mainly in the Mid-West and North Eastern 'rust belt', including Detroit, Philadelphia, Pittsburgh, Baltimore and Memphis. The analogy is made to pruning an overgrown tree so that it can bear fruit again.[13]

In Australia and other auto-oriented societies, the situation is not so bad, although there are many declining outer areas and even some middle suburbs that are in 'negative equity'[14] or right on the edge, meaning that they are increasingly less tenable as places to live.

The above strategy of pruning cities is a radical way of greening the city, though the primary motivation for the move is to improve economic viability. There are, of course, less extreme ways of urban greening, including urban agriculture, community gardens and urban reforestation on areas of land that lend themselves to this kind of renewal. Community gardens are to be found already in many places worldwide, including central London on sites previously slated for office development (the Calthorpe Project and the Phoenix Community Garden). Denver also has numerous community gardens facilitated by a group called Denver Urban Gardens (Newman and Kenworthy, 1999). In European cities, community allotments are a major part of the urban landscape, ensuring that a lot more green space is interwoven within the urban region than in automobile cities. Compact development intrinsically lends itself to having more land to express nature.

New vehicle technology

Some of the negative impact of the automobile can be attributed to the type of technology used – namely, the internal combustion engine powered by liquid fossil fuels. Any city repair strategy needs to consider the introduction of alternative technologies for private vehicles. The most promising to date is perhaps the Vehicle to Grid (V2G) electric plug-in vehicle systems, which also act as storage systems for renewable energy generation. However, such systems only make sense in the context of much reduced travel demand since the infrastructure requirements are so large and expensive, and it is not possible to replace the current huge levels of private travel with any known combinations of new fuels or vehicle systems.

Regeneration, repair and renewal of the social and cultural environment

This addresses some of the deep underlying assumptions and cultural norms upon which human society has been built over many decades. It portends a shift in collective consciousness on many levels. Specific examples of social and cultural regeneration, repair and renewal include:

- active transportation and healthy communities by design;
- car-free movements;
- car-sharing;
- mending and renewing the social fabric and overcoming transportation inequities.

These examples are discussed in the following sections.

Active transportation and healthy communities by design

Understanding of the link between the design of communities, auto dependence, sedentary lifestyles and negative health effects is growing rapidly (Frank et al, 2003). Auto-based societies are all seeing increases in the rate of obesity in all age groups, but especially in children who live increasingly chauffeured lifestyles. There is thus a strong alliance developing between urban planning, transportation planning and the health professions, which is working towards awareness of the need for more 'active transportation' and community design that promotes walking, bicycling and walk-to (as opposed to 'drive-to') transit both for obligatory travel as well as recreation. The emphasis is simultaneously on improving individual health, creating healthy communities and healthy cities, and reducing the cost burden on the health system of obesity-related diseases. The creation of more walkable communities is at the heart of these efforts. Physical health is not the only objective here. It is also to improve social and psychological health by creating communities where there are again connections between people and an informal network of support that operates because there is more contact between people in transit, on the street, across front fences and in local shops. This helps to repair both the physical and mental health of the individual and the community.

Car-free movements

There are several social movements around the world that are attempting to draw attention to the issues that are the subject of this book. They range in order of scale downwards, from the now well-established car-free cities movement, to car-free communities and car-free

Figure 8.8 'Divide cities into two sections: Driving and non-driving'

Source: Andy Singer (www.andysinger.com)

housing movements. In practice, they are all strongly networked and linked, especially through conferences and the internet, so the boundaries between these different levels of car-free activities are quite blurred.[15]

The push for car-free cities is a worldwide movement that espouses the qualities of traditional walking cities, such as Sienna and Venice.[16] J. H. Crawford (2002, 2009) explains in detail the precedents for car-free cities, their benefits and how to design car-free cities based on walking, bicycling and transit, including a method for involving citizens in the process. There have been a number of car-free cities conferences dating back to 1997 in Lyon, France, and Timisoara, Romania (2000), attended by representatives of activist organizations around the world who share an interest in creating car-free cities. Car-busters, an organization in Prague, is involved in the conferences and other activism supporting the concept of car-free cities through their magazine. Eric Britton has been a leader in providing valuable sources of information and numerous discussions about car-free cities and related matters at his website www.newmobility.org.

As with car-free cities, there is a worldwide social movement that focuses on perhaps the more manageable and achievable task of creating car-free communities or car-free housing developments (e.g. the organization Carfree UK).[17] Such organizations try to promote car-free development by explaining why it is needed and how to go about achieving it. There is a larger umbrella organization called the World Carfree Network, which facilitates World Carfree Day:

Every 22 September, people from around the world get together in the streets, intersections and neighbourhood blocks to remind the world that we don't have to accept our car-dominated society.

On their website they explain the following aim:

By following ecological and socially inclusive principles, we can build exciting, beautiful and harmonious environments on a human scale. By creating pedestrian-oriented, bicycle-friendly human habitats, we can reintroduce routine physical activity into people's daily lives. We can make destinations easily accessible to children, the elderly, the poor and the physically handicapped. We can transform existing villages, towns and cities into more desirable places to live and work, with a healthy density and mix of homes, shops, businesses and cultural destinations. We can at the same time minimize our ecological footprint by dramatically reducing our contribution to oil dependence and climate change.[18]

Commonly quoted car-free communities are Vauban in Freiburg (see Chapter 9), which does allow car ownership but keeps nearly all of the community space free of cars by requiring car-owning residents to park in two large garages at the edge of the development, where a parking space costs US$40,000. Another is GWL Terrein, a development from 1998 near the centre of Amsterdam, which has 591 apartments but only 135 parking bays on one side of the development with a surrounding controlled parking zone, with residents of GWL Terrein being ineligible for parking permits.[19]

There are many more attempts to produce housing developments that are car free, or that in practice are close to car free. The unfortunate reality is, especially in the US, that it is extremely difficult to build significant car-free housing developments because of investor reluctance and obstacles posed in the municipal codes that regulate planning and development. A car-free development has been proposed in 2009 for Hayward, a suburb in the San Francisco Bay area:

Quarry Village is a proposed 1000-unit neighbourhood that would fill a former quarry near Cal State East Bay and 1.5 miles from the Hayward BART Station. It's the brainchild of Sherman Lewis, a professor emeritus in political science at Cal State East Bay who created a non-profit organization to promote the idea with local officials, investors and developers. According to Lewis, 69, people would rent or buy eco-friendly garage-free homes in the densely built community with interconnected pathways. Residents would receive transit passes with the cost of their home but could pay separately for one of just 100 parking spaces. A village square would feature a grocery store and other services. Shuttles would ferry passengers to the campus and BART. While Lewis said he already has 100 people signed up to buy a home if the village is ever built, he is not funding the project himself, and it's unclear whether real estate investors will take a risk on his unconventional proposition.[20]

Scheurer (2001) also provides a very detailed review of the performance of a selection of car-free housing areas.

Overall, the ever-increasing global movement involving conferences, web networking and other means to promote car-free development at various scales constitutes a significant change in the social and cultural underpinnings of urban and transportation planning development, and collectively this movement is constantly challenging, repairing and renewing, bit by bit, the norms that have shaped human settlements for the last 65 years or so.

Car-sharing

In Europe it is becoming increasingly popular not to own an automobile and to avoid all the associated expenses and problems of finding parking spaces and paying all the costs, but rather to join a car-sharing scheme, where one can gain access to a vehicle relatively easily and with a lot less administrative effort and expense. Car-sharing has spread all over the world, including a well-developed network in North America:[21]

> By the end of 2003 the number of professional car-sharing services in European cities exceeded 250, with a total membership of more than 200,000. North America has quickly followed Europe with successful services now operating in more than 60 cities in the US and Canada and a combined membership of over 80,000 ... In November 2004 CarShare Australia presented in partnership with futureeffect a seminar series in Sydney and Melbourne on car-sharing titled *Reinventing the Private Car – Changing Personal Mobility in the 21st Century*.[22]

Figure 8.9 When small lanes, trees and shrubs replace large streets, surprisingly dense single-family residential neighbourhoods can be achieved: Pedestrianized neighbourhood (bottom); tetra-cycle (top), both at Toronto Islands

Source: Preston L. Schiller

Car-sharing, although in its relatively early stages, is part of a process of social and cultural change towards how society manages the need for automobile transportation.

Mending and renewing the social fabric; overcoming transportation inequities

Many attempts at reducing automobile dependence focus on the physical aspects of producing an inherently less auto-dependent environment. It is less common to find examples that explicitly address issues to do with socio-economic groups, age and race and the need to repair and renew these aspects in planning for lower auto dependence. The Fruitvale TOD in Oakland (San Francisco Bay Area, California) on the BART system was built on a former Park & Ride lot and has developed into a very attractive, dense, mixed-use development, which caters very much to older people and people of lesser means:

> The Fruitvale Village is a successful national model for liveable communities created by the Unity Council in the early 1990s. Initially conceived as a multi-phase revitalization development project, the Fruitvale Village expanded successfully beyond the initial goals of coordination of public transportation and

land-use planning between a low-income inner-city community, transit agency and local municipality. Combining the older Fruitvale with the new village produced a distinctive urban space for daily visitors to experience an opportunity to shop, eat and rest in a safe and pleasant setting.[23]

The development has a housing area for aged persons, as well as significant affordable housing for lower-income people and facilities for families, such as a daycare centre. It is situated in a low-income area of mainly Hispanic composition and ongoing management of the development, including security issues, has been an important part of its continued success. The development ensures that many lower-income families have quality housing in a well-managed development rich in shops and community facilities and close to transit. Further development of the site involves green buildings and energy saving systems.

Regeneration, repair and renewal of governance and decision-making institutions, and the economic assumptions underpinning them

This dimension of the '3 Rs' (regeneration, repair and renewal) involves the rolling-up of sleeves and the strenuous but often rewarding work of reforming important decision-making bodies, as well as moving policy deliberations in the direction of greater sustainability in transportation.

This chapter, up to this point, has attempted to advance the discussion of ST and develop a model of how it is structured. The next step is to develop a shorter list of priorities and agenda items for its realization based upon the lessons learned from this and previous chapters. Some of the most pressing priorities include the regeneration, repair and renewal of governance, decision-making institutions and the economic assumptions underpinning them.

Fortunately, there are several exemplary efforts to redefine the relationship between citizens and governance and decision-making institutions that may be drawn upon. Often such efforts are led by citizens but may involve or attract the attention and participation of government officials and business leaders. Chapter 7 cites or discusses several examples of effective citizen participation that have made a difference. Four more innovative and low-cost ways in which citizens can empower themselves and help government and transportation agencies move towards sustainability are:

1   *Rescue Muni*: an example of a citizen-initiated effort that has led to organizational, fiscal and service improvements at a major transit agency.
2   *City Repair*: a citizens' effort to traffic calm, and expand, beautify and celebrate the public realm in streets and parks.
3   *Transit Camp*: an innovative way for transit enthusiastic computer and website experts to help their local transit agencies improve information services, planning and operations.
4   *Jane's Walk*: a grass-roots movement honouring Jane Jacobs by organizing free urban walking tours that bring activists, experts, government officials and just plain folks together to learn and share thoughts about community.

Box 8.3 Rescue Muni: A transit riders' association for San Francisco

Rescue Muni is a transit riders' organization for customers of Muni, San Francisco's Municipal Transportation Agency (SFMTA), which offers bus (conventional and electric trolleys), light rail streetcar and the famed cable car services. It was founded in 1996 by Muni riders to improve the system's reliability, service and safety. Muni had been plagued for years by uncertain and uneven year-to-year funding, organizational and operational issues and some areas of friction with its ridership base. From its outset Rescue Muni has been oriented to placing Muni on a better financial footing, as well as working in a variety of ways to foster organizational, public participation, informational and service improvements. It has played an important role in stabilizing funding, and setting performance and operational standards for the transit service. It advocates walkable streets and other non-motorized improvements that benefit transit and the quality of urban life. The organization conducts an annual riders' survey, serves as a citizens' watchdog group for Muni, and promotes expansion of transit service in San Francisco. Rescue Muni co-sponsored November 1999's Proposition E for Muni reform after circulating its own charter amendment earlier that year and participating in city hall negotiations. Rescue Muni is an independent non-partisan group that meets regularly in downtown San Francisco.[24]

Figure 8.10 Joining hands after transforming an intersection into 'Share It Square', Portland, Oregon

Source: City Repair, Portland, Oregon

City Repair, in Portland, Oregon, is a citizens' effort that began in a limited number of neighbourhoods and then spread to many others, as well as a few other cities and suburbs.

Transit Camp is not a summer getaway for bus drivers and their families, nor is it an attempt to apply Andy Warholisms to the decoration of transit vehicles. Rather, it is a citizen-initiated and led effort to improve transit in several Canadian and US cities.

Jane's Walk is a citizen-initiated effort to honour the legacy of urbanologist Jane Jacobs through locally organized and led walks to and through urban attractions and neighbourhoods. The walks often attract elected officials, such as Toronto's Mayor David Miller, and planners, in addition to civic enthusiasts and neighbourhood activists.

Box 8.4 Portland's City Repair

Part of the reason for Portland's success in developing sustainable transportation (ST) policies and projects has been the willingness of its city and regional governments and its transit agency to interact effectively with its citizenry, and often accommodate or incorporate citizen initiatives within its ongoing planning framework.

The City of Portland has responded well to the 'bottom-up' example of City Repair, a neighbourhood-based citizens' effort that began in the mid 1990s in a few neighbourhoods and has since spread to many others, as well as to other jurisdictions. Its Intersection Repair programme has been reclaiming and 'repairing' intersections in neighbourhoods where traffic was degrading pedestrian conditions and neighbourhood amenity. By decorating intersections and sidewalks and staging celebratory events, the variety of functions that streets can serve was demonstrated. The city's transportation department has co-operated with this effort and the city has changed or adapted policy to assist in these efforts.[25]

Figure 8.11 Celebrating 'Freda's Tree', another 'repaired' intersection, Portland, Oregon

Source: City Repair, Portland, Oregon

Each of the four efforts encapsulated above bring different types of approaches and energies to the issues they are addressing. Three of the efforts, City Repair, Rescue Muni and Jane's Walk, are rooted in community and ongoing organizations' approaches to issues. Transit Camp is more of the sort of shorter-term intense effort one finds in other parts of the virtual landscape. It will be very interesting to compare the admirable efforts of Transit Camp to influence well-established agency practices with those of the other 'more into it for the long haul' efforts.

Box 8.5 Transit Camp

Transit Camp is an effort led by citizens in a few cities to upgrade the image and services offered by transit agencies. It originated in Toronto, Ontario. It has been inspired by the phenomenon of 'BarCamp', user-generated 'un-conferences' and participatory workshops that bring together persons in semi-formal and often playful problem-solving explorations. Transit Camp attracts many computer and website experts, as well as a range of talented citizens enthusiastic about improving transit. It offers a transit agency the opportunity to take advantage of the expertise, resources and creative energy of many people whose contributions are often overlooked in the everyday world of public transportation bureaucracies.

Its format is generally that of an intense workshop usually occurring over a weekend. Sometimes there are follow-up evening meetings and workshops. Transit Camps in Toronto, San Francisco's Bay area and Vancouver have focused on various issues, including website improvements, web-based trip planners, improving the image and marketing of transit, developing a 'transit culture', overcoming agency stodginess and inertia, and improving security around transit.[26]

Figure 8.12 Taking a Jane's Walk to discuss how to repair and improve a pedestrian pathway

Source: Jane Farrow, director, Jane's Walk

Box 8.6 Jane's Walk

Jane's Walk developed as a commemoration of Jane Jacobs in Toronto in 2007. It has since been emulated in dozens of cities across Canada and the US. Citizens volunteer to lead a neighbourhood walk, which becomes a strolling conversation that can range from history and heritage to architecture and neighbourhood problems and solutions. At its outset, many of the walks were led by people with special expertise or interest in urban design and historic neighbourhoods, such as former Toronto Mayor David Crombie.

Under the direction of Jane Farrow, the walks have been reaching out to more marginalized neighbourhoods with large minority populations, often in suburbs or urban fringes. Local neighbours, including youths, are recruited to organize and lead walks, such as in the Dorset Park neighbourhood of Scarborough, Toronto – formerly a suburb, now incorporated as part of the enlarged Toronto municipality. One problem that Jane's Walkers in Dorset Park, an area with many residents of Middle Eastern heritage, have identified and started to address is a narrow fenced sidewalk extending several hundred metres through an industrial area between the junior public school and adjacent park and a dense residential development. The sidewalk and its chain-link fence have badly deteriorated. The fence is sagging, occasionally snaring children who brush against it. In winter the sidewalk is often not properly cleared, forcing residents and schoolchildren to march single file, at times through deep snow. Neighbourhood residents are now organizing to resolve this problem as their walking conversation evolves into community action.[27]

Figure 8.13 Jane Jacobs and other Stop Spadina veterans, joined by Wolfgang Zuckermann and Katie Alvord, at the 20th-anniversary celebration and Eco-City Conference, Toronto Islands, 1991

Source: Preston L. Schiller

Sustainable transportation agenda and priorities

The examples above and the bulk of this chapter suggest some of the priorities for an ST agenda. Priorities would include:

- The unequivocal need for strategic increases in density and mixed land uses, not across an entire city, but certainly at critical nodes or sub-centres to develop a polycentric urban form.
- The need to prioritize investment in transit, walking and cycling in a biased way to overcome many decades of neglect and favouring of PMVs. First-rate transit systems must be built and land uses integrated around them (TOD).
- The need for transit systems to be given clear speed advantages over private traffic, especially through many more dedicated rights of way and much more traffic light priority.
- The need for the reform of public transportation agencies that have for too long focused on maintaining their status quo and BAU, rather than becoming bold innovators and agents of change. Citizen-led efforts, such as Rescue Muni and Transit Camp, point to ways in which citizen energy can renew such agencies.
- The central importance of the public realm and its influence on non-motorized mobility and the social life of the city. The public realm must be protected and restored in all cities to ensure a liveable, beautiful, connected city.
- Changing the ways in which citizens interact with governance and planning bodies. Examples of more productive forms of public participation have been presented in this chapter and Chapter 7. More will be presented in Chapter 9.

These are priorities that have been realized in some ways in several of the exemplary cities explored in the next chapter.

Agenda items for reforms that need to be accomplished but are difficult, especially at the city and metropolitan levels, because they require change at state–provincial, business, national and even some at international levels include:

- the overcoming of transportation inequities; cities may or may not be able to improve transit, walking and bicycling independent of national reforms or funding, but creating effective railway networks or reducing levels of air transport must be addressed at higher levels;
- major economic and transportation pricing reforms;
- the de-subsidization of driving and other harmful dimensions of transportation.

From the new paradigm to its embodiment

In the next chapter we will explore several examples of cities that have engaged in the process of introducing sustainable transportation. Some of the ways in which these exemplary cities have demonstrated different

Box 8.7 Kenneth R. Schneider: Fighting for change

Jeffrey R. Kenworthy

The writings of Kenneth R. Schneider in his books *Autokind vs Mankind: An Analysis of Tyranny – A Proposal for Rebellion, A Plan for Reconstruction* and *On the Nature of Cities: Towards Enduring and Creative Human Environments* remain today probably the most powerful and convincing dissections one can read about the excesses of automobile dependence and the irrationality of continuing down that path. Alas, in the early and even late 1970s in the USA, these were not the kind of analyses or exposés that the majority of people in the transportation policy and decision-making community wanted to read, and even less respond to constructively. His writings at the time were truly voices crying in the wilderness, and yet for those of us beginning to see the lunacy of the transportation trajectories of that time, his words were a great source of inspiration, a challenge and a call to action. Today, his words are part of an accepted wisdom about the need to tackle monocultural approaches to transportation systems.

When I, as a young student, wrote to Ken in 1979 after reading his second book and praising its contents, he wrote back to me saying that my letter was the only one he had ever received – indeed the only positive thing anyone had ever said at the time about *On The Nature of Cities* or his other writings. He said he might just as well have written the book in Sanskrit. Ken became a good friend and I visited with him in Flagstaff, Arizona, where he lived at the time, and learned much from him about cities and their problems, and the foibles of modern auto-based planning, especially as it was practiced in the developing world (he was part of a UN Commission to help plan a new capital for Nigeria, an exercise that left him quite depressed because of the impregnable auto-orientation of all those around him). But Ken also provided wonderful insights into the desert and canyon country of Arizona and Utah, which he deeply loved, and the Hopi Indians with whom he worked as a teacher before turning his sights on the automobile.

Ken shared with me a still unpublished manuscript called *The Community Spaceframe*, an impassioned 'built environment' response to the disconnected and inhuman ways he saw human settlements being built all around him. The community spaceframe in simple terms was a dense walking settlement, connected to high quality transit, but it was above all a vision of a way of life where people again had human community, where they provided mutual support in an environment that did not build in isolation. He understood density; he understood that cities by their nature had to have certain threshold densities for their well-functioning. Low density, for him, was the disease of the automobile, which, in essence, eliminated the very nature of what a city was all about. Of course, he was in good company here with Mumford and Jacobs.

Ken also confided that the book he really wanted to write about cities and transportation would be called *The City Fight Book*. This was not a wanton call to conflict. It was his clear thinking and experience that cities and their transportation systems can never change without a fight, whether that is a community-led rebellion against BAU or the headlong clash between different planning and transportation ideologies within the realm of government. Time has certainly proven him correct on this point.

Ken is no longer with us and he never got to write that book. But he still stands as one of the great thinkers and dreamers about transportation and the cities they shape. He sounded among the clearest, most passionate and most articulate warnings and calls to action against the dominance of auto-based planning of any writer. Above all he always had the 'common good' in cities foremost in his thoughts. He is sorely missed, but his writings helped shape a generation of thinkers and urban activists, and are still highly relevant as lucid reminders of where we have come from and the fights that remain to be won.

aspects of the new paradigm have been highlighted to a limited extent. What is clear from this chapter is that a truly significant task for any one city or country is to embrace all the potential factors that contribute to the success of ST. As the exemplars demonstrate, this is not a cause for discouragement because success in different aspects of this new paradigm tends to trigger a much larger process of change, in much the same way as a pebble cast into the centre of a pond sends out ripples that embrace the whole pond. The clear message seems to be that change begets change, so the first steps towards paradigm change in any of the areas discussed in this chapter can have a much bigger impact than the mere sum of the individual parts. They can be part of a regeneration, repair and renewal process. Cities, in particular, are ecosystems, and in ecosystems every factor and part is linked to every other factor and part.

The exemplars in Chapter 9 demonstrate, in many ways, the processes of regeneration, renewal and repair discussed above. For example, Surubaya's Kampung Improvement Programme has fundamentally restored the physical environment for residents of these former slums. The social and cultural traditions of interaction and commerce in public space have been given the quality public realm in which to find proper expression. Seoul's removal of a central city freeway has restored and greened the physical environment, giving citizens a whole new space in which to walk and interact with other people. Its successful freeway removal has inspired more fundamental changes in the culture within planning organizations and the city's transportation planning orientation towards transit, walking and cycling. The Portland, Freiburg and Boulder exemplars also have elements of regeneration, repair and renewal of the physical, social, governance, decision-making and economic aspects of their cities. Certainly, it would seem that these cities give much needed hope to other cities grappling with the need to regenerate their urban environments.

Questions for discussion

- Identify at least one significant difference between business as usual (BAU)/predict and provide and mobility management / transportation demand management (TDM) approaches and orientations to urban transportation planning and provision.
- Discuss the differences between 'mobility' and 'accessibility' in terms of the differing approaches to planning and investment of each and some of their consequences for urban form, the economy and the environment.
- Compare a few of the differences between forecasting and the 'old paradigm' of business as usual (BAU) with backcasting and the 'new paradigm' of integrated planning, participation and policy-making in terms of likely outcomes.
- Why does it currently appear to be easier to advance a sustainable transportation programme at the level of cities and regions than at the level of states/provinces or nations?

Notes

1 As it was then called; now it is known as 'transportation engineering'.

2 Norman Kennedy (1963) 'Evolving concept of transportation engineering', *Traffic Engineering and Control*, cited in Plowden (1972).

3 See Schwedler (2007); also see his endnote 1 and www.thepep.org/en/workplan/ia4pi/ia4pi.htm.

4 For more on this topic, see the excellent resources at the Victoria Transport Policy Institute (2008, 2009a,b,c).

5 This is similar to the perverse tax incentives in the US that benefit motorists far more than commuters by transit or non-motorized modes.

6 See critique of HOV in Chapter 6; see discussion of transit priority in Chapter 4 and the transit primer in Appendix 1.

7 For more detailed information about some of these, see the excellent resources available at Victoria Transport Policy Institute (2009c), www.vtpi.org/tdm/index.php#incentives.

8 See www.re-energy.ca/ridethewind/backgrounder.shtml.

9 See www.completestreets.org/, www.tc.gc.ca/programs/environment/utsp/sidewalkCafes.htm, www.squirepark.org/project_pages/reclaiming-streets-for-the-people/ and www.bellinghamherald.com/102/story/1076038.html.

10 See www.preservenet.com/freeways/FreewaysInducedReduced.html.

11 See www.newurbannews.com/Mar08Malls.html.

12 See www.sierraclub.org/sprawl/community/transformations/.

13 See www.telegraph.co.uk/finance/financetopics/financialcrisis/5516536/US-cities-may-have-to-be-bulldozed-in-order-to-survive.html.

14 Carrying mortgages that are more than the house is now worth.

15 Critical mass bike rides that are held in some 300 cities all around the world to draw attention to the bicycle as a legitimate means of transportations could be considered another manifestation of this worldwide car-free movement; see http://en.wikipedia.org/wiki/Critical_Mass.

16 See www.carfree.com/.

17 See www.carfree.org.uk/.

18 See www.worldcarfree.net/about_us/global/charter.php.

19 See www.carfree.org.uk/043.

20 See www.sfgate.com/cgi-bin/article.cgi?f=/c/a/2009/06/08/BA2D17THSA.DTL.

21 See www.carsharing.net/.

22 See www.goget.com.au/car-sharing-worldwide.html.

23 See www.unitycouncil.org/fruitvale/overview1.htm.

24 See www.rescuemuni.org/ and www.sfmta.com/cms/home/sfmta.php.

25 Thanks to City Repair's Matt Phillips and Michael Cook for their helpful information and photos; for more, see http://cityrepair.org/.

26 See Toronto, http://transitcamp.wik.is/; see also http://transitcamp.wik.is/2007_Transit_Camp/The_Story_of_TransitCamp; Bay Area Transit Camp, http://barcamp.org/TransitCampBayArea; Vancouver Transit Camp, http://justagwailo.com/2007/12/18/vancouver-transit-camp-recap, www.canada.com/vancouvercourier/news/story.html?id=9588298d-6139-4b9e-ac4e-aed3bd7d0216 and http://skytrainunconference.ca/ – thanks to Karen Quinn Fung for sharing information about Vancouver's Transit Camp.

27 See Jane's Walk Canada, www.janeswalk.net/; Jane's Walk US, www.janeswalkusa.org/; Micallef (2009). Many thanks to Jane Farrow, director of Jane's Walk, for much useful background information.

References and further reading

Britton, E. (2009) 'The new mobility agenda', www.newmobility.org, accessed 1 October 2009

Brög, W. and Erl, E. (2003) '(Auto) mobility in the conurbation: Is mobility dominated by the car?', *Socialdata*, Munich, www.socialdata.de/.../(Auto)%20Mobility%20in%20the%20Conurbation.pdf, accessed 15 September 2009

Buchanan, C. (Head of Working Group) (1963) *Traffic in Towns: A Study of the Long Term Problems of Traffic in Urban Areas*, The Buchanan Report, Reports of the Steering Group and Working Group appointed by the Minister of Transport, HMSO, London

City Repair (2009) http://cityrepair.org/

Crawford J. H. (2002) *Carfree Cities*, International Books, Utrecht, The Netherlands

Crawford J. H. (2009) *Carfree Design Manual*, International Books, Utrecht, The Netherlands

Engwicht, D. (ed) (1989) *Traffic Calming: The Solution to Urban Traffic and a New Vision for Neighborhood Livability*, CART (Citizens Advocating Responsible Transportation), Ashgrove, Australia, reprinted (1993) STOP (Sensible Transportation Options for People), Tigard, OR

Engwicht, D. (1993) *Reclaiming our Cities and Towns: Better Living with Less Traffic*, New Society Publishers, Gabriola Island, British Columbia

Engwicht, D. (2005) *Mental Speed Bumps*, Envirobooks. Sydney, Australia

Frank, L., Engelke, P. and Schmid, T. (2003) *Health and Community Design: The Impact of the Built Environment on Physical Activity*, Island Press, Washington, DC

Goodwin, P. E., Hallett, S., Kenny, F. and Stokes, G. (1991) *Transport: The New Realism*, Transport Studies Unit, Oxford University Press, Oxford, UK

Jane's Walk (2009) www.janeswalk.net

Kenworthy, J. (2008) 'An international review of the significance of rail in developing more sustainable urban transport systems in higher income cities', *World Transport Policy and Practice*, vol 14, no 2, pp21–37

Komanoff, C. (1994) 'Pollution taxes for roadway transportation', *Pace Environmental Law Review*, vol 12, no 1, pp121–184

Litman, T. (2003) *Exploring the Paradigm Shift Needed for Sustainable Transportation*, www.vtpi.org/reinvent.pdf, accessed 15 September 2009

Micallef, S. (2009) 'The (sub)urban village', *Spacing*, summer–fall, pp60–63

Newman, P. W. G. and Kenworthy, J. R. (1984) 'The use and abuse of driving cycle research: Clarifying the relationship between traffic congestion, energy and emissions', *Transportation Quarterly*, vol 38, pp615–635

Newman, P. W. G. and Kenworthy, J. R. (1989) *Cities and Automobile Dependence: A Sourcebook*, Gower Technical, Aldershot, UK, and Brookfield, VT

Newman, P. W. G. and Kenworthy, J. R. (1999) *Sustainability and Cities: Overcoming Automobile Dependence*, Island Press, Washington, DC

Newman, P. W. G., Kenworthy, J. R. and Lyons, T. J. (1988) 'Does free-flowing traffic save energy and lower emissions in cities?', *Search*, vol 19, no 5/6, September–November, pp267–272

Nowlan, D. M. and Stewart, G. (1991) 'Downtown population growth and commuting trips: Recent Toronto experience', *Journal of the American Planning Association*, vol 57, no 2, pp165–182

Penalosa, E. (2003) *Sustainable Transportation: A Sourcebook for Policy-Makers in Developing Countries*, Sustainable Urban Transport Project, www.sutp.org, www.vtpi.org/gtz_module.pdf, accessed 15 September 2009

Plowden, S. (1972) *Towns against Traffic,* Deutsch, London

Rescue Muni (undated) 'A transit riders' association for San Francisco', www.rescuemuni.org/, accessed 15 September 2009

Scheurer, J. (2001) *Urban Ecology, Innovations in Housing Policy and the Future of Cities: Towards Sustainability in Neighbourhood Communities*, PhD thesis, Murdoch University at Perth, Australia

Schwedler, H.-U. (2007) 'Supportive institutional conditions for policy integration of transport, environment and health', European Academy of the Urban Environment, Berlin, www.eaue.de/PUBS.HTM, accessed 17 June 2009

Socialdata (undated) http://socialdata.us/links.php, www.socialdata.de

Swift, P. (undated) 'New urbanism: Clustered, mixed-use, multi-modal neighborhood design', www.vtpi.org/tdm/tdm24.htm, accessed 15 September 2009

Transit Camp (San Francisco Bay Area) (2009) http://barcamp.org/TransitCampBayArea, accessed 15 September 2009

Transit Camp (Toronto) (2009) http://transitcamp.wik.is/, accessed 15 September 2009

Victoria Transport Policy Institute (2008) *Road Pricing*, Victoria Transport Policy Institute, www.vtpi.org/tdm/tdm35.htm, accessed 15 September 2009

Victoria Transport Policy Institute (2009a) *Transportation Management Programs*, Victoria Transport Policy Institute, www.vtpi.org/tdm/tdm42.htm, accessed 15 September 2009

Victoria Transport Policy Institute (2009b) 'Online TDM Encyclopedia', Victoria Transport Policy Institute, www.vtpi.org/tdm, accessed 15 September 2009

Victoria Transport Policy Institute (2009c) 'Incentives to use alternative modes and reduce driving', www.vtpi.org/tdm/index.php#incentives, accessed 15 September 2009

9

Exemplars of Sustainable Transportation: Walking the Talk in Vancouver, Portland, Boulder, Freiburg, Seoul and Surubaya

Introduction

Most of the ideas underpinning the quest for more sustainable urban transportation systems are not 'rocket science'. Everyone knows that cities need to transfer more travel onto the green modes – transit, walking and cycling – and to use one of the more recent terms in the lexicon of transportation professionals: 'feral transportation'. Feral transportation comprises all those 'wild' and sometimes noisy or possibly annoying modes used predominantly, though not exclusively, by youth, ranging from skateboards, dirt surfers, in-line skates, scooters and the like to perhaps even the Segway, or the small electric buggies used increasingly by older people to do their shopping, to sit and socialize together in small pocket parks and generally to maintain their independent mobility. Whatever modes we are talking about here, the most basic unifying element of sustainable transportation is to ensure that use of the high energy-consuming and space-demanding private automobile, enemy number one of a high-quality public realm in cities and the pillar of 'business as usual', is minimized. This is, of course, as much about urban land use as it is about particular modes of transportation or technologies, so the discussion here is critically concerned with those elements of land-use planning that are facilitating the use of more sustainable modes – for example, transit-oriented development (TOD).

This chapter provides an overview of a number of cities around the world that are achieving significant gains in the endeavour towards more sustainable transportation. It highlights some of their most significant achievements and also some ways in which they are doing this.[1] Where possible, some recent and previously unpublished research results of trends in cities in transportation-related indicators are presented to highlight, more generally, the success or otherwise of the world's cities towards becoming more sustainable in transportation.[2]

Choosing cities for this chapter is, unfortunately, not an overly difficult task since there are not many cities in the world that one can highlight as making truly significant, widespread, continuous and consistent strides in the desired direction. Partial evidence of this is the almost deity-like status of Curitiba, Brazil, and, more lately, Bogotá, Colombia, for the highly successful bus rapid transit (BRT) systems that these cities have implemented, particularly so for the fact that they have done so in the context of a highly polarized socio-economic situation with a large proportion of very low-income inhabitants and slum-dwellers. Not wishing to repeat the already copious information available about Curitiba's famous bus system, as well as its less successful efforts to encourage walking and cycling championed worldwide by former Mayor Jaime Lerner, or Bogotá's TransMilenio bus rapid transit system, publicized effectively by the previous Mayor Enrique Penalosa, this chapter leaves these excellent examples for readers to explore themselves.

Curitiba is often seen as a 'silver bullet' for other cities. One point that is infrequently recognized about this city, however, is that some of its most famous achievements, such as the weekend conversion of a major downtown street to a pedestrian mall, were done in the military dictatorship period prior to democracy when it was not unusual for elected officials to act with impunity in public matters, whether philanthropic or otherwise.[3] Because of the special conditions prevalent there, it is not possible simply to transplant the Curitiba model to other cities, though many, including Los Angeles, have toyed with the idea. For example, land use and transportation development are under the same regulatory control in Curitiba and, hence, dense development is directed at the structural axis of the city linked to the bus rapid transit system, a power most cities would give a lot to be able wield with such alacrity. In a more usual political situation, probably only Stockholm has ever achieved such tight coordination of land-use and transportation development when it developed its Tunnelbana metro system and high-density satellite centres, commencing in the 1950s (Cervero, 1995, 1998; Newman and Kenworthy, 1999).

This chapter has therefore chosen six cities from diverse urban cultural and socio-economic contexts that represent comprehensive achievements towards sustainable transportation. Five of these are Vancouver (British Columbia), Portland (Oregon), Boulder (Colorado)[4], Freiburg im Breisgau (Germany) and Seoul (South Korea). It also looks at perhaps a less well-known but significant advancement in sustainable transportation undertaken in Surubaya (in East Java, Indonesia): the Kampung Improvement Programme (KIP). This sample of cities provides an instructive range of exemplars from the more auto-oriented and wealthy North American environment, both Canada and the US, through the more human-scale, compact European context, to the giant and rapidly industrializing megacity context in Asia, and finally to a large lower-income Asian city in Indonesia. By no means are these the only case examples worthy of attention; but they are among the more significant and instructive ones. There are others and the number grows steadily.

The exemplars

Vancouver, British Columbia – automobile city to a planner's pilgrimage

Vancouver is a metropolitan area of some 2.2 million people. Perhaps its most distinguishing feature in a North American context is that the City of Vancouver at the core of the region[5] has no urban freeways.

Vancouver has become to urban planners what Stockholm achieved in the 1950s when it built its Tunnelbana, or modern metro system, and proceeded to build whole communities of satellite towns around its stations, such as Valingby and Kista. Stockholm became an official global pilgrimage site for planners to view the best in TOD, complete separation of cars from pedestrians and cyclists, and other excellent urban design features encouraging walking and cycling.

Vancouver's transformation from a typical auto city with a relatively short urban history compared to its East Coast North American counterparts really commenced during the early 1970s with the successful community-led fight to rid the city of all planned freeway construction within the City of Vancouver boundaries. This fight involved a then shop front lawyer named Michael Harcourt who helped the Chinatown community to remove the threat of a freeway. He later became a Vancouver city councillor, mayor of Vancouver and, finally, premier of British Columbia, a political career built significantly on fighting freeways and campaigning for more liveable neighbourhoods in their place. Instead of large clover leaf freeway junctions punctuating the downtown area, Vancouver is home to perhaps one of the most dynamic and lively central and inner-city populations of any city in the auto-dependent world at places such as False Creek North and South, Yaletown, the city's West End, Coal Harbour Redevelopment, as well as many other sites. The absence of high-speed road travel has meant that premium locations, near the heart of most amenities and speedy transit, have become the most popular places in which to live in order to maintain accessibility and acceptable daily travel times. The Vancouver region's average road traffic speed in 2006 was only 38.6kmph, whereas metro areas in the US and Australia average between 43kmph and 52kmph (Kenworthy, 2009).

This case study explores various facets of Vancouver's success in sustainable transportation.

Table 9.1 Vancouver key figures

Population (2006)	2,116,581
Metropolitan GDP per capita (US$ 1995; 2006 adjusted)	US$29,582
Urban density (persons per hectare; 2006)	25.2
Road length per person (metres; 2006)	4.7
Car use per person (vehicle kilometres travelled, or vkt, per year; 2006)	6971
Transit use (boardings per person; 2006)	134

Source: Jeffrey R. Kenworthy

Figure 9.1 View of False Creek South, Vancouver, British Columbia – an area that would have been lost to freeway infrastructure and is now a walkable neighbourhood

Source: Jeffrey R. Kenworthy

Figure 9.2
Coal Harbour Redevelopment, downtown Vancouver, British Columbia, with its fine attention to the walkability of the public realm

Vancouver comparisons

We can compare the Vancouver metropolitan area[6] to other Canadian and international metropolitan areas and examine the trends in some key factors over the 1996 to 2006 period and earlier. In land-use terms, Vancouver had trends typical of North American cities between 1961 and 1981. Urban density declined from 24.9 persons per hectare in 1961, to 21.6 per hectare in 1971, to 18.4 per hectare in 1981. At the time that its strong re-urbanization policies began to cut in (discussed later), assisted significantly by the absence of high-speed private transportation options, it then started to increase in density. In 1991 it rose back to 20.8 persons per hectare; 1996 saw 21.6 persons per hectare; and in 2006 it exceeded its 1961 density and was sitting at 25.2 persons per hectare, a 17 per cent increase in ten years (Kenworthy and Laube, 1999; Kenworthy, 2009). Land-use change of this magnitude that is focused mainly in central and inner areas, but which generates a significant increase in density across an entire region of between 1 million and 2 million people, is hard to achieve, especially since some parts of the region are continuing to grow with lower suburban densities. One factor that has probably helped to raise the acceptability and success of high density in Vancouver is the large number of ex-Hong Kong residents who were courted by Vancouver prior to the return of Hong Kong to Chinese rule.

In terms of car use, per capita annual car kilometres in 1981 were 6756km, which rose to 8361km in 1991. By 1996 this was down to 6746km and in 2006 it had risen slightly (3.3 per cent) to 6971km. But the net effect is that in 15 years between 1991 and 2006, car use per person in the Greater Vancouver Regional District (GVRD) decreased by 17 per cent. Part of the reason for this change is no doubt due to increases in density, which, in turn, have helped to increase transit usage. But density is not the only factor in increased transit use. Vancouver also commenced in 1986 to develop a rail backbone to its transit system in the form of its newly opened Skytrain system, which afforded much faster urban travel.

In 1981 transit use was 111 annual trips per person, which had declined to 95 per person by 1991. In 1996 it rose to 118 and in 2006 stood at 134 trips per person per annum.[7] This is just short of its 1961 figure of 138 trips per person, when car ownership in Vancouver was a mere 285 cars per 1000 people. Now, with almost the same transit use as in 1961, the region has 506 cars per 1000 people. Clearly, even in the context of high car ownership, transit is becoming more attractive and popular with Vancouverites due to a combination of better, speedier and more diversified services, more attractive ticket offers especially to students, but also because many more people are now living within walking distance to transit stops and feeder services to speedier rail, and bus services have improved greatly. Perhaps as a consequence, Vancouver's car ownership was even down by 3 per cent in 2006 from its 1996 figure of 520 per 1000. On the downside, transit – especially around Skytrain stations – has experienced increasing crime levels in the last few years, giving rise to many concerns in Vancouver.

Part of this process of change is also reflected in central business district (CBD, downtown) parking per 1000 jobs, which in 1971 stood at 341, rising to 342 in 1981 and then blowing out to 443 in 1991 and 444 in 1996. In 2006, CBD parking supply took a drop back to 389 spaces per 1000 CBD jobs. For comparison, in 2005, US cities averaged 509 spaces per 1000 CBD jobs, or 31 per cent more than in Vancouver. The low level of freeway provision in the region is also significant.[8] Freeway length per person fell from 0.077m to 0.069m between 1996 and 2006, while US cities in 2005 stood at 0.159m per person, some 130 per cent more than in Vancouver. Other positive features of Vancouver's transportation trajectory are an increase in transit service per capita (seat kilometres per person), up by 12 per cent from 1996 to 2006, and also a fall in transportation-related deaths from 6.5 to 5.4 per 100,000 people.[9]

Better transit service

Compared to most American cities, Vancouver enjoys high levels of transit use (134 trips per person in 2006), or exactly double that of the average for ten large US cities of 67 trips per person in 2005. The New York–New Jersey–Connecticut (tri-state) metropolitan region is by far the most transit-oriented US urban area and has 168 trips per person, so that Vancouver is not so far behind this top-performing region. On the other hand, it does have a considerable way to go to catch up with some of its Canadian peers – for example, the Montreal region with 206 trips per person, or even Toronto with 154. However, between 1996 and 2006 both these cities were either stagnant or slightly declining in transit use (Kenworthy, 2009), while Vancouver's use of transit is still growing (13 per cent increase from 1996 to 2006) and could overhaul these other traditional Canadian transit metropolises if such trends continue.

Vancouver's transit system consists of a comprehensive network of both diesel and trolley buses; specialized bus services for people with disabilities; an advanced elevated and driverless light rail transit (LRT) system called Skytrain operating at about two-minute intervals in the peak and six-minute intervals in the off-peak; a commuter rail line called the West Coast Express, servicing distant suburban communities; and a ferry service called the Sea Bus. As well, there is a new fully automated 18.5km partially underground, partially elevated and partially at-grade rail line from the city to the airport and a branch into the Richmond suburbs, which opened in August 2009. It will operate on headways of six minutes, have expected ridership of 100,000 per day by 2010 and a travel time of 24 minutes.[10] If we assume a more modest patronage of 80,000 per day over the whole 365 days and a population of 2.3 million, this line alone will add about 13 transit trips per capita in Vancouver (an increase of 10 per cent), excluding increased associated new boardings on access transit lines.

Within the City of Vancouver, which is built on a fine-grained traditional street grid, the bus system is relatively frequent with buses operating north–south and east–west, providing good radial and cross-city travel opportunities, with speedier services called the B-Line in some areas. Overall, however, bus average speeds are mostly below 20kmph due to frequent stops, many intersections,[11] moderate traffic congestion and passenger loads that are often horrendously high, affording poor passenger comfort. The buses do, however, interconnect well with each other in many locations and transfers to Skytrain, the West Coast Express, the Sea Bus and the recently opened Canada Line are also well catered for, meaning that mobility in all directions across the whole region on transit is feasible without necessarily passing through the central area, and transit trips are often competitive in speed terms. The lack of freeways in the city of Vancouver means that although the bus system is often slow, travel speeds can still be competitive with the car, especially where a rail segment or B-line bus is involved.

The major challenges in Vancouver, due to its transit-conducive urban form and growing transit ridership, are to increase transit speed, frequency, capacity and comfort for riders, as well as to extend the rail system and bus rapid transit service options into other parts of the region. This is happening with plans for a light rail line along the desperately crowded and densely developed Broadway Corridor (where B-Line buses currently run) and a possible extension of Skytrain technology from the existing Millennium Skytrain line in Coquitlam to Port Moody through the Coquitlam suburbs (the Evergreen Line). Interestingly, the Canada Line has been constructed with a cost-sharing arrangement reported as being Cdn$970 million from private-sector and Vancouver airport sources,[12] with Cdn$930 million from federal, provincial, Translink and City of Vancouver funds,[13] which may bode well for further development of Vancouver's transit system.

Transit-oriented development (TOD)

A major success factor of transit development in Vancouver over the last 25 years has been the strong efforts to integrate high-density residential and mixed-use development in significant nodes around selected stations on Skytrain, redevelopment of highly favoured waterfront areas such as False Creek and Coal Harbour, and even, in some cases, the development of strong town centres around bus-only or bus plus commuter rail nodes such as Port Moody. From before its inception, Skytrain's development has gone hand in hand with planned TOD high-density development from which it draws a lot of its patronage. Park & Ride around stations in the City of Vancouver, City of Burnaby and City of New Westminster have been expressly excluded in favour of high-density uses clustered close to the station entrances. These developments exist at numerous stations such as major centres at Metrotown, New Westminster and smaller developments at other stations such as Joyce–Collingwood and Edmonds Stations. South of the Fraser River in the Surrey suburbs, Park & Ride surrounds some stations such as Surrey Central, with development set back from the station. The resulting urban design outcomes are very poor compared to those north of the Fraser.

Figure 9.3 High-density clustering of mixed-use development at Joyce–Collingwood Station, Burnaby, Vancouver

Source: Jeffrey R. Kenworthy

The larger nodes on Skytrain have mixed commercial, office, residential, retail and markets within a short walk of the station. The new housing consists of quality high-rise towers, three- to four-storey condominium-style developments and townhouses. Some of the housing consists of individual housing co-operatives that have provided more affordable housing options. The TOD at New Westminster is set along an attractive landscaped boardwalk on the Fraser River that includes playgrounds for children and extensive gardens, trees and grassed areas. The family units have inner courtyards in which families and friends congregate. The farmers' market where residents do their shopping is communally orientated with open eating areas and a more relaxed, less structured, less sterile atmosphere than a supermarket. The landscaped boardwalk is partly maintained by the 7/11 supermarket chain.

Some significant evidence for the preference of Vancouverites for such well-located, short-distance, non-auto travel option sites comes from the Canadian Censuses of 1991 to 2006. Over this 15-year period, the population of the City of Vancouver, the core of the whole region, grew from 471,844 to 578,041 people, an increase of 23 per cent, and this was in the context of falling household occupancy.[14] Even prior to 1991, the City of Vancouver population was on the rise and increased by 40,000 people between 1986 and 1991.

As well as the obvious nodes that have sprung up within the existing urbanized area around Skytrain in the 25 years since its opening, the re-urbanization trend leading to the significant population increases just described has resulted in an enormous amount of other new development along the major diesel and trolley bus lines in the city where a lot of mixed-use shopping and business activities already exist (e.g. the Arbutus Lands development). This development consists of medium- to high-density housing

Figure 9.4 Arbutus Lands inner-city redevelopment, Vancouver, British Columbia

Source: Jeffrey R. Kenworthy

(sometimes shop-top housing) with special attention to the needs of families wishing to escape the car-dependent suburbs. Specific design manuals are aimed at producing compact environments suitable for a whole range of household types.

Perhaps the star attraction in this redevelopment is the staggering intensity and quality of development at False Creek, located at the foot of the CBD or downtown area and serviced by frequent trolley and diesel bus services and some Skytrain stations at points near its periphery.

The provincial electoral district of False Creek had a population of nearly 44,000 in 2006.[15] Development at both False Creek South and North (Yaletown), as well as the new South-East False Creek, being developed at even higher densities and as something of an 'ecological model', provide excellent examples of how to build high-density transit-oriented urban villages in central locations with extensive and beautifully designed open spaces, together with adjacent mixed land uses such as markets, hotels, cultural activities, shops and restaurants (e.g. Granville Island). There is an enormous variety in housing forms and styles in these areas, including townhouses, terraced units, medium-rise and high-rise apartments, with many of the earlier ones being co-operative housing ventures. The extensive public spaces and children's play areas are traffic free, the only direct road access on the south side of False Creek being essentially from a two-lane road at the rear of the development, with parking mostly under the buildings.

The whole of False Creek North and South and even beyond this area is knitted together with first-class, wide pedestrian- and bicycle-only facilities, and it is this environment at ground level, below the often towering residential complexes, that gives people the option of sustainable transportation, as well as conviviality and convenience. Along this pedestrian spine there are local shops, community facilities, child-minding centres, professional suites for dentists and doctors, meeting areas, community playgrounds and sports areas, all integrated within walking or cycling distance of most residences. For a central city location, False Creek provides an exceptionally quiet oasis and, yet, a dynamic and varied urban location for residents and the many visitors who use the area for social and recreational purposes.

Developments such as this and others, such as Coal Harbour, and the ongoing evolution of Vancouver's West End, have helped to minimize Vancouver's growth in car use in inner areas by increasing transit use and making the use of non-motorized modes more feasible and attractive. The important point here is that Vancouver is limiting outward sprawl and gradually reshaping itself into a more transit-oriented region.

Apart from these waterfront areas, the Skytrain stations and high-density residential precincts in the inner city of Vancouver, other focal points for high-density development have been created in areas such as the Fraserlands Development, connected by feeder buses to Skytrain stations. Still other very attractive and significant high-density mixed-use developments have occurred in areas only serviced by buses, or buses and commuter rail, such as Port Moody, though, as mentioned, there are plans to build the Evergreen Line of the Skytrain to this area (or light rail). Within these centres pedestrians and cyclists are given attractive and comparatively safe conditions and there exists

Figure 9.5 Port Moody town centre's attractive public realm, suburban Vancouver

Source: Jeffrey R. Kenworthy

a civic life in the city spaces that is atypical for a majority of North American cities where 'big box' retail centres and office parks tend to be the norm.

This process has been partly shaped by the Greater Vancouver's regional planning strategy (Livable Region), which effectively creates a green belt for the region and limits the amount of suburban land that can be developed. This is on top of an already topographically constrained city due to mountainous terrain and the narrow Fraser River Valley.

It has been public policy since the mid 1970s to try to concentrate much development in transit-rich locations. Indeed, public consultations with communities affected by Skytrain-linked redevelopments occurred as early as 1978, eight years ahead of the opening of the first Skytrain segment in 1986 for the Expo that occurred on the land now known as False Creek North, or Yaletown. This high density has occurred at stations in Vancouver as well as neighbouring Burnaby and further down the line in New Westminster, at stations such as Joyce–Collingwood, Metrotown, Edmonds and New Westminster. Such TODs are gradually reshaping the Vancouver region into a genuine polycentric 'transit metropolis' (Cervero, 1998). Some key factors in this land-use evolution have been:

- Part funding of rail by the British Columbia provincial government occurred and strong direction was made by the province to local authorities to actively support the transit investment through appropriate zoning of station precinct land.
- There was involvement of provincial government in assembly and re-servicing of land for TOD. For example, at New Westminster, land for the very high-density TOD that has developed with superb public space centred on a boardwalk along the Fraser River was former logging industry land that needed rehabilitation and servicing with new infrastructure before land parcels could be released for high-density redevelopment.
- There was strong support for the idea of less car-oriented regional centres based on the Skytrain, with excellent conditions for pedestrians and cyclists. Each of the new centres on Skytrain pays particular attention to the quality of urban design and to facilitating comfortable and convenient bicycle access from surrounding areas and within the centre itself.

- Successful partnerships between BC Transit and private developers occurred: location and development of stations in the first stage of Skytrain was a joint exercise, including some joint financing of station costs.
- Early consultation and engagement with communities was a hallmark of TOD. Local area strategies were established for the 800m radius of stations. Public meetings and local advisory committees were created to address citizen concerns, particularly in relation to crime and traffic.
- Land with highest densities was rezoned from derelict industrial uses; opposition was therefore minimal because it was a big improvement on existing conditions. Such sites were the 'low hanging fruit' in a wide range of redevelopment opportunities and gave government the opportunity to demonstrate the quality and liveability that could be achieved at much higher densities on sites that presented the least problematic options in terms of community resistance. It was a smart strategy because much opposition to higher densities is based on fear of the unknown, so cities have to go through a process of acceptance of such changes. Successful demonstration projects of compact, liveable developments have created snowball effects in numerous cities (e.g. Perth, Western Australia).
- Despite huge criticism, BC Transit decided to not allow any Park & Ride at stations north of the Fraser River. Instead, strong bus feeders and improvements for pedestrians and cyclists leading to stations were implemented. The absence of this policy at stations south of the Fraser River, such as at Surrey Central, where although there is a substantial bulk of new development (even architectural award-winning buildings) means that the difference in the public realm is tangible. At Surrey Central, buildings are set back from the station and large car parks hug the station environs, whereas at non-Park & Ride stations, high-density development and pedestrian environments are connected directly to station entries and exits.
- The City of Vancouver abolished all freeway development within its borders during the early 1970s. This has meant that any higher-speed segregated rail service can offer a speed of service that is very often much higher than the equivalent car trip. For example, the Skytrain operates at

Figure 9.6 Less attractive transit-oriented development (TOD), car parking and Park & Ride, Surrey Central, Vancouver region

Source: Jeffrey R. Kenworthy

an average speed of 40.3kmph, a little higher than average 24 hour car speed and significantly higher than peak period traffic speed. Likewise, the West Coast Express, the relatively new commuter rail service, achieves an average speed of 37kmph, which again is higher than peak period road speeds in Vancouver and nearly the same as the 24 hour speed. The recently opened Canada Line has an average speed of 46kmph.

Importantly, Vancouver has conducted research that suggests a strong synergy between urban form, economic performance and liveability. The *BC Sprawl Report 2004* (Alexander et al, 2004) used indicators of urban form, economic vitality and liveability to compare neighbourhoods across the Vancouver region. It found a statistically significant positive link between higher densities and mixed uses, positive economic features and enhanced liveability, which suggests a three-way winning scenario for policies that are aimed at creating less auto-dependent living and more walkable and sociable environments.

Development of liveable public places

Vancouver is not a city that has major pedestrian areas or extensive traffic calming of neighbourhoods, as in many European cities. However, the City of Vancouver has become a highly liveable place characterized by an exceptional amount of human activity along lively and interesting streets and in its public spaces. For example, one of the most interesting and liveable public environments is Robson Street, the long avenue that connects the downtown with Stanley Park through the West End. The sidewalks are packed with pedestrians, notwithstanding the often bumper-to-bumper traffic and high-frequency trolley bus services that operate along the street.

Punter (2003) describes this strong human dimension and Vancouver's detailed attention to urban design of the public realm as a hallmark of Vancouver's success as one of the world's most liveable cities. This is in stark contrast to cities in the US, which all too frequently have very hostile street environments due to automobile-oriented development, particularly large freeways and interchanges. An interesting aspect of this 'culture of care' or public civility which pervades Vancouver is the way in which drivers in the City of Vancouver can invariably be relied upon to stop in both directions as soon as a pedestrian looks like he or she wants to cross the street, regardless of whether there is a crosswalk or not.

Vancouver's transportation plans were nevertheless the same as in US cities during the 1960s. However, through the community-led process already described, the exclusion of all freeway development from within the City of Vancouver's borders has meant that this part of the region, in particular, has developed much more around the transit system, with a high level of walking and cycling for other trips. If freeways had been built, not only would the land that currently houses these developments have been alienated and occupied with clover leaf junctions, quality of life would have also been reduced due to fumes, noise and severance.

For example, the West End of Vancouver is the second highest-density residential area in North America outside Manhattan and enjoys thriving and diverse activities along its main roads, not only Robson, but also Denman and

Davies Streets, while the grid-based, tree-lined residential streets that run across these major streets have numerous pocket parks created from selective street closures between blocks in the fine-grained street grid. The area also has the extensive Stanley Park and foreshore at its doorstep.

The latest phase in Vancouver's efforts to be a more sustainable 'eco-city' is its concept of eco-density.[16] This is a commitment by the City of Vancouver to become a more compact, ecologically oriented city in every way, including minimizing and reducing current levels of automobile use.

Portland, Oregon: From 'a streetcar named expire' to an aspiring 'streetcar city'

Table 9.2 Portland key figures

Population (2005)	1,918,188
Metropolitan GDP per capita (US$; 1995, 2005 adjusted)	US$37,342
Urban density (persons per hectare; 2005)	12.9
Road length per person (metres; 2005)	9.9
Car use per person (vehicle kilometres travelled, or vkt, per year; 2005)	10,753
Transit use (boardings per person; 2005)	58

Source: Jeffrey R. Kenworthy

Oregon has always been the leading US state in terms of environmental initiatives. It was the first to introduce recycling and deposits on return of glass bottles and it was the first US city to abandon plans for a giant freeway in favour of an LRT system or, in the old lexicon, a modern trolley or streetcar. San Diego beat Portland in reinstalling the first 'trolleys' in the US during the post-war period;[17] but the more fundamental and broader changes towards sustainable transportation are not as evident there as in Portland.

Brief history and comparisons

Sustainable transportation in Portland has been on an upward trajectory since the mid 1980s. For example, data for 2005 show that, by comparison, in the 15 years between 1990 and 2005, San Diego transit boardings per capita have only risen from 28.9 to 31.8 (10 per cent increase), while Portland has grown from 46.2 to 58.2 per capita, or a 26 per cent increase, and, of course, the actual level of use is approaching twice as high as in San Diego. Interestingly, the metropolitan population density of San Diego in 1990 was 13.1 persons per hectare, whereas Portland was 11.7 persons per hectare. Even so, during that year Portland still had 1.6 times more transit use per capita, four years after the opening of the first light rail line, whereas by that time San Diego had nine years of experience with LRT. The data suggest a somewhat better focused and integrated transit system in Portland, notwithstanding its overall lower population density in 1990.

The path to achieving these comparative successes in Portland was not smooth. The idea for an electric transit option was born in Portland in 1973 during the Arab oil embargo, an idea championed by a number of visionaries in Portland at the time.[18] The campaign to get better transit in Portland was linked to a major campaign by Sensible Transportation Options for Portland (STOP), originally formed in 1972 to stop the Mount Hood Freeway (Carlson et al, 1995). The 13 years that followed up to the opening of the first light rail line eastwards to Gresham from the central city was not easy and was punctuated with fights (Edner and Arrington, 1985). The local newspaper ran a competition to name the new trolley line and awarded first prize to 'A Streetcar Named Expire'.[19] The new transit line immediately proved itself, however, with very good levels of patronage. For some time, patronage was higher at weekends than on weekdays, affording people the easy opportunity of visiting the crowded downtown area for the Saturday market, later extended to Sundays due to immense popularity. Later on, an historic trolley car service was piggybacked onto part of the new LRT line, with a short spur being built in a side-street just outside downtown in order to provide an early turnaround

Figure 9.7 Metropolitan Area Express (MAX) passing through the Saturday market, downtown Portland, Oregon, is beginning to look a bit like the centre of a European city

Figure 9.8 Sand sculpture event at Pioneer Square Courthouse park, formerly a parking lot, Portland, Oregon

Source: Jeffrey R. Kenworthy

point. This synergy between LRT and the revitalized CBD is sometimes referred to as the 'MAX factor'.

There are a number of key features that distinguish Portland from other US cities. The most obvious physical manifestations of the difference are Portland's beautiful high-profile central city area and inner-city neighbourhoods, which since 1986, with the opening of the LRT called Metropolitan Area Express (MAX), have become more and more anchored around this growing light rail system and the more recent inner-city tram or streetcar system.

Going in the direction of most US cities during the 1960s and 1970s of a declining downtown with a rapid loss of retail opportunities to the suburbs, no rail-based or electric transit alternative and plans for many new freeways, Portland has completely reversed this process and now has a downtown area that competes in human quality, interest and activities with many cities in Europe today and a much greater emphasis on transit system development than on freeways, although the metropolitan region as a whole still squarely fits in the auto-dependent category. The key difference is that it is changing: the trajectory is different. The rest of this brief case study explores the basis of Portland's success in more sustainable transportation.

The land use–transit connection

Any discussion of the distinction between transportation in Portland and other US cities or, indeed, many cities in the world today inevitably involves land-use policy and the practical implementation measures that Portland has adopted, mainly in the last 25 years. However, Portland's planning pedigree predates the latest generation of activity, even back to the latter years of the Great Depression when Lewis Mumford, the great urban historian and spokesperson for 'cities for people, not cars', encouraged Portland to protect its downtown area of fine-grained street blocks and human scale, and also to adopt a system of regional governance. Portland did both. It established Metro, which includes the Metropolitan Planning Organization (MPO) role for transportation planning and funding.

But the roots of Portland's performance over the last 25 years or more in land-use and transportation development date back to the 1970s when Governor Tom McCall spearheaded a state-wide growth management strategy – in particular, the establishment and maintenance of urban growth boundaries (UGBs) in Oregon. Portland established such a boundary inside which all urban growth had to occur. This boundary has not only withstood numerous ballot and legal challenges, but has been linked to transportation through the 1991 Oregon Transportation Planning Rule, which applies a growth rule to limit increases in vehicle miles travelled (vmt), the most fundamental measure of car use. It is interesting, then, that the latest status report in spring 2009 from Tri-Met and its various jurisdictional partners shows data that indicate that between 1996 and 2006, daily vmt increased only 19 per cent in the face of a 27 per cent increase in population, while Tri-Met patronage rose 46 per cent (Tri-Met, 2009). The data show that in 2007, Portland ranked seventh nationally in per capita transit ridership, behind only Chicago, Boston, Honolulu, Washington, DC, San Francisco and New York.

This is a significant success for a comparatively young metropolitan area of around 2 million people, which has not had the historical advantage of extensive transit era system development in the form of large rail systems that cities such as New York, Boston and Chicago have been blessed with. However, it also has to be said that at an annual ridership of 58 trips per capita, or even 64 trips per capita (depending upon the boundaries of Portland's transit service area that one assumes) is not high in an international context.[20] This highlights the uphill battle that has to be fought in any US city to gain traction in sustainable transportation and to overcome a long history of urban sprawl and auto-based development.

Figure 9.9 Tom McCall Park, the site of a former freeway in downtown Portland, Oregon

Source: Jeffrey R. Kenworthy

The beginnings of the comparatively strong transit success of Portland in a US context can also be traced to the land use–transportation integration evident in Portland's 1973 Downtown Plan. A transit mall, which opened in 1978, was envisioned as the centrepiece of downtown revitalization and marked the beginnings of a trend to leverage broader community-building objectives through transit investment. Other achievements began to punctuate where Portland was going as a city: the conversion of a downtown parking lot to a park; the creation of Pioneer Courthouse Square out of a parking lot, now a major community meeting point in downtown between the one-way pair of streets along which MAX operates; and the tearing up of a freeway spur along the Willamette River downtown and conversion of it to Tom McCall Park, the site of Portland's annual Rose Festival. The River Place urban village redevelopment adjacent to the new park, itself built on a commuter parking lot, sprang up along the river with a hotel, shops at ground level and several floors of apartments above. Pioneer Courthouse Square's success is due partly to the staging of regular formal events there and its amphitheatre-like space fringed with food and drink outlets.

Further important steps in Portland's efforts to reinvent itself as a more sustainable and liveable city came with the successful civil society opposition to the Western Bypass loop of the I-5 freeway through rural lands just outside the growth boundary. The initial opposition came from a revamped version of the community group STOP. The success of this opposition led to a study that was undertaken jointly with the US Environmental Protection Agency (USEPA) and the growth management advocacy organization, 1000 Friends of Oregon, to develop a new approach to the problem, which culminated in a new planning model called land use, transportation, air quality (LUTRAQ). The solution to building the freeway was to cluster and moderately densify housing and mixed land uses together with transit provision and infrastructure for walking and cycling and traffic calming of streets. The freeway was scrapped and now transit-oriented development is evident on the Westside light rail line that opened in 1998.[21]

This approach has continuously gained ground in Portland since then. Planning in the 1990s for Portland's streetcar system was predicated on central city revitalization, especially in the Pearl District. Since opening in 2001, there has been over US$3.4 billion in new development and over 10,000 dwellings constructed along its route. Planning of the airport LRT extension was predicated on TOD and involved private-sector contributions to construction costs, and the interstate LRT line, opened in 2004, was located to achieve land development rather than speed. The extension to the streetcar and the new aerial tramway opened up the waterfront adjacent to downtown and will become the city's highest-density and most sustainable TOD with 10,000 jobs and 3000 housing units expected by 2015. Today Portland has 44 miles (71km) of LRT and 4 miles (6.4km) of streetcar. Along this network over US$9 billion of development has occurred using transit-friendly land-use planning (Arrington, 2009). Portland has arguably the most aggressive approach of any US city to TOD. Its 2040 Growth Management Strategy of 'build up, not out' is built around transit. According to Arrington (2009, p4), the plan:

> ... features a tight urban growth boundary, focusing growth in existing built-up areas and requiring local governments to limit parking and adopt zoning and comprehensive plan changes that are consistent with the growth management strategy. By 2040, two-thirds of jobs and 40 per cent of households are to be located in and around centres and corridors served by buses and light rail transit.

Arrington (2009) also explains in detail how TOD policy and implementation strategies have come a long way since the first LRT line was opened in 1986 without a lot of thought to TOD. Today the toolbox used by planners to secure a very successful TOD programme is at a state, regional and local level. At a state level there is the UGB and the complementary Transportation Planning Rule. The 1993 Transportation and Growth Management Program also promotes and helps to fund high-quality community planning, the 1995 TOD

Figure 9.10 New TOD on the Gresham MAX line, Portland, Oregon

Source: Jeffrey R. Kenworthy

Figure 9.11
Portland's streetcar running through the new high-density revitalized Pearl District

Source: Jeffrey R. Kenworthy

Tax Exemption allows for up to a ten-year residential property tax exemption and the 2001 Vertical Housing Program encourages density and mixed land use in community-designated areas, with up to an 80 per cent property tax exemption over ten years.

At a regional scale there is the 1994 Regional Growth Management plan, which is behind the 2040 vision and requires local government compliance through growth targets, parking maximums, density minimums and street connectivity standards to encourage walking and cycling and easy routing of buses. There is also the 1998 TOD Implementation Program, which has access to local and federal funds, mainly for supporting TOD construction through site acquisition and TOD easements.

Local tools include joint development (1997) where Tri-Met has written down the value of TOD project land to get the highest and best transit use, and the 1996 TOD Tax Exemption in the cities of Gresham and Portland.[22] Tax increment financing is used by the City of Portland in urban renewal districts for public investments, increasing densities and to secure affordable housing. Finally, the Westside Station Area Planning (1993 to 1997) helps local governments to prepare and adopt plans for 0.5 mile radii (800m) around stations to ensure that density levels are adequate (a minimum density standard), parking spaces are minimized (through a maximum permitted parking supply), the right building orientation to transit and prohibition of automobile uses. Tri-Met, Metro and the Oregon Department of Transportation (DOT) help to fund the programme.

Figure 9.12 Bus mall shelters (top) and Yamhill Market station (bottom): Good design-planning in Portland

Note: Portland has planned shelter for transit users' comfort wisely and aesthetically: elegant shelters on the bus mall with much useful rider information inside. Here, bicycle security personnel stop for coffee at the downtown Yamhill Market MAX stop – the convenience store nearby offers snacks and 'passive security' to waiting riders during the day and evening.

Source: Preston L. Schiller

Table 9.3 Boulder/Denver key figures

Area	Boulder	Denver
Population (2005)	City: 83,432	2,256,442
	County: 271,934	
Metropolitan GDP per capita (US$; 1995, 2005 adjusted)	na	US$43,779
Urban density (persons per hectare; 2005)	12.1 (Boulder County)	14.7
Road length per person (metres; 2005)	na	8.7
Car use per person (vehicle kilometres travelled, or vkt, per year; 2005)	15,372 (Boulder County)	14,176
Transit use (boardings per person; 2005)	na	38

Notes: Denver's metro area population includes Boulder County. The City of Boulder has greater density, lower vkt per person and higher rates of walking, bicycling and transit use than does its surrounding Boulder County, or even much of the Denver metro region, although some of this data is difficult to obtain and disaggregate from regional or county-level data. na = not available.

Source: Jeffrey R. Kenworthy

Some large-scale results of this overall approach are that, today, Portland area residents travel about 20 per cent fewer miles every day and are twice as likely to use transit for the journey to work and seven times more likely to bicycle to work that the average metropolitan resident in the US. Interestingly, it is reported that 80 per cent of Tri-Met's riders either have a car available for that trip or choose not to own a car. As a result, Portlanders spend 15.1 per cent of their household budget on transportation compared to 19.1 per cent nationally (Arrington, 2009).

Overall, Portland presents probably the best example of a coordinated and long-term effort to change a large highly car-dependent US metropolitan region into a more sustainable one. A comparison of Portland, Seattle and Vancouver based on a 1990s perspective showed Portland neatly positioned between the more extreme auto orientation of Seattle and the more transit-oriented Vancouver (Schiller and Kenworthy, 1999). The mammoth nature of the task of turning around an auto city cannot be underestimated, and while Portland represents a very significant success in a US context, it must be remembered that when the comparisons are drawn more widely it is still a car-dependent region. However, it is changing and will continue to change by building on past successes and developing new and stronger approaches to sustainable transportation, as it already has shown over many decades now (see also Chapter 8, Box 8.4).

Boulder, Colorado: Small is beautiful and effective

Boulder is a small university town with a 2005 population of 83,432 people situated in the larger Boulder County area of 271,934 people.[23] Boulder County is part of the even larger and very highly automobile-dependent Denver metropolitan region of about 2.5 million people, although Boulder separates itself from the march of urban sprawl by a strong green belt. The city has a very progressive history in sustainable settlement terms, and in 1959 was the first US community to introduce such a green belt to prevent both its own urban sprawl and the urban encroachment around it, and especially to protect the impressive landscape vista of the Rocky Mountain foothills. It did this through an innovative community organization called Plan Boulder, which still maintains an active involvement in Boulder's development.[24] Boulder has set itself apart in transportation terms from nearly all American communities of its size in a number of ways.

Up until about 1990, although it had achieved some successes, such as the innovative Pearl Street pedestrian mall in the city's centre (dedicated 6 August

1977),[25] as well as improved pedestrian and cycling facilities, as a whole the city had maintained a traditional 'predict-and-provide' supply-side road-building approach to future transportation development. However, financial, political and physical realities intervened to make this approach unsustainable. In 1996 the Transportation Master Plan set a transportation demand management (TDM) goal to hold traffic levels to 1994 levels and to reduce single-occupant vehicle (SOV) mode share to 25 per cent (Havlick, 2004). In order to do this the city had to focus on travel choices, rather than being locked into compulsory car use for a majority of trips. This involved improving transit services, creating demand for transit trips, enhancing the bicycle and pedestrian system, marketing and providing good information about the new choices, changing land use and urban design approaches, tackling parking pricing and establishing some dynamic relationships between the city and the University of Colorado (CU) – a 'town–gown' partnership (Toor and Havlick, 2004). It also involved effectively stopping some large-scale road expansion in neighbouring counties, mainly through public purchase of properties and development rights to prevent development that did not fit with Boulder's growth management and TDM strategies.

Comparisons and trends

Before detailing more of how Boulder made changes to its transportation system, it is useful to look at some of the current perspectives. Since 1990 there has been a 17 per cent shift from SOV work trips to other modes. Daily vehicle miles of travel in 1994 were 2.4 million miles (4 million kilometres) and this has remained largely flat compared to the modelled potential growth in vmt to 2001 of 3.8 million vmt (6.3 million kilometres). Growth in non-auto modes has been very significant, making Boulder noticeably different from the average US city. Using year 2000 resident trip diaries compared to the US 1995 National Passenger Transportation Survey, Boulder's comparative position is shown in Table 9.4.

The results show that Boulder residents are roughly four times more likely to walk, about ten times more likely to ride a bicycle and twice as likely to use transit than an average US urbanite. The lower school bus usage is most likely

Figure 9.13 Residents and visitors listen to music at the Pearl Street pedestrian mall, Boulder, Colorado

Note: A few decades ago the music would have been drowned out by the traffic of a once motorized main street.

Source: Norman Koren (www.normankoren.com)

Table 9.4 Boulder's travel patterns compared to US averages

Mode	Boulder	US
(percentage of daily person trips)		
Walk	19.8	5.4
Bicycle	10.0	0.9
Transit	4.2	1.8
School bus	0.7	1.7

Source: Havlick (2004)

due to the greater independent mobility afforded to children in Boulder.[26] It is also possible to highlight some differences between Boulder and Denver. In 2000, bicycle and pedestrian mode share to the CBD of Boulder (a relatively tiny CBD) was 29 per cent, while Denver, the CBD of the whole region containing some 103,000 jobs (Kenworthy, 2009), achieved only slightly better at 33 per cent. For total non-auto modes to the CBD, Boulder achieved 47 per cent and the Denver CBD just slightly more (54 per cent), even though it is the focal point for the entire metro region transit system. The success of Boulder's 'town–gown' partnership and the significant improvements in the transit system (see later) are highlighted by the fact that in 1990, 2 per cent of students used transit to the campus, but in 2003 this was 17 per cent, and 67 per cent of students travel to the campus by bicycle or on foot.

In terms of transit ridership, the trends are very revealing. Regional transportation district (RTD) data from 1982 through to 2004 show that in Boulder (local services) there has been a threefold increase in annual usage from 2.12 million to 6.34 million, while in Denver all local services grew from 29.80 million to 40.23 million, or only a 1.3 times increase.

For per capita comparative purposes, if we take the low point in Boulder County's transit evolution,[27] using US Census data on the population of Boulder County (225,339), the data show that per capita ridership was ten trips per capita. By 2005 (population 271,934) this had risen to 6,476,841, or a per capita utilization of 24 trips per capita, a 140 per cent increase in a county of very suburban character. By comparison, in 1990, the Denver metropolitan region as a whole, embracing some more urbanized areas of higher density,[28] had annual per capita ridership of 30 trips (all modes). By 2005 this was 38 trips per capita, or only a 27 per cent increase.[29]

Boulder's success in sustainable transportation

The above comparative data point to a significant and coordinated programme of sustainable transportation. This sub-section briefly reviews the pillars of this success.

The bicycle programme

Boulder has improved its cycling network through a programme of new bicycle routes, bicycle paths and 374 miles (602km) of bicycle lanes involving 74 bicycle underpasses.[30] It has introduced bicycle-actuated crossings at intersections and placed bicycle racks on all buses. These policy-driven changes, which commenced during the 1980s, were aimed at a fundamental change in transportation direction that stressed transportation demand management, walking, bicycling and transit.

One of the biggest successes has been on the campus of the University of Colorado (CU), where during the 1990s it was realized that building new parking structures to accommodate auto commuting by staff and students was a mistake and the university cancelled them. Instead, the university worked with the city to foster a better transit system (see following sub-section) and to encourage greater walking and bicycling. Bicycle stations were set up to repair bicycles and provide information and there are now free CU bicycles that students can check out for immediate travel needs. However, perhaps the biggest success has been the acceptance that it is simply much cheaper to provide for non-auto access on campus than it is to cater for car commuting. By examining the existing infrastructure costs per round trip to the campus by faculty, staff and students and the costs of accommodating an additional new round trip, sustainable modes have achieved huge advantages. A report by Nelson/Nygaard Consulting Associates (2003) provides data[31] that shows orders of magnitude differences in infrastructure costs for an existing and new trip to the campus by foot or bicycle compared to the same trips accommodated by car. Although it is not clear from the graph, the data presented in their report are annualized costs per trip.

The transit programme

Probably the biggest and most successful innovation has been the Boulder Community Transit Network (CTN), a network of six differently branded types of routes that are part of the GO Boulder network, whose goal is to shift 19 per cent of commuters from their cars onto other modes. In 1990 CTN transit ridership was reportedly 5000 per day and by 2002 had risen to 26,000 per day or a 420 per cent increase (Bruun, 2004). The routes are referred to as the Hop, Skip, Jump, Bound, Stampede and Dash and buses are accordingly branded and are of different sizes. The Hop services are the shortest routes and the service distances get progressively greater towards the Dash.

The CTN is, as the name implies, the product of a community consultation process. Boulder undertook its highly successful transit innovations[32] only after a year of extensive public involvement. A broad-based citizens' group of some 50 community leaders, working with several City of Boulder and transit agency staff, devoted a great deal of time and energy to this effort, with larger public meetings being held as well. Boulder did not adopt a business as usual approach where an agency gets consultants to take a look at part of the transit 'problem' and then perhaps does a little tinkering to fine tune it. Significant changes to transit need to be undertaken with the enlistment of public support to ensure usage and ownership of transit systems, and that is what Boulder did. They formed a new unit called GO Boulder as a way of going around the Public Works Department, which was operating on a business as usual approach. They also established the longstanding City of Boulder Transportation Committee, which ensured citizen interest in the issues.[33] But it took approximately ten years to establish the CTN, and involved about one year of citizen-involved planning per route.

The CTN is now a well-supported, community-based design using buses that are family friendly and bus drivers are employed as community ambassadors. Strong transit use was developed through innovative pass programmes described below, marketing and education, seamless interfaces between bus, bicycle and pedestrian facilities, good connections to regional services, and transit-supportive land-use and urban design (Bruun, 2004).

The development of the CTN has gone hand in hand with effective ways of generating new demand for transit through ticketing innovations. First, the city has its Ecopass unlimited transit access programme. Ecopasses with photo ID are only issued at a low-cost group rate to residents once enough households have joined up.[34] Pricing is based on location, number of people or number of households and the level of transit service. Businesses generally get Ecopasses for employees through deals negotiated with the human resources manager. Pass programmes are also available to all downtown employees and all CU staff and students. In 2001 there were some 60,000 RTD Ecopasses and discount passes issued, 25,000 of which were for students, 6500 were for CU staff, 22,200 were for businesses and 3800 were for neighbourhoods; an additional 2500 were other passes. The goal as it stands now is to issue 100,000 transit passes (Havlick, 2004). CU students were able to have the Ecopass in 1991, and annual ridership went from 300,000 to 1.5 million trips in the first five years.

The economic rationale for these improvements to transit for students and employees at the university is also evident in the same data from Nelson/Nygaard Consulting Associates (2003) outlined above for bicycles, which shows that the annualized costs of existing and new trips to campus by faculty, staff and students on transit are dramatically below the costs of accommodating existing and new trips by car to the campus.

Overall, Boulder demonstrates what can be done in a smaller community with genuine rather than token public involvement and the positive effect of consistent and complementary public policies and political support for land-use planning, urban design and transportation strategies that have supported sustainability over a period approaching two decades.

Freiburg im Breisgau, Germany: The pin-up sustainable city

Freiburg im Breisgau is a small university city of 219,345 people[35] nestled in the Black Forest area of southern Germany and occupying 150 square kilometres, 40 per cent of which is forest (Salomon, 2009). With the sunniest microclimate in Germany, it boasts one of the most comprehensive approaches in the world to transit, walking and cycling from both a transportation and a land-use perspective. Perhaps its most striking feature is its obvious attention to high-quality coherent urban design throughout the city. All development has to pass through strict urban design guidelines before being implemented and there is strong citizen awareness of the need to protect the city's liveability, especially from problems generated by reliance on private transportation.[36]

Freiburg has for many years been the 'pin-up' city for sustainable transportation and more generally for developing a much more sustainable city environment based on ecological building principles, prioritizing public transportation, walking and cycling,

Table 9.5 Freiburg key figures

Population (2008)	219,345
Metropolitan GDP per capita (US$; 1995, 2009 adjusted)	US$28,236
Urban density (persons per hectare; 2005)	45.0
Road length per person (metres; 2005)	2.3
Car use per person (vehicle kilometres travelled, or vkt, per year; 2005)	not available
Transit use (boardings per person; 2005)	328

Source: Jeffrey R. Kenworthy

and all supported by superb urban design of the public realm. If one wants a watershed event to help explain the strength of the 'Freiburg phenomenon', it was probably the state government of Baden-Württemberg's decision in 1975 to build a nuclear reactor. Opposition to the move was very intense and successful and spawned a civil society movement with heavy university involvement to ensure that Freiburg could then meet its future energy needs in a sustainable way. The 1980s was the period of the energy supply concept for Freiburg. That meant renewable energies and it meant doing everything possible to curb demand for energy, including focusing on transit, walking and cycling and creating a built form and public realm that favoured these modes and minimized the need to travel (Peirce, 2009). As early as 1989 it was referred to by John Roberts in *Quality Streets* as the 'green planner's dream' (Roberts, 1989). During the 1990s Freiburg further responded to sustainability by basing its future development on a climate protection concept and from 2007 on a climate protection action plan that aims for 40 per cent of the current carbon dioxide (CO_2) level by 2030 through a focus on sustainable transportation and building and construction standards (Salomon, 2009).

Freiburg's development for decades now has been strongly based on citizen action and participation. Citizens are shareholders in solar and wind power stations. There is direct participation in the spatial development plan and the municipal budget. Citizens act as technical experts on committees and there is much citizen-led environmental education and many campaigns. This citizen participation and commitment and the networks of stakeholders have helped to create a vision of integral sustainable development, which has formed a consensus across all political parties (Salomon, 2009)

Freiburg comparisons

In order to appreciate the City of Freiburg in relation to other cities, it is useful to assemble some basic transport-related data about the city and to compare it to some typical data on European and other cities from the unpublished update of Kenworthy and Laube (2001). Table 9.6 depicts data for Freiburg against averages for cities in other parts of the world and some other German cities.

Freiburg is a typical German city with a density of 45 persons per hectare,[37] which is approximately three times the density of a typical auto cities in the US and Australia, but not quite double the density of cities in Canada. Freiburg's car ownership of 374 cars per 1000 people is relatively modest even in a German context. Berlin, Frankfurt, Hamburg and Munich average 472 cars per 100 people, or 26 per cent more, so it would appear that Freiburg's longstanding commitment to more sustainable transportation has helped to suppress the need for car ownership. It is also partly to be explained by the nature of urban development in Freiburg, discussed later in the chapter, with its partial emphasis on car-free or car-reduced housing environments such as Vauban, Rieselfeld and Der Seepark. As a group, the auto cities of North America and Australia average over 600 cars per 1000 people.

In terms of motorcycle ownership, which has been increasing significantly everywhere in the world over the last ten years, Freiburg is a typical German

Table 9.6 Some basic transportation-related data for Freiburg compared to other cities, 2005–2008

Factor	Freiburg	Berlin	Hamburg	Munich	US cities	Australian cities	Canadian cities
Population (averages)	219,345	3,395,189	1,743,627	1,288,307	6,425,359	2,840,875	2,655,793
Urban density (persons per ha)	44.0	54.1	38.0	55.0	15.4	14.0	25.8
Car ownership (cars per 1000)	374	361	484	531	640	647	522
Motor cycle ownership (motorcycles per 1000)	31	28	28	42	17	21	14
Road length per person (metres)	2.3	2.0	2.5	1.8	6.0	7.6	5.4
Transit trips per capita per year	328	410	266	577	67	96	151
Transport deaths per 100,000	3.27	1.97	2.47	?	9.51	6.21	6.26

Source: Unpublished data from Jeffrey R. Kenworthy from update of the Millennium Cities Database for Sustainable Transport; Freiburg data sourced from official online statistics of City of Freiburg im Breisgau, http://wiki.stadt.freiburg.de/

city with 31 motorcycles per 1000 people[38] and is not quite double the typical level of ownership in the auto cities. Throughout German cities there is, in particular, a proliferation of small motor scooters (50cc to 150cc), apparently in response to fuel prices, but also to overcome congestion and to assist in more easily finding a parking space in increasingly auto-crowded environments with limited parking.[39]

In road supply, Freiburg does not particularly distinguish itself in Germany, having 2.3m per person, while the average for the four German cities here is 2.2m. However, this is, on average, about one third of the level to be found in the auto cities in Table 9.6 and this lesser orientation around roads helps to explain not only Freiburg's more sustainable transportation, but European cities in general.

Where Freiburg does distinguish itself is in transit use, which stands at 328 trips per person, or almost one transit trip by every man, woman and child every day of the year. In Hamburg, a city of 1.7 million, the usage is only 266 trips per person, while in the US cities transit usage is a mere 67 trips per person,[40] or 20 per cent of Freiburg's level. This is in stark contrast to cities in Canada, which average 151 trips per capita or getting on towards half the transit use per person of Freiburg.

Unfortunately, transport deaths in Freiburg stand at 3.27 per 100,000 people, which is higher than in both Berlin and Hamburg,[41] although significantly below the auto cities.[42]

Essentially, Freiburg is a 'city of short distances' with a policy of decentralized but concentrated services and markets, focused on limiting urban sprawl and encouraging inner-city redevelopment.

Apart from progressive transportation policies themselves, Freiburg's success in transportation revolves around a series of other factors.

Table 9.7 Relative share of non-pedestrian trips by mode in Freiburg

Mode	1976 (percentage)	1991 (percentage)
Cars	60	47
Public transport	22	26
Bicycles	18	27

Source: Pucher and Clorer (1992)

Better public transport

Freiburg's success in sustainable transportation was established relatively early. In 1969 it had some critical decisions to make about its old tram system. It decided to keep and extend the tram system, with new lines appearing in 1979. In 1973 it also began to restrict inner-city car traffic through large-scale pedestrianization of central city shopping streets, while still allowing access to trams and buses. Pucher and Clorer (1992) show in Table 9.7 how in 1976 the percentage of daily *non-walking* trips by automobile was 60 per cent, but by 1991 this had reduced to 47 per cent. Likewise, transit trips had risen from 22 to 26 per cent and bicycle trips had gone from 18 to 27 per cent. For *all* daily trips, in 1991 Freiburg had achieved a situation where walking and cycling together accounted for 40 per cent of daily trips, and public transport 18 per cent, leaving only a 42 per cent share for cars (Bratzel, 1999). There was, over this 15-year period, only a net increase of 1 per cent in car trip-making, while transit ridership rose 53 per cent and bicycle traffic rose 100 per cent (Pucher and Clorer, 1992). By 1999, in Freiburg, 50 per cent of all daily trips were walking and cycling, 18 per cent transit and 32 per cent car. The goal for 2020 is 51 per cent walking and cycling, 20 per cent transit and 29 per cent car (Salomon, 2009).

Light rail has become the backbone of Freiburg's public transit. In places, the light rail lines run along grassed track beds either on their own rights of way through parkland settings, or in the centre of roads. Buses have become primarily feeders to the light rail system and mobility by transit has improved greatly (Pucher and Clorer, 1992). The central city has benefited environmentally by having a clean, quiet mode of transport servicing it. Transit has been very cleverly and aggressively promoted through marketing campaigns to encourage people out of their cars and through attractive ticketing offers linked to environmental awareness. In 1984 Freiburg introduced the rainbow ticket, a monthly environmental travel card, initially resisted by the transit operator, but then strongly embraced in a much wider public transport zone, when its success in attracting customers was evident (Bratzel, 1999).

Along with the improvements to transit and its consequent upsurge in usage, the large increase in the use of bicycles has also been underpinned by many off-road facilities for cyclists (and pedestrians), as well as bicycle storage facilities around the city. Some of the main segregated bicycle spines run parallel to the grassed light rail track beds and, in sections, run through small 'urban forests'. This attention to both the safety and aesthetics of the environment for pedestrians and bicycle users is very conducive to high levels of non-motorized transport.

Figure 9.14 Bicycle-and pedestrian-friendly Freiburg, Baden-Württemberg, Germany

Source: Jeffrey R. Kenworthy

Development of liveable public places

Freiburg has created a people-friendly, liveable city. A key part of the strategy has been detailed attention to the quality of the city's public realm. The improvements in this area have been at least partly responsible for the big increase in the use of bicycles, as indicated above, and a progressive enhancement in the quality of the pedestrian experience in Freiburg. Pedestrianization of almost the entire central area has played a large role in enhancing the liveability of the city. People of all ages can be seen enjoying the city's spaces. The central area has many outdoor cafés and restaurants and an open-air market place. All of the pedestrianized streets have been resurfaced with a wide variety of cobbled surface designs. Trees have been introduced and many flower planters bring colour to the city in warmer months. Creepers have been strategically planted for the purpose of greening many building surfaces. They have also been encouraged to grow across trellises to form bridges linking both sides of the street, as well as to form arched entry statements into traffic-calmed or pedestrianized streets.

A feature of the pedestrianized centre and, indeed, the whole city is its water theme. The city celebrates water in its public areas. In the days before modern waste disposal systems, Freiburg, in common with other cities, had small open drains along all streets. This unusual system of 'gutters' is termed '*Bächle*'. In Freiburg, these *Bächle* were once used to provide water for fire fighting and to refresh livestock. Today the water theme continues with freshwater running in small channels throughout the city and continuing into residential areas and new developments, such as those described below. Children, one of the most vulnerable and disadvantaged groups in cities from a transportation perspective, are given great independence in Freiburg's streets and can be seen playing in the *Bächle*.

Many cities have pedestrianized centres and some are quite extensive and beautiful (e.g. Copenhagen and Munich). However, in Freiburg, the combined effect of the elements described, plus the street furniture, such as seating and lighting, provide perhaps one of the most coherent and attractive urban environments in any city, one that is inclusive of all members of the population, regardless of age or ability.

Another factor that is very important in extending this central city amenity throughout Freiburg is the extensive traffic calming of streets or, in the German, '*Verkehrsberuhigung*'. Many streets have been made safer and friendlier for bicycles and pedestrians through traffic-calming treatments. These treatments include mid-block neck downs,[43] strong entry statements leading into residential areas such as those described above using creepers, canyons of trees to reduce perceptible width, changes in street surface to signal lower speed

Figure 9.15 The central pedestrian zone in the centre of Freiburg

Source: Jeffrey R. Kenworthy

areas, strategic use of parked cars to increase separation between the sidewalk and road, and so on. Spaces such as parking areas have been reclaimed for civic uses and children's play areas as the city has become less car oriented. At least some surface parking areas in inner neighbourhoods have been placed underground and the area above turned into open space.

Less auto-dependent urban development

There is a concerted effort to provide for Freiburg's population growth in planned urban communities linked to transit. Freiburg has a number of 'model neighbourhoods' in this regard. Three are briefly described here, der Seepark, Rieselfeld and Vauban, in roughly chronological order.

Der Seepark

Der Seepark is a large urban village consisting of a variety of different types of multi-family dwellings. It is set adjacent to a light rail stop and its central feature is the large integrated lake and parkland on city property. The entire environment is mostly traffic free and internal circulation is all on foot and bicycle. Parking is underground or restricted to on-street bays along traffic-calmed peripheral streets. The public spaces were designed for a short-term and long-term purpose – initially as the site of the state garden show in 1986 and then as a multipurpose public park which melds with the surrounding housing as a seamless whole. The result is a very attractive, integrated and convenient living environment. People who reside there and people from other parts of Freiburg, of all ages, can be seen sharing the public spaces. Activities include children's play areas; swimming in the central lake; cycling; strolling; in-line skating; eating in the on-site facilities; enjoying open-air concerts; using adjacent formal sports facilities; sunning in the 'meadows' and resting in formal gardens. A very high proportion of the access to this neighbourhood is by non-auto means and virtually all of the people seen using the public realm of the neighbourhood have arrived by transit, foot or bicycle.

Freiburg–Rieselfeld

The district of Freiburg–Rieselfeld was developed out of a need to provide for a very high demand for new housing during the late 1980s and early 1990s and accommodates 11,000 people. Rieselfeld was only possible through an extension of Freiburg's excellent LRT system, along which there are several stops serving the new district. The LRT runs on a grass track bed through the new district, where there is a linear neighbourhood centre with a rich mix of shops, food stores, restaurants, professional suites and other uses, and sitting above those are several floors of housing. The whole of Rieselfeld is accessible by foot to the LRT stops, and both the main street and the residential streets connecting to it are very bicycle and walking friendly – indeed, children frequently ride bicycles, walk and play in the general street environment. Along this main LRT street are also civic functions, such as a library, churches and a large square where, during summer, children enjoy the computerized water fountains. Rieselfeld is an excellent example of TOD linked in a linear rather than nodal form to new urban development.[44]

Figure 9.16 Walkable, and transit- and ecologically oriented developments, Vauban and Rieselfeld

Note: Notice the mother and child easily crossing the LRT line (bottom).

Source: Jeffrey R. Kenworthy

Vauban

Vauban is a redevelopment area on a site near the city, including an old French military barracks, and is linked to the rest of the city by an extension of the LRT system, again running along a green track bed. Some of the old buildings have been retained and recycled into a kindergarten and other civic uses. Vauban again is a dense mixed-use new neighbourhood of 5000 people, but with the added feature that it is strongly focused on environmental technologies, especially for renewable energy. It has passive and plus-energy houses, meaning that these latter dwellings generate net energy, which is fed back into the grid, and it has its own power plant burning waste organic material, mainly wood waste. It is a 'car-free' neighbourhood, meaning that if one wants to have a car one has to store it in a solar parking structure on the fringe of the neighbourhood. Vauban is strongly oriented towards transit, walking and cycling, and one of its most evident and endearing features is its family-friendly public realm. Throughout the development men and women can be seen pushing children in prams, and children can be seen independently walking and riding bicycles around the area, simply because the street environments are comparatively safe with 30kmph (19mph) residential zones. There are also many attractive parks that are intensively used by parents with children. Overall, Vauban is probably one of the most attractive sustainable transportation neighbourhoods in the world, successfully blending high-density housing, mixed uses, green spaces, transit and walking facilities into a rich and highly liveable, socially gregarious and safe public environment.

To summarize, the three policies which Pucher and Clorer (1992, p386) suggest were used by Freiburg to 'tame the auto' and which are still being used, are:

> First, it has sharply restricted auto use in the city. Second, it has provided affordable, convenient and safe alternatives to auto use. Finally, it has strictly regulated development to ensure a compact land-use pattern that is conducive to public transport, bicycling and walking.

Seoul, South Korea: Rivers of cars to rivers of water and people

Background and Seoul comparisons

Seoul is a megacity of enormous proportions. The City of Seoul, at the heart of the metropolitan region, is a megacity in its own right with 10.4 million people, but the metropolitan area involving Seoul, Inch'on and Kyonggi-do embraces 23 million people. Seoul has a more sustainable transportation system than all the other cities in this chapter by virtue of its very high density of 230 persons per hectare, a very well-developed transit system and relatively conducive conditions for walking and cycling, where some 53 per cent of daily trips are by these green modes and 47 per cent by private transport – cars and motorcycles (Kenworthy and Laube, 2001).

Table 9.9 provides a sample of the key land use and transportation data for Seoul in 1995 compared to the average values for a range of other regional groupings of cities. It shows that Seoul had only 160 cars per 1000 in 1995 and 3667 passenger kilometres per person driven in cars. Both figures are a fraction of the US and other auto cities. But in terms of transit use, it stands out with nearly six times the per capita usage of US cities and, indeed, nearly two times the Western European cities' figure. Its well-developed transit system with a significant rail component gives it nearly 1.5 times more transit travel than the very poor low-income Asian cities in the sample. It is, however, weaker in the use of non-motorized modes, being only a few percentage points higher than that achieved in Australian cities, though more than double the US figure.

Table 9.8 Seoul key figures

Population (1995)	20,576,272
Metropolitan GDP per capita (US$, 1995)	10,305
Urban density (persons per hectare; 1995)	230.4
Road length per person (metres; 1995)	0.9
Car use per person (vehicle kilometres travelled, or vkt, per year; 1995)	2564
Transit use (boardings per person; 1995)	359

Source: Jeffrey R. Kenworthy

The Cheonggye Freeway demolition and Cheonggyecheon River restoration project

What currently most distinguishes Seoul from other cities is perhaps the boldest ever example of 'trip de-generation' ever undertaken. This involved the tearing down of 5.8km of the Cheonggye four-lane freeway and surface street below, which carried together 168,000 vehicles per day through the very heart of the city, in order to exhume the culturally significant Cheonggyecheon River.[45] The freeway alignment has been transformed into a linear green heart for the city, a place to promenade and enjoy. All of this occurred without any significant traffic disruption and furthermore changed the direction of transportation planning in the city towards prioritizing transit and non-motorized modes. The

Table 9.9 Seoul's transportation characteristics compared to other global cities, 1995

Factor	Urban density	Car ownership (cars/1000)	Car pass km per person	Transit pass km per person	Per cent of motorized pass km on transit	Per cent of daily trips by non-motorized modes
Seoul	230.4	160	3,667	2,781	37.6 per cent	17.9 per cent
USA	14.9	587	18,155	488	2.9 per cent	8.1 per cent
ANZ	15.0	575	11,387	918	7.5 per cent	15.8 pe rcent
CAN	26.2	530	8,645	918	9.8 per cent	10.4 per cent
WEU	54.9	414	6,202	1,524	19.0 per cent	31.3 per cent
HIA	150.3	210	3,614	3,636	45.9 per cent	28.5 per cent
EEU	52.9	332	2,907	3,240	53.0 per cent	26.2 per cent
MEA	118.9	134	3,262	1,118	29.5 per cent	26.6 per cent
AFR	59.9	135	2,652	2,924	50.8 per cent	41.4 per cent
LIA	204.1	105	1,855	1,944	41.0 per cent	32.4 per cent
LAM	74.7	202	2,862	2,754	48.2 per cent	30.7 per cent
CHN	146.2	26	814	1,897	55.0 per cent	65.0 per cent

Source: Kenworthy and Laube (2001)

project was a large-scale example of the idea of traffic behaving more like a gas than a liquid. Traffic engineers and transportation planners are trained to think of traffic as a liquid that holds its volume and will flow over everything if blocked or allowed to grow in excess of its current 'container'. However, traffic tends to shrink when road capacity is removed, as has been proven time and again when pedestrian zones have been created (Kenworthy, 2006).

The full story of this project can be viewed online in a 25-minute documentary called *Seoul: The Stream of Consciousness.*[46] The concept for the project started with two engineers turning over memories of the past and the idea of restoring the Cheonggyecheon River, which lay beneath, because the Cheonggye District had become one of the dirtiest and noisiest parts of the city and would continue this way so long as the freeway remained.

The district and river have a long history dating back to at least the early 1400s. Part of this history was the turning of the river into a sewerage system and the development of squatter settlements of Korean War refugees along its banks. By the 1950s the whole area had become a symbol of poverty and the legacy of 50 years of colonialism and war. The only way to remove the blight this caused to Seoul during a period of great economic hardship was to cover it over with a road, which occurred between 1955 and 1977, and at the time, like most freeway building enterprises, became a symbol of progress and modernization. However, by 2001 when Lee Myung-bak successfully ran for mayor, he made his top political priority the tearing down of this freeway and surface road, converting it to a green river boulevard. He also happened to be, in a previous life, the chief executive officer (CEO) of the company that built the road in the first place, so was in the unique position of knowing in intimate detail the realities of getting rid of it. The demolition and river restoration were to revitalize the area economically, but also to set Seoul on a new path in attracting tourism and investment, giving the city green credentials internationally and emphasizing quality of life. This radical road deconstruction project set Lee Myung-bak on a successful political career and he was elected president of South Korea in December 2007.[47] This follows a similar pattern to political figures such as Jaime Lerner in Curitiba and Michael Harcourt in British Columbia developing high-level political careers on the basis of moves towards sustainable transportation.

Figure 9.17 High densities, mixed uses and traffic-calmed streets make central Seoul, South Korea, quite walkable

Source: Jeffrey R. Kenworthy

Project context and results

Prior to the removal of the roads between 2003 and 2005, Seoul had already embarked upon a number of strategies to try to better manage private transportation in the city as a whole. In 1996, modest tolls of about US$2 were introduced on two major entry points into the CBD. Traffic fell by 14 per cent and speeds improved by 38 per cent. Traffic returned to pre-toll levels, but occupancy improved and average speeds remained higher. In 1997 regular fee increases were introduced for public parking, parking requirements were lowered for commercial buildings and a parking permit system was introduced for residential parking. In 2003 a voluntary No Driving Day was introduced, including financial inducements to participants.

The corridor in which the demolished roads were located is served

Figure 9.18 Cheonggye Freeway corridor, 1980s (left), and construction progress on the new river boulevard after demolition of the Cheonggye Freeway (right), Seoul, South Korea

Source: Jeffrey R. Kenworthy

by multiple subway lines; but importantly the city overhauled the bus system. This included an expansion of a bus rapid transit system operating in exclusive median lanes, which had been introduced already in 1996. By 2005 there were four routes covering 22 miles (35km); by 2007 there were seven routes covering 42 miles (68km) and by 2010 it is planned to have 12 routes over 73 miles (118km). Kerb-side bus-only lanes were also expanded, the fares and timetables were coordinated, including use of a smart card and intelligent transportation systems (ITS) technology, and services were integrated with the subway system and the various services colour coded for ease of use and identity. The changes were also widely publicized leading up to the roads coming down. The results were very good. Within months, transit user satisfaction had reached 90 per cent, speeds for the BRT had improved by between 33 and 100 per cent and accidents and injuries on all routes had fallen by one third. But the litmus test of all of this was that in five months between January and May 2005, bus patronage rose by almost 1 million per day, or almost 25 per cent, and the volume of private traffic through central Seoul dropped 9.1 per cent and citywide traffic by 5.9 per cent. The project planner Kee Yeon Hwang also said: 'as soon as we destroyed the road, the cars just disappeared and drivers changed their habits'. Other benefits of the project included:

- average 30 per cent increases of adjacent land value;
- temperatures in the green corridor that are about 7° Fahrenheit below those of areas 0.25 miles away (400m);
- extra water, open space access and recreational opportunities with a jump in the quality of life of city centre residents, workers and visitors;
- a re-branding of Seoul's image internationally to one of a more sustainability-focused city;
- long-term economic benefits of the project estimated by the Seoul Development Institute to be US$8.5 billion to $25 billion and 113,000 new jobs.[48]

Finally, the success of this project and the fact that it won a prestigious international sustainability award in Washington, DC, in 2006 has inspired a proliferation of further projects to focus even more on transit in Seoul and especially to enhance conditions for pedestrians and cyclists and to continue improvements to the public realm.[49] The aim of the Seoul Development Institute charged with coordination of the projects is to cut the use of private vehicles by more than half and to convert all diesel buses to natural gas.[50]

Surubaya, Indonesia: Islands of green – walking villages in a sea of motorization

Surubaya is a low-income city in East Java of around 3 million people, surrounded by at least a further 7 million rural inhabitants. In common with other Asian cities, it is very dense at about 177 persons per hectare (Kenworthy and Laube, 1999), although it typically lacks the very high-rise residential towers that characterize cities such as Hong Kong and Seoul. Surubaya suffers just like so many rapidly developing cities from rampant motorization based on a chaotic and often lethal mixture of cars, motorcycles and trucks, all mixed in with pedestrians and bicycles and the non-motorized Indonesian rickshaws called *becaks*. However, in this traffic nightmare typical of the main roads, there exist the traditional residential areas called *kampung*, and while many of these were slums, many have also been the subject of a venture between community, city government and university – the Kampung Improvement Programme (KIP), which has seen them revitalized with good transportation results.

Table 9.10 Surubaya key figures

Population (1990)	2,473,272
Metropolitan GDP per capita (US$; 1990)	US$726
Urban density (persons per hectare; 1990)	176.9
Road length per person (metres; 1990)	0.3
Car use per person (vehicle kilometres travelled, or vkt, per year; 1990)	1064
Transit use (boardings per person; 1990)	174

Note: No later data for Surabaya are systematically available.

Source: Kenworthy and Laube (1999)

The KIP has led to greatly enhanced sustainability of the communities participating in the scheme, not only from a physical perspective, but also in social, cultural and economic terms. KIP and its sister programme of 'soft' urban renewal based on walk-up flats have been very active and successful in East Java, particularly in Surabaya, where they have enjoyed the collaboration and strong support of the Institute Technology 10 November Surabaya (ITS)[51] and the City of Surabaya. KIP is now applied in 500 Indonesian cities and towns, including Jakarta, Bandung and Semarang.

In order to provide the necessary context for understanding the unique nature of the Indonesian *kampung*, this case study commences with a general description of what a *kampung* is, followed by an 'after KIP' description of a *kampung* environment, as well as something of the wider environment in which the *kampung* exists. This is followed by a simple description of the achievements of KIP and the planning and implementation processes employed, focused on transportation.

KIP as a model of how urban greening and reduced travel needs can go together

Kampungs are the traditional form of indigenous urban development in Indonesia, and have grown organically and incrementally over many years without planning guidance or regulations, building codes or centralized, coordinated service provision. *Kampungs* are found in all areas of Indonesian cities and are formally recognized as part of the urban housing system. In fact, in Surabaya they house 63 per cent of the population on only 7 per cent of the total urban area and can be found in the CBD, government and civic areas, shopping districts and expensive housing areas. A *kampung* can be described as having the following features (Silas, 1993):

- It is not a squatter settlement or a slum; it is a tight agglomeration of continuous and incrementally developed self-help housing, built mostly on traditionally owned land in traditional ways.
- It is an indigenous concept of housing and community of various sizes, shapes and densities, catering for mostly low- and middle- to low-income families at different dwelling price levels.

- It generates within itself vast home industries ranging from manufacturing of leather, cloth and metal goods to various foods and services.

A typical *kampung* after KIP

The *kampung* environment presents a rich, dense tapestry of self-built houses of varying quality and size, narrow paths and lanes alive with people walking, riding bicycles and talking, children playing, residents selling tropical fruits, fish and other produce, and women drying washing in these relatively clean and quiet streets. Street vendors ply the sidewalks with their bicycles selling a variety of foodstuffs and other wares from elaborate, multi-level, purpose-built contraptions sitting astride the rear of the bicycle. Home industries such as traditional mask-making and footwear manufacture spill out onto the paths in these spatially constrained living environments.

The paths, of course, form the basic access for every property in the *kampung*; but in reality they are at once front yard, market stall, playground, meeting place and thoroughfare to the thousands of residents of each *kampung*. *Kampung* streets express that melding of transportation, social, economic and cultural functions that was common in the pre-automobile city of the West, but which has been lost in favour of the street as merely a conduit for automobiles.

Physically, *kampungs* consist of low-rise, extremely compact small houses, each with a doorway directly onto the pathway. This interface between public and private worlds is frequently straddled by the residents sitting in their doorways, talking, working and selling goods and produce. From above, the urban form appears as an almost contiguous, tight matrix of red-tiled roofs and the densities achieved in such environments bear witness to the frugal use of land and the relatively large household sizes.[52]

The narrow paths are barely visible from above, identifiable only as corridors of green fruit-bearing trees which shade these public access ways from the tropical heat. Larger streets are relatively few and car traffic is discouraged. Houses are mixed together with an intense variety of other uses, such as schools, mosques, small shops, manufacturing establishments, community centres and so on.

The paths that knit the urban fabric together are almost exclusively for non-motorized traffic, mainly pedestrians, bicycles or *becaks*, the traditional three-wheel bicycle taxis which still ply the streets of Surabaya, but which have been banished in Jakarta by the central government. Small motorcycles owned by residents also use the narrow streets, but strict speed limits of 5kmph apply. Motorcycles are more often just pushed through the *kampung*.

Ringing most *kampungs* in Surabaya are major traffic arteries, along which residents of the *kampungs* travel to other destinations within the city, mostly on foot or bicycle or by using the overcrowded mini- and midi-buses. These buses, along with a burgeoning fleet of private cars, trucks and motorcycles, help to fill the main roads with noise and black diesel fumes and contribute to an increasingly hostile and dangerous world for pedestrians and bicyclists. Each *kampung* has a direct entrance onto the main road from one of its small paths and the entrance is punctuated with an entry statement bearing the name of the *kampung* and signs displaying some basic rules of the community such as speed limits and curfews. Within *kampungs* there are small 'guardhouses' on some corners which are used through the night to maintain security ... a tradition learned from the Japanese during the occupation in the World War II.

Inside the *kampung*, away from the main road, and in an environment which is essentially pedestrianized, there is little noise other than human sounds and the songs of the many birds which are kept in bamboo cages hanging outside the entrances to the dwellings or in windows. The air is also a good deal more breathable than along the main roads, filtered by the vegetation along the paths and reduced in pollutants by distance separation.

KIP: What it has achieved and how

The Kampung Improvement Programme is a neighbourhood improvement programme aimed at facilitating better roads and sidewalks, drains, water supply, sanitary facilities, solid waste management and better social and educational conditions among the inhabitants. It is, above all, a partnership programme between urban communities and government, with a strong facilitation and guidance role performed by ITS's Laboratory of Housing and Human Settlements.

According to Silas (1993, p36):

> The programme is based on the idea that sustainable local development can only be achieved by linking the public sector and the community, with the Institute Technology 10 November Surabaya (ITS) having a catalytic role. Important elements in this relation are regular consultation, mutual commitment, a shared contribution to development, and care for and development of the living environment.

KIP, in its recent manifestations, commenced in 1968 and was borne out of a need to do something about the increasingly degraded and unhealthy conditions characteristic of *kampungs* as they had evolved in larger Indonesian cities. In the physical improvements made under KIP, the centrepiece has been the

Figure 9.19 Aerial view of *kampung* density (top); traffic chaos and danger outside the *kampung* (bottom), Surubaya, Indonesia

Source: Jeffrey R. Kenworthy

Figure 9.20 Commerce and socializing on a *kampung* pedestrianized tree-lined street (left); *kampung* street used only for walking and non-motorized transportation ('*becaks*') (right)

Source: Jeffrey R. Kenworthy

provision of the sidewalks described earlier to improve movement within and around the *kampung* and to seal what were previously just mud paths. This has been the single biggest investment under KIP. Both roads and sidewalks are also provided with deep side-drains to cope with tropical rainfall.

Roads for motor vehicles are deliberately kept to a minimum since most *kampung* dwellers do not own cars and want to discourage the interest of middle-income people invading the improved *kampungs*. In constructing the new sidewalks, almost continuous side borders of garden beds are also provided, along with space for painted concrete receptacles for both disposable waste (yellow containers) and, more recently, recyclable waste (blue containers).

These garden beds are richly planted with fruit-bearing and decorative trees, shrubs and flowers, with women playing a major role in these activities. The greening of the streets happens very rapidly and seems to be a catalyst for other initiatives. The local community also provides street lighting and entrance gates to the *kampungs*. The resulting improvement in the urban environment from these simple changes supports and encourages an ongoing process of upgrading the construction quality and appearance of houses and other private infrastructure such as toilets, garbage bins, water supply and electricity. The KIP has improved the living conditions of 1.2 million people living in only 3008ha of *kampungs*.[53]

The Kampung Improvement Programme is a successful model of enhanced urban sustainability in developing countries. It has simultaneously improved the social, economic and environmental sustainability of the communities that it has embraced and it has done so through a process that is strongly community based and respectful of all people, preserving and strengthening local culture, as well as being very efficient in its use of scarce financial and human resources. Government capital is at least partially matched by locally raised funds and multiplied by the time and labour inputs of the residents of the *kampungs*. The programme has also benefited from the constructive catalytic role played by an involved, community-oriented academic sector, without whose support the programme would probably have faltered.

As KIP strengthens the local community and builds on the structure which provides most services within the *kampung*, the result is an urban settlement pattern which is not car dependent. It is the equivalent of an urban village concept. Outside the *kampung*, Indonesian cities still need to prioritize transit rather than large roads; but within the *kampung* it is a model of non-motorized land use. The greening of these *kampungs* has occurred without them losing their density.

Conclusions

This chapter has shown that it is possible to forge new directions in transportation in all kinds of cities, whether they are large or small, auto-oriented cities in North America, traditional European cities, or poor or wealthier megacities in the Asian region. Good ideas abound in sustainable transportation; but if there is one single lesson binding all of these examples together, it is that without either strong leadership or effective civil society, or a dynamic combination of both, good ideas are not enough. In all six case studies, political commitment and vision, as well as strong civil society involvement, have been key factors in driving the achievements in each place. And, of course, in other iconic examples not dealt with in this chapter, such as Bogotá and Curitiba, leadership and genuine respect for and engagement with the broader community, especially the poor and others generally without a strong voice, have been a hallmark of their success too.

Questions for discussion

- What are some common themes that run through the examples of success in sustainable transportation?
- What other cities have had success in sustainable transportation? What did they achieve and how?
- Why are major comprehensive successes in sustainable transportation relatively few and far between?

Notes

1   E.g. engagement with urban communities.
2   Update in progress of *The Millennium Cities Database for Sustainable Transportation* (Kenworthy and Laube, 2001).
3   Based on personal communication with Klaus Frey.
4   Part of the Denver metropolitan area.
5   Circa 578,000, or more than 25 per cent of the population.
6   Greater Vancouver Regional District (GVRD).
7   The data are for the whole transit region; ridership is likely to be significantly higher within the city limits.
8   The freeway ban applied to the City of Vancouver only, so the region as a whole does have some freeways.

9   In contrast to US cities at 9.5 deaths per 100,000 people in 2005, or 76 per cent more than Vancouver, despite the US cities themselves having also fallen by 25 per cent over this period in transport deaths per 100,000 people.

10 The Canada Line: www.canadaline.ca, accessed 27 May 2009.

11 Because of the fine-grained grid along which they operate.

12 US$720 million and $250 million, respectively.

13 See www.air-rail.co.uk/resources/09-Mehr+-+Vancouver+Air+Rail.pdf.

14 E.g. 2.2 persons per occupied dwelling in 1996 to 2.1 in 2001; www12.statcan.ca/census-recensement/2006/dp-pd/prof/92-591/index.cfm?Lang=E.

15 See http://en.wikipedia.org/wiki/Vancouver-False_Creek.

16 See www.vancouver-ecodensity.ca/content.php?id=48.

17 1981, compared to 1986 in Portland.

18 Among the leaders was Neil Goldschmidt, the Governor of Oregon, who later became President Carter's Secretary for Transportation.

19 With no apologies to the theatrical play.

20 E.g. the five Canadian cities in Kenworthy (2009) in 2006 had an average of 151 transit trips per capita, or about 2.6 times that of Portland, and the five mainland capitals in Australia averaged 96.

21 According to Arrington (2009), at the time of opening 7000 transit-supportive residential units were already under construction in station precincts.

22 Similar tool as at the state level.

23 US Bureau of Census (2005) *American Factfinder*, http://factfinder.census.gov/servlet/ACSSAFFFacts?_event=Search&geo_id=&_geoContext=&_street=&_county=Boulder&_cityTown=Boulder&_state=04000US08&_zip=&_lang=en&_sse=on&pctxt=fph&pgsl=010.

24 See www.planbouldercounty.org/.

25 See www.boulderdowntown.com/discover/pearlstreethistory.html, accessed 29 June 2009.

26 The author lived in Boulder with three boys aged 11, 8 and 3, for four months. The eldest two boys walked to school every day unaccompanied and the eldest boy rode a bicycle independently around Boulder, something he was never allowed to do at home in Australia.

27 2,178,998 annual transit trips in 1990; Boulder and Longmont local services.

28 Counties of Adams, Arapahoe, Boulder, Denver and Jefferson.

29 Some of which was, of course, accounted for by the increase in Boulder County.

30 Based on personal communication with Spenser Havlick, 16 May 2009.

31 In Figure 10.3 of their report.

32 Defining certain major corridors as high-frequency all-day, all-evening and weekend services.

33 E.g. the current Boulder County Commission and former mayor, Will Toor, who started his civic involvement with this committee.

34 A minimum of US$5000 from at least 100 households.

35 30 June 2008: www.freiburg.de/servlet/PB/menu/1156563/index.html.

36 Based on personal communication with Jürgen Dickmann, City of Freiburg, 1990.

37 The average for the German sample is 48 per hectare.

38 The German city average here is 32.

39 The ubiquitous Smart Cars, the tiny autos made by a consortium of Swatch and Daimler–Benz, have the same advantages and people often park them at right angles to the street between two cars that are parallel parked.

40 One trip every 5.5 days.

41 66 per cent and 32 per cent higher, respectively.

42 65 per cent less than in US cities, 47 per cent less than in Australia and 36 per cent less than in the Canadian cities.

43 Room for only one vehicle at a time.

44 Although the new district as a whole is a 'node' within the city structure.

45 *Seattle Urban Mobility Plan* (2008); The Preservation Institute: www.preservenet.com/freeways/FreewaysCheonggye.html.

46 For more information, see www.e2-series.com.

47 The Preservation Institute, www.preservenet.com/freeways/FreewaysCheonggye.html; *Seattle Urban Mobility Plan* (2008), www.cityofseattle.net/Transportation/docs/ump/06%20SEATTLE%20Case%20studies%20in%20urban%20freeway%20removal.pdf.

48 *Seattle Urban Mobility Plan* (2008), www.cityofseattle.net/Transportation/docs/ump/06%20SEATTLE%20Case%20studies%20in%20urban%20freeway%20removal.pdf.

49 See 'London, the price of traffic' at www.e2-series.com.

50 See the Preservation Institute at www.preservenet.com/freeways/FreewaysCheonggye.html.

51 Mostly under the guidance of Professor Johan Silas of the Laboratory of Housing and Human Settlements.

52 In some cases over 1000 persons per hectare, compared to typical figures of 10 to 15 per hectare in US and Australian cities.

53 Almost 400 persons per hectare, or almost 30 times typical urban densities in US and Australian cities.

References and further reading

Alexander, D., Tomalty, R. and Anielski, M. (2004) *BC Sprawl Report: Economic Vitality and Livable Communities*, Smart Growth BC, Vancouver, British Columbia

Arrington, G. B. (2009) 'Portland's TOD evolution: from planning to lifestyle', in C. Curtis, J. L. Renne and L. Bertolini (eds) *Transit Oriented Development: Making It Happen*, Ashgate, Surrey, UK

Bratzel, S. (1999) 'Conditions of success in sustainable urban transport policy – policy change in relatively successful European cities', *Transport Reviews*, vol 19, no 2, pp177–190

Bruun, E. (2004) *Community Oriented Transit Best Practices*, Working Paper 1, Independent Assessment Study of District 2 Transit Services, Alameda–Contra Costa Transit District, Transit Resource Center, Florida

Carlson, D. Wormser, L. and Ulberg, C. (1995) *At Road's End: Transportation and Land-Use Choices for Communities*, Island Press, Washington, DC

Cervero, R. (1995) 'Sustainable new towns: Stockholm's rail served satellites', *Cities*, vol 12, no 1, pp41–51

Cervero, R. (1998) *The Transit Metropolis: A Global Inquiry*, Island Press, Washington, DC

Edner, S. M. and Arrington, G. B. (1985) *Urban Decision Making for Transportation Investment: Portland's Light Rail Transit Line*, US Department of Transportation, Technology Sharing Program, Report No DOT-I-85-03, US Government Printing office, Washington, DC

Havlick, S. (2004) *TDM in Boulder: A Town–Gown Partnership*, Powerpoint presentation, The University of Colorado, Boulder, CO

Kenworthy, J. R. (2006) 'The Eco-City: Ten key transport and planning dimensions for sustainable city development', *Environment and Urbanization*, Special Issue, April, pp67–85

Kenworthy, J. R. (2009) *Update of the Millennium Cities Database*, Research in progress

Kenworthy, J. R and Laube, F. B. (1999) *An International Sourcebook of Automobile Dependence in Cities, 1960 to 1990*, University Press of Colorado, Niwot, CO

Kenworthy, J. R. and Laube, F. (2001) *The Millennium Cities Database for Sustainable Transport*, UITP, Brussels and ISTP, Murdoch University, Perth, Australia

Nelson/Nygaard Consulting Associates (2003) *Parking and Transportation Micro-Master Transportation Plan: Existing Conditions*, University of Colorado at Boulder, Boulder, CO

Newman, P. W. G. and Kenworthy, J. R. (1999) *Sustainability and Cities: Overcoming Automobile Dependence*, Island Press, Washington, DC

Peirce, N. (2009) 'German city emerges as a world class energy saver', *Washington Post Writers Group*, http://citiwire.net/post/973/, accessed 30 July 2009

Pucher, J. and Clorer, S. (1992) 'Taming the automobile in Germany', *Transportation Quarterly*, vol 46, no 3, pp383–395

Punter, J. (2003) *The Vancouver Achievement: Urban Planning and Design*, UBC Press, Vancouver, British Columbia

Roberts, J. (1989) *Quality Streets: How Traditional Urban Centres Benefit from Traffic Calming*, Transport and Environment Studies (TEST), London

Salomon, D. (2009) 'Freiburg Green City: Approaches to sustainability. Presentation to European Green Capital Award, 1 December 2009', http://ec.europa.eu/environment/europeangreencapital/docs/cities/2010-2011/freiburg_presentation.pdf, accessed 30 July 2009

Schiller, P. and Kenworthy, J. R. (1999) 'Prospects for sustainable transportation in the Pacific Northwest: A comparison of Vancouver, Seattle and Portland', *World Transport Policy and Practice*, vol 5, no 1, pp30–38

Seattle Urban Mobility Plan (2008) 'Case studies in urban freeway removal', Chapter 6, www.cityofseattle.net/Transportation/docs/ump/06%20SEATTLE%20Case%20studies%20in%20urban%20freeway%20removal.pdf, accessed 10 August 2009

Silas, J. (1993) *Surubaya 1293 to 1993: A City of Partnership*, Municipal Government of Surubaya, Surubaya, Indonesia

Toor, W. and Havlick, S. (2004) *Transportation and Sustainable Campus Communities: Issues, Examples, Solutions*, Island Press, Washington, DC

Tri-Met (2009) *Status Report, Spring*, Tri-Met, Portland, Oregon

10
Conclusion: Growing More Exemplars

Necessities for growing more exemplars

The exemplary cities highlighted in Chapter 9 demonstrate that movement towards sustainable transportation can occur in diverse places under differing and often difficult circumstances. Chapter 8 presented a model for approaching sustainable transportation and an outline of what an agenda for accomplishing it might entail. In this concluding chapter, some of the ingredients and lessons learned from the two preceding chapters, in terms of themes or threads that run through successes in sustainable transportation, are distilled into a few of the critical and defining items necessary to 'grow' more exemplars.

Political leadership

In many of the cases cited in Chapter 9 and elsewhere in the text, bold political leaders, especially mayors and other senior political figures, played a key role in working with citizens in developing and realizing a vision for change from business as usual (BAU) to sustainable transportation (ST). Very often, this political leadership required the politicians to go against the advice of their own bureaucracies and even to endure threats of legal action from business interests who felt threatened by the changes proposed. When one considers a wide range of the success stories in sustainable transportation, it is difficult to deny the importance of political leadership as a thread running through so many of the successes. Bold political leadership is needed at all levels of society and international arrangements. It will take leadership at national and international levels to promote effective passenger and freight rail systems and to reduce the excessive transporting of freight and individuals by the least sustainable modes, trucking and aviation, as well as reversing the destructive patterns of freight globalization.

Political leadership has demonstrated its capabilities effectively at the level of many cities and mayorships around the planet. In Europe during the 1960s and 1970s, mayors of many cities were behind the pedestrianization schemes in their central cities and were threatened with legal action from shop-owners who saw their businesses being ruined. The moves also went against the trajectories of growing motorization in European cities and the prescriptions of the transportation models and planners for more road infrastructure and parking. In practice, when the schemes were undertaken, the success of the pedestrianized areas was so strong that the mayors often had delegations of shop-owners asking that the schemes be extended to include their shops.

A similar thing happened in Curitiba, Brazil, with the first pedestrianized street being introduced over one weekend. It required strong political leadership to carry it through against very strong opposition. Mayor Jaime Lerner of Curitiba, as well as Mayor Enrique Penalosa of Bogotá, Colombia, have been leading lights in the extraordinary progress in sustainable transportation made by these cities. Likewise, without Mayor Lee Myung-bak's political support, Seoul's demolition of the Cheonggye Freeway in South Korea would likely not have occurred. Mayor Ken Livingstone of London, UK, is best known for the ground-breaking central London congestion charge, which was a major success in reducing traffic and emissions, and also raised funds for more sustainable transportation. In Perth in Western Australia, Labor Party Minister for Transport Julian Grill was instrumental in the electrification of Perth's suburban rail system and the decision to build a 31km line to the northern suburbs. This latter decision went against the advice of the transport bureaucracy and consultants at the time, which favoured a busway. In the current decade, Alannah MacTiernan, minister for planning and transport, was instrumental in the complex fight to realize Perth's 74km southern suburbs railway against considerable opposition from many quarters.

Strong and consistent political leadership on sustainable transportation in Boulder, Colorado, over a very extended period through local political figures such as Spenser Havlick and Will Toor, has been instrumental in ensuring a consistent and clear message on the directions needed in the city in order to become more sustainable.

The list of politically driven changes towards more sustainable transportation could be greatly extended. In most cases, something deeper lies behind this overtly political leadership. This is the more complex, private and personal desire and belief, which is inherent to an individual's character, upbringing and underlying ethics – a determination that it is important to make a positive difference in the world, to change things and to leave a good legacy, which supports the 'common good'. This is a side to political figures that is rarely explored in the cut and thrust of politics, and hardly ever becomes a point of public discussion; but without it, the political actions, courage and endurance to undertake projects that totally change the existing paradigm and status quo would most likely be lacking. It is perhaps the key difference that determines whether places are gifted with good political leadership, mediocre or worse.

Community or grassroots leadership

Many successful transformations of cities or aspects of them began as citizen efforts that ended in political and institutional changes. Often such efforts spawned activists who became accomplished experts and brought new perspectives and creative energy to their cities. One example is that of David Engwicht (1989, 1993, 2005), who emerged as a leader of a movement to block the building of a major road through the centre of established inner residential areas in Brisbane, Australia. From a base of little or no knowledge of transportation, but with great creative energy and an ability to innovate, he embarked on a steep learning curve producing extraordinarily valuable documents about traffic calming as a concept and a way to set a new direction in transportation thinking. His books have made large impacts in cities and towns around the world. His unique ways of engaging citizen participation have been able to draw attention to thorny transportation issues and to help find solutions.

Community-based citizens' organizations and non-governmental organizations (NGOs) (discussed below in this chapter) are well positioned to watchdog and monitor changes once under way. Portland, Oregon's Meeky Blizzard led the 1990s effort to defeat a massive suburban highway expansion proposal and, working with the very dedicated 1000 Friends of Oregon, turned this sow's ear highway proposal into a silk planning purse that demonstrated the strength of urban development around improved transit, walking, bicycling and compact mixed land uses. She now heads the Liveable Communities effort in the office of progressive Congressman Earl Blumenauer who, as a Portland city council member, played an important role in changing that city's transportation direction.

A key part of the Vancouver, British Columbia, success story is the role of Michael Harcourt, then a young shop-front lawyer, commissioned by residents of Chinatown in downtown Vancouver to help them fight destructive freeway plans. The proposed freeways and interchanges would now occupy the key sites that are today the hallmarks of Vancouver's success in building beautiful neighbourhoods and a more sustainable city with more sustainable transportation. Harcourt went on to become a Vancouver city councillor, the mayor of Vancouver and, ultimately, premier of British Columbia – a political career built significantly on an agenda of preventing freeway development and, instead, the construction of world-class walkable neighbourhoods. In practice, there were many others involved in the evolution of Vancouver in a positive direction. Vancouver today collectively demonstrates the inherent power of grassroots community and political leadership.

There are many unsung heroes of environmental stewardship and progressive transportation in cities the world over. These people work tirelessly without remuneration and over many years to achieve more sustainable objectives. To give due credit to this inestimably valuable work and to explore the achievements of such people would require a book in its own right. Suffice it to say that without the leadership and skills of such people in so many cities around the world, there would be far fewer examples today to provide hope about what can be achieved in sustainable transportation.

Leadership and responsiveness within government

The best-laid plans of political and community leaders could easily 'go awry' without the enthusiastic support and technical skills of career government officials. By the same token, a hostile institutional environment can stymie and delay change, and sometimes government officials may be 'forced' to obey political dictates about transportation and planning matters that run against their personal beliefs or philosophies. In the worst cases, bureaucratic opposition actually leads to the undermining or even stoppage of often valuable politically led projects.

On the other hand, there are also many leaders within government organizations who, by the nature of their position, toil quietly behind the scenes, mostly out of the public eye, and are often instrumental in changing the political climate through their influence on elected representatives. Because of the 'public service' nature of their employment, they do not necessarily receive the recognition due to them; but they are an essential part of what ultimately unfolds. In significant projects and plans to change the paradigm in transportation, the interplay and dynamics between elected representatives and the government officials upon whom they rely determine the quality of the final outcome. Of course, the timeframe of career government officials most often extends way beyond typical political terms, and so their leadership, consistency or, importantly, their ability to change their ideas and to innovate, comprise an essential element in the story of sustainable transportation in most places.

Academic and professional expertise, the 'long haul' and subverting the dominant paradigm

Another necessity is the joining of civic energies with the depth and expertise that comes from years of research and study. The academic and professional expertise that lies outside, and is independent of government, can be a very important part of the propagation and implementation of ideas in sustainable transportation. This is especially true when that expertise is combined with activism or government work for periods of time. There are many such academics, whose works are cited in the chapter references and endnotes, who have been very effective in combining the diverse worlds of academia, government and community activism. They have been notable actors in combating highway expansion and promoting visions involving better transit, bicycling, walking conditions and improved land-use planning because they have spent years researching these areas and applying results to real world situations. Naturally, the critical attention of great thinkers such as Lewis Mumford, Jane Jacobs, Ivan Illich, Peter Hall and many others has been, and still is, a necessary ingredient in the history of ideas that forge positive change.

An important aspect to acknowledge here is the influence of writers who were considerably ahead of their day. They gave voice to arguments, which in their times had little support or popularity from within any sector of society and yet stood as beacons of hope, change and intellectual influence to a younger generation whose ideas were only just forming. One such writer was Kenneth R. Schneider (1971, 1979), whose seminal books are among the earliest and best anatomies of the problem of the automobile and ideas for change. Where humanity is today in its thinking and evolution about more sustainable transportation is at least partially a tribute to the power of such 'voices in the wilderness', who provided the first tentative steps in changing the seeming path dependence of automobile-based planning.

The influence of academics and other professionals whose ideas promote paradigm change is probably most effective when combined with some form of direct public contribution to political discourse and involvement in the direct support of community organizations and political parties or figures who are committed to change. The danger of this kind of high-profile position for the people concerned is that they can be labelled with having lost their 'academic objectivity' and have become, rather, 'advocates'. As with politicians, this then boils down to the motivations and ideals of the individuals concerned and whether they feel compelled to change the course of transportation and planning or to take a more hands-off approach. In practice, it is possible for academics, writers and other professionals to successfully straddle both worlds, conducting sound new research, which points in particular directions, while at the same time ensuring that it does not just gather dust on a shelf. For example, Jane Jacobs, most remembered for her books, was also a prominent figure in her home city of Toronto, Ontario, in successfully fighting against the construction of the Spadina Expressway.

A major advantage on the part of academics, professionals and writers in the transportation field is that, like government officials, they are generally there for the 'long haul' and can transcend changing political agendas. But unlike government people, they are not gagged from public comment on important issues. This enables them to continue working in the public sphere, bringing a consistent long-term message that challenges political policy positions when the winds of political change blow contrary to the aims of greater sustainability. They can also support, assist and give needed strength and credibility to progressive sustainability policy positions in transportation and planning when the political climate is amenable.

A significant role, then, of academics, professionals and writers is persistence in keeping issues alive, telling the same story over and over and in many different ways. These are among the people who are in the best position to be sturdy pioneers and to go out on a limb to forge change. New ideas are not accepted immediately; thus, it is important to have a strong voice with consistency and clarity over a long period of time, with mounting evidence. Eventually, and almost imperceptibly, ideas that once seemed radical and subversive become mainstream, and change then happens.[1]

Environmental and other non-governmental organizations

Well-organized and effective groups that fight for sustainability in the transportation and planning field are an important component in the mix of factors and forces that determine change. They can the make the difference between political decisions against sustainable transportation succeeding or being defeated due to adverse publicity against such moves. Organizations such as the Public Transport Users Association in Australia and similar groups the world over, who lobby and engage in political action that supports public transportation; the Coalition of Tollway Action Groups in Sydney, who have fought freeway development in the Sydney region for many years; bicycle users and advocacy groups around the world; and many more who provide skilled community action, are all important players in achieving sustainable transportation. Historically, we can see the mark of groups such as the Centre for Urban Research and Action (CURA), a Melbourne group who fought the planned freeway system there, which today has significant missing links dating

Box 10.1 Jane Jacobs: An enduring legacy

Jeffrey R. Kenworthy

Writer and activist Jane Jacobs was almost prophetic of current urban agendas in her observations about the true nature of cities and what they require to function properly and fairly. In particular, *The Death and Life of Great American Cities* (Jacobs, 1961), *The Economy of Cities* (Jacobs, 1970) and *Cities and the Wealth of Nations: Principles of Economic Life* (Jacobs, 1984), which identified cities rather than nations as the primary engines of economies, have left a legacy that is as relevant today as when she wrote them. Her work prefigures the invention of traffic calming and the current ascendancy of concepts such as 'complete streets', 'eyes on the street' and transit-oriented development (TOD). In *The Death and Life of Great American Cities* (Jacobs, 1961, p377) she states:

> Attrition of automobiles operates by making conditions *less* convenient for cars. Attrition as a steady, gradual process would steadily decrease the numbers of persons using private automobiles in a city ... attrition of automobiles by cities is probably the only means by which absolute numbers of vehicles can be cut down ... Tactics are suitable which give room to other necessary and desired city uses that happen to be in competition with automobile traffic needs.

Some of the important moves to create more sustainable transportation systems today – rebuilding strip malls by constructing buildings to the sidewalk and building over parking lots; widening sidewalks; providing cycle-ways and taking traffic lanes for light rail; building out of whole commuter parking lots to create public squares in the centres of cities such as Portland; taking parking lots for the creation of mixed-use urban villages with exemplary public space; and transforming shopping centres into mixed-use high-density centres – all demonstrate that uniquely simple idea from 1961: the 'attrition of automobiles by cities'.

Perhaps the greatest legacies of her writings are the minutely described workings of neighbourhoods: dense mixed-use neighbourhoods such as Greenwich Village and the North End of Boston. Here we learn how cities are meant to work on the basis of pedestrian traffic, interactions on the street, connections between people in local shops, and the natural surveillance and security systems that no amount of policing can replace. Ultimately, as Lasch describes in his praise of Jacobs (cited in Chapter 2 of this text), such well-functioning neighbourhoods and the public realm that knits them together help to establish a fundamental social order and instruct children in the principles of civic life. Such environments are not car dependent. They can only work on the basis of non-motorized modes and transit.

Jane Jacobs's writings are so eloquent and yet so easily read and understood that they open up, and will continue to open up, the true nature of cities to anyone prepared to read them. As is often the case, the truth of this kind of claim is perhaps best illustrated by a short story, in this case a personal one.

As a young student in the mid 1970s, quite serendipitously, the first thing I was required to read was the chapter in *Death and Life* where Jacobs describes how the North End of Boston operates as a community and how street security was maintained by the local Italian community. The writing was so clear and passionate, so richly human and so interesting that it stood out like a beacon of light amidst often dull and convoluted academic discourse. It left an enduring impression and was central to a decision two and half years later to change the entire focus of my studies and research to cities.

Jane Jacobs's astute observations of the nature of cities and how to sustain them remain as an enduring legacy of an extraordinarily perceptive thinker and writer, one who is essential to all students of transportation and other urban disciplines.

back to their actions. Within hours, in the pre-internet and pre-mobile phone age of the 1960s and 1970s, this group could get hundreds of people together to protest against imminent freeway construction activities. A former deputy prime minister of Australia was involved in CURA. In his later role as a senior political figure, he was also a key player in the Building Better Cities programme, an Australian federal government initiative during the 1990s to provide funds to support innovations in urban development and transportation, and to promote greater equity in Australian cities.

Many environmental organizations in the US and Canada are engaged in transportation issues at local, state and provincial, federal and even international levels. These include the Sierra Club(s), Environmental Defense Fund (EDF), Natural Resources Defense Council (NRDC), Friends of the Earth (FoE), the David Suzuki Foundation and Canada's Transport 2000. More examples, including international efforts, may be found in the resources toolbox in Appendix 2.

The number of such action groups, both big and small, around the world is impossible to count. But they can be collectively acknowledged as forming an important force, particularly where political leadership favouring sustainability is lacking and communities themselves need to try to shape changes in a more favourable direction. It also has to be said that some of these organizations can be extremely effective at stopping change, such as groups in Los Angeles and San Diego who have fought successfully in the past to keep rail out of their communities for a number of reasons, especially those related to fear of crime being introduced. Other groups fight effectively to keep more compact development out of their neighbourhoods, a move that in general thwarts progress towards sustainability.

Figure 10.1 Jane Jacobs, who used to cycle to her job at *Fortune* magazine in 1950s Manhattan, inspects a functioning bicycle transformed into mobile artwork as part of the 'Bicycles as Art' competition, Toronto, Ontario (1991)

Source: Preston L. Schiller

Private-sector leadership

Sustainable transportation requires the integration of government, the community and the private business sector in order to implement change. No single sector can do everything by itself. The private sector is driven by a profit motive and is inherently keyed to innovation and change in order to find new business opportunities, whereas government is often more geared towards stability, order and established ways of doing things.

Sometimes it is the private sector that can come knocking on the doors of government, seeking to pursue bold and unusual ventures that stretch existing planning and transportation frameworks and also challenge existing communities and vested interests with their proposals. In Perth and Adelaide there have been private-sector proposals to government to fully fund the development of urban rail systems in return for favourable land development opportunities close to railway stations. In both cases the proposals were considered too bold for current thinking within government. In particular, the transportation bureaucracies found it too challenging and potentially complex to have funding of a major infrastructure project tied to the private sector instead of the simpler tried and tested way of getting capital funds through a state treasury borrowing for themselves to manage.

The disadvantage of this lack of government receptivity to potential innovation is that the rail projects were seen mainly as technical matters of engineering and construction, rather than being intimately concerned with integrated land-use development. The private-sector proposals inherently had the potential to involve land-use planning to a greater extent and to integrate high-density mixed-use developments, whereas the government-led projects focused more on the traditional Park & Ride lots at rail stations.

Similarly in Fremantle, Western Australia, there is a controversial private-sector proposal to build a dense, mixed-use, carbon-neutral development in the coastal waters adjacent to Fremantle, which would involve strong linkage to transit and the use of electric vehicles.[2] The merits of the project are hotly debated, and regardless of its pros and cons, it demonstrates that the private sector can come forward with ideas that challenge both government and established communities to push the boundaries of thinking about what is possible in sustainable transportation and planning.

Many examples of innovative ideas emanating from private-sector developers and architects are presented through efforts such as those of the Congress for the New Urbanism[3] and the Prince's Foundation for the Built Environment,[4] among many other efforts around the planet to overcome the weight of overly restrictive or archaic building codes and development practices.

Sometimes rethinking of the current business paradigm or a reassessment of its harmful effects emerges from within major corporations. Such was the case when Elmer Johnson, the former executive vice president and director of General Motors Corporation, led a study project of the American Academy of Arts and Sciences that produced a study highly critical of the impacts of unbridled automobility on urban areas (Johnson, 1993). And many were surprised when the (then) California-based Bank of America (1995) joined with the Greenbelt Alliance, the California Resources Agency and the Low Income Housing Fund to produce a research paper highly critical of sprawl development.

The important message is that in order to implement sustainability, the private sector with its capital, skills and innovation is a key player in the push for greater sustainability. Its frequent aggressiveness needs, of course, to be always balanced against 'common good' interests; but its role should not be underestimated or rejected simply on an all too glibly handed-out stereotype of the 'ugly, greedy developer', driven only by a profit motive. People with vision and commitment to positive change, or even equality, do not just come from government or the general community; they also exist in the private sector. Where this does exist, it needs to be harnessed.

The creative class: Breathing imagination into urban and transportation planning

Another source of energy that needs to be better used in the development of sustainable cities and transportation systems is that of creative people: musicians, artists, urban ecologists and a host of mostly younger individuals who are breathing life back into decaying neighbourhoods, finding affordable

Figure 10.2 While waiting for the new Portland, Oregon, suburban Westside Diesel Multiple Unit (DMU), regional train riders can amuse themselves at this unique 'talking heads' board game

Source: Preston L. Schiller

Figure 10.3 Stilt-walkers and other street performers in car-free Old Havana, Cuba

Source: Preston L. Schiller

Figure 10.4 It takes imagination and creativity to introduce a Japanese restaurant on wheels to Zurich's streetcar tracks, Switzerland

Source: Jeffrey R. Kenworthy

housing in interesting communities, promoting community gardens and co-operatives, finding their niches and *modus vivendi* (which often involve alternative modes of getting around their communities), and, in the process, bringing fresh insight into addressing a range of urban and transportation issues. Urban observer and analyst Richard Florida[5] has coined the term 'the creative class' (Florida, 2002) in his effort to analyse why some US cities were doing well in attracting talented and innovative younger persons, while others appeared to be declining, due in part to what he termed, borrowing from economist Mancur Olson, 'institutional sclerosis'.

Artists such as Andy Singer (2001, andysinger.com) whose car-toons pepper several chapters of this book, capture the absurdities of BAU transportation and the playful energies that can be associated with bicycling, walking, community-building and even transit. David Byrne (2009), creator of the Talking Heads band, has made bicycling a part of his daily life for over 25 years and derives much creative energy for his work from pedalling about New York and the cities where he tours. In conjunction with the release of his latest work, *Bicycle Diaries* (2009), Byrne organized an autumn 2009 tour, 'Cities, Bicycles and the Future of Getting Around', in which he shared the podium with local civic leaders, planning experts and bicycle advocates at numerous cities in the US and Canada.[6] More energies like these need to be harnessed to advance sustainable cities and sustainable transportation.

Success builds success: The power of demonstration projects

This discussion has set out some of the key factors or themes in achieving successes in sustainable transportation. In the end, it is the power of the projects themselves, what they demonstrate and how they can lead to more change that really matters. It is always possible to criticize and snipe at new ideas and proposals; but what is often most needed is to actually build something new that shows in concrete terms the power of such transformations. It is often the only way to silence critics and opposition and create a new direction. To draw an analogy, in chemistry there is a term called the 'rate-limiting', 'rate-determining'

Figure 10.5 Kirkland, Washington, in the Seattle area rerouted a lakefront road and converted the original one to a mile-long promenade for bicyclists and pedestrians; many generations can now pedal, stroll, watch birds and enjoy the restored shoreline

Source: Preston L. Schiller

or 'rate-setting step' in a chemical reaction. It is the slowest step in the reaction, which, once transcended, leads to an accelerated reaction. The absence of any projects that demonstrate the desired direction in sustainable transportation and planning frequently constitutes the 'rate-limiting step' in particular places.

Portland's light rail transit (LRT) system, the Metropolitan Area Express (MAX), was roundly and relentlessly criticized by the press during its planning and construction, as were new rail developments in Perth. After opening, the success of the systems built a new direction. In the case of Portland, the arguments were no longer over the wisdom of building more new rail transit systems, but over which community should get the next extension. The City of Portland also went on to build a streetcar system on its own when it was not a high funding priority for the regional transit agency. Likewise, pedestrianization of city centres and the economic success of businesses located in them led to a desire for further extensions, as opposed to threats of lawsuits.

It is frequently argued that people are wedded to their cars and low-density forms of living; but this is often due to a paucity of choices. Once such choices become available, such as the high-density transit-oriented developments in Vancouver, it begins to break the stereotype of a city of only suburban house dwellers and car owners by showing people that high-quality alternatives are available which offer a different but also very liveable, more sustainable way of life. The success of such new offers in the marketplace gives the private sector confidence to break out of some of their 'cookie cutter' approaches that have proven successful and to diversify their lifestyle offers.

In the end, people must experience and feel the difference between unsustainable transportation and sustainable transportation-based ways of life, and the kind of overall environments and 'lifestyle packages' that this can create. It must bring to them personal benefits, not just accrue benefits to society as a whole. Somewhere along the line every place needs a successful project, something that can be experienced, felt and enjoyed. With successful projects to prove the worthiness of sustainable transportation, all the efforts of politicians, bureaucrats, academics, writers and community groups will gather momentum and gain direction, creating a 'virtuous circle' of change.

David Brower, an environmental 'archdruid', would engage audiences when the issue of transportation arose in discussion with: 'All in favour of sustainable transportation, raise your right foot!'

Are you raising your right foot? Now, how about your left? That's it: keep on walking or pedalling or ambling to the transit stop.

Questions for discussion

- Discuss the different types of leadership that are needed to make a community 'exemplary'.
- Using Jane Jacobs as an example, what are some of the issues around being a researcher or urban analyst *and* a community activist?
- How can your university and community become exemplars?

Notes

1   For a discussion of the subversiveness of such ideas and paradigm changes, see Bradbury (1998).
2   The North Port Quay development: www.northportquay.com.au/.
3   See www.cnu.org.
4   See www.princes-foundation.org.
5   See www.creativeclass.com/richard_florida/.
6   See www.davidbyrne.com/art/books/bicycle_diaries/index.php#events.

References and further reading

Bank of America, Greenbelt Alliance, the California Resources Agency and the Low Income Housing Fund (1995) *Beyond Sprawl: New Patterns of Growth to Fit the New California*, Bank of America (Environmental Division), San Francisco, CA

Bradbury, R. H. (1998) 'Sustainable development as a subversive issue', *Nature & Resources*, (UNESCO), www.tjurunga.com/thinking/papers/sustain.html, accessed 15 September 2009

Byrne, D. (2009) *Bicycle Diaries*, Viking, New York, NY

Engwicht, D. (ed) (1989) *Traffic Calming: The Solution to Urban Traffic and a New Vision for Neighborhood Livability*, CART (Citizens Advocating Responsible Transportation), Ashgrove, Australia, reprinted (1993) STOP (Sensible Transportation Options for People), Tigard, OR

Engwicht, D. (1993) *Reclaiming Our Cities and Towns: Better Living with Less Traffic*, New Society Publishers, Gabriola Island, BC

Engwicht, D. (2005) *Mental Speed Bumps*, Envirobooks, Sydney, Australia

Florida, R. (2002) 'The rise of the creative class: Why cities without gays and rock bands are losing the economic development race', *Washington Monthly*, www.washingtonmonthly.com/features/2001/0205.florida.html, accessed 15 September 2009

Jacobs, J. (1961) *The Death and Life of Great American Cities*, Penguin Books, Harmondsworth, UK

Jacobs, J. (1970) *The Economy of Cities*, Vintage, New York, NY

Jacobs, J. (1984) *Cities and the Wealth of Nations: Principles of Economic Life*, Random House, New York, NY

Johnson, E. W. (1993) *Avoiding the Collision of Cities and Cars: Urban Transportation Policy for the Twenty-First Century*, American Academy of Arts and Sciences, Chicago, IL

Schneider, K. R. (1971) *Autokind vs Mankind: An Analysis of Tyranny – A Proposal for Rebellion, a Plan for Reconstruction*, Norton, New York, NY

Schneider, K. R. (1979) *On the Nature of Cities: Towards Enduring and Creative Human Environments*, Jossey-Bass Publishers, San Francisco, CA

Singer, A. (2001) *CARtoons*, Car Busters, Prague, and www.andysinger.com

Appendix 1

Transit Primer
Major Categories of Public Transport Modes and Planning Considerations[1]

Eric C. Bruun

Public transport can be divided into two branches: fixed-route and demand-responsive modes. The former carry by far the most individuals in any system that plays a major transport role within a city or region. However, the latter also play a complementary role and must co-exist. The following section focuses on fixed routes, vehicle types and Rights of Way (RoW), with more about demand-responsive services in the proceeding sections.

Fixed-route vehicle types: Rubber-tyred and steel-on-steel

Fixed-route modes can also be divided into two major categories: rubber-tyred vehicles and steel-on-steel contact vehicles. The latter are typically known as rail vehicles. Rubber-tyred vehicles are common to the everyday existence of most readers. They have the following major features:

- require manual guidance;
- have substantial resistance to motion between tyres and contact surfaces;
- have good adhesion – they can start on slippery surfaces and climb steep grades;
- are limited to about 10 tonnes per axle due to stress on tyres.

Steel-on-steel contact has different properties, many of which are highly useful to public transport:

- positive guidance for safety;
- very little rolling resistance for high-energy efficiency;
- limited adhesion – limited steepness of gradients and oils can prevent starting;
- axle weights can exceed 20 tonnes so that very large vehicles can be built;
- steel rails help electric traction for more power and less pollution;
- electric traction permits regenerative braking for reduced wear energy and consumption;
- rails and catenary for power increase image and visibility of mode.

Conventional bus transit

Rubber-tyred vehicles are predominantly two-axled buses. The most common length in more developed countries is 12m (40 feet), but lengths can vary down to 8m (26 feet) or up to 18m (60 feet) with the use of an articulated joint. The less organized public transport networks characterized by owner operators and syndicates, rather than public agency-sponsored vehicles, tend to use vehicles smaller than 12m. The seat layouts can vary depending upon the demand levels and strength of competition from the automobile. For very high demand and/or weak competition from autos, there tend to be fewer seats and far more standees. Conversely, for more moderate demand and/or riders with an automobile option, there tend to be more seats and a generally higher comfort level.

The vast majority of rubber-tyred vehicles operating on fixed routes operate on RoW C. Bus stops tend to be no more than 50m to 100m (164–328 feet) apart, and only the more popular stops will have shelters. A significant advantage with buses is that they can be installed onto routes quite quickly and easily. Service levels can also be rapidly adjusted as demand reveals itself. Major stops, transfer points and terminals can, however, require elaborate infrastructure and substantial space. There are a limited number of cases of busways elevated above traffic to achieve RoW A. Generally, these will have limited stops and the buses using them will distribute themselves onto RoW A roads.

Traditional rail transit: Streetcars and rapid transit

Rail vehicles, mostly steel-on-steel, are seen on all different types of RoW. Historically, streetcars operated on RoW C, by definition. As the space came to be shared with too many autos, reliability of services deteriorated. This was the reason for the demise of most streetcar services. Stop spacings tended to be short since they played a similar role to buses. Stops were also affected by traffic – accessing vehicles in the middle of the street came to be difficult. Streetcars still exist, mostly in places that have a strong culture of traffic enforcement and encouragement of public transport.

Rapid transit (as well as its predecessor, the elevated steam railroads) and most regional rail systems operate on RoW A for high reliability, speed and safety. Indeed, that is usually their defining feature. Station spacings tend to be shorter in central areas, perhaps only 400m (1300 feet), but can increase to several kilometres in more outlying areas. Capacity can vary a great deal, even over the course of a day. This is one of the major advantages of rail technology – coupling or uncoupling of railcars depending upon demand. This translates into cost savings, as far fewer vehicle operators are needed to accommodate peaks in demand, which are common during rush hours. On the other hand, infrastructure and vehicles are costly and it can take years to expand stations for longer trains and to extend lines.

Newer rail and bus transit forms: Light rail transit and bus rapid transit

During the 1970s, it came to be recognized that there was a need for modes somewhere in between the streetcar and rapid transit. This was especially true in places where the streetcar did not receive protection from the private automobile. The result is what came to be known as light rail transit (LRT). This system operates for significant sections of its length on RoW B – that is, laterally separated from traffic between intersections. It also has longer station spacings than regular buses or streetcars. Its investment cost and capacity/speed performance fall somewhere between the two earlier options. It is the most common rail mode being constructed in North America and in Europe, but is also seeing some application in developing countries.

More recently, there has been a parallel evolution of rubber-tyred modes with the development of bus rapid transit (BRT). This mode was developed in Curitiba, Brazil, and Bogotá, Colombia, and runs with frequent service using very large buses to provide rail-like capacity. Many other places have now followed suit, but usually with much lower capacity. Instead, they are focusing on attracting users who might have an automobile. Like LRT, they have longer station spacings and operate largely or exclusively on RoW B. If they do not operate on RoW C, then vehicles larger than 18m (60 feet) can be used.

Although it is considered controversial, many believe that BRT can replace LRT, and perhaps even rapid transit, in virtually all newly contemplated design projects. While this is doubtful, it is clear that it has immediate application in both rich and underdeveloped countries. It can be built quickly, and in more corridors than steel-wheel modes, facilitating much needed change in many of the highly congested cities of the developing world. In richer countries, it can bring major service improvements to moderate demand corridors that would receive lower funding priority in the queue for rail mode projects.

It should also be pointed out that there are almost infinite variations so that modal distinctions are blurring. Just a couple of examples will suffice. Previously, rubber-tyred vehicles that operated on guideways were found only on short-haul applications such as airports or as circulators. Now there are systems that operate in networks and are fully automated. These could be described as light rail rapid transit or automated light rail transit. There are also vehicles that look very much like the latest light rail vehicles, but are, in fact, buses on rubber tyres. They have one guidance track in the middle of the lane, but are also free to operate in mixed traffic.[2] The active planner must keep up with a continuous flow of intriguing new possibilities.

Vehicle speed and service frequency as important considerations

People who choose to use transit will do several legs in a trip – accessing the transit, waiting for the transit to come while at the stop, time onboard the vehicle and egress time (time spent reaching the final destination). If a transfer must occur, then one must add another wait time and another onboard vehicle time. Compare this to using a bicycle or personal motor vehicle (PMV) for the whole trip – there is no access, wait time or egress time, as one goes directly from origin to destination. This has implications for the type of service that must be provided in order to attract choice users. The time for transit need not be as short as the alternative, but it cannot be too much longer or anyone with other options will use them.

In order to attract short trips, transit must be frequent otherwise the person might still be waiting at the boarding point when they could already have arrived at their destination. However, because the trip onboard is for a short distance, the actual speed does not make much difference. By comparison, in order to attract long trips, speed must be relatively high otherwise the person will consider how much time is 'wasted' and will likely reject transit. On the other hand, frequency is not as important, as people are more willing to consult a schedule and adjust their plans a little, especially if transit is faster once on board. Larger cities with well-designed and ubiquitous transit systems will have services catering to both short trips and long trips. Indeed, they reinforce each other by making connections an attractive possibility for far more origin–destination pairs than if only one type of service existed.

Routes and networks should be analysed together

A transit route's performance should be evaluated as an element in a network. The difference between individual route performance and network performance is important because of transfers. When deciding what type of network(s) to use in a city or region, the relevant assumption should be one of equal operating budgets for several alternative bundles of services within the same area.

As an example, assume that there are three basic candidate service configurations that might serve a corridor heading towards the central business district (CBD). Assuming a similar operating budget for each one, the first is direct service to the centre on each route, the second merges them so that the routes run on a common trunk section as they get closer to the CBD, and the third breaks the routes into segments, both terminating at a transfer point between outer and trunk sections. This last one now mandates a transfer to continue towards the centre. This corresponds to many BRT and LRT proposals in which bus lines become feeders instead of 'one seat rides'.

The first candidate configuration provides direct routing towards the CBD, the shortest travel time onboard and direct service. However, it requires travellers going to destinations on other routes in the corridor to transfer in the CBD as there are no direct connections between outer points along the routes, which is not realistic when there is low demand. Thus, except for destinations on the same route, routing is circuitous and travel time is long. The second candidate, of radial branches sharing a common trunk section, reroutes travellers to and from the outer branches to the common trunk section. It opens up the possibility of transfers between outer points on the other branches without going all of the way to the CBD first. This will increase travel time somewhat for people on the outer sections; but an offsetting positive point is the existence of shorter connections between outer origins and destination. There is another potential offsetting that is positive as well – the common trunk increases the frequency of service and capacity along the corridor into which all of the routes have been funnelled. Thus, this reconfiguration would be very attractive in situations where one street needs more service.

One way to increase frequency on particular routes is to replace larger vehicles with smaller ones. This, however, is often impractical since operating costs do not go down in direct proportion to vehicle size, and total capacity is

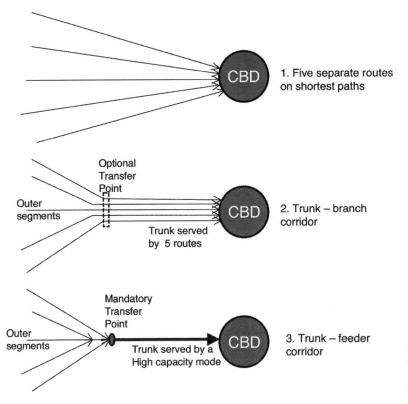

1. Five separate routes
on shortest paths

2. Trunk – branch
corridor

3. Trunk – feeder
corridor

Figure A1.1 Diagram of three
different route configurations

Source: Eric C. Bruun

reduced. Moreover, if a common trunk configuration is used and it is already congested, more vehicles will aggravate the situation.

Another possibility is to increase vehicle size in order to increase capacity. This represents the third candidate configuration. A co-operative use of modes can improve frequency on the feeders as well as the trunk. Large vehicles operate on the trunk, and smaller vehicles on the feeders. This necessitates a transfer for all riders traversing the inner and outer segments. However, there is an offsetting benefit – by operating fewer but higher-capacity transit units on the trunk section, the saved vehicle hours that otherwise would have operated on this section can be reinvested into increasing the frequency along the feeders. This will attract more short trips and reduce travel time between points on the outer segments since connections also occur more frequently.

Evaluation of alternative investment proposals should always consider not only the single route that may be receiving improvements, but the interaction with potential candidate-restructured route networks. On balance, 'forcing' transfers can often be a good thing.

Transit priority and service reliability

Even when transit speed is not important, the reliability of travel time is. When transit can be counted on to be on time more than PMVs, travellers can remove

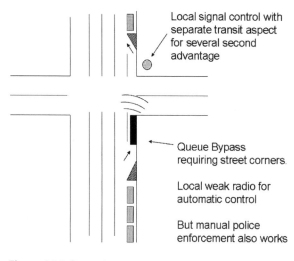

Local signal control with separate transit aspect for several second advantage

Queue Bypass requiring street corners.

Local weak radio for automatic control

But manual police enforcement also works

Figure A1.2 Queue bypass

Source: Eric C. Bruun

the cushion they allow for traffic conditions when using PMVs. Furthermore, the image of transit is boosted when it is apparent that it provides more reliable service. From the operators' perspective, it both reduces operating costs and subsidy needs. Vehicles can be scheduled more tightly and, thus, more work can be performed per day. Revenue collected also increases with more ridership.

When speed is important, the benefits from travel time reliability improvements only increase. The average time saved per run can become considerable, allowing more work from each vehicle over the course of the day; but substantial ridership increases when the tighter schedules are noted by the travelling public.

Transit signal priority (TSP) is an important means to improve reliability. It is an application of intelligent transportation systems (ITS) that has come down in cost and in ease of application. It involves the local detection of approaching transit vehicles, such that the signal is kept at green for longer or turns green earlier, so that the vehicle can cross through intersections without delay. On RoW A there is no need, by definition. But for RoW B, it can be effective in bringing average operating speeds up to those approaching RoW A. For RoW C, its effectiveness depends upon site-specific conditions. If a bus is caught in traffic far from the intersection, it can make little difference. In such cases, a compromise design, such as queue bypasses for buses combined with TSP, can be quite effective.

Notes

1   For excellent graphics and information about transit modes, see Beimborn (2006) and many other highly informative materials about transit at his website: http://www4.uwm.edu/cuts/.
2   See Figure 4.19 for a photo of the Translohr in Padua.

Reference

Beimborn, E. (2006) *Transit Technology Alternatives*, http://www4.uwm.edu/cuts/utp/techno.pdf, accessed 15 September 2009

Appendix 2

Sustainable Transportation Resources Toolbox

Selected Organizations and Websites with Information, Policy, Planning, Research and Advocacy Information

A fully inclusive listing of web resources is beyond the scope of this text. On the following pages is a selected listing of a range of sites that we believe to be useful to those wishing to explore the book's topics further. Most of these websites will have links to many others. For instance, carsharing.net has links to many local and regional car-sharing organizations. Many of the contemporary authors whose work is cited in the text have excellent websites and blogs, which can be readily found. Due to space limitations, we have included only one author's website below, that of Professor Edward Beimborn, because of its important graphics, web-links and resources.

Name/topic	Description	Address
America Walks	Studies, network, conferences, advocacy	www.americawalks.org
APA (American Planning Association)	Publications, conferences	www.planning.org
Association of German Transport Companies	Guidebooks for public transport and freight	www.vdv.de
BTS (Bureau of Transportation Statistics)	Statistical materials, studies, analyses	www.bts.gov (US, some international)
Car-sharing	Worldwide resources on car-sharing	www.carsharing.net
Carfree.com (related to Carfree Cities)	Solutions, case studies, graphics	www.carfree.com
CarfreeUK	Planning in the UK for a car-free society	www.carfree.org.uk
Centre for Sustainable Transportation	Publications, policy analysis	http://cst.uwinnipeg.ca
Center for Urban Transportation Studies	Studies, graphics, references, links	www4.uwm.edu/cuts (Dr Beimborn)
City Repair (Portland, Oregon, US)	Streets for pedestrians, community-building	http://cityrepair.org
CIVITAS (CIty-VITAlity-Sustainability)	EU cities, interests; sustainability, transport	www.civitas-initiative.org
CNU (Congress for the New Urbanism)	Traditional neighbourhood design (TND), policy, conferences, some transport	www.cnu.org
CODATU	Transport training and planning assistance	www.codatu.org
EMBARQ (World Resources Institute)	NGO for sustainable transport assistance	www.embarq.org
Eno Transportation Foundation (US)	Studies, analysis, data, standards	www.enotrans.com
FoE (Friends of the Earth)	US, UK, international environmental NGO; sustainability, transport	www.foe.org (US), www.foe.co.uk (UK), www.foei.org (international)
IAPP (International Association for Public Participation)	Information, case studies, network resources	www.iap2.org
IBF (International Bicycle Fund)	Non-motorized planning, bicycle tours	www.ibike.org
International Transport Forum	Data, studies, conferences, freight logistics	www.internationaltransportforum.org
IPPR (Institute for Public Policy Research)	Public involvement programme, information, network	www.ippr.org.uk/home
ITDP (Institute for Transportation and Development Policy)	Sustainable transport, especially bicycling and transit	www.itdp.org
IUTP (International Union for Public Transport)	Publications, conferences, advocacy	www.uitp.org

Organization	Description	Website
Jane's Walk	Jane Jacobs-inspired community planning for safer walking, etc.	www.janeswalk.net (Canada), www.janeswalkusa.org (US)
Jefferson Center	NGO advocating the use of citizens' juries	www.jefferson-center.org
League of American Bicyclists	Education, policy, publications, meetings	www.bikeleague.org
LGC (Local Government Commission)	Design, policy, conferences, participation	www.lgc.org
National Complete Streets Coalition (US)	Streets for all users; design, policy, safety	www.completestreets.org
New Mobility Agenda	Information, networking, car-free cities	www.newmobility.org
OECD (Organisation for Economic Co-operation and Development)	Research, publications, conferences; economics, energy, transport	www.oecd.org
PPS (Project for Public Spaces)	Place-making, design, transportation	www.pps.org
Prince's Foundation for the Built Environment	Ecological planning, designing and building	www.princes-foundation.org
Project ACTION (mostly US)	Best practices, advocacy; disabled transport	www.projectaction.easterseals.com
SD Gateway (Sustainable Development Communications Network)	Public participation, environmental emphasis	www.sdgateway.net (Canada-based)
SGA (Smart Growth America)	Design, policy, development, transportation	www.smartgrowthamerica.org
Sierra Club (US/Canadian NGO)	General environmental, transportation, anti-sprawl, sustainable urban design	www.sierraclub.org (US), www.sierraclub.ca (Canada)
STATTAUTO (Berlin, Germany)	Car-sharing, various vehicles, passes, etc.	www.stattauto-berlin.de
STELLA	Web resources for sustainable transportation	www.stellaproject.org
STPP (Surface Transportation Policy Partnership)	Policy reform, publications, activist network links	www.transact.org (US)
SURBAN (Sustainable Urban Development)	EU; comprehensive case studies, links	www.eaue.de/winuwd/default.htm
SustainabiliTank (sustainable development media think-tank)	International media, news, resources	www.sustainabilitank.info
Sustran-discuss list (e-forum)	Studies, Global South, development	www.geocities.com/sustrannet
Sustrans (UK)	Non-motorized, education, policy, resources	www.sustrans.org.uk
SUTP (Sustainable Urban Transport Project)	NGO; training, dissemination, assistance to developing cities	www.sutp.org

Name/topic	Description	Address
T & E (European Federation for Transport and Environment)	Information, advocacy, sustainable transportation policy, practices; Europe	www.transportenvironment.org/
T-2000 (Transport 2000)	Promoting transit, intercity rail in Canada	www.transport2000.ca (affiliate links)
T4A (Transportation for America)	Campaign for sustainable transportation systems in the US	http://t4america.org
TCRP (Transit Cooperative Research Program, US)	Best practice syntheses, studies, innovation in transit	www.tcrponline.org
THE PEP (Transport, Health and Environment Pan-European Programme)	UN-sponsored; publications, conferences, information clearinghouse	www.thepep.org
Transit Camp	Citizens helping agencies to improve information, websites, marketing, security	http://transitcamp.wik.is (Toronto), http://barcamp.org (San Francisco Bay)
TRB (Transportation Research Board)	Publications, conferences (all aspects)	www.trb.org (US)
Viva Cities	Car-free residential and business districts	www.vivacities.org
VTPI (Victoria Transport Policy Institute)	Online TDM encyclopaedia, studies	www.vtpi.org
Walk and Bike for Life (Canada-based)	Promotion of active transportation	www.walkandbikeforlife.org
WHO (World Health Organization)	Health, safety research and dissemination	www.who.int (UN)
World Carfree Network (Carbusters)	Clearinghouse; sustainable car-free future	www.worldcarfree.net
World Transport Policy and Practice	Sustainable policy, research, opinion	www.eco-logica.co.uk/worldtransport.html
Worldwatch Institute	Research, policy, energy, transportation	www.worldwatch.org
Wuppertal Institute (Germany)	Cutting-edge sustainability research	www.wupperinst.org/en/home/

List of Acronyms and Abbreviations

AAA	Automobile Association of America
AHP	analytic hierarchy process
BAU	business as usual
BCE	before the Christian Era
BCR	benefit–cost ratio
BRT	bus rapid transit
CAFE	corporate average fuel efficiency
CBD	central business district
CEO	chief executive officer
CNG	compressed natural gas
CO_2	carbon dioxide
CSS	context-sensitive solutions
CTN	community transit network
CTR	commute trip reduction
CU	University of Colorado
CURA	Centre for Urban Research and Action
DDT	dichlorodiphenyltrichloroethane
DOT	Department of Transportation
EDF	Environmental Defense Fund
EIA	environmental impact assessment
EMU	electric multiple unit
EOQ	economic order quantity
EU	European Union
FoE	Friends of the Earth
GDP	gross domestic product
GHG	greenhouse gas
GM	General Motors
GVRD	Greater Vancouver Regional District
ha	hectare
hr	hour
HOT	high-occupancy toll (lane)
HOV	high-occupancy vehicle (lane)
HPV	human-powered vehicle
IBF	International Bicycle Fund
ICC	US Interstate Commerce Commission
ICE	internal combustion engine
ID	identification
IRR	internal rate of return
ISTEA	Intermodal Surface Transportation Efficiency Act
ITDB	Institute for Transportation and Development Policy
ITS	Institute Technology 10 November Surabaya
ITS	intelligent transportation systems
JIT	just in time
KIP	Kampung Improvement Programme

km	kilometre
kmph	kilometres per hour
LAW	League of American Wheelmen
LOS	level of service
LRT	light rail transit
LTL	less than truckload
LUTRAQ	land use, transportation, air quality
LVT	land value taxation
m	metre
MagLev	magnetic levitation
MARR	minimum allowable rate of return
MAX	Metropolitan Area (LRT) Express
MCE	multi-criteria evaluation
MM	mobility management
mph	miles per hour
MPO	Metropolitan Planning Organization
MSC	marginal social cost
MVET	US Motor Vehicle Excise Tax
NAFTA	North American Free Trade Agreement
NASCAR	National Association for Stock Car Auto Racing
NGO	non-governmental organization
NPR	National Public Radio
NPV	net present value
NRDC	Natural Resources Defense Council
ORV	off-road vehicle
pkm	passenger kilometres
pkt	passenger kilometres travelled
pmi	passenger miles
pmt	passenger miles travelled
PMV	personal motor vehicle
PPP	public–private partnership
P&R	Park & Ride
PRT	personal rapid transit
RATP	Régie Autonome des Transports Parisiens (Autonomous Operator of Parisian Transports)
RGR	regional rail
RORO	roll on, roll off
RoW	right(s) of way
RRT	rail rapid transit
RTD	regional transit district
RV	recreational vehicle
SCM	supply chain management
SFMTA	San Francisco's Municipal Transportation Agency
SOV	single-occupant vehicle
ST	sustainable transportation
STOL	short take-off and landing
STOP	Sensible Transportation Options for Portland
SUV	sports utility vehicle

TAZ	transportation analysis zone
TDM	transportation demand management
TEST	Transport & Environment Studies
teu	20 Foot equivalent unit(s)
TGV	*train à grande vitesse* (high-speed train)
THE PEP	Transport, Health and Environment Pan-European Programme
TIF	tax increment financing
tkm	tonne kilometres
TLC	total logistics cost
TMA	transportation management association
tmi	tonne miles
TND	traditional neighbourhood design
TOD	transit-oriented development
TOFC	trailer on flatcar
TOT	trucks on trains
TSP	transit signal priority
UGB	urban growth boundary
UK	United Kingdom
US	United States
USEPA	US Environmental Protection Agency
V2G	Vehicle to Grid
VAMPIRE	Vulnerability Assessment for Mortgage, Petrol and Inflation Risks and Expenses index
vkm	vehicle kilometres
vkt	vehicle kilometres travelled
vmi	vehicle miles
vmt	vehicle miles travelled
VTO	vertical take-off
WTO	World Trade Organization

Glossary

Readers are also referred to the Index for specific locations and definition usages in this volume.

Analytic hierarchy process (AHP) A technique for the weighting of incommensurable inputs and then comparing a variety of alternative projects with the intent of selecting the best one.

Automobile The major type of personal motor vehicle (PMV), which includes light trucks and sports utility vehicles (SUVs).

Back-casting Working backwards from a vision of a preferred future to its planning and enactment (distinct from the use of historic data to evaluate a project, used in other contexts).

Bus rapid transit (BRT) Service designed to emulate most of the features of light rail transit (LRT), including use of right of way B, longer station spacings than regular bus services, transit signal priority, and other intelligent transportation systems (ITS) features and passenger amenities.

Car-share(ing) A co-operatively or privately available vehicle service.

Charrette Planning exercise; community representatives and experts create, comment upon or change proposed project alternatives, often involving visual renderings or computer simulations.

Ciclovia Spanish for bicycle-way; also a celebration of walking and bicycling.

Community transit network (CTN) Boulder, Colorado, transit system.

Discounting The concept of reducing the future value of money to reflect the fact that money is worth more if it is used in the present.

Fordism Pattern of industrial production initiated by Henry Ford's automobile assembly line.

Hybrid (vehicles) Combining more than one power source.

Intelligent transportation systems (ITS) Hardware and software specifically designed for improving transportation operations, information to the public and service planning.

Intermodal Travel involving connections between modes.

Kampung Improvement Programmes (KIP) Improvement programmes for Indonesian cities.

Light rail transit (LRT) Streetcars, trolleys, trams, light rail.

Metropolitan Area Express (MAX) Portland area LRT transit system.

Metropolitan Planning Organization (MPO) Governmental body conducting transportation forecasting, planning and funds distribution for a metro region (US; similar forms elsewhere).

Minimum allowable rate of return (MARR) The lowest discount rate for which the net present value (NPV) of an investment must be greater than zero, typically set by public policy for public agencies, by minimum profit requirements for private firms.

Mode The way in which travel occurs; walking, bicycling, types of public transit (bus, rail), ships and ferries, aviation.

Multi-modal Involves the use or availability of more than one transportation mode.

Net present value (NPV) The set of discounted benefits minus discounted costs for an investment or project alternative.

Opportunity cost The forgone possibilities when resources are committed to a particular project alternative.

Paradigm A framework within which a complex phenomenon operates and defines activities such as planning, financing, attitudes, etc.

Passenger kilometres travelled / passenger miles travelled (pkt/pmt) Measure of passenger travel.

Peak (demand, hour) Time and/or direction of greatest road traffic volume.

Public–private partnership (PPP) A method of project development in which responsibilities and finances are divided among various parties in recognition of the benefits that each can receive.

Regional transit district (RTD) Denver, Colorado, area regional transit system.

Right of way A (RoW A) A right of way with full physical separation from all other paths, providing the highest operating speeds and most reliable travel times.

Right of way B (RoW B) A right of way where transit vehicles have lateral separation from other traffic, but still share intersections with cross-traffic.

Right of way C (RoW C) A right of way where transit vehicles operate in mixed traffic, providing the slowest operating speeds and least reliable travel times.

Sloanism The marketing strategy initiated by General Motor's Alfred P. Sloan.

Tax increment financing (TIF) A method based on assessing a charge on properties close to new transit services which assumes that property owners benefit from the new public investment.

Teu 20 foot equivalent unit; measure of cargo container equivalence.

Time–area A resource consumption measure multiplying the space required by a vehicle and the time for which it occupies it; computed for both parked vehicles and vehicles in the traffic stream.

Tonne kilometre (tkm) Measure of distance that freight travels (1 tonne travels 1km = 1tkm). The measure can also be expressed in miles (tmi).

Transit Public transportation

Trip Travel between two points, often between an origin and a destination, but sometimes meaningless (not to be confused with drug-induced states where origin/destination does not matter).

Trip de-generation Opposite of trip generation; elimination of trips, especially by PMVs.

Trip generation The factors that lead to PMV travel; also the first step in the four-step sequential model where trips are created based on the type and size of activity occurring at a given location.

Vehicle kilometres travelled / vehicle miles travelled (vkt/vmt) Measure of vehicle travel.

Verkehrsberuhigung German term for traffic calming.

Index